Rethinking right-wing women

MANCHESTER
1824
Manchester University Press

New
Perspectives
on the Right

Series editor
Richard Hayton

The study of conservative politics, broadly defined, is of enduring scholarly interest and importance, and is also of great significance beyond the academy. In spite of this, for a variety of reasons the study of conservatism and conservative politics was traditionally regarded as something of a poor relation in comparison to the intellectual interest in 'the Left'. In the British context this changed with the emergence of Thatcherism, which prompted a greater critical focus on the Conservative Party and its ideology, and a revitalisation of Conservative historiography. *New Perspectives on the Right* aims to build on this legacy by establishing a series identity for work in this field. It will publish the best and most innovative titles drawn from the fields of sociology, history, cultural studies and political science and hopes to stimulate debate and interest across disciplinary boundaries. *New Perspectives* is not limited in its historical coverage or geographical scope, but is united by its concern to critically interrogate and better understand the history, development, intellectual basis and impact of the Right. Nor is the series restricted by its methodological approach: it will encourage original research from a plurality of perspectives. Consequently, the series will act as a voice and forum for work by scholars engaging with the politics of the right in new and imaginative ways.

Reconstructing conservatism? The Conservative Party in opposition, 1997–2010
Richard Hayton

Conservative orators from Baldwin to Cameron
Edited by Richard Hayton and Andrew S. Crines

The right and the recession
Edward Ashbee

The territorial Conservative Party: Devolution and party change in Scotland and Wales
Alan Convery

David Cameron and Conservative renewal: The limits of modernisation?
Edited by Gillian Peele and John Francis

Rethinking right-wing women

Gender and the Conservative Party,
1880s to the present

Edited by

Clarisse Berthezène and Julie V. Gottlieb

Manchester University Press

Published by Manchester University Press
Altrincham Street, Manchester M1 7JA
www.manchesteruniversitypress.co.uk

British Library Cataloguing-in-Publication Data
A catalogue record for this book is available from the British Library

ISBN   978 1 7849 9438 9   hardback

First published 2018

Typeset in Arno Pro by
Servis Filmsetting Ltd, Stockport, Cheshire
Printed in Great Britain by
CPI Group (UK) Ltd, Croydon, CR0 4YY

Contents

Figures and tables

Figures

Tables

Notes on contributors

Laura Beers is a Birmingham Fellow at the University of Birmingham, specialising in modern British political history. She is the author of *Your Britain: Media and the Making of the Labour Party* (Harvard, 2010) and *Red Ellen: The Life of Ellen Wilkinson, Socialist, Feminist, Internationalist* (Harvard, 2016), and the co-editor, with Geraint Thomas, of *Brave New World: Imperial and Democratic Nation-Building in Britain between the Wars* (London, Institute of Historical Studies, 2012).

Clarisse Berthezène is a senior lecturer at the University of Paris Diderot. She is the author of *Training Minds for the War of Ideas. Ashridge College, the Conservative Party and the Cultural Politics of Britain, 1929–1954* (Manchester University Press, 2015) which was awarded the PSA Group Prize 2016 for the best publication on conservative politics and the study of conservatism, and (with Jean-Christian Vinel) *Postwar Conservatism, a Transnational investigation. Britain, France and the United States, 1930–1990* (Palgrave Macmillan, 2017). She is currently working on Conservative women, voluntary associations and local government, 1918–1951.

Adrian Bingham is Professor of Modern History at the University of Sheffield. He has written extensively on the national popular press in the decades after 1918, examining the ways in which newspapers both reflected and shaped attitudes to gender, sexuality and class. He is author of three books: *Gender, Modernity and the Popular Press in Inter-War Britain* (Oxford University Press, 2004), *Family Newspapers? Sex, Private Life, and the British Popular Press 1918–1978* (Oxford University Press, 2009) and (with Martin Conboy), *Tabloid Century: The Popular Press in Britain, 1896 to the Present* (Peter Lang, 2015). He is currently working on a new project entitled 'Everyday Politics, Ordinary Lives: Democratic Engagement in Britain, 1918–1992'.

Rosie Campbell is Professor of Politics at Birkbeck University of London. She has recently written on parliamentary candidates, the politics of diversity and gender voting behaviour and political recruitment. She is the principal investigator of the ESRC-funded *Representative Audit of Britain*, which surveyed all candidates standing in the 2015 British general election, and co-investigator of a Leverhulme-funded study of British parliamentary candidates and MPs from 1945 to 2015 (www.parliamentarycandidates.org). She has co-authored reports on gender and political participation for BBC Radio Four's *Woman's Hour*, The Electoral Commission, The Fabian Women's Network and The Hansard Society. Rosie has recently been interviewed by the *Today Programme*, *Westminster Hour*, *Woman's Hour*, *Newsnight* and *Good Morning Britain*. Rosie presented two episodes of Radio Four's *Analysis* on *How Voters Decide* in February 2017 (www.bbc.co.uk/programmes/b08ff18d).

Sarah Childs is Professor of Politics and Gender at the University of Bristol, UK. She has published widely on women's political representation. Her most recent research book, *Sex, Gender and the Conservative Party: From Iron Lady to Kitten Heels'*, written with Paul Webb, was published by Palgrave in 2012. In 2015 she published two edited books *Gender, Conservatism and Representation*, and *Deeds and Words* with Celis and Campbell respectively, both in ECPR press. The publication of *The Good Parliament Report* in 2016 followed a secondment to the UK House of Commons (www.bristol.ac.uk/media-library/sites/news/2016/july/20%20Jul%20Prof%20Sarah%20Childs%20The%20Good%20Parliament%20report.pdf). This identifies the diversity insensitivities in the House and provides a comprehensive blueprint for reform.

Krista Cowman is Professor of History and Director of Research in the College of Arts, University of Lincoln. She has published widely on women and politics in twentieth-century Britain and is currently working on women's quotidian activism in post-war British cities.

Julie V. Gottlieb is a Reader in Modern History at the University of Sheffield. She has published extensively on the history of women and politics in Britain, including *Feminine Fascism: Women in Britain's Fascist Movement, 1923–1945* (I. B. Tauris, 2000) and *'Guilty Women', Foreign Policy and Appeasement in Inter-war Britain* (Palgrave Macmillan, 2015). She has also explored these and related themes on radio, television, in print media and as podcasts, and written blogs for various outlets including *History Matters*, the *Huffington Post*, and *The Conversation*. With Clarisse Berthezene and the Conservative Party Archive, she co-ogranised the conference upon which this volume is based in June 2015.

Matthew C. Hendley received his PhD in Modern British History from the University of Toronto. A full professor at the State University of New York College at Oneonta, he is the author of *Organized Patriotism and the Crucible of War: Popular Imperialism in Britain, 1914–1932* (McGill-Queen's University Press,

2012), the co-editor of *Imagining Globalization: Language, Identities and Boundaries* (Palgrave Macmillan, 2009) and author of three chapters in edited book collections and five journal articles. His main published research interests are in popular imperialism and popular Conservatism in early twentieth-century Britain and their intersections with gender and culture.

Anne Jenkin has worked in and around the Conservative Party and the Westminster village for most of her life. In 2005 there were 17 Conservative women MPs (9 per cent of the Parliamentary Party) and she and Theresa May founded Women2Win, the campaign to get more Conservative women elected to Parliament. She became a Conservative member of the House of Lords in 2011. She founded the Conservative Friends of International Development and is active in various anti-waste campaigns. She has held various positions of responsibility, sat on select committees and is an officer of a number of All-Party Parliamentary Groups (APPGs), but her passion remains getting more women actively involved in public life.

Jeremy McIllwaine studied history at Ulster University before taking an MA in Archive Administration at Liverpool University between 1992 and 1993. After qualifying as an archivist in 1993, he worked primarily on local authority archives – including Hertfordshire Archives (1993–2001), the Corporation of London Record Office (2001–5) and London Metropolitan Archives (2005–6). Since May 2006 he has held the post of Conservative Party Archivist, based at the Bodleian Library in Oxford.

June Purvis is Emeritus Professor of Women's and Gender History at the University of Portsmouth. She has published widely on the history of women's education and on the suffragette movement in Edwardian Britain, including *Emmeline Pankhurst: a Biography* (Routledge, 2002). Two recent collections include *Women's Activism: Global Perspectives from the 1890s to the Present* (Routledge, 2013), co-edited with Francisca de Haan, Margaret Allen and Krassimira Daskalova and *Connecting Women's Histories: the Local and the Global*, Special Issue of *Women's History Review*, August 2016, co-edited with Barbara Bush. June is the Founding and Managing Editor of *Women's History Review* and the Editor for a Women's and Gender Book Series with Routledge. She is currently the Chair of Women's History Network and the Secretary and Treasurer of the International Federation for the History of Women.

David Thackeray is a Senior Lecturer at the University of Exeter. His first book *Conservatism for the Democratic Age* (2013) explored the Conservatives efforts to develop a mass party in the twentieth century. His current research explores the growth and decline of 'British World' trade networks between the 1900s and 1970s.

Richard Toye is Professor of Modern History at the University of Exeter. He is the author of three books on Winston Churchill, the most recent of which is *The Roar of the Lion: The Untold Story of Churchill's World War II Speeches* (Oxford University Press, 2013). Together with Julie V. Gottlieb, he edited *The Aftermath of Suffrage: Women, Gender, and Politics in Britain, 1918–1945* (Palgrave Macmillan, 2013).

Diane Urquhart is a Reader in modern Irish history at the Institute of Irish Studies of the University of Liverpool. She is a graduate of Queen's University, Belfast and a former postdoctoral fellow of the Institute of Irish Studies at Queen's. She has published widely on women and political activism and legislative reform. She is the author of *The Ladies of Londonderry: Women and Political Patronage, 1800–1959* (I. B. Tauris, 2008) and *Women in Ulster Politics, 1890–1940: A History Not Yet Told* (Irish Academic Press, 2007). She is the editor of *The Papers of the Ulster Women's Unionist Council and Executive Committee, 1911–40* (Irish Manuscripts Commission, 2001) and co-editor of *Irish Women at War: the Twentieth Century* (Irish Academic Press, 2010); *Irish Women's History* (Irish Academic Press, 2004); *The Irish Women's History Reader* (Routledge, 2000) and *Coming into the Light: The Work, Politics and Religion of Women in Ulster, 1840–1940* (Institute of Irish Studies, 1994). Diane is currently completing a history of Irish divorce.

Acknowledgements

We are grateful to a number of individuals and institutions for supporting the conference and the broader research project that has developed into this volume. First and foremost, the Conservatives and Conservatism Group of the Political Studies Association, then under the leadership of Dr Richard Hayton, made a significant financial and organisational contribution to the conference, facilitating the coming together of historians, political scientists, political sociologists and politicians. The conference 'Rethinking Right-Wing Women: Gender, Women and the Conservative Party, 1880s to the Present', took place at the Conservative Party Archive at the Bodleian, Oxford, in June 2015. The Chief Archivist of the CPA, Jeremy McIllwaine, was the most attentive host and co-organiser, and we couldn't have had a better setting than the new Weston Library. A number of others were most generous with their time and offered various insights into the archiving of vital material – past, present, and for the future – especially Stephen Parkinson, Professor Stuart Ball, and Ann Baroness Jenkins. Our respective universities, the University of Sheffield and Paris-Diderot (SPC)/LARCA UMR 8225, have provided us with financial support, helped with publicity, and offered much encouragement. The University of Sheffield's Arts Enterprise Scheme funded a research assistant and conference administrator, Dr David Swift. Additional support was provided by the Royal Historical Society and the Maison Francaise d'Oxford. The editorial team at Manchester University Press have been friendly, efficient, highly professional, and consistently helpful. Both our editor, Tony Mason, and the series editor, Richard Hayton, have provided much appreciated support from the outset.

We would also like to thank the contributors to this volume for their efforts and for engaging so thoughtfully with the themes and mission of the project. Further, we thank the authors for adjusting some of their initial conclusions with great alacrity yet all the while with unfailing intellectual rigour in light of the dramatic remapping of the political landscape in the UK at just the time when we were preparing our chapters. These have been dramatic changes that could not have been more resonant and pertinent to the story of women in the Conservative Party and the place of gender in conservative political culture.

The editors would also like to thank their families for their support, patience and forbearance.

Clarisse Berthezene and Julie V. Gottlieb, 2017

Introduction

Clarisse Berthezène and Julie V. Gottlieb

Historians and political scientists have deemed the twentieth century 'the Conservative Century', owing to the electoral and cultural dominance of the Conservative Party in Britain. While the turn of the twenty-first century portended something rather different, as a Cool Britannia-Blairite-New Labourite political class inaugurated the new millennium, and the Labour Party governed from 1997 to 2010, since then, and even more so in the fallout of Britain's recent EU Referendum (June 2016), it looks increasingly likely that the twenty-first century may also be a 'Conservative Century'. There are many historical, political, sociological and cultural explanations for the hegemony of the Conservative Party. One aspect that has been under-explored, however, is the party's mobilisation of women and its positioning on gender issues. By any measure, the Conservative Party has been successful at organising women and engaging them at the grass roots, and women have supported the party at and between elections.

This collection is the product of a collaborative research project embarked on soon after the death of former Prime Minister Margaret Thatcher in April 2013. We could not have predicted that we would be putting the finishing touches on the book just as Theresa May became the second Conservative woman Prime Minister of the United Kingdom. May's achievement is one more powerful example of the ascendancy of women to pinnacle leadership positions and, arguably, this pattern is even more pronounced on the Right and among conservative, nationalist and inward-looking and exclusionist parties worldwide than on the Left. Therefore, a fundamental anomaly emerges whereby women have been as, or even more, successful in those parties that have been, to varying degrees, hostile to feminist and women's liberationist agendas.

Theresa May is not simply a replica of the first woman Prime Minister, no matter how easily that was assumed due to the suddenness of her stepping into No. 10 Downing Street three weeks after the Brexit vote. There is much that distinguishes the two, including May's self-identification with feminism. That said, she was quick to disappoint hopes that she would feminise government in significant ways, and she appointed eight women to her Cabinet against the seven in her predecessor David Cameron's last Cabinet. Indeed, as we survey the period from the 1880s to the present, more complex patterns and personalities come to view, suggesting that not all roads lead to and from Thatcher.

Nonetheless, the Thatcher legacy is a very powerful one, exemplified by the media frenzy and the re-enactment of the visceral political divisions of the 1980s that greeted her death. It was quite evident that Britain's first woman Prime Minister was largely perceived as an aberrant figure who had emerged from a party of men and, in any case, was herself a 'man' in well-tailored women's clothing. From the point of view of those more sympathetic to her political and personal achievements, she was cast as a heroic outsider who had risen *sui generis* from a hostile environment. Conversely, generations of her detractors marked the occasion by propelling 'Ding Dong the Wicked Witch is Dead' to the top of the charts. But what else became especially evident in those days and weeks of memorialisation and national reflection was that journalists were ill-served by social scientists and the historical profession in qualifying and clarifying the Thatcher phenomenon. This volume traces the relationship among women, gender and the Conservative Party from the 1880s to the present, and thereby seeks to fill that gap.

Conservative women have been under-researched for the paradoxical reason that they have not been of much interest to androcentric historians of the Tory Party, while they have never been embraced by women's historians because of their presumed reactionary views and their complicity with the patriarchal establishment. By casting our attention to Conservative women, women leaders and the changing features of institutionalisation of the party's attitudes to gender issues and sexual equality, we aim to unpack and contest these assumptions that have prevented serious and sustained study of gender politics in the most electorally successful political party of the twentieth century, the so-called 'Conservative Century'. The foregrounding of gender in political history is often understood as simply meaning the integration of women into a pre-existing narrative structure. Conversely, foregrounding conservatives in gender studies will undoubtedly lead to rethinking the too often unquestioned equation between feminism and socialism, which has implied a form of refusal to consider Conservative activists. There is therefore a need to challenge the focus, agenda and paradigms of both orthodox political history and gender studies and think, in Thompsonian terms, about the *making* of Conservative women.[1]

One implicit prejudice that demands closer interrogation concerns women's '*natural* conservatism'. On the other hand, an assumption that equally calls for contestation concerns feminists' '*natural* leftism'. Historicising the process of *becoming* Conservative women, as opposed to simply *being* women, is part and parcel of the enterprise of rewriting women, as well as historicising the process of becoming Conservative feminists. One of the most important and lively debates that the contributors will conduct, and that will be more widely relevant to many sections of the public, is the tenability of 'Conservative feminism'. Is there a fundamental contradiction in terms between feminism and British conservatism? Do we need to differentiate between feminism and other forms of women's political empowerment? Is it more helpful to make a distinction between women in party politics and women in politics to advance a feminist agenda?

To illuminate this debate we need to know first how the Conservative Party organised women. Women gained the local government vote in 1869, if they were independent householders, mainly as widows or single women with good incomes. They could be elected to school boards and Poor Law boards from the 1870s, rural and urban district councils from the 1890s and town and county councils from 1906 – and many were.[2] Tory women were mobilised as party workers – they were crucial for fund-raising and canvassing, and electioneering work. In fact, they were politicised long before they were granted the franchise. In the Victorian period, they participated in a range of extra-parliamentary auxiliary organisations including the Primrose League. Founded in 1883, the League helped the Conservative Party get around the restrictions on election expenditure of the Corrupt Practices Act. Over the next two decades, the Primrose League became a mass organisation central to the electoral fortunes of the Conservative Party and the development of a 'tory democracy', as many scholars have now shown.[3] It was women's philanthropic networking that provided the League with its activist infrastructure. Women's successful mobilisation for the party before they became citizens and, later, in the wake of women's suffrage in 1918 and universal suffrage in 1928, was instrumental in the Conservative Party's transformation and reinvention from elite to mass democratic party.[4]

In the interwar period, the Conservative Party offered training and examinations for women organisers in the party, who were full-time paid officials. The reinvention of the Conservative Party in the twentieth century had much to do with the place occupied by women within the party hierarchy and within the party's social activities, but also within the numerous non-political associations that emerged during the First World War and flourished in the interwar period. Non-party civic organisations were initially seen as a competing form of politics by the Conservative Party, as political ideas were being debated. However, Conservative activists, and women in particular, devoted much time to working in non-party organisations and played a vital role in turning these associations into platforms to combat the development of what they identified as divisive class politics, by which was meant Socialist politics. Clearly, the Conservative party's ascendancy in interwar British politics was built, in large part, on its ability to develop an important women's movement.

Against this backdrop, is it really so incongruous that there have been two women Conservative Prime Ministers? Given the party's historical appeals to a settled domesticity and the promotion of forthright women moved by the spirit of public service (women's responsibilities rather than rights), is it at all surprising that in 2010 David Cameron's Conservatives won the 'Mumsnet' election?

Historiographical framework

There was a brief moment in the late 1980s and early 1990s when a 'turn to gender' in the historiography of the Conservative Party seemed under way, but it petered out within a few years and today remains isolated and marginalised. The ground-breaking study by journalist Beatrix Campbell, *The Iron Ladies: Why Do Women Vote Tory?* (1987),[5] designed as much as anti-Thatcher polemic as a definitive history, explored the views of the 'iron ladies' and gave them a voice. Martin Pugh's work on popular conservatism (1988) and David Jarvis's illuminating article on the Conservative appeal to women voters in the 1920s and the reinvention of the 'Conservative woman',[6] showed how the Conservative Party had designed specific policies to court the new female electorate and how effective these strategies had been. Neil McCrillis's study of the *British Conservative Party in the Age of Universal Suffrage* (1998)[7] charts the party's concerted response to the challenge of an expanded electorate and how the Women's Unionist Organisation transformed the party into a popular organisation. Finally, the first and only scholarly monograph on the feminisation of the Conservative party, Lori Maguire's study of *Conservative Women: A History of Women and the Conservative Party* (1998), probably over-emphasised the direct agency of women, but raised interesting questions about prevailing definitions of feminism and the complexity of Conservative definitions of gender.[8] Ina Zweiniger-Bargielowska's research into the gender gap in the post-war age of affluence and austerity has shed light on the concomitant success of the Conservative party and failure of the Labour party in appealing to women.[9]

The insights of these scholars were not followed up, and women's activity within the party system is still largely peripheral to the dominant historical narratives of party development, policy and electoral tactics.[10] As the subjects of historical investigation and sociological inquiry, Conservative women have been doubly discriminated against. Indeed, within the larger field of British conservatism and the history of the Tory Party specifically, the study of women is often regarded as secondary and relegated to an academic ghetto – a sectional interest in 'the politics of gender'. While 'gender' as an analytical category has indeed been considered by most political historians as an 'optional extra',[11] the interest of which was unproven, feminist historians have shown little interest in Conservative women. On the flip side, the history of feminism has largely been written as a history of women's emancipation and, as such, inextricably aligned with a progressive tradition defended by the Left.[12] Of course, what came to be known as 'domestic feminism' within the Conservative Party may seem very far from feminism as defined by gender historians. Yet, these women Conservatives felt they addressed specifically 'women's issues'. The vice-chair of the Conservative Party organisation in 1945, Marjorie

Maxse, was concerned with 'the formulation of policy of special interest for women'.[13] In 1948, along with Lady Tweedsmuir and Lady Emmet, she worked on a 'Women's Charter' to attack discrimination experienced at different levels and call for equal pay. How far can these female bastions of conservatism also be considered feminist?

We have set out to consider the impact of Conservative political culture on women, and of women on the Conservative Party from the 1880s to the present. The choice of a chronology going from the 1880s is to enable us to trace 'The making of Conservative women' – that is to say the process by which, stemming from the feminine philanthropic tradition of the nineteenth century, the women's Conservative movement came into being and endowed it with a new language that received mass support and contributed to redefining its identity. We explore the construction and performance of gender identities by Conservative politicians at local, national and international levels. Bringing together scholars with a specialist interest in the dynamics between British Conservatism and gender at various junctures and in related contexts since the 1880s when the party 'modernised' and took on the form that we recognise today, our chapters are tied together by particular themes. The most prominent of these are the relationship between Conservatism and feminism; causes and levels of sexual antagonism within the Tory Party; and the feminisation of the party and Conservative culture and identity – here the processes to discern are cyclical rather than linear.

Starting in the 1880s, Urquhart demonstrates that the alliance between Conservatives and Unionists, typified by the Tories' name change to the Conservative and Unionist Party in 1912, was hugely significant in the history of female politicisation. Using the legislative frame of the Corrupt and Illegal Practices Act of 1883, which forbade the payment of political canvassers, and the 1884 Reform Act, which enfranchised the majority of men in Britain, as well as the backdrop of three successful Irish Home Rule bills, she explores the processes by which an unprecedented number women became politically active for the first time. From the introduction of the first Home Rule Bill in 1886, women became involved in unionism in ever increasing numbers. Northern and southern Irish female unionist organisations were subsequently established, the largest of which, the Ulster Women's Unionist Council, had amassed over 100,000 members by 1913, thus becoming the largest female political force ever mobilised in Ireland's history.

But what of the relationship between Conservative women and the suffrage movement? Christabel Pankhurst's biographer, June Purvis, traces her famous subject's encounters with the Conservative Party, demonstrating Christabel's growing scepticism about the Independent Labour Party (ILP), the Labour Party, and a class-based feminism. Yet this does not mean she was, at least in the heyday of the suffragette movement, right wing and, by implication, reactionary. Purvis shows how Christabel engaged with Conservatives, and gives some insight into the lesser strain of Conservative suffragism. There is a more tangled history of Toryism and suffragism, more complicated than the historiographical focus on Tory anti-suffragism has tended to allow for.

Thackeray reflects on new research on women in the party – their activities, organisation and representation – in the first decade after enfranchisement. In May 1918, Mary Maxse, the outgoing chairman of the Women's Unionist Association, met her organisation's decision to disband and form a Conservative Party women's organisation with foreboding. She despaired that her supporters had 'amalgamated like lambs with the official Unionist men'. Yet ten years later, the Conservative Women's Organisation claimed one million supporters, comfortably more than its rivals, and Maxse's successor, Caroline Bridgeman, chaired the party's National Union. Thackeray considers what these successes meant and whether they proved that women had become fully integrated into the Conservative Party. Clearly, there was a marked disparity between women's importance to grassroots organisation and the four female MPs who sat on the Conservative benches after the 1929 election. Moreover, women's position within the wider party organisation, so unclear in 1918, remained problematic.

Hendley carries on examining how women were mobilised for party political work before attaining citizenship. With a hierarchical and vaguely medieval structure, the Primrose League peaked at two million members (most of them female). It was well known for its political propaganda and electoral canvassing. It also promoted social integrative functions through large-scale entertainments, garden fetes and whist drives. The League played an important role in Victorian Conservative politics through operating in the 'social sphere' in which politics could be mixed with conviviality in a non-confrontational setting and absorbed almost unconsciously. Hendley examines how the Primrose League reacted to a shifting political landscape from 1900 to 1918, arguing that by 1918, though it was no longer the crucial body of female auxiliaries to the Conservative Party it had been in the past, the League had avoided the fate of becoming a body of superfluous women. The adaptability of the Conservative Party and its related organisations was a key to the long-term success of Conservatism.

What difference did the vote make to the status and organisation of women in the party? These are the questions raised by Gottlieb and Berthezène. Gottlieb takes a more biographical approach, focusing on some of the first Conservative women MPs. The valuable work performed by Conservative women at grassroots has been acknowledged in the scholarship, as have the strategies developed by the party to mobilise women as both party workers and voters, while much less attention has been conferred on those Conservative women who became virtual national celebrities. By the late 1930s the two women Conservative MPs to achieve this celebrity and notoriety were Lady Nancy Astor, the first woman MP to take her seat, a committed feminist and hostess of the so-called Cliveden set, and the Duchess of Atholl, the first woman MP from Scotland, an avowed anti-(non) feminist and the Chamberlain scourge at the height of appeasement. Both defied stereotypes of Tory femininity with their own personal styles, by taking an abiding interest in international affairs when most Conservative women were expected to be focused on the local and parochial, and by engaging with women across party lines to advance their favoured policies. The early Tory women MPs achieved public-facing leadership positions in the Conservative Party, and they were, inevitably (unacknowledged) role models for and forerunners of Thatcher's construction of female leadership.

Berthezène examines the contribution Conservative women made to the formulation of Conservative principles. She reflects on their claim that they were 'practical', 'commonsense' women, as opposed to what they saw as their cerebral, theoretically minded Labour and Liberal counterparts. The deliberate cultivation of the identity of 'the middlebrow' was an important means to embrace democracy and speak to all social classes, which led them to develop a particular view of 'responsible womanhood' and citizenship, notions which they felt had been inappropriately annexed by 'the Left'. It was also a response to the emergence of a new culture of non-partisan organisations, which provided an important challenge to the position of political parties in interwar Britain. Women's voluntary associations were particularly instrumental in educating in citizenship and provided a female sphere of political activity that was removed from the rough-and-tumble of party politics. Looking at the Women's Voluntary Services, which were set up in 1938 by Lady Reading, at the request of the Home Office, Berthezène shows how they played the role of antechambers to the political world.

How have Conservative men reacted to women's new roles in the party? How accepting and welcoming was the patrician, paternalist and patriarchal male leadership to women pioneers in Parliament and to the new strategies developed to capture the 'women's vote'? Toye, one of Churchill's biographers, offers a case study of the 'great man's' relationships with women and his stand on gender issues, from his famous opposition to women's enfranchisement to a more accommodating attitude later in the course of his varied career. In turn, Toye draws on the available evidence to try to understand what women voters made of Churchill over the span of his political life.

It is the question of political engagement and party appeals to women that is the focus of Bingham's investigation. By the 1950s, Conservative Party politicians, strategists and activists had developed a range of appeals to female voters which centred on the relevance of politics to everyday life, and which celebrated women's domestic roles as chief consumer, guardian of the family purse and prime defender of the household. Party propaganda warned that under the Labour Party, the state and the unions would encroach and intervene into the private sphere and reduce individual and family freedoms. The party gradually developed and refined these appeals as more women moved into work, calls for gender equality increased, and affluence and permissiveness raised new political and social issues: nevertheless, many of the key underlying messages about the politics of everyday life remained in place. Yet while some historians have traced the formulation and articulation of these gendered appeals, they have been far less attentive to the ways in which this resonated with ordinary women and their understanding of the politics of everyday life. Bingham's chapter draws on opinion polls, social surveys, diaries, memoirs and media sources to seek to address this important gap, examining the ways in which different groups of women perceived the Conservative Party and their various ideological appeals from the 1950s to the 1980s.

It is the same relatively neglected period that concerns Cowman as she offers a new portrayal of Margaret Thatcher from the vantage point of her early years as an MP. Thatcher is usually represented as having no time for feminism or the feminist movement. Throughout her tenure as leader of the Conservative Party she has been characterised as derisive of the contemporary women's movement, cutting local authorities' funding for women's groups and committees and being slow to promote women within the ranks of her own government. Cowman's chapter suggests that the reality may have been more complicated. Although recent portrayals (such as Abi Morgan's film script) have focused on Thatcher as a 'woman alone' in a man's world, other sources suggest that she may have had a more fruitful working relationship with other political women, especially in her early political career as a backbencher. Exploring Thatcher's early work for women's issues and with women's groups as well as her early relations with other women MPs reveals her to be a less one-dimensional political figure than critics of her later political career have suggested, and help unpick further the complexity of her appeal to women.

The thorny issue of Conservatism and women's liberation is illuminated by Beers in her study of feminist responses to Thatcher and Thatcherism. The polarisation of feminism and Thatcherism facilitated a rapprochement between the Women's Liberation Movement (WLM) and the Labour Party. Beers offers new insight into Thatcher's ambivalent relationship to other women. She never identified herself as a feminist. In fact, she remained derisive of the 'dungarees only, no skirts allowed' unfeminine pose of the 'strident' feminists who so vehemently opposed her administration. Thatcher did not understand feminists, and they in turn were slow to appreciate her appeal to a substantial sector of British women. Feminists, in turn, launched a scathing critique of female Thatcherites. Women who supported Thatcher were either dupes, or hang 'em and flog 'em old biddies, the blue-rinse foot soldiers of the Conservative army.

Childs' and Campbell's contribution, from the point of view of political sociology, reflects on the post-Thatcher era of Tory success, and the attempted feminisation of the party, or certain aspects of it, under David Cameron's leadership. The UK Conservative Party at the general election of 2010 was undoubtedly a more feminised institution: it was to more than double the number of its women MPs returned to Westminster; had established new women's forums for policy debate among its women members; and had fought on a much more competitive women's agenda, reflecting the interventions of key women party and parliamentary actors. Almost immediately feminist criticism surfaced: suggestions that anonymity would be given to men accused of rape were met with the accusation that the Coalition was being sealed over women's bodies; economic austerity was soon revealed to have a female face, as state benefits and welfare were cut, disproportionately and negatively impacting women. The charge was clear: Cameron's commitment to feminisation had been mere electoral opportunism masking both a neo-liberalism that fails to see how gender structures society, and a social conservatism that valorises the traditional gendered division of labour. Feminisation – the integration of women and women's issues in politics[14] – is best understood as a process rather than an end point. The 2015 general election is an obvious moment to hold the party to account. To establish whether its commitment to the greater participation and descriptive representation has been maintained; and to explore the nature of its representational claim for women, and to investigate the relationship of these to the party's wider political programme: in sum, to subject the contemporary Conservative Party to a gendered audit.

The final two contributions bring us right up to the present and will no doubt inspire future research on gender and Conservatism. The contributors to this volume all took part in a conference hosted by the Conservative Party Archives (CPA), Bodleian Library, Oxford, in June 2015. A major issue that scholars have faced in researching Conservative women is the limitations or inaccessibility of the source material. Certainly for the pre-1945 period, the record of Conservative women's activism is patchy. The CPA's archivist, Jeremy McIlwaine, offers here an invaluable insight and guide to the archival situation, and draws our attention to collections and records that are recent deposits or that have never been properly exploited. Scholars do not always understand the constraints and strains faced by archivists – and the politics of the archive – and McIlwaine presents a refreshingly honest and revealing behind-the-scenes perspective.

Finally, the Baroness Anne Jenkin of Kennington tells the story of the creation of Women2Win, which she founded with Theresa May in 2005, when the under-representation of Conservative women in politics was particularly conspicuous. Indeed, there were only seventeen Conservative women MPs in 2005 when they decided to make party feminisation their mission and to create Women2Win to ensure the Conservative Party fairly represented women at all levels of politics. After the election in 2010 the number of Conservative women MPs increased from 17 to 49 MPs, from 9 per cent of the Parliamentary Party to 16 per cent.

As a whole, our research taps into ever-current debates about women's political preferences, the politicisation of gender and the gendering of politics. It attempts to make sense of why women have, and have not, voted Conservative since the 1880s and their relationship with the party. It aims to discard stereotypes that essentialise women as being innate Conservatives or that present them as 'the power behind the throne'. It documents the contingent nature of female support for the Conservative

Party and the constant need for the party to construct political identities compatible with women's agendas. Finally, it asserts the agency/instrumentalism of women within the Conservative Party.

Notes

1 David Jarvis, 'Review of G. E. Maguire, *Conservative Women: A History of Women and the Conservative Party, 1874–1997* (1998); and Karen Hunt, *Equivocal Feminists: The Social Democratic Federation and the Woman Question, 1884–1911* (1996)', *Twentieth Century British History*, 10: 4 (1999), 540–51.
2 Patricia Hollis, *Ladies Elect. Women in English Local Government 1865–1914* (Cambridge: Cambridge University Press, 1987).
3 Alistair Cooke, *A Gift from the Churchills: the Primrose League, 1883–2004* (London: Conservative Research Department, 2010); M. Pugh, *The Tories and the People, 1880–1935* (Oxford: Blackwell, 1985); Janet Robb, *The Primrose League, 1883–1906* (New York: Columbia University Press, 1942).
4 Pugh, *The Tories and the People.*
5 Beatrix Campbell, *The Iron Ladies: Why Do Women Vote Tory?* (London: Virago, 1987).
6 Martin Pugh, 'Popular Conservatism in Britain: Continuity and Change, 1880–1987', *Journal of British Studies*, 27: 3 (The Dilemmas of Democratic Politics) (July 1988), pp. 254–82; *Women and the Women Movement in Britain, 1914–1999* (Marlowe & Co, 1995); David Jarvis, 'Mrs Maggs and Betty: The Conservative Appeal to Women Voters in the 1920s', *Twentieth Century British History*, 5 (1994), 129–52.
7 Neil McCrillis's study of the *British Conservative Party in the Age of Universal Suffrage* (Columbus: Ohio State University Press, 1998).
8 G. E. Maguire, *Conservative Women: A History of Women and the Conservative Party, 1874 to the Present* (Basingstoke: Palgrave Macmillan, 1998).
9 I. Zweiniger-Bargielowska, *Austerity in Britain: Rationing, Controls and Consumption, 1939–1955* (Oxford: Oxford University Press, 2000).
10 The classic example is the Longman's series, *The History of the Conservative Party*. A notable exception is David Thackeray's recent study of Conservative cultures, *Conservatism for the Democratic Age. Conservative Cultures and the Challenge of Mass Politics in Early Twentieth Century England* (Manchester: Manchester University Press, 2013), which shows how the Conservative party focussed on addressing women as consumers at the beginning of the twentieth century.
11 David Jarvis discusses this in his review of books by G. E. Maguire and Karen Hunt (see note 1).
12 Laura Lee Downs, *Writing Gender History* (London: Bloomsbury Publishing, 2004); Françoise Thébaud, *Ecrire l'histoire des femmes et du genre* (Lyon: ENS Editions, 2007).
13 Maguire, *Conservative Women*, p. 141.
14 Joni Lovenduski, *Feminizing Politics* (Cambridge: Polity Press, 2005).

1

'Open the eyes of England': female unionism and conservatism, 1886–1914[1]

Diane Urquhart

Women were often active agents of change. Their involvement in elections, political protests and petitioning pre-dated the establishment of formal women's political associations in the 1880s and partial female enfranchisement in 1918. Women could, and did, influence the voting practices of men and female political writings were commonplace, although they frequently obscured their identity by the means of pseudonyms or anonymity which raises the question of gendered political boundaries. Involvement in national reform campaigns for married women's property rights, women's suffrage, the repeal of the Contagious Diseases Acts and Irish land reform also prompted Irish and British female political cooperation in the mid- to late nineteenth century.

However, social class often dictated the type of political activity women could perform with the upper-class political hostess typifying the heady influence that some women exerted as conduits between the conjoined socio-political domains of the Victorian and Edwardian eras. Yet, despite the visibility of politically active women, they have often been understudied and excluded from histories of party and popular politics. In relation to conservatism and unionism, this lacuna minimised considerations of women's political contribution and led to both ideologies being depicted as largely and – at times – wholly male manifestations.[2] Women are being written back into these histories and it is an indication of the maturity of women's history that the female Unionist movement can now be placed into a broader backdrop of popular conservatism. A gender inclusive approach also allows for a more nuanced understanding of political machinations, power and the unprecedented popularity of both conservatism and unionism in the late nineteenth and early twentieth centuries.

Women were drawn into more formal political associations not by any evolutionary process from their early political activism, but by a combination of party self-interest and the impending political crisis over Irish home rule. Conservatives were conscious of the need to widen their support base beyond the traditional rural heartland by the early 1880s, but the Corrupt and Illegal Practices Prevention Act of 1883 had a more pressing impact on the need to popularise conservatism. This Act inadvertently changed the political worth of women as party workers. Expectations of the Act were high as it was hoped that it would 'work well in the interests of electoral purity' to establish 'a new form of electioneering law'[3] and 'confer upon the constituencies much greater freedom in the choice of candidates'.[4] Despite the passage of the Corrupt Practices Act of 1854 and the Ballot Act of 1872, the 1880 election saw eighteen members unseated, owing to electoral corruption, and cumulative electoral expenses were estimated at £2–3 million.[5] Many thus welcomed the 1883 Act which forbade treating, undue influence, bribery, personation and the payment of canvassers and workers taking voters to the polls or posting electoral posters.[6] The number of electoral agents, meetings and expenditure was also tightly regulated by constituency size. Fines, imprisonment, bans on voting and candidature were the fate of those who attempted to evade its strictures.

However, from the Act's passage in September 1883 there were concerns that it would be violated or, to use the press's more colloquial expression, that the 'proverbial four-horse coach will be driven' through it.[7] There was also consternation regarding the practicalities of levelling political expenses: 'the rich man' was still in possession of 'an enormous pull over his poorer neighbour … but it [the 1883 Act] seeks to interpose an effectual barrier to the production of swollen election bills'.[8] Candidates could still amass £100 personal expenses during electoral contests and, as the Trades Union Congress averred, more support might have been forthcoming for Labour candidates. However, a Commons' motion to pay Labour candidates' expenses from the rates was defeated by 167 to 80 votes.[9] There were further charges of undue state influence with 'many' reportedly 'afraid of legislation of this kind getting too "grandmotherly"'.[10] The press's adoption of this female idiom underscored the widely held view of women's political unsuitability. The Act, however, also impacted on political party organisation beyond that likely envisaged by its Liberal sponsors; women were quickly encouraged to become politically active on an unprecedented scale.

As Rix suggests, the 'obvious solution' to the electoral conundrum posed by the 1883 Act was to augment existing party organisations, but this too had its critics. Many Conservatives were 'suspicious of the much-reviled caucus' and the associated curtailment of candidates' independence. To the *Saturday Review*, for example, candidates would become 'practically the slaves of local associations'.[11] Some Conservatives also believed that the Liberals would benefit more from increased volunteer political labour, but this proved ill-founded. Any remaining Conservative misgivings on popularising the party association were also countered by the increase in the electorate in 1884 and their subsequent electoral defeat in 1885: the percentage of enfranchised adult males in England and Wales rose from 18.1 per cent in 1861 to 62.2 per cent in 1891 and in Ireland, over the same period, from 13.4 per cent to 58.3 per cent.[12] Conservative expediency thus led them to form the first politically inclusive organisation. This was the Primrose League, established as a male-only association in November 1883, but women were admitted to its ranks in the following month. The reach of this new body thus went beyond the enfranchised and the elite; it was a defender of tradition with a clear attachment to the Anglican Church, monarchy and empire.[13]

Using a potent mix of imperialism, heraldry and Masonic modelling, Primrose League habitations (the name for male, female and mixed-sex branches) with male Knights, female Dames and Junior Leagues of 'Buds' became the largest party association. In 1884 its membership comprised 747 Knights and 153 Dames; by 1891 it recorded 63,251 Knights, 50,973 Dames and 887,068 associate members and by 1899 it had a million and a half members.[14] Some degree of inflation was caused by the organisation's practice of including lapsed members in its figures, but its entertainments were hugely popular although Lady Salisbury expressed this somewhat differently: 'Vulgar … of course it's vulgar. But that is why we have gone on so well.'[15]

The role of women within the League was carefully defined from the outset and these gender boundaries were rarely breached. This built on women's earlier philanthropic work, political hostessing and involvement in bodies like the Anti-Corn Law League, which was 'conceptualised as an extension … of domestic concerns, not as an intrusion into the 'male' political arena'.[16] The led to domesticity being foregrounded for Primrose League Dames. In consequence, women's work centred on political education, canvassing and 'political sociability' which developed 'into a strong associational culture'.[17]

Owing to Lord Claude Hamilton's initiatives, Irish Unionists formed a distinct grouping within the Conservative Party from 1886.[18] An unwavering attachment to notions of a ruling elite, monarchy and especially empire also placed the Primrose League firmly within the Unionist camp. With Randolph Churchill, author of the 'Ulster will fight, and Ulster will be right' mantra, as a key League promoter, links to the augmenting Unionist campaign of the 1880s were perhaps inevitable.[19] Theresa, 6th Marchioness of Londonderry also typified the connection between conservatism and unionism. This leading Conservative hostess, Primrose League Dame and member of its executive committee, was later president of the Ulster Women's Unionist Council (UWUC). Her portrayal of the Conservative's Party's defining principles as Anglicanism, education and opposition to Home Rule further underscores the affinity with unionism.[20] The Irish question was also, at times, 'an excellent recruiting sergeant' for the Primrose League; Pugh estimates that the first home rule bill and the Nationalist plan of campaign increased membership by 550,000 in the twelve months from March 1886.[21]

The League was also active in Ireland. By 1888 there were thirty-five Irish Primrose League habitations. However, the three Belfast habitations, which were in operation in the 1890s, constituted a third of the total Ulster representation. Indeed, the League was never overly popular in the heartland of unionism, the north-east of Ireland, where it faced competition from indigenous male and female Unionist associations as well as the Orange Order.[22] By comparison, there was an identifiable Primrose concentration in the south and west of Ireland. Membership and gender profiles are not clear for all habitations, but few of the Ulster branches shared the popularity, albeit self-proclaimed, of St Patrick's in Cork, with over 3,500 members in 1888. This was one of eight local Cork habitations, comprising 23 per cent of the total Irish branches, which established this city as the Irish centre of the Primrose League.[23]

There was a clear identification with the Unionist cause in the Irish habitations. In 1902, William Ellison Macartney, Conservative MP for Tyrone, addressed those attending a mixed-sex meeting of the Kingstown habitation in Co. Dublin as Unionists: 'Every one of them was imbued with the principles of loyalty to the person of the Sovereign, and also to the Constitution.' Yet, they were also branded as imperialists with a duty to support the government in bringing the Boer conflict to a successful conclusion despite the same administration having 'neglected' Ireland: 'whatever legislation had been passed for Ireland, was, so far as it affected Unionists, to their detriment'.

The bulk of Macartney's address, however, exhibited a preoccupation with maintaining the union and Irish affairs: land agitation; municipal politics and the Nationalist United Irish League.[24] As such, his address underlined a variation in right-wing political priorities as interest in unionism outside of Ireland waned from the 1890s to such an extent that Henderson Robb claims that the 'public bored' of home rule.[25] This is not without foundation; interest in the home rule issue temporarily diminished after the defeat of the first and second Home Rule bills in 1886 and 1893 and a heightened imperialism was evident in many English Primrose League habitations, especially during the Boer War era.[26]

'Ulster raises its voice of solemn warning'[27]

Although interest in the Irish question vacillated, opposition to home rule generated a similar response within unionism as the electoral reforms of the 1880s encouraged within conservatism: a process of political popularisation that brought women into the political fold. Gladstone's first Home Rule Bill of 1886 was modest in ambition, proposing the establishment of an Irish Parliament with restricted powers, but home rule came to represent the aspirations and anxieties of an increasingly divided Irish nation. Opposition to the 1886 Bill spawned the first organisation of Unionist women, but its roots lie not within conservatism, but in the newer creation of Liberal Unionism. Isabella Tod was an experienced political activist by the time of the first Unionist campaign. As one of Ireland's leading feminists, Tod had been involved in various campaigns for married women's property reform, temperance, suffrage, female educational reform and the repeal of the Contagious Diseases Acts. It was, however, indicative of the perceived threat of home rule that she largely devoted the remaining decade of her life to unionism. Tod, believing that the successes of the earlier reforms would be negated by home rule, established a branch of the London-based Women's Liberal Unionist Association in Belfast in 1886.

Although Tod went on a tour of England with a male delegation from the Ulster Liberal Unionist Association, she, in consequence of a deservedly renowned oratorical reputation, was the sole female representative. For most women political work at this juncture meant conducting auxiliary 'spadework'.[28] Indeed, the emphasis on women's supposed suitability for certain avenues of political engagement which was apparent within the Primrose League was also evident within unionism. Women were, for example, excluded from the Unionist Belfast convention of 1892 as it was feared their presence might deride the proceedings. Tod therefore organised what she referred to as a 'social gathering' on the day preceding the convention, but this was a façade; the *conversazione* was a mixed-sex assembly attended by several hundred and her address was distinctly political: she depicted home rule as 'the furnace of revolution'.[29]

Independent of the Liberal Unionist fold, the Ladies' Committee of the indigenous Irish Unionist Alliance had a central office in Dublin in the 1890s and small local female Unionist associations were active in Ulster in the early twentieth century.[30] Their work remained characterised by petitioning, fund-raising, didactic and electoral work. The inauguration of the Ulster Women's Unionist Council (UWUC) in 1911, however, gave a new permanency to female unionism which soon overshadowed liberal unionism, local initiatives and female southern unionism.[31] Their motto, 'Union is strength', exemplified the earlier fixation with Ireland's constitutional relationship while the organisation's name was indicative of an increased preoccupation with the future of Ulster rather than Ireland as a whole. Like the Primrose League, the UWUC became hugely popular within a relatively short time. This was part of a broader process which saw unionism become popular for the first time in its history.[32] By the end of 1911 thirty-two branches were formed throughout Ulster with an estimated membership of 40,000–50,000. Two years later figures of between 115,000–200,000 members were cited. Although a margin of exaggeration is to be expected, the sheer scale of their activities, attendances at their public demonstrations as well as signatories to their petitions confirms this as a very sizeable organisation.[33]

Much of the explanation for this popularisation lies in the escalation of Unionists' fears of home rule from 1911. The Parliament Act of that year removed the last constitutional safeguard against home rule, limiting the power of the House of Lords to a two-year veto; any future bill could no longer be defeated outright. For Unionists this gained a grim reality when the Government of Ireland Bill of 1912 was defeated in the Lords and hence delayed for two years.[34] This helped to further unite unionism and conservatism: the parties formally amalgamated in 1912 to become the Conservative and Unionist Party.[35] The Parliament Act also girded the determination of Unionists to resist home rule. Unionist leader, Edward Carson, declared this as his last political contest and, although 'much overwhelmed at all that lies before us', resolved to 'make a big effort (my last in politics) to stir up some life over this Home Rule fight'.[36]

Elite leadership also aided the propagation of female political associations. The Primrose League was led by women such as the Marchioness of Salisbury, Lady Jersey and the Duchess of Marlborough, and earlier female Unionist organisations in North Tyrone and Londonderry were under the presidency of the Duchess of Abercorn and the Marchioness of Hamilton respectively. Although the rank and file of the UWUC, like the Primrose League, was middle and working class, the organisation was led by members of Ulster's aristocracy who were related by familial or marital ties to the male leaders of unionism.[37] All of the UWUC's presidents to the mid-twentieth century were titled and women of this class possessed the time and economic freedom to participate in political life, often on a daily basis.[38] The UWUC's ruling body, its executive committee, for instance, not only met on weekdays but also during normal working hours, which obviously precluded working women's involvement. This elite leadership also added respectability to female political engagement which was particularly significant when endeavouring to mobilise the first generation of women en masse.

Both the Primrose League and the UWUC positively promoted their ancillary status. As Primrose League Dame, Lady Jersey opined in 1890: 'We ladies ... are not in the least desirous of trenching on any department which does not belong to us; we don't wish to govern the country.'[39] The UWUC declared a similar desire to work by means of 'gentleness, tact and quiet influence'.[40] Both associations thus emphasised maternal and domestic roles which helped to reassure women that they had a political part to play. Thus, while League Dames advocated raising children 'in the principles of religion and devotion to their country and of patriotism',[41] Unionist women developed a gendered argument which highlighted the sanctity of the home. Indeed, in both organisations, female political participation was aligned to the protection of familial life. As one local Unionist women's association declared in 1911:

> If our homes are not sacred from the priest under the existing laws, what can we expect from a priest-governed Ireland ... let each woman in Ulster do a woman's part to stem the tide of Home Rule ... the Union ... meant everything to them – their civil and religious liberty, their homes and children ... once the Union was severed there could be no outlook in Ulster but strife and bitterness ... Home was a woman's first consideration ... in the event of Home Rule being granted, the sanctity and happiness of home life in Ulster would be permanently destroyed.[42]

The focus of the UWUC was, however, narrower than that of the Primrose League. The former identified the defeat of home rule as its sole concern and would not engage with the women's suffrage debate. This stance was likely inspired by the Primrose League whose Grand Council declared suffrage off the agenda in 1899 although it would not intervene if local habitations discussed the issue. By comparison, the UWUC's suffrage avoidance was all-embracing. The discrepancy between the two associations' views can be explained by the more charged Irish political terrain where any variance from opposing home rule was seen as prejudicial to the Unionist cause.[43]

'Arousing the conscience of England'[44]

From 1885 to 1911 much of the Unionist campaign focused on Britain as many believed that home rule would be defeated at Westminster. The creation and maintenance of a strong pro-Unionist parliamentary base was therefore seen as paramount. As Conservative leader, Walter Long advised, 'steps [should] be taken to get in touch with individual [British] electors and friendly associations as to open the Irish question in various constituencies and prepare to follow up'.[45] A British campaign also allowed unionism to be considered within a broader imperial context: one of the most active female Unionist workers, Edith Mercier-Clements appealed for Unionists to 'speak to the English electors, telling them that Home Rule for Ireland meant complete separation – a cleavage of the Empire at its very heart'.[46]

To coordinate this campaign, from the 1890s Unionist clubs had a linkage system, matching Irish branches to English and Scottish Unionists which inspired the forerunners of the UWUC. [47] The Ladies' Committee of the Irish Unionist Alliance, for instance, linked its branches to English constituencies and sent literature to marginal Liberal constituencies in the 1890s, and an early twentieth-century local incarnation of female unionism, North Tyrone Women's Unionist Association (WUA) was connected to sympathetic bodies in English constituencies and sent speakers to England from 1907. Two months later a campaign involving twelve speakers and twenty-five workers was being devised for Darlington and Cornwall.[48]

Political education and canvassing work in marginal British constituencies was a Unionist priority, but Theresa Londonderry acknowledged the challenges of an augmented electorate: 'every election is not now won by speeches and meetings, but on the doorsteps – by distributing literature and by personally canvassing the people'.[49] Such prioritisation explains why, just two months after its foundation, the UWUC created a Literature Committee with remit for English and Scottish propaganda. They subsequently distributed leaflets such as 'Reasons Why the English Workingman Should Vote Against Home Rule' and 'The Irish Question in Brief for Busy English People', which formed part of a huge propaganda campaign. By September 1913 a hundred Unionist women in Belfast sent 10,000 leaflets and newspapers weekly to Britain, with some sent directly to public houses as 'both Radicals and Conservatives met there and discussed the [home rule] question in a less partisan spirit than in their own clubs', as well as to Protestant clergy and working men's clubs.[50] Although it is difficult to measure the impact of this aspect of the campaign, correspondents claimed radicals were converted to the Unionist cause.[51]

To the same end, women worked as 'unionist missionaries' in Britain; twenty-six women were based permanently in England and Scotland at the height of the third home rule crisis of 1912–14, seeking 'to address Radical' and working-class audiences.[52] Each was issued with an introduction slip, reaffirming the constraints of the Unionist remit: 'I want to make it clear that I am here as an Irishwomen to explain the dangers that will arise to your country and mine by the adoption of the government policy of Home Rule, and that I do not concern myself with other questions in which English Unionist may be interested.'[53] Thus, in addition to the suffrage question, other areas of British Conservative and Unionist interest, like tariff reform and local government, would not be entertained. This was a long-standing Unionist conundrum. Bonar Law, for example, caused Irish consternation in 1913 by 'making so much of Tariff Reform':

> Why can't he leave it alone and let you [Carson] win the battle on Ulster and Home Rule? Several of us know that it is just what Birrell and some other members of the Cabinet want, that Tariff Reform should be brought in again, and then they think they are certain to win the election ... [to] befog the electors' minds with Tariff Reform, is very serious'.[54]

Rallying working-class interest was also testing. Lantern slides were the routine fodder of the political canvasser and UWUC 'missionary', but Mrs Sinclair, electioneering in Maidstone in 1912, also used the services of a conjurer. In this work Unionist women cooperated with an array of pro-Unionist bodies including the Primrose League, the Women's Protestant Union, English and Scottish Women's Unionist Associations, the Unionist Defence League and the Women's Amalgamated Unionist and Tariff Reform Association (WAUTRA) to update electoral registers, address meetings and canvass. This interaction was furthered by a revival of the linkage system pioneered by the Unionist clubs: the UWUC connected its local Women's Unionist Associations (WUA) to sympathetic English and Scottish organisations. By 1913 twenty-one of the thirty-two WUAs in Ulster were twinned in this way. For example, Dunmurray WUA in South Belfast was linked to its Macclesfield equivalent, sending literature to a 150 known radicals whose names and addresses were supplied by the Macclesfield organisation. Unionists subsequently enjoyed some by-election victories. Leith Burghs in Scotland was won for Unionists in 1914 for the first time since 1832 and there were further successes in South Buckinghamshire and Bethnal Green which the seven UWUC literature workers, collaborating with two female southern Unionists, claimed as a personal victory, being 'convinced it is entirely due to our pamphlets'.[55]

By comparison, interaction with the Irish habitations of the Primrose League, with an estimated membership of 1,500 representing just 0.2 per cent of the overall organisation by 1912, was limited.[56] This was an extreme example of growing Primrose malaise and Unionist contact with the Women's Unionist and Tariff Reform Association was more sustained and significant. WAUTRA developed from the Women's Unionist Tariff Reform Association formed in 1906. In 1909 it merged with surviving Liberal Unionist women's bodies to establish WAUTRA and in 1912 the larger summation of the Conservatives and Liberal Unionists further aided WAUTRA's growth. Indeed, the *Primrose League Gazette* acknowledged that it faced increased competition for members and WAUTRA emerged victorious. With over 500 branches, the latter became 'the forerunner of the official women's arm of the Conservative Party'.[57]

WAUTRA organised an anti-home rule conference in 1911, raised funds for visiting female Unionist speakers (twenty of whom were invited to England and Scotland in mid-1911) and offered various English newspapers material relating to the UWUC and its workers. WAUTRA president, Mary Maxse also addressed the women's council in Belfast in 1916 and workers were sent to Ulster where the UWUC escorted them to Nationalist areas in the north-west of Ulster and then to so-called 'loyal districts in the East to contrast the prosperity and industry which prevailed there'.[58] Yet, there was always an element of Unionist expediency to such interactions; cooperation with WAUTRA was only sanctioned where 'it seemed likely to be of use to … [unionism] and … in other places we should work independently'.[59] The UWUC also sought support from beyond established British women's associations and beyond conservatism, initiating an Association of Unionist Ulsterwomen in London, which attracted 175 members by 1913.[60]

A different political emphasis also characterised their British campaign. The fear that Irish home rule would equate to Rome Rule and Catholic domination of the Protestant minority was the Unionists' most pressing concern. However, this was played down in British Unionist propaganda in favour of empire as Unionists sought to widen their appeal and align with an entity that was larger than any party. This reprioritisation was also, at times, at the request of organisations like the Scottish Women's Unionist Association which asked 'that Ulster workers should not touch on the question of Religion in Ireland when speaking in the West of Scotland'.[61] This was particularly marked in aftermath of the Unionist disquiet which accompanied the 1911 McCann mixed-marriage case in Belfast where children were removed from their Protestant mother by their Catholic father in the wake of the 1908 *Ne Temere* papal decree of Pius X. The UWUC amassed close to mile of signatures on an anti-*Ne Temere* petition by April 1912 and sought to issue this in pamphlet form in England and Scotland 'as an appeal to … women … for help':

> Serious dangers would arise from investing legislative function to a body of which a large and permanent majority would be under ecclesiastical control … of the Roman Catholic Church … [which] claims uncontrolled jurisdiction in the provinces of

education and marriage law … in an Irish parliament the natural instincts of humanity would be of no avail … against the dictates of the Roman Church … No valid reason has been advanced for depriving Irish women of the rights and privileges which they now enjoy.[62]

Given this heightened apprehension, the UWUC's response to the Scottish Women's Unionist Association's request was somewhat predictable: religion could not be wholly avoided, but Unionist workers were advised 'in doubtful cases to refer to it as a 'majority question' and to speak of the opinion of 'Political Priests'.[63]

Unionists also became increasingly concerned that Britain simply failed to comprehend their predicament. The Parliament Act of 1911, the associated delay, but not defeat, of the third home rule bill in 1912 and disappointing Conservative electoral performances, cumulatively shook Unionist faith. As early as 1911, in the midst of political backbiting over the Parliament Act, Carson wrote to confidante Theresa Londonderry with a characteristic despondency: 'I am sick to death of the Home Rule tragedy. It … will spilt the Party to pieces and, should it turn out to be true, I earnestly hope the Conservatives will never again be in office during my life.'[64] Writing from England in the following year, Carson reiterated his disillusion: 'No one cares here and everyone does there [in Ireland] – that is the whole difference.'[65] The increased urgency of the Unionist campaign in the post-1911 period is evidenced by the growing number of UWUC speakers in Britain: in 1911 twenty women addressed six English constituencies; by the close of 1913 ninety-six women in ninety-three constituencies addressed 230 meetings and between June 1913 and March 1914 the UWUC canvassed 14,000 electors in sixty-five British constituencies at a cost of £95. Such work entailed long periods away from home and explains the preponderance of unmarried female unionist 'missionaries': over two thirds of Unionist women working in this capacity were unmarried in 1914.[66] A process of acclimatisation removed the most marked bias toward female speakers by the time of the third home rule crisis, but class considerations remained: 'ladies' were sought for small cottage meetings, drawing rooms, village schools and larger meetings whereas 'women of any class' were believed capable of 'house to house' work.[67]

The Unionist crisis of confidence ultimately led them to be become less focused on Parliament and Britain. This resulted in a process of 'Ulsterisation' whereby Unionist loyalty became conditional on home rule not being foisted upon them.[68] As Todd notes, this defensive stance materialised when Unionists felt threatened.[69] A growing defiance was certainly evident in both male and female unionism. A printed UWUC statement of 1912, for example, declared:

we make it known to all whom it may concern that we will stand by our men folk in resisting to the uppermost the domination and control of a rebel parliament in Dublin … should Home Rule be forced upon Ireland … we shall remain as we are, with unimpaired citizenship in the UK and with representation as we now have it in the Imperial Parliament.[70]

The scheme for 'Ulster Day' on 28 September 1912, when with men and women signed the Ulster Solemn League and Covenant and Women's Declaration respectively, stands as a striking example of both the introspective process of 'Ulsterisation' and conditional Unionist loyalty. The text of the Women's Declaration, although having words like 'calamity' in common with the covenant, also reinforced women's place within unionism; they would 'associate themselves' with men as part of a Unionist movement now determined to use whatever means were necessary to defeat home rule.[71] Unionist plans for a provisional government in Belfast were announced in September 1913 and signalled another move away from reliance on Westminster.[72] The formation of the Ulster Volunteer Force (UVF) in the same year was the clearest indication that Unionists were moving from constitutionalism to militarism and preparing for civil war.[73] The UVF was backed by female Nursing, Driving and Signalling Corps which the women's council helped to administer, drafting training schemes, organising first aid classes and securing equipment and supplies for medical units which were established throughout Ulster. Some women were also involved in intelligence work, deciphering police messages, for example, and a smaller number were involved in gun running. A concern that Unionist propaganda destined for Britain was being intercepted in Belfast Post Office in 1914 led the UWUC to encourage members to send material to known sympathisers and take leaflets with them if they were travelling to Britain. This pragmatism did not materially diminish the scale of the campaign: 3,184 packets of leaflets were, for instance, taken to England in January 1914.[74]

Despite the growing belligerence, support was still forthcoming from bodies like WAUTRA who sent resolutions of a support during this phase of the fight against home rule.[75] Theresa Londonderry's patronage of the Conservative leader Andrew Bonar Law after his accession in late 1911 helped him to better understand the Unionist position and British Unionists like F. E. Smith remained steadfast.[76] In 1913 the Primrose League also changed its oath to affirm its allegiance to maintaining the union.[77] There were, however, concerns amidst a faction of the UWUC of Conservative Party puppetry: 'the [UWU] Council is allowing itself to be made the fool of the English Conservative Party and its agents and organizations, who have no regard for Ulster except as a lever for securing their own return to power'.[78] Conservative apprehension that this more militant manifestation of unionism would not be an election winner also emerged and Balfour and Chamberlain distanced themselves. Their former faith in Unionist loyalty to crown and empire and the notion of a Protestant ascendancy ruling class became increasingly hard to align with militarism. Loyalty to unionism was no longer absolute throughout the Conservative Party; only 300 Primrose League habitations, for example, signed a memorial to Carson in 1914 and a similar number were active in the UWUC's ongoing campaign.[79] Thus, as Rodner highlights, the majority of British Unionists distanced themselves from the military preparations while pledging their support in the event of civil war over home rule.[80]

This was evident within the British associations that the UWUC collaborated with on the most regular basis; evacuation schemes for women and children from Ulster to Britain in the event of a civil war reached the planning stages in a 1913 joint venture, which temporarily overcame organisational jealousies, by WAUTRA and the Primrose League. The former also launched an appeal to offer accommodation 'to the women and children whose fathers and sons have fought Great Britain's battles in Great Britain's hour of need. Alas that they should be reaping Great Britain's ingratitude.'[81] The League's Help the Ulster Women Committee further secured accommodation for 8,000 and donations totalling £17,000.[82] Others made individual approaches to the UWUC; the Duchess of Somerset pledged to send an equipped medical unit to Ulster on 'the day the first shot is fired'.[83] The Duchess of Newcastle also tried to rally Unionist women in Nottinghamshire to donate to 'show some appreciation for Ulster fellow Unionists, who by their deeds are giving everything including their lives, if needs be, to the cause ... If this government remains in power much longer no one can tell what will happen.'[84] Others offered to nurse the wounded if war broke out,[85] while Lord Curzon's 1914 new year address averred that it was 'the duty of every Primrose Leaguer ... to support those who are so bravely fighting the battle of the Union in Ireland and to insist that the least words on the Home Rule Bill shall be spoken ... by the British democracy'.[86]

Conservatives 'behaving too badly over Ulster'[87]

The conflict which occurred was not a civil war over home rule, but the First World War. The delayed third home rule bill of 1912 passed in 1914, but was immediately suspended for the duration of the war with special treatment promised for Ulster. In consequence of their ancillary status, women were not consulted on the Unionist political truce which was subsequently declared, but their workers in English and Scottish constituencies were recalled. Unionist interaction with Conservative bodies such as WAUTRA and the Primrose League and the Association of Unionist Ulsterwomen in London were all subsequent casualties of the wartime truce.

Ultimately, the war made Unionist concerns look 'very small'.[88] Following the 1916 Irish rising, some Unionists expected a compromise from Lloyd George which would invalidate all that was agreed in Asquith's 1914 Act and the special position promised for Ulster in any subsequent home rule settlement.[89] However, there was mounting mistrust of previous allies including the former Conservative Party leader, Bonar Law. As Ruby Carson, wife of the Unionist leader, recorded in her diary: 'Bonar Law and Co. ... have quite gone for Home Rule and are altogether beneath contempt – but it's all very worrying in the middle of a war ... [they] ought to have decent feelings – I hope to never have to meet one of them again.'.[90] Unionist fears that an unpalatable salve for Ireland would come in the midst of the war intensified: 'The Unionists in the Cabinet are now trying to throw over ... Ulster and say they never knew there were to be negotiations which is a lie. They are more contemptible than Asquith himself.'[91] Relations with Lloyd George became very strained; he 'turned against' Carson 'completely and is doing his best, very successfully, to turn everyone else in the Government against him. If Sir Edward writes to him now on any Irish question, he doesn't even answer.'[92] The need for Unionist representation at the Irish convention ultimately overcame Carson and Craig's commitment to the wartime coalition: they withdrew from the cabinet in January 1918.[93]

Post-war, with moves towards partition for the six north-eastern counties of Ulster and dominion status for a new Irish Free State, the bonds between female unionism and conservatism were largely lost. Never one of its more popular initiatives, the practice of associate UWUC membership was not revived and this was characteristic of the continued autonomy of Ulster unionism in the post-war period. Although in the early 1920s female Unionist representatives attended the annual Women's Conference of Conservative and Unionist Associations in England, the UWUC funded female scholarships to attend the Bonar Law College, literature was sent to Britain and female Unionist speakers were requested to work in English and Scottish constituencies, this work never regained the dynamism of the third home rule crisis and arguably neither did unionism. The Irish Unionist Alliance split in 1919 and the Ulster Women's Unionist Council of the early twentieth century remains the largest female political force in Ireland's history.[94]

This consideration of the inter-relationship between female conservatism and unionism provides a gendered example of political partiality. Resisting home rule was always Unionists' raison d'être while, as Boyce has observed, 'as far as British conservative opinion was concerned, the fate of Ulster, or of any part of Ulster, was always secondary to what were regarded as the interests of England and of the British empire'.[95] Thus, by 1920, the UWUC highlighted that 'The English and Scotch electors, unfortunately, seem to have lost interest in the Irish Question, being more deeply concerned with the Labour situation' and post-war reconstruction. Although the organisation distributed propaganda on 'The Cause of Loyal Ulster', they averred: 'The future holds much uncertainty for the loyal population of the Six Counties … our watchword is still "UNION".' Indeed, their claim that 'The struggle against the enemies of the Empire and of Ulster is not at an end, it is merely transferred to a new field', could only conclude that 'Ulster stands alone as never before'.[96]

Notes

1 The title is an extract from the Countess of Erne's reaction to Bonar Law's Blenheim speech of 27 July 1912, *Belfast News-Letter*, 2 August 1912.

2 See, for example, E. H. H. Green, *Ideologies of Conservatism: Conservative Political Ideas in the 20th Century* (Oxford University Press: Oxford, 2002).

3 *Trewman's Exeter Flying Post*, 5 September 1883.

4 *Leicester Chronicle*, 8 September 1883. A number of guides to the complexities of the

Corrupt and Illegal Practices Prevention Act were produced, including J. E. Gorst's *Election Manual*; Ernest A. Jelf, The *Corrupt and Illegal Practices Prevention Act* which ran to a second edition in 1885; J. C. Carter's *Corrupt and Illegal Practices Prevention Act* and a Conservative Central Office election abstract. *The Pall Mall Gazette* offered one of the clearest overviews of the Act on 12 October 1883. The Conservative Primrose League also advertised that anyone found in breach of the Act would cease to be a member of its organisation (*Weekly Irish Times*, 26 June 1886).

5 Kathryn Rix, '"The Elimination of Corrupt Practices at British Elections?" Reassessing the Impact of the 1883 Corrupt Practices Act', *English Historical Review*, 123: 500 (February 2008), 67 and 70.

6 The term personation refers to fraudulent voting in consequence of assuming another voter's identity.

7 *Trewman's Exeter Flying Post*, 5 September 1883.

8 *Aberdeen Weekly Journal*, 20 September 1883.

9 *Sheffield and Rotherham Independent*, 12 September 1883.

10 *Aberdeen Weekly Journal*, 20 September 1883.

11 Rix, 'The Elimination of Corrupt Practices', pp. 79, 80 and cited p. 90.

12 K. Theodore Hoppen, 'Roads to Democracy: Electioneering and Corruption in 19th-century England and Ireland', in *History*, 81: 264 (October 1996), 554.

13 Krista Cowman, *Women in British Politics, c.1689–1979* (Palgrave Macmillan: Basingstoke, 2010), p. 91.

14 Associate members paid lower membership fees and comprised the majority of members by the end of the nineteenth century. The League's mixed-sex habitations were the most popular. For a full list of membership figures from 1884 to 1900 see Linda Walker, 'Party Political Women: A Comparative Study of Liberal Women and the Primrose League, 1890–1914', in Jane Rendall (ed.), *Equal or Different: Women's Politics, 1800–1914* (Blackwell: Oxford, 1987), p. 171.

15 F. G. Marcham, 'Review of J. H. Robb, *The Primrose League*', *Journal of Economic History*, 4: 1 (May 1944), p. 100.

16 Ben Griffin, T*he Politics of Gender in Victorian Britain. Masculinity, Political Culture and the Struggle for Women's Rights* (Cambridge University Press: Cambridge, 2012), pp. 264–5.

17 Cowman, *Women in British Politics*, p. 99.

18 See John F. Harbinson, *The Ulster Unionist Party, 1882–1973, its Development and Organisation* (Belfast: Blackstaff Press, 1973). Colonel Edward Saunderson was the first leader of the Irish group. Liberal Unionists were also in an anti-home rule alliance with Conservatives from 1886, but remained a distinct organisation until 1912.

19 Randolph Churchill became the first Chancellor of the Primrose League in 1884. He was later succeeded by another Unionist stalwart, the Earl of Abercorn in 1883.

20 H. Montgomery Hyde, *Carson* (Heinemann: London, 1953), p. 297. See Diane Urquhart, *The Ladies of Londonderry. Women and political patronage, 1800–1959* (I. B. Tauris: London and New York, 2007). The Dowager Marchioness of Waterford and Julia, Marchioness of Waterford also sat on the League's first Ladies' Grand Council. For the Ordinances of the Ladies' Grand Council, see the *Primrose League Gazette*, 2 January 1899.

21 Martin Pugh, *The Tories and the People* (Oxford University Press: Oxford, 1985), p. 90. Henderson Robb concurs, suggesting a 'gargantuan increase … after the injection of the Home Rule issue into the political picture' in 1886 (Janet Henderson Robb, *The Primrose League, 1883–1906* (Columbia University Press: New York, 1968), p. 58. The Plan of Campaign sought to secure rent reductions for Irish tenants in the period 1886–91.

22 Irish branches of bodies like the Girls' Friendly Society also distributed anti-home rule material in 1890s.

23 Pugh, *Tories and the People*, pp. 89 and 215.

24 *Irish Times*, 8 January 1902. The meeting opened with a rendition of 'Rule Britannia'.

25 Henderson Robb, *Primrose League*, p. 60.

26 Liberal premier, W. E. Gladstone introduced the first home rule bill to the House of Commons in April 1886. The bill proposed the establishment of an Irish legislature with restricted functions, but was defeated in the Commons in June 1886. Gladstone also introduced the second home rule bill in January 1893. It passed its third reading in the Commons with the repeated use of closure, but was subsequently rejected by the Lords in September 1893.

27 Isabella Tod speaking at the 1892 *conversazione*, F. J. Biggar Collection, Central Library, Belfast, Q. 126, *Report of the general meeting of 12,000 delegates at the Ulster convention* (np: Belfast, 1892), p. 104.

28 The comment was made by the Ulster Unionist Council's Thomas Sinclair addressing the inaugural meeting of the UWUC in 1911 (*Belfast News-Letter*, 24 January 1911).

29 Isabella Tod speaking at the 1892 *conversazione*, p. 104.

30 For example, in North Tyrone from 1907 and in Londonderry from 1909.

31 Work on the UWUC includes Nancy Kinghan, *United We Stood: Official history of the Ulster Women's Unionist Council, 1911–75* (Belfast: Appletree Press, 1975); Diane Urquhart, *Women in Ulster Politics, 1890–1940: A History Not Yet Told* (Dublin: Irish Academic Press, 2000); Diane Urquhart (ed.), *The Minutes of the Ulster Women's Unionist Council and Executive Committee, 1911–40* (Dublin: Irish Manuscripts Commission, 2001); Diane Urquhart, '"The Female of the Species is more Deadlier than the Male"?: The Ulster Women's Unionist Council, 1911–40', in Janice Holmes and Diane Urquhart (eds), *Coming into the Light: The Work, Politics and Religion of Women in Ulster, 1840–1940* (Belfast: Institute of Irish Studies, 1994), pp. 93–123 and Diane Urquhart, 'In Defence of Ulster and the Empire: The Ulster Women's Unionist Council, 1886–1940', *Galway Women's Studies Centre Review*, 4 (1996), 31–40.

32 See Alvin Jackson, 'Unionist Politics and Protestant Society in Edwardian Ireland', in *The Historical Journal*, 33: 4 (December 1990), 839–66.

33 For example, an estimated 25,000 women greeted Carson on his first visit to west Belfast in 1913 which was believed to be the largest assemblage of women in Ireland's history (PRONI, D2688/1/3, UWUC Annual Report for 1913).

34 The Liberal government of H. H. Asquith introduced the Parliament Act of 1911.

35 Conservative patrons of unionism included F. E. Smith, Arthur Balfour, Austen Chamberlain, Lords Milner and Roberts. See T. A. Jackson, *The Ulster Party: Irish Unionists in the House of Commons, 1884–1911* (Oxford: Clarendon Press, 1989). As noted, Liberal Unionists also remained separate from the Conservatives until the 1912

creation of the National Unionist Association of Conservative and Liberal Unionist Associations, often abbreviated to the Unionist Association.

36 Hyde, *Carson*, cited p. 418. Carson was true to his word; he passed the mantle of Unionist leader to James Craig in 1921. Craig subsequently became the first Prime Minister of Northern Ireland.

37 For example, spouse of the UWUC's first president, Mary Anne, 2nd Duchess of Abercorn, was a Unionist MP for Co. Donegal from 1860, the leading spokesman for unionism in the Lords from 1895 and first president of the Unionist Association of Ireland.

38 Mary Anne, 2nd Duchess of Abercorn was the first president of the UWUC (1911–13). She was succeeded by Theresa, 6th Marchioness of Londonderry (1913–19). Theresa Londonderry was replaced by Rosalind, 3rd Duchess of Abercorn (1919–22). She was succeeded by Lady Cecil Craig, later Viscountess Craigavon (1922–42).

39 Walker, 'Party Political Women', p. 173.

40 *Belfast News-Letter*, 24 January 1911. This caused minimal protest in UWUC ranks. One of the few complaints came from one of the UWUC's most active workers, Edith Mercier-Clements who was frustrated at their tentative approach to politics: 'The time was long past when women had to make an apology for mixing in such affairs, because any woman could do as much to influence public opinion as any man' (*Northern Whig*, 10 January 1912).

41 Walker, 'Party Political Women', p. 173.

42 Public Record Office of Northern Ireland (hereafter PRONI), D3790/4, minute book of Lurgan Women's Unionist Association, 13 May 1911.

43 The women's Unionist leader, Theresa Londonderry and the Unionist leader, Edward Carson were both staunch anti-suffragists. On the Ulster suffrage movement, see Diane Urquhart, '"An articulate and definite cry for political freedom": the Ulster suffrage movement, 1870–1918', *Women's History Review*, 11: 2 (2002), 273–92.

44 PRONI, D3790/4, Miss Sinclair speaking at Lurgan Women's Unionist Association, 5 May 1911.

45 PRONI, D1098/2/1/1, North Tyrone Women's Unionist Association, 28 May 1907.

46 *Ibid.*

47 Unionist Clubs were first established in 1893, but were revived in 1911. See Harbinson, *Ulster Unionist Party*.

48 PRONI, D1098/2/1/1, North Tyrone Women's Unionist Association minute book, 28 May and 30 July 1907.

49 Theresa, 6th Marchioness of Londonderry, *Belfast News-Letter*, 24 January 1911.

50 The UWUC's Literary Sub-Committee, established in May 1913, scanned both the Unionist and Nationalist press for articles of interest to send to England and Scotland. See PRONI, D1089/1/1, UWUC Executive Committee minutes, 22 September 1911.

51 See, for example, PRONI, D1460/11, letter of Col. R. H. Wallace read at a June 1912 UWUC meeting.

52 PRONI, D/2688/1/3, UWUC Active Workers' Committee minutes, 15 November 1912.

53 PRONI, D1098/1/1, UWUC Executive Committee minutes, 7 June 1911. Irish women were admitted to the local government franchise later than their English counterparts

in a series of piecemeal reforms introduced from 1887. See Urquhart, *Women in Ulster Politics*, pp. 118–74.

54 PRONI, D1507/A/4/14, Rt. Hon. Frederick Wrench, Dublin to Edward Carson, 14 November 1913.

55 PRONI, D1633/2/19, Lilian Spender diary entry, 23 February 1914.

56 Pugh, *Tories and the People*, p. 168.

57 Mitzi Auchterlonie, *Conservative Suffragists. The Women's Vote and the Tory Party* (London and New York: I. B. Tauris, 2007), p. 87.

58 PRONI, D1098/1/1, UWUC Executive Committee minutes, 21 July 1911.

59 *Ibid.*, 27 October 1911.

60 *Ibid.*, 15 October 1912.

61 PRONI, D2688/1/3, UWUC Standing Committee and Active Workers minutes, 6 December 1912.

62 PRONI, D1098/1/1, UWUC Executive Committee minutes, 27 March 1912. The *Ne Temere* decree declared mixed marriages null and void unless solemnised according to the rites of the Catholic Church. The petition bore the names of over 100,000 women and was presented to Parliament by Sir John Lonsdale. The UWUC also aimed to have Dublin women sign the petition.

63 PRONI, D2688/1/3, UWUC Standing Committee and Active Workers minutes, 6 December 1912.

64 Hyde, *Carson*, p. 279.

65 Carson to Theresa Londonderry, 13 August 1912 in Hyde, *Carson*, cited, p. 316.

66 Kinghan, *United We Stood*, p. 14; PRONI, D2846/1/2/7 and D1098/1/1. In 1913–14 the UWUC expended £2,259 on workers' travelling expenses. Of the ninety-seven UWUC workers in June 1914, sixty-six (representing 68 per cent) were unmarried.

67 PRONI, D1089/1/1, UWUC Executive Committee minutes, 7 April 1911.

68 Jackson, *Ulster Party*, p. 326. The term 'Ulsteria' was also in contemporary use. The *Westminster Gazette* referred to it, for example, as 'not so much an argument as a disease' (20 April 1987).

69 See Jennifer Todd, 'Two Traditions in Unionist Political Culture', *Irish Political Studies*, 2 (1897), 1–26.

70 PRONI, D1098/1/1, UWUC annual meeting, 18 January 1912.

71 See PRONI, D1313/1 for the text of the Women's Declaration. Just under 229,000 women signed the declaration compared to 218,000 male signatories to the Covenant (figure for female signatories cited in PRONI, D/1089/1/1, UWUC Executive Committee minutes, 16 January 1913. Figure for male signatories cited in A. T. Q. Stewart, *The Ulster Crisis. Resistance to Home Rule, 1912–14* (London: Faber, 1969), p. 66. Ulster women resident elsewhere in Ireland signed in much smaller numbers, for example, 768 in Dublin and just twenty-six in Waterford. A British covenant and declaration was also signed by those of Ulster birth, but unlike its Ulster equivalent, this attracted more male signatories than female; 19,162 men signed in comparison to 5,047 women. With British and Ulster signatories combined, 237,368 men signed, compared to 234,046 women. Another British covenant was signed by over two million men and women in 1914.

72 These plans included an unconfirmed commitment to women's suffrage.

73 See Jane G. V. McGaughey, *Ulster's Men. Protestant Unionist Masculinities and Militarization in the North of Ireland, 1912–23* (Montreal and Kingston: McGill-Queen's University Press, 2012).

74 PRONI, D1098/1/1, UWUC Executive Committee minutes, 17 February 1914.

75 See, for example, PRONI, D/1089/1/1, letter from the North Lambert branch of the Women's Tariff Reform League.

76 Contemporaries acknowledged that Theresa's influential political connections allowed the UWUC to act on a much wider stage by securing 'openings in Great Britain for its workers'. *Ulster Women's Unionist Council Year Book* (Belfast: Ulster Women's Unionist Council, 1920).

77 Pugh, *Tories and the People*, p. 174.

78 PRONI, D2688/1/5, UWUC Advisory Committee minutes, June 1914.

79 Pugh, *Tories and the People*, p. 165.

80 William S. Rodner, 'Leaguers, Covenanters, Moderates. British Support for Ulster, 1913–14', *Eire-Ireland*, 17: 3 (Fall 1982), 84.

81 PRONI, D1098/2/4. WAUTRA's Miss Austen Park attended a UWUC meeting in late 1913 to offer shelter for Ulster women and children (see PRONI, D2866/1/5, UWUC Advisory Committee minutes, 20 December 1913).

82 Pugh, *Tories and the People*, p. 152.

83 PRONI, D1507/1/6/41, January 1914.

84 Seventeen women subsequently raised £670 and the Duchess of Newcastle donated £100 in April 1914 (PRONI, D2846/1/11/37).

85 PRONI, D2846/1/11/12.

86 *Weekly Irish Times*, 3 January 1914.

87 PRONI, D1507/C/2, diary of Lady Ruby Carson, 26 April 1916.

88 PRONI, D1295/17/3, letter extracts of Lady Lilian Spender, 2 May 1917.

89 PRONI, D1507/C/2, diary of Lady Ruby Carson, 27 April 1916. The 1920 Government of Ireland Act repealed Asquith's Act of 1914.

90 PRONI, D1507/C/2, diary of Lady Ruby Carson, 26–7 April 1916.

91 *Ibid.*, 14 June 1916.

92 A. T. Q. Stewart, *Edward Carson* (Dublin: Gill & Macmillan, 1981), p. 115.

93 Carson was Attorney General and Craig was Treasurer of the Household and government whip.

94 Membership of the Irish suffrage movement, for example, peaked at an estimated 3,500 members whilst membership of the Irish Nationalist organisation, Cumann na mBan (the Women's Council) peaked at *c*.12,000 in 1919.

95 D. G. Boyce, 'British Conservative Opinion, the Ulster Question, and the Partition of Ireland, 1912–21', *Irish Historical Studies*, 17: 65 (March 1970), 89.

96 PRONI, D2688/1/9, UWUC annual report in *Ulster Year Book*, 1920. The UWUC is still in existence today.

2

Christabel Pankhurst:
a Conservative suffragette?

June Purvis

A biographical approach to the writing of history can help us elucidate some of the issues involved when 'rewriting' right-wing women, and offer us a way to understand the complexities and apparent paradoxes of the human personality, as well as the process of writing history. The suffragette Christabel Pankhurst (1880–1958) is a case in point. In her suffrage heyday, she was regarded as a charismatic, radical figure who, with her mother Emmeline Pankhurst, was the co-leader of the Women's Social and Political Union (WSPU), the most notorious of the many suffrage organisations campaigning for the parliamentary vote for women in Edwardian Britain.[1]

The WSPU was founded by Emmeline Pankhurst on 10 October 1903 at her home, 62 Nelson Street, Manchester. Christabel was present, as were some local socialist women who were members of the Independent Labour Party (ILP).[2] All the Pankhurst family – Emmeline and her three daughters, Christabel, Sylvia and Adela, as well as her son, Harry – were ILP members of the local Manchester Central Branch.[3] However, Emmeline and Christabel had become disillusioned with Labour men who seemed to think that there were more important matters than women's enfranchisement. The women-only WSPU, founded on 10 October with its slogan, 'Deeds, not words', was to be 'an independent non-party, non-class organisation', recollected Christabel. It was not officially affiliated to the ILP although it ran parallel to it.[4]

At this time the parliamentary vote was based on the ownership of property or occupation of property of a minimum value and restricted to men, about 59 per cent of the adult male population being thus enfranchised. All women – as well as criminals and patients in lunatic asylums – remained voteless, irrespective of these property qualifications.[5] It was this sex discrimination that Christabel, the WSPU's Chief Organiser and key strategist, sought to end. From 1903 until the outbreak of the First World War, she and her mother campaigned tirelessly for votes for women on the same terms as men, enlisting the support of thousands of 'suffragettes', as members of the WSPU came to be named.[6]

In its early years, the WSPU engaged in peaceful tactics but as the Liberal government of the day refused to grant women the parliamentary vote, more violent, illegal forms of protest were adopted, especially from 1912 – attacks on private and public buildings, setting fire to mail in post boxes, large-scale window smashing of shops in London's West End and arson. Such militancy was only suspended in August 1914 when war was declared. Both WSPU leaders patriotically supported their county in its hour of need.

When Christabel died in 1958, many tributes were paid to her. Christabel Pankhurst, with her 'magnetic personality' was 'the driving force' behind the militant suffragette movement, asserted *The Times*, and 'possibly its most brilliant orator'. It continued: 'A most attractive young woman with fresh colouring, delicate features, and a mass of soft brown hair, a graceful figure on the platform, she spoke with a warmth, a passion, and a highly effective *raillerie*, which few who were prepared to give her a hearing could resist ... Courageous and resourceful ... she was a force to be reckoned with.'[7] The *New York Times* went further, suggesting that Christabel Pankhurst 'probably did more than any other individual to make women's suffrage come true in Britain in 1918'.[8]

The British state obviously considered Christabel Pankhurst an important figure since during her lifetime, in 1936, she was honoured by being made a Dame Commander of the Order of the British Empire. Yet despite this state recognition and the various favourable press pronouncements about her importance in British political history, she has been consistently denigrated by historians and feminist scholars as 'right wing'. Thus Les Garner speaks of 'the growing conservatism' of Christabel and her mother during their suffrage years as do Martin Pugh and G. E. Maguire.[9] David Mitchell describes Christabel in unflattering terms as ruthless, bourgeois, man-hating, autocratic and right wing while Martin Pugh in his collective biography of the Pankhurst family even makes the unconvincing assertion that by 1917, she was 'on the high road that leads to fascism'.[10]

My aim in this chapter is to challenge this frequently made claim that Christabel Pankhurst was right wing, a 'Conservative Suffragette'. In order to engage in such an appraisal, I discuss the influential socialist feminist historiography about the suffragette movement that cast her in such a light. I then offer an alternative analysis that places her much more fairly within a different feminist tradition.

One of the earliest and most influential accounts of the suffragette movement was written by a former participant and younger sister of Christabel. Sylvia Pankhurst's *The Suffragette Movement*, was first published in 1931. Partly historical and partly autobiographical, Sylvia subtitled her book 'an intimate account of persons and ideals'. The text was not only a history of the suffragette movement but also an account of the Pankhurst family, all told through the lens of socialist feminism and through the various tensions that were only too apparent between Emmeline Pankhurst and her middle daughter, and between the daughters themselves.

In the preface to her book, Sylvia states that her book is largely made up of memories. Certainly memories of her disagreements with her mother and Christabel are evident throughout the text, shaping her interpretation of events, providing self-justification. Sylvia devotes ten chapters to her family background and childhood, describing how she, Christabel and Adela, the youngest Pankhurst daughter, were taken to political gatherings by their parents who were involved in the radical causes of their day, especially socialism and women's suffrage. Sylvia idolised her father, Richard, and felt neglected by her mother whose favourite child, she claims, was the clever and pretty Christabel, 'the apple of her eye'.[11] The rivalry between the two eldest Pankhurst girls is carried over into their adult lives so that Christabel is portrayed in the suffragette movement as an evil force upon their supposedly easily swayed, widowed, weak mother who is led from the true path of socialism: 'Mrs. Pankhurst, to whom her first-born had ever been the dearest of her children, proudly and openly proclaimed her eldest daughter to be her leader.'[12]

As noted, all the Pankhurst women were paid-up members of the ILP when the WSPU was founded, so when Christabel resigned from the ILP, four years later, in order to recruit more middle-class women of *all* political persuasions, Sylvia demonised her as the betrayer of socialist feminism: 'What interest she had ever possessed in the Socialist movement, in which she had reared, she had shed as readily as a garment'.[13] And as a separatist feminist who did not want to affiliate the WSPU to socialism or any male political party but to recruit women across the class divide, Sylvia accused her sister of marginalising the importance of class and of being a Conservative – 'I detested her incipient Toryism.'[14] As Jane Marcus has commented, Sylvia went further than merely criticising her mother and Christabel presenting herself as the 'heroine' of the suffragette campaign. From 1913, Sylvia had begun re-building WSPU branches among the poor in the East End of London, forming her own grouping, the East London Federation of the Suffragettes. And in *The Suffragette Movement* she suggests it is her success in getting the Liberal Prime Minister Herbert Asquith, an ardent anti-suffragist, to received her East London delegation of working women in June 1914 that was the key to winning the vote. Thus suffrage victory was claimed not in the name of separatist feminism but in the name of socialist feminism, a victory less over the government, asserts Marcus, than over Sylvia's 'real enemies, her mother and her sister'.[15]

Sylvia's account of the suffragette movement – and of the Pankhurst family – is a compelling one. Vividly written with lots of detail, it has become the dominant narrative in the historiography of the movement, eagerly read by feminists in the so-called 'Second Wave' of the women's movement in Western Europe and the USA. As feminists in the late 1960s and 1970s met in conscious-raising groups, many women on the Left looked to the past, to try to find out what their foremothers had been doing. *Hidden from History: 300 years of Women's Oppression and the Fight Against it*, the title of Sheila Rowbotham's path-breaking 1973 text, summed up the mood.[16] Women were largely absent from history, whether written from a socialist, liberal or mainstream perspective. Rowbotham's book was regarded as the 'taking-off' point for the development of women's history in Britain and it was socialist feminists who set the agenda – women like Rowbotham, Sally Alexander, Anna Davin, Barbara Taylor, Jill Norris and Jill Liddington who, at that time, were not employed in higher education but were closely linked to the socialist publication *History Workshop Journal*. The writing of women's history in Britain at this time was largely forged by socialist feminists who focused primarily on researching working-class women, exploring the ways in which their lives were shaped by capitalist exploitation, the class struggle and the sexual division of labour, both within the home and in paid work. And it was Sylvia Pankhurst's interpretation of the suffragette movement that these influential socialist feminists embraced, not the alternative memoirs written by Christabel or Emmeline Pankhurst.[17]

Rowbotham, for example, finds the WSPU focus on 'uniting women' through the 'single issue' of the vote wanting. 'It is curious', she writes, 'that at a time when increasing sections of the labour movement were becoming disillusioned with parliament, the women were ready to risk and suffer so much for the vote.'[18] After Christabel and Emmeline resigned from the ILP in 1907, it is claimed that they deliberately adopted a dubious policy of 'courting upper-class women'.[19] As they moved further and further away from their socialist roots, they clearly settled 'on the other side', becoming 'right-wing feminists' who supported the First World War.[20] The campaign for the vote was 'undoubtedly mainly middle class', it is asserted. Despite Rowbotham's plea that it 'was not a simple question of reactionary middle-class feminists versus enlightened working-class socialists', it is clear throughout her analysis that this is so.[21] Since for Rowbotham, the only form of valid political organisation is that adopted by the Left of mobilising workers in the class struggle against their capitalist employers, the WSPU is downgraded to a 'pressure group … Emmeline and Christabel did not think in terms of building a mass organisation or of mobilising workers to strike, but of making ever more dramatic gestures.'[22]

Liddington and Norris's account of the involvement of working-class women in radical suffragist politics in early twentieth-century Lancashire continues in the same vein – that the only significant form of struggle is against class exploitation. The suffragettes, it is claimed, 'represented no one but themselves; they could speak for no mass movement, and they could exert no pressure as trade unionists'.[23] Rather than criticise the Liberal government for refusing to grant women their democratic right to the parliamentary vote, Christabel is blamed for the 'bitter divisions and destructive splits' that occurred in the suffrage movement: 'co-operation' was not in her nature. And since Christabel supported the principle of 'votes for women' rather than putting first issues of social class, she is represented as right wing.[24]

I have always found such analyses problematic since these influential feminist historians judge Christabel Pankhurst from a socialist feminist perspective – and find her wanting. Christabel was not oblivious to the class inequalities between women, but she did not put social class relationships and the class struggle at the heart of her feminist perspective. For Christabel Pankhurst, the subjection and subordinate status of women in Edwardian society, evident in the denial of that most basic of human rights, the right to the parliamentary franchise, was due to the power of men. She emphasised the commonalities that all women shared, despite their differences, and the primary importance of putting women first rather than considerations of class conflict and class struggle. She saw the suffrage struggle as a 'sex war', where men were the main enemy.[25] It is only through exploring Christabel's feminist ideas, and placing her as a pioneer of what in the 1970s would become known as 'radical feminism' that we can interrogate and critically assess these widely cited claims that she was a Conservative suffragette.[26]

Christabel Pankhurst was already active in the WSPU in 1906 when, at the age of 25, she was awarded a first-class honours degree in Law from Manchester University. Yet, despite her highly prized graduate qualification, she was barred from entering the legal profession because she was a woman. Women had been campaigning for the vote at least from 1866, when the first women's suffrage petition was presented to Parliament, and this more personal insult undoubtedly added to her determination to do something about changing the subordinate status of women. After all, she had been for a number of years a member of the National Union of Women's Suffrage Societies (NUWSS) that advocated legal, constitutional and peaceful means of campaigning; but all the effort had not produced a successful result. Nor did the early years of peaceful campaigning by the WSPU catch the notice of MPs and the press. Women, Christabel believed, had for too long been patient and submissive – they needed to be roused, to become assertive about their democratic rights, to demand rather than ask politely for the parliamentary vote. So she decided on a more confrontational policy that drew on socialist traditions of political protest as well as the more radical currents within the women's movement.

On 13 October 1905, together with Annie Kenney, a working-class recruit to the WSPU, Christabel attended a Liberal Party meeting at Manchester Free Trade Hall. There was no mention of women's suffrage in the speech given by Sir Edward Grey and so Annie asked the question, worded in advance by Christabel: 'Will the Liberal Government give votes to women?' As expected, no answer was given and so Christabel hastily unfurled a small home-made banner of white calico on which had been written 'Votes for women'– and repeated the question. Angry cries broke out. The Chief Constable of Manchester invited the women to put their question in writing, so that it could be given to the speaker. But Sir Edward Grey did not reply. After the vote of thanks was given, Annie jumped onto a chair and shouted out the question again. During the pandemonium that broke out, Christabel and Annie were roughly handled and dragged outside the hall where Christabel deliberately spat at a policeman in order to court arrest. In the police court the next day, she and Annie pleaded guilty and chose imprisonment rather than pay a fine. Christabel served seven days in Strangeways, Annie three.[27] As Christabel expected, their assertive action became headline news in the press, which almost universally condemned such 'unladylike' behaviour. But many letters of sympathy were also sent to the two prisoners and recruits flocked to join the WSPU. As Christabel recollected, 'where peaceful means had failed, one act of militancy succeeded'.[28] From now on, the heckling of MPs and a willingness to go to prison became key tactics of the suffragettes, forms of protest that were eagerly covered by both local and national newspapers.

Christabel Pankhurst, the Chief Organiser and key strategist of the WSPU, firmly believed that the WSPU could only succeed if it became a national movement that embraced women of all social classes and all political persuasions. The first issue of *Votes for Women*, in October 1907, the WSPU's first newspaper, made this clear:

> [W]e refuse to ally ourselves with any of the other political parties ... By accepting a place as one of the sections supporting a particular party, the women's suffrage party loses its identity and the cause is robbed of its importance as a distinct political issue ... It is only upon an independent basis that women of diverse political views can be united, and in union with one another women will find their best strength.[29]

Unlike her sister Sylvia, Christabel did not want the WSPU to be tied to socialist politics and to attract predominantly working-class women. Even before the founding of the WSPU she had become disillusioned with socialist men and became increasingly so throughout the suffragette campaign as the Labour Party refused to give priority to women's suffrage. As early as August 1903, two months before the WSPU was established, Christabel was expressing her views on the matter in the *I.L.P. News*. 'It is not at all impossible to have tyranny under Socialism', she pointed out. 'Why are women expected to have such confidence in the men of the Labour Party? Working men are as unjust to women as are those of other classes.'[30] In January 1905, Emmeline Pankhurst attended the Labour Party conference, hoping it would endorse a Women's Enfranchisement Bill which was set down for debate in Parliament on 12 May. Christabel too strongly supported the measure since it would enfranchise a substantial number of working women on the same property qualification as men, and therefore 'put an end to the rule of one sex by the other'.[31] But the Labour Party conference voted against the bill, arguing instead for adult suffrage.[32] The labour movement's emphasis on class rather than gender issues, on a unified working class of comradeship between women and men, would always bedevil Christabel's efforts to bring in a women's suffrage measure.

One year later, in the 1906 January general election, twenty-nine Labour MPs were returned to Parliament and five of their number drew places for private members' bills to be presented in the House of Commons. Although Keir Hardie, the leader of the ILP, wanted one of these bills to be devoted to women suffrage, the other Labour MPs decided instead to focus on class issues in the party programme – old age pensions, feeding of destitute schoolchildren and the right of the unemployed to work. When one of the private members' bills remained in doubt, Emmeline Pankhurst demanded that it be given to 'votes for women'. But the Labour MPs refused, deciding instead that it should be given to a checkweighing bill that would protect the earnings of workmen. Christabel received the news with disdain. 'From what I have heard it is quite necessary to keep an eye on them [Labour MPs]', she wrote to a friend. 'J.K.H[ardie] is the one who really wants to help. The further one goes the plainer one sees that men (even Labour men) think more of their own interests than of ours.'[33]

It was experiences such as this that reinforced Christabel's view that the problem of the subordinate and inferior status of women in Edwardian Britain was not a class issue but a problem of the inequality between the sexes, specifically the power of men. The WSPU, she argued, had to become free from class politics, not 'a frill on the sleeve of any political party' but an organisation that would 'rally women of all three parties [Labour, Conservative and Liberal] and women of no party, and unite them as one independent force'.[34]

In August 1906, at the Cockermouth by-election, Christabel first put into practice the tactic of independence from all men's political parties. The policy worked in that women who would not have supported a Labour-affiliated organisation joined a women's organisation that was independent of Labour, at least at the central level – although at the local level many suffragettes retained an allegiance to socialism.[35] Nonetheless, the policy of independence from Labour caused tensions and bitter disagreements with many socialist suffragettes. In September 1907, Charlotte Despard and Teresa Billington-Greig, with other disgruntled socialists, left the WSPU and formed their own organisation, later called the Women's Freedom League. Shortly afterwards, to the dismay of Sylvia and Adela, Christabel and their mother resigned their ILP membership.[36]

By 1907 the WSPU had expanded rapidly with forty-seven branches established and nine paid organisers. Two years later, the number of paid organisers had risen to thirty and the WSPU, now located in London, occupied nineteen rooms in Clement's Inn. Additionally, eleven regional WSPU offices had been established in Bristol, Torquay, Manchester, Preston, Rochdale, Birmingham, Leeds and Bradford, Newcastle, Glasgow, Edinburgh and Aberdeen, while yearly income had risen to the substantial sum of £21,214.[37] It would appear that women of all political persuasions, and none, had now joined the WSPU although more Liberal women could be found in the NUWSS and more Conservative women in the Conservative and Unionist Women's Franchise Association (CUWFA) which, like the NUWSS, upheld peaceful, constitutional and legal means of campaigning. How many Conservative women joined the WSPU is debatable but both G. E. Maguire and Mitzi Auchterlonie suggest that the number was few.[38] The CUWFA often publicly denounced the assertive tactics of the WSPU, especially the violent tactics adopted from 1912. However, as Maguire points out it was not as straightforward as that. 'Some Conservative women actually belonged to the WSPU, others contributed [financially] ... some sought an alliance ... while still more sympathised quietly and refused all attempts at condemnation.'[39]

One well-known Conservative who did join the WSPU, in January 1909, was Lady Constance Lytton, a member of the aristocracy. As her biographer points out, Constance was unusual among women of her class in having relations who were active in the suffrage struggle, including her sister Emily who was already a WSPU member.[40] Constance Lytton engaged in window smashing, was imprisoned and forcibly fed, actions that only ceased after she suffered a second stroke in May 1912 and became an invalid for the rest of her short life. How she reconciled her feminist militancy with her conservatism is debatable. But it would appear that Constance no longer thought of herself as a Conservative. 'Party politics of all kinds sicken me', she wrote to a friend before she joined the WSPU. 'I'm still on the look-out for a label that will fit my various creeds ... This clumsy combination is the nearest: – "Advanced – radical –socialist – individualist."'[41]

Neither of the two main political parties, the Conservatives and the Liberals, were prepared to adopt women's suffrage as party policy since both parties were divided on the issue and could not agree on what grounds women should be enfranchised. A narrow measure, based on property qualifications, would bring in wealthier women who were more likely to vote Conservative while a wider measure would include more working-class women who would be more likely to vote Liberal. The desire to seek 'party advantage' stalled any reform.[42] Time and time again, the machinery of the House of Commons was used to block women suffrage bills, despite numerous peaceful processions to Parliament. Christabel and Emmeline Pankhurst knew that their cause was just, and democratic, but after a large Hyde Park demonstration on 21 June 1908, called to show the extent of popular support for women's enfranchise-ment, they felt that argument had been exhausted. That day, 'Women's Sunday' as it was called, Christabel in a green silk dress and graduate cap and gown was one of about 42,000 women who converged in the park, attracting crowds of about half a million. Discarding her academic robes in the heat of the day, she spoke on one of twenty platforms. Although she was initially jeered, her skill in handling a hostile crowd was now legendary, and she did it to great effect. If you want to know why this most derided of movements has emerged from obscurity to brilliant popularity, opined the *Daily News*, you have only to listen to Christabel Pankhurst. '[H]er hair loosened in the breeze, her eyes sparkling with the fighting spirit, her face shining with confidence in her cause. She was born to command crowds.'[43] From now on militancy, which had largely involved heckling MPs, civil disobedience and peaceful processions broadened to include more violent deeds, initially in 'undirected and uncoordinated individual acts', such as window breaking.[44]

During 1908 Christabel was at the peak of her fame, particularly after the Bow Street trial held in October 1908 when she acted as lawyer for the defendants – namely her mother, Flora Drummond and herself. For some time the WSPU had been planning another procession to Parliament, to take place on 13 October.

Emmeline Pankhurst had said that this time the suffragettes would 'enter the House [of Commons], and, if, possible, the Chamber itself'.[45] Christabel promptly set about advertising the event by printing thousands of handbills which invited men and women to 'Help the Suffragettes to Rush the House of Commons on Tuesday Evening, 13th October 1908, at 7.30.' Summons were issued against the three women who, on 13 October, eluded the police for most of the day before presenting themselves for arrest at 6 p.m. When they appeared at Bow Street, Christabel took the unusual step of acting as lawyer for the defence. In a brilliant publicity coup, she subpoenaed as witnesses two Cabinet Ministers, Lloyd George and Herbert Gladstone who had been in the vicinity of Trafalgar Square when the demonstration took place. Christabel's witty exchanges with Lloyd George over the meaning of 'rush' delighted the court room – and the press. In a brilliant summing up, the articulate, charming Christabel placed the WSPU's campaign within the longer, historical struggle for constitutional liberties, accusing the Liberal government of having 'practically torn up' Magna Carta, the 1215 charter that was the cornerstone of civil liberties. Women were not only denied their legal right of trial by jury but also their constitutional right to lay their grievances in person before the House of Commons.[46] Although all three women were found guilty for inciting to riot and sent to prison – Christabel for ten weeks – the widespread publicity given to the case by an admiring press brought much needed publicity for the women's cause and more converts.

A theme at the Bow Street trial, that it was the duty of women, as voteless citizens, to resist tyrannous governments, was frequently reiterated by the charismatic Christabel. At the heart of her notion of 'militancy' was the idea that women should throw off the false dignity that came with submission and earn true dignity, through revolt. 'Remember the dignity of your womanhood: do not appeal, do not beg, do not grovel, take courage, join hands, stand beside us, fight with us', she pleaded to one audience at a packed Albert Hall meeting in April 1909.[47]

By now, suffragette protests at Liberal Party public meetings were difficult since women were excluded from such gatherings unless they had a signed ticket. By the end of September 1909 too, the Liberal government had begun to force feed hunger-striking imprisoned suffragettes. Since forcible feeding was accompanied by overpowering physical force as feeding tubes were thrust by male doctors into women's struggling bodies, it was often experienced as a form of rape by a powerful male state.[48] The leadership of the WSPU was outraged at such treatment, condemning the 'brutality' of a Liberal government that 'violated' the bodies of women.[49] When Keir Hardie made a protest in the House of Commons, many MPs laughed.[50] 'The despots of the world, in their blindness and folly, have always thought that Might would be stronger than Right', thundered the angry Christabel, 'and they have never learned, except by their own overthrow, that the arm of the weak is made strong to defeat the evil-doer.' The result of the government's latest move was that women of the WSPU were 'more determined than ever to proceed with their militant agitation'.[51]

The suffragettes campaigned vigorously against the Liberals in the January 1910 election and Christabel hoped that a Conservative government might be returned. For some time she had been corresponding with Arthur Balfour, the leader of the Conservatives, trying to persuade him to adopt women's suffrage as party policy. However, Balfour informed Christabel that although he supported women's suffrage in theory, it was difficult for him to act since his party did not agree on the issue. Before the election result was known, a displeased but polite Christabel sent him a frank reply:

> Your statement on woman suffrage has naturally disappointed us. You tell us that there is a division of opinion in the [Conservative and] Unionist party on this question. That we know, but the same thing is true of every other question until the leader speaks ... Four years ago you told us that you could do nothing because the matter was not rife for settlement & we were not in the swim. We have worked unceasingly from that day to this to fulfil the conditions implied in those words of yours ... Of course if we had had your help during the past four years, militant methods & all the hardship & sacrifice they involve would have been unnecessary. You will forgive me, I know, for saying that woman suffrage ought to be viewed from the high ground of public duty and national interest. Your reply to us seems to take account only of party convenience.[52]

The Liberals lost their overall majority in the January general election, winning just 275 seats against 273 Conservative, 83 Irish Nationalist and 40 Labour. Yet again, it was the anti-suffragist Asquith who formed the new government, aware that the success of any new legislation would be dependent on the support of MPs outside his own party.[53] Realising that the new political situation might be useful to the women's cause, Henry Brailsford, a journalist, set about forming a Conciliation Committee for Women's Suffrage, which eventually consisted of 54 MPs across the political spectrum. Despite her private reservations about the committee's support of a private member's women's suffrage bill, Christabel publicly supported the initiative. Meanwhile, her mother called a suspension of all militant activities, only constitutional methods to be adopted. The so-called 'truce' with the Liberal government remained until 21 November 1911, apart from one week during November 1910.

During June and July 1910, the WSPU sponsored several large peaceful demonstrations. One held on 18 June, which included more than twenty other suffrage societies, provided an occasion for Christabel once again to emphasise her feminist views, about the bond of sisterhood that united all women, irrespective of class and wealth, and of the importance of women working together in a common cause:

> [T]the Procession ... will include women who are rich as well as those who are poor, and women of every social degree. Everything which separates will be forgotten, and only that which unites will be remembered ... it will be a festival at which we shall celebrate the sisterhood of women. According to the old tale of men's making, it is not in women to unite and to work with one another. Women have only now discovered the falsity of this, and they are rejoicing in their new-found sisterhood.[54]

That the WSPU attracted women of all social classes is often forgotten. One former suffragette recollected that when in prison in 1912 she found 'rich and poor … young professional women … countless poor women of the working class, nurses, typists, shop girls, and the like'.[55]

Determined to do all she could to help the promised reform bill, deliberately drawn up on narrow lines in order to win Tory support, Christabel again contacted the Conservatives who, despite their criticisms of militant methods, were prepared to work with her. 'Heard from Christabel yesterday down the telephone and we have now arranged for a meeting of the Conservative suffragists in the House of Commons to be held on July 10th', Lord Robert Cecil informed his sister, Maud Selborne. 'Christabel is evidently anxious that the Bill should not be extended … she wishes us to strengthen her hands in her negotiations … by saying that we are strongly opposed to any extension of the Bill.'[56] Maguire erroneously interpreted this as a sign of Christabel moving to the right, rather than as a pragmatic move to win support for a women's suffrage measure that would end the sex discrimination preventing all women exercising the parliamentary vote.[57] However, despite Christabel's efforts, the Conciliation Bill did not become law. Although it passed its second reading with a majority of 109, Asquith killed it off when he announced that there was no time for the bill that year. Two further Conciliation Bills in 1911 and 1911–12 also failed to come to fruition.

On 7 November 1911, Asquith suddenly announced that his government would introduce in the next session a Manhood Suffrage Bill that would admit a women suffrage amendment. For Christabel, such a 'crooked and discreditable scheme' which would not give equal voting rights to women and men was inspired by the wheeler-dealing of Lloyd George, Chancellor of the Exchequer.[58] On 1 March 1912, suffragettes for the first time struck without warning, engaging in mass shop window smashing in London's West End. Three days later, the police swooped on WSPU headquarters. Although the other WSPU leaders were arrested, Christabel was not there. She had been forewarned about what was happening and, as agreed beforehand, fled to France where a political offender could not be extradited. It was from Paris that Christabel now attempted to lead the WSPU, aided by frequent visits from her mother, in between her numerous imprisonments, and by loyal friends such as Annie Kenney who carried messages back and forth across the Channel.

From then until the outbreak of the First World War in August 1914, a minority of the militant suffragettes engaged in violent, illegal tactics, including destroying mail in post boxes and secret arson attacks. Many of these acts of vandalism were introduced by the rank and file but Christabel supported the new directions, just as she had endorsed window-smashing. The burning of letters, she insisted, had as its aim the abolition of the sexual and economic exploitation of women, including the stopping of 'hideous assaults on little girls'.[59] The all-male government, she believed, would never grant women the vote until they were forced to do so. Men in the past, she pointed out, had not been given the vote by asking nicely; in Bristol in 1831 they had burned the bishop's palace and other public buildings.[60]

The WSPU had never been a single-issue organisation, just focused on the vote, as Sylvia had claimed in *The Suffragette Movement*.[61] The gender divisions between men and women which disadvantaged women in the law, in employment, in pay and in public life had frequently been voiced by both Christabel and Emmeline, as they argued for equality for women in all walks of life.[62] These wider reform issues, especially the double sexual standard, female prostitution and VD, now came much more to the fore in Christabel's writings. In her influential book *The Great Scourge and How to End It* she argued that in a male-dominated society, man-made morality and man-made law upheld a double moral standard whereby sexuality was organised in men's interests and around notions of men's uncontrollable sexual urges. Bringing the issue of women's enfranchisement into the bedroom, the uncompromising Christabel suggested that the only solution for this state of affairs was twofold, 'Votes for Women, which will give to women more self-reliance and a stronger economic position, and chastity for men'.[63] Men had to be educated on sexual matters, exercise control over their sexual appetite, just as women did, and not see prostitution as inevitable. Women could reject the male authority to which they were supposed to submit and reclaim their bodies for themselves. Such views were not welcomed by many socialist feminists of the time, including Christabel's unmarried sister Sylvia who had been having an affair with Keir Hardie, a man much older than herself. But Christabel was arguing for the right of women to live independent 'pure' lives, if they wished, without following the expected path for their sex in Edwardian Britain, namely marriage and motherhood.[64]

By April 1914, Christabel was thoroughly disillusioned with male party politics. Her ire was especially directed at the Labour Party which, though it upheld the principle of equality for men and women, had propped up the Liberal government. '[T]the cause of votes for women has not profited in the smallest degree from the presence of the Labour members in the House of Commons', she told WSPU members. 'For Suffragists to put their faith in any men's party, whatever it may call itself, is recklessly to disregard the lessons of the past forty years … The truth is that women must work out their own salvation. Men will not do it for them.'[65]

On 4 August, Britain declared war against Germany. Militancy was suspended and both Christabel and Emmeline Pankhurst patriotically supported their country in its hour of need. However, the women's cause was not forgotten but a new strategy adopted, namely encouraging women to support the war effort as a way to earn their enfranchisement.[66] Such an approach was alien to Sylvia Pankhurst, a pacifist, who saw the First World War as a capitalist enterprise. That Christabel became not a socialist in the interwar years but a Second Adventist, that is a Christian who is expecting the imminent return of Christ, did not add to her allure either, nor her future successful career as a preacher and writer of religious books.[67]

By the autumn of 1917, Christabel and Emmeline knew that the following year a clause in the Representation of the People Bill would grant the parliamentary vote for women aged 30 and over who were householders, the wives of householders, occupiers of property of £5 or more annual value, or university graduates. Since the WSPU would be redundant, the WSPU was re-launched as the Women's Party, an organisation that would prepare women for their impending citizenship. With the slogan 'Victory, National Security and Progress', the Women's Party conflated the winning of the war with the women's cause. Such views did not endear Christabel to Sylvia, nor to most future historians who see the Women's Party, with its attack on pacifism, Marxism and the labour movement, as a move to the right.[68] However, the separatist Women's Party with its hybrid Conservative policies and progressive feminist initiatives, such as equal opportunities in pay, law, employment and public service, was a more complex organisation than often portrayed. It was shaped not only by the local British context of nationalism and feminist politics, but also by the global context of a world war and the arrival of Bolshevism in Russia, which both Christabel and her mother detested as undemocratic.[69]

On 6 February 1918, under a coalition government, the Representation of the People Act became law. Although women were not enfranchised on equal terms with men, Christabel was thankful that the principle of sex discrimination had been broken.[70] In 1919, with the Coalition government's approval, she stood unsuccessfully for election to Parliament against a Labour candidate. Subsequently, she dropped out of electoral politics. It was no surprise to her that when a Labour government came to power in 1924 it resisted attempts to bring in an equal franchise bill, despite the efforts of a number of feminist groups. It was a Conservative government, led by Stanley Baldwin, which granted equal franchise in 1928.

In this chapter I have argued that, contrary to popular opinion, during the pre-1914 period, Christabel Pankhurst was not a 'Conservative' but a 'Radical' suffragette. Although she was critical of socialism and of the Labour Party during her suffrage years, this does not make her right wing. Her sister Sylvia, had difficulty in understanding this, as do many socialist feminists today, since they associate feminism only with the left of politics. But the feminist movement has always been more complex than this, and has had many differing ideological strands. Nor does that fact that Christabel undoubtedly supported the Conservatives in 1927, when her mother stood as a Conservative parliamentary candidate, make her a Conservative in her younger days. It is always problematic to read any biography 'backwards' since feminists, like other individuals, journey through life.

Christabel Pankhurst in her suffrage years developed a women-centred approach to politics. She advocated a separatist feminist position which called on women to organise together, independent of male political parties. This was a powerful rallying call that politicised thousands of women. It was a form of consciousness raising about the wrongs that voteless women shared, irrespective of their class or income.

It was a means whereby a sense of sisterhood was fostered that enabled women to stand on their own two feet and articulate their demands. Christabel Pankhurst pioneered a feminist viewpoint which, if out of tune with feminism in 1920s and 1930s Britain, became important to radical feminists in the Women's Liberation Movement in the late 1960s and 1970s.

Notes

1 This chapter draws on some of my other publications including 'A "Pair of … Infernal Queens"? A Reassessment of the Dominant Representations of Emmeline and Christabel Pankhurst, First Wave Feminists in Edwardian Britain', *Women's History Review*, 5 (1996), 259–80; 'Christabel Pankhurst and the Women's Social and Political Union', in Maroula Joannou and June Purvis (eds), *The Women's Suffrage Movement: New Feminist Perspectives* (Manchester: Manchester University Press, 1998), pp. 157–69; 'Christabel Pankhurst and the Struggle for Suffrage Reform in Edwardian Britain', in Irma Sulkunen, Seija-Leena Nevala-Nurmi and Pirjo Markkola (eds), *Suffrage, Gender and Citizenship: International Perspectives on Parliamentary Reforms* (Newcastle upon Tyne: Cambridge Scholars Press, 2009), pp. 278–98 and *Christabel Pankhurst: a Biography* (Routledge, forthcoming). I follow the conventions of the day and frequently refer to Christabel and Emmeline Pankhurst only by their first names.

2 Christabel Pankhurst, *Unshackled: The Story of How We Won The Vote* (London: Hutchinson, 1959), p. 44.

3 They all attended a meeting at the Central Manchester ILP branch on 8 August 1905, Manchester Central ILP Minute Book, 8 August 1905, Manchester Central Library.

4 Christabel Pankhurst, *Unshackled*, p. 44, and June Purvis, *Emmeline Pankhurst: a Biography* (London and New York: Routledge, 2002), p. 67.

5 See Neil Blewett, 'The Franchise in the United Kingdom 1885–1918', *Past and Present*, 32 (1965), 27–56.

6 E. Sylvia Pankhurst, *The Suffragette Movement: An Intimate Account of Persons and Ideals* (London: Longman, 1931), p. 199, notes that by 1906 the *Daily Mail* had christened WSPU women 'suffragettes'.

7 *The Times*, 15 February 1958.

8 *New York Times*, 15 February 1958.

9 Les Garner, *Stepping Stones to Women's Liberty: Feminist Ideas in the Women's Suffrage Movement 1900–1918* (London: Heinemann Educational, 1984), p. 29, Martin Pugh, *The March of the Women: a Revisionist Analysis of the Campaign for Women's Suffrage, 1866–1914* (Oxford: Oxford University Press, 2000), p. 103, and G. E. Maguire, *Conservative Women: a History of Women and the Conservative Party, 1874–1997* (Basingstoke: Macmillan, 1998), p. 58.

10 David Mitchell, *Queen Christabel: a Biography of Christabel Pankhurst* (London: MacDonald and Jane's, 1977) and Martin Pugh, *The Pankhursts* (London: Allen Lane, The Penguin Press, 2001), p. 342.

11 Sylvia Pankhurst, *The Suffragette Movement*, p. 267.

12 *Ibid.*, pp. 191–2.

13 *Ibid.*, pp. 247–8.

14 *Ibid.*, p. 221.

15 Jane Marcus, Introduction, to her edited *Suffrage and the Pankhursts* (London: Routledge, 1987), pp. 5–6.

16 Sheila Rowbotham, *Hidden From History: 300 Years of Women's Oppression and the Fight Against it* (London: Pluto Press, 1973).

17 Christabel Pankhurst, *Unshackled* and Emmeline Pankhurst, *My Own Story* (London: Eveleigh Nash, 1914).

18 Rowbotham, *Hidden From History*, p. 82.

19 *Ibid.*, p. 79.

20 *Ibid.*, p. 160.

21 *Ibid,,* p. 79.

22 Rowbotham, *Hidden From History*, p. 88.

23 Jill Liddington and Jill Norris, *One Hand Tied Behind Us: the Rise of the Women's Suffrage Movement* (London: Virago, 1978), pp. 188–9.

24 *Ibid.*, pp. 183 and 192.

25 Susan Kingsley Kent, *Sex and Suffrage in Britain, 1860–1914* (New Jersey: Princeton University Press, 1987), p. 5.

26 For the links between Christabel's feminism and radical feminism see Dale Spender, *Women of Ideas and What Men Have Done to Them* (London: Routledge, 1982), pp. 397–434; Elizabeth Sarah, 'Christabel Pankhurst: Reclaiming her Power', in Dale Spender (ed.), *Feminist Theorists* (London: The Women's Press, 1983), pp. 256–284; Olive Banks, *The Biographical Dictionary of British Feminists Volume One 1800–1930* (Brighton: Harvester Press, 1985), 'Christabel Pankhurst', pp. 146–149 and Purvis, 'A "Pair of ... Infernal Queens"?'

27 *Manchester Guardian*, 16 October 1905.

28 Christabel Pankhurst, *Unshackled*, p. 55.

29 Christabel Pankhurst, *Votes for Women Supplement*, October 1907, p. ii.

30 Christabel Pankhurst, 'Women and the Independent Labour Party', *I.L.P. News*, 77, August 1903.

31 *Labour Leader*, 23 April 1904.

32 *Ibid.*, 3 February 1905.

33 Mary Gawthorpe, *Uphill To Holloway* (Penobscot, Maine: Traversity Press, 1962), p. 210.

34 Christabel Pankhurst, *Unshackled*, p. 69.

35 On this theme see Krista Cowman, '"Incipient Toryism"? The Women's Social and Political Union and the Independent Labour Party, 1903–14', *History Workshop Journal*, 53, 2002, pp. 129–148; June Hannam and Karen Hunt, *Socialist Women Britain, 1880s to 1920s* (London: Routledge, 2002), chapter 5, and Christine Collette, *The Newer Eve: Women, Feminists and the Labour Party* (Houndmills: Palgrave, 2009), Part I.

36 Purvis, *Emmeline Pankhurst*, p. 99.

37 Andrew Rosen, *Rise Up Women! The Militant Campaign of the Women's Social and Political Union 1903–1912* (London: Routledge), pp. 83 and 114–15.

38 Maguire, *Conservative Women*, pp. 56–57, and Mitzi Auchterlonie, *Conservative Suffragists: The Women's Vote and the Tory Party* (London: I. B. Tauris, 2007), p. 89.

39 Lori Maguire, 'The Conservative Party and Women's Suffrage', in Myriam Boussahba-Bravard (ed.), *Suffrage Outside Suffragism: Women's Vote in Britain, 1880–1914* (Houndsmills: Palgrave, 2007), p. 57.

40 Lyndsey Jenkins, *Lady Constance Lytton: Aristocrat, Suffragette, Martyr* (London: Biteback, 2015), p. 79.

41 Betty Balfour, *Letters of Constance Lytton* (London: Heinemann, 1925), pp. 132–3.

42 Richard Toye, *Lloyd George & Churchill: Rivals for Greatness* (London: Macmillan, 2007), p. 77.

43 *Daily News*, 22 June 1908.

44 Sandra Stanley Holton, *Suffrage Days: Stories from the Women's Suffrage Movement* (London: Routledge, 1996), p. 134.

45 *Votes for Women*, 8 October 1908.

46 *Votes for Women*, 29 October 1908; Ian Fletcher, '"A Star Chamber of the Twentieth Century": Suffragettes, Liberals, and the 1908 "Rush the Commons" Case', *Journal of British Studies*, 35 (October 1996), 504–30.

47 *Votes for Women*, 7 May 1909, p. 634.

48 See June Purvis, 'The Prison Experiences of the Suffragettes in Edwardian Britain', *Women's History Review*, 4 (1995), 103–133.

49 *The Times*, 29 September 1909, letter signed by Emmeline Pankhurst, Emmeline Pethick-Lawrence, Mabel Tuke and Christabel. Members of the public also protested against forcible feeding, as did a few in the medical profession; see J. F. Geddes, 'Culpable Complicity: the Medical Profession and the Forcible Feeding of Suffragettes, 1909–1914', *Women's History Review*, 17 (2008), 79–94.

50 Mitchell, *Queen Christabel*, p. 145

51 *Votes for Women*, 15 October 1909, pp. 36 and 40.

52 Christabel Pankhurst to Arthur Balfour, 1 January 1910, Balfour Papers, British Library, Ms Add 49793, folios 61–63.

53 Rosen, *Rise Up Women!*, p. 130.

54 *Votes for Women*, 29 May 1910, p. 550.

55 Ethel Smyth, *Female Pipings in Eden* (London, Peter Davies, 1933), p. 211.

56 Quoted in Maguire, *Conservative Women*, p. 57.

57 Maguire, *Conservative Women*, p. 58.

58 *Votes for Women*, 10 November 1911, p. 88.

59 *The Suffragette*, 6 December 1912, p. 114.

60 Front cover of *The Suffragette*, 16 January 1914.

61 Sylvia Pankhurst, *The Suffragette Movement*, p. 242.

62 See, for example, Emmeline's 1908 speech on 'The Importance of the Vote', discussed in Purvis, *Emmeline Pankhurst*, p. 106.

63 Christabel Pankhurst, *The Great Scourge and How To End It* (London: E. Pankhurst, 1913), p. 37.

64 June Purvis, 'Fighting the Double Moral Standard in Edwardian Britain: Suffragette Militancy, Sexuality and the Nation in the Writings of the Early Twentieth-century British Feminist Christabel Pankhurst', in Francisca de Haan, Margaret Allen, June Purvis and Krassimira Daskalova (eds), *Women's Activism: Global Perspectives from the 1890s to the Present* (London: Routledge, 2013), pp. 125 and 131.

65 *The Suffragette*, 17 April 1914, p. 10.
66 Purvis, *Emmeline Pankhurst*, chapter 19 and Nicoletta F. Gullace, *'The Blood of Our Sons': Men, Women, and the Renegotiation of British Citizenship During the Great War* (Houndmills: Palgrave Macmillan, 2002), chapter 6.
67 In 1940, Christabel settled in the USA.
68 Sylvia Pankhurst, *The Suffragette Movement*, p. 595; Brian Harrison, *Prudent Revolutionaries: Portraits of British Feminists Between The Wars* (Oxford: Oxford University Press, 1987), p. 35; Julie V. Gottlieb, *Feminine Fascism: Women in Britain's Fascist Movement 1923–1945* (London: I. B. Tauris, 2000), p. 157; Pugh, *The Pankhursts*, p. 340 and Nicoletta F. Gullace, 'Christabel Pankhurst and the Smethwick Election: Right-Wing Feminism, the Great War and the Ideology of Consumption', *Women's History Review*, 23 (2014), pp. 330–46.
69 June Purvis, 'The Women's Party of Great Britain (1917–1919): A Forgotten Episode in British Women's Political History', *Women's History Review*, 25 (2016), 638–51.
70 Christabel Pankhurst, *Unshackled*, p. 292.

3

At the heart of the party?
The women's Conservative organisation
in the age of partial suffrage, 1914–28

David Thackeray

In 1928 Lady Iveagh, Vice-Chairman of the National Union of Conservative Associations (NUCA), claimed that one million women were members of the Conservative Party. While it would be prudent to question how many of these were active members, it was undoubtedly true that the Conservatives had been more successful than their rivals in attracting women members. At this time, the Conservative Women's Organisation was around four times the size of its Labour rival, and much larger than the Women's National Liberal Federation, which had a paper membership of around 100,000.[1] This achievement was all the more impressive given that the women's organisation had only been part of the formal Conservative Party structure since 1918. And yet, while women came to be seen as essential to grassroots electoral politics they remained woefully under-represented within most of the key positions within the party. The Conservative Party fielded 35 female candidates across the five elections between 1918 and 1929. Even so, there were never more than three women sitting on the Conservative benches in the House of Commons during this time (although 13 Conservative women MPs were returned in the National Government's landslide victory in 1931).

While the history of women's involvement in the Conservative Party during the early twentieth century has received some attention from scholars, there has been a tendency to focus on aspects of the organisational story, rather than exploring the cultures of female activism within the party more broadly.[2] An important exception to this trend is a series of essays produced by David Jarvis, which considers issues such as the class-based appeals of the 'Mrs Maggs and Betty' stories in the party magazine *Home and Politics*, women's relationship with male activists in constituency politics, and the importance of home-based issues in the Conservative appeal to female voters.[3] I have built on this work with a history of the Conservative Women's Organisation, which focuses, in part, on the range of regional appeals that the party developed to female voters and activists in the 1920s, and a comparative study of the activities of the Liberal, Labour and Conservative women's organisations in the 1920s.[4] Despite the growth of this literature there are still many gaps in our knowledge of women's involvement in Conservative politics during the interwar period and there has been no full-length study to compare with Pamela Graves's history of Labour women or Cheryl Law's analysis of the post-suffrage British women's movement.[5]

The following analysis offers an overview of the Conservative women's association, considering its relationship with male politicians both at constituency level and at Conservative Central Office. It breaks new ground in considering how debates about welfare in the early 1920s reshaped Conservative understandings of gender roles, and explores representations of masculinity and femininity in electoral culture via a detailed study of election addresses. Female activists had begun to develop a significant presence in the organisation of Unionist electoral politics in the 1900s through the activities of the Women's Unionist and Tariff Reform Association, which focused on appealing to housewives' interests as consumers. There was little significant change in the nature of the Conservative appeal to women after the partial enfranchisement of 1918, with female voters still being addressed overwhelmingly as housewives rather than as wage-workers. Conservative women candidates did little to challenge the status quo, chiefly presenting themselves as the guardians of the interests of the home and family welfare, much as women councillors in local government had done before 1918.[6]

Working with the men: at central office and the constituencies

In May 1918 the Women's Unionist and Tariff Reform Association (WUTRA), which had been the leading voice for Conservative women since its foundation in 1906, disbanded and formed the backbone of the new Conservative Party women's organisation. It might have been expected that WUTRA chairman Mary Maxse would greet this achievement enthusiastically. Instead she was despondent, confiding to her husband: 'I have been feeling that all those years of work have been absolutely thrown away when I see the women handed over to a body so completely dead as the Unionist Central Office.' Claiming that her supporters had 'amalgamated like lambs with the official Unionist men', Maxse retired from work for the party forthwith and was replaced as leader of the Conservative Women's Organisation by her former deputy, Caroline Bridgeman, the wife of a party whip.[7]

In Edwardian Britain WUTRA had developed a widespread following, at least in areas of high Conservative and Liberal Unionist support, and it claimed a membership of 300,000 in 1913.[8] The organisation's main activity had been to encourage women to support the cause of tariff reform, presenting it as a housewives' question. However, it also promoted a wider anti-socialist politics and focused chiefly on opposition to Irish home rule in the years immediately before the First World War.[9] WUTRA undertook operations in 175 constituencies during the January 1910 election; 41 of these seats were already held by Unionists, but an additional 62 were captured at this election, and in another 50 cases the majority of the incumbent Liberal or Labour MP was reduced.[10]

Given that branches of this women's organisation did not receive financial support from Conservative Central Office, and relied on voluntary effort, the effectiveness of WUTRA branches varied widely. For example, in the West Midlands a series of notes compiled around 1912 by local party leaders and agents indicate a variety of opinions on the usefulness of women's branches. Of the twenty WUTRA branches that are discussed in the notebook seventeen were considered as offering an effective service to the party. Of the others, Smethwick was recorded as being 'of very little use except at Parliamentary Elections'. Neighbouring Handsworth 'would be a useful body were it not almost entirely stultified by its respectability'.[11] This claim that WUTRA was overly reliant on well-to-do women organisers was a common complaint nationally.[12] Meanwhile, in Wolverhampton South there were:

> upwards of 5000 members but only 200 or 300 are worth anything in the way of assisting the Unionist Association and, even then, care has to be exercised in the kind of work they are given to do – their canvassing is unreliable. The great bulk of the Women Members are very illiterate but, by giving them a badge and a certificate a sort of hold is gained on them to call themselves Unionists, and one can appeal to them to influence the male members of their families. If we did not get hold of them the other side would.[13]

Such dismissive attitudes towards the women's organisation on the part of male party leaders would become a significant cause of acrimony during the 1920s. But other judgements of WUTRA in the region were more complimentary. For example, Stanley Baldwin MP for West Worcestershire since 1908, saw the women's association as a great boon to the Unionist organisation in his constituency. They formed a branch in nearly every polling district, held extensive campaigns in outlying villages, and organised fund-raising social events. By 1914 over two thousand women were WUTRA members in West Worcestershire.[14]

Of course, the First World War, and the enactment of a party truce, severely disrupted WUTRA's organisation. In October 1917 Caroline Bridgeman expressed concern at how the association could meet the task of winning the support of the new women voters given the depleted state of its organisation and finances.[15] The leaders of WUTRA devoted significantly more time to bodies such as the Women's Institutes and Land Army during the war than party activism.[16] Anxieties over post-war organisation framed WUTRA's subsequent discussions over amalgamation with the Conservative Party. A memorandum drawn up by the party chairman, Sir George Younger, in January 1918 proposed the creation of a small women's department within central office noting that: 'the WUTRA has a number of efficient branches and a few really good organisers but its Central Organisation neither possesses sufficient authority nor adequate funds for the task of a national organisation'. Under this arrangement WUTRA would be 'placed at the disposal of Central Office' in return for the allocation of a number of seats on the National Union Council.[17] Bridgeman considered that this arrangement did not provide her organisation with enough power and autonomy.[18] A subsequent memorandum, which left the matter of organisation open, proved more satisfactory and paved the way for WUTRA's amalgamation into the Conservative Party. From 1918 onwards, depending on the views of individual constituencies, men and women could either join a mixed local association or separate constituency organisations linked by a single executive and agent. Either way they would have equal representation in regional organisations and in sending delegates to NUCA conferences.[19]

Over the following years there were various debates within the Conservative Party about whether women would be best served by establishing their own single-sex associations or joining mixed constituency organisations.[20] In an address reported in the *Conservative Agent's Journal* in 1920, Leigh Maclachlan, a party agent, advocated separate organisations as 'in a mixed Association a woman is a mere unit, and no particular appeal is made to her as a woman'. Maclachlan claimed that of most women 'unless she were a very determined person she would not thrust herself forward at a mixed meeting, especially if she is a working woman. Her political education is less advanced than that of the majority of men.' Women operating in single-sex associations, it was claimed, were more effective than those working in mixed organisations.[21]

Within the Conservative Club movement there was hostility towards allowing women to join following the advent of female suffrage.[22] According to Mr F. de Lisle Solbe, the Secretary of the Conservative Club Association, men wanted a homo-social environment: 'The tastes of men and women from the club viewpoint are utterly and entirely different. Immediately there would be friction, feathers would fly, and the Club would "bust up",' According to de Lisle Solbe, club life appealed to men as it was a place they could drink 'without being subjected to feminine observation and strictures'.[23] As David Jarvis has shown, male activists often reacted ambivalently towards the growing influence of women within the Conservative Party during the 1920s. While it was common for activists to celebrate the organisational vitality of women's constituency associations, men were also alarmed by the increasing feminisation of the party's grassroots organisation.[24]

Given the history of tensions between the women's organisation and male-led Conservative associations, it is perhaps unsurprising that this could lead to distrust in election work. In 1924 Herbert Jessel, the chief Conservative organiser for London, claimed that the women's association was the least satisfactory cog in the party organisation in the capital, noting 'there is no co-operation between the Women's Organisation in the Central Office and the London Department'.[25] Referring to the 1923 election he claimed that 'election applications for women speakers came to the men District agents and were allotted without consultation with the women Agents'. This rendered 'useless the knowledge we have been able to gain of the type of audience and the capacity of women speakers'.[26] Echoing

Maclachlan, Jessel claimed that women would be best served by developing their own associations if there was demand thereby giving them greater freedom and responsibility. Introducing a paid woman organiser in each constituency was vital to improving the prospects of the Conservative party among female voters: 'We cannot hope for the average woman in the East End of London to have either the ability or the time to organise themselves. A paid worker would be the only solution and even then progress would be slow.'[27] However, in practice most constituencies were unwilling to meet the costs of employing a paid woman organiser, in addition to paying a (invariably male) constituency agent. Where a female constituency worker was employed, their salary was usually underwritten by the local women's branch of the party. Given fears that the employment of two constituency organisers might lead to a duplication of effort and the type of poorly coordinated election planning which Jessel outlined, the woman party worker was usually made subordinate to the male constituency agent.[28]

Although the model of homosocial branch activism may have limited the abilities of women to play a leading role in constituency activism, its appeal to women appears to have been important to the Conservative Party's significant expansion in membership during the 1920s. Whereas there were 1,300 women's branches in 1921, this number had risen to 4,067 by 1924.[29] One of the biggest success stories was in the West Midlands, where Annie Chamberlain, wife of Conservative MP Neville Chamberlain, launched the Unionist Women's Institute movement. The institutes offered an opportunity for working women to congregate in an informal setting quite different from the drawing-room meetings in the home of a well-to-do local lady which had been a common feature of WUTRA's pre-war social culture. Unionist Women's Institutes provided simple political talks such as 'The A.B.C. of Unionism' and 'What the City is Doing for the Children'.[30] In Birmingham Chamberlain's model of activism helped the women's branches become a key part of the party's grassroots organisation, particularly in poorer districts where Labour was making significant advances. In inner-city Duddeston there were 60 male subscribers to the Conservative association in early 1927 and 500 female subscribers. A few miles south, in leafy Edgbaston there was less disparity between the sexes, with 546 men subscribing to party funds and 1,039 women.[31] In Leeds too, the Conservative Women's Organisation made significant advances during the 1920s in response to Labour inroads in the city. Party activities were publicised by a periodical *The Conservative Woman*, established in 1921. As well as the usual branch news relating to local women's associations, this publication attempted to foster a wider female Conservative worldview, including sections on lifestyle and the home. A regular feature offered household hints, providing advice on economical cookery and domestic management.[32]

The position of the women's Conservative organisation was improved by increasing cooperation with Conservative Central Office in the years after women gained the parliamentary vote. In 1926 a National Association of Conservative and

Unionist Women Organisers was formed, and the following year women made up 36 per cent of delegates at the NUCA conference.[33] J. C. C. Davidson, appointed party chairman in 1926, sought to improve relations between men and women within the Conservative organisation, making Lady Iveagh Vice-Chairman of the NUCA and Marjorie Maxse Deputy Principal Agent of the party.[34] However, while women had cemented a position of influence within the Conservative Party over the course of the 1920s, this success was largely based on the growth of single-sex branch organisations rather than a wider effort to reform the culture of party activism more broadly. In fact, in 1925 the *Daily Herald* claimed that no women spoke at that year's NUCA conference.[35] A 1927 article by Marjorie Maxse highlighted the difficult relations between the women's organisation and constituency party leaders:

> Women have nothing to hide from the men; do not seek to usurp their place or power; and do not work for feminism but for the Party. Nor do women wish to become Agents. They do, however, wish to become efficient Women District Secretaries … On the other hand, it is unwise to drive the women or expect them to work 'under' the Agent … Instead give them their own field of work and let them accomplish quickly and efficiently the work which only women can do.[36]

Women's associations appear to have had little influence over the selection of parliamentary candidates and women remained excluded from the Conservative Club movement and the National Society of Conservative Agents. Women party agents received significantly lower salaries than their male counterparts and were commonly expected to resign their posts on marriage.[37] Throughout the interwar period it remained extremely rare for women to rise to the position of constituency association chairman.[38] As Marjorie Maxse indicates, female Conservative activists tended to commonly devote their attention to the particular activities of women's branches or sub-committees rather than reaching for more general leadership positions within the party organisation at a local or national level. Those women who tended to take a leading role in the party's organisation in the 1920s, such as Caroline Bridgeman, Annie Chamberlain and Marjorie Maxse (none of whom ever stood as parliamentary candidates) were invariably related to men who had an established position in Conservative politics.

Home and politics: the Conservative appeal to women

In 1922 the *Conservative Campaign Guide* ended with a discussion of the challenges of appealing to women to support the Conservative Party, noting that 'the problems of a changeful time need the co-operation of the woman, who sees them from the kitchen and nursery window, with the man, who looks through that of an office or workshop'.[39] This focus on women voters as housewives was typical of much Conservative literature of the time, as well as political coverage in the right-wing press, with little attention paid to women's employment outside the home.[40] For example, housewives developed a totemic role in the economy debate of the early 1920s, which led to the press magnates lords Rothermere and Northcliffe sponsoring a series of Anti-Waste League candidates at by-elections in support of cutbacks in government spending. Papers such as the *Daily Mail* and *The Times* claimed that the anti-waste cause had a particular appeal for housewives as they were the section of society who best understood the strains which high prices and taxation placed on the household budget.[41] Anti-Waste League candidates at by-elections took pains to claim that they had widespread female support. Admiral Sueter, the victorious candidate at the Hertford by-election of June 1921, even styled himself the 'Anti-Waste and Housewives Candidate'.[42] However, the press lords' claims to represent the housewives' interest did not go without challenge from the women's Conservative organisation. Their magazine *Home and Politics* highlighted the anti-waste MPs' poor attendance record in the Commons and observed that the Rothermere press was in the habit of publishing advertisements for luxurious fashions hardly in keeping with the owner's position as a champion of stringent retrenchment.[43]

The Conservative valorisation of the housewife contrasted sharply with the party's hostile treatment of young women wage workers in contemporaneous debates about unemployment insurance. Gendered conceptions of provision based on perceptions of the value of wartime service played an important role in shaping the unemployment insurance system after 1918. In particular, Conservatives claimed that the entitlement of ex-servicemen to a fair income in times of unemployment was paramount. With the unemployment insurance fund coming under strain as a result of ongoing recession, the Conservative-backed Lloyd George government took measures to prevent ex-servicemen facing hardship in March 1921. Not only were men who had fought under the colours brought into the state insurance scheme, but the original draft of the Unemployment Insurance Act (1920) Amendment Bill recommended that they receive 20*s.* of weekly benefit, as opposed to 18*s.* for ordinary male civilian workers.[44] Eventually a universal rate of 20*s.* was introduced for all men and 15*s.* for women.[45] Alfred Law, Conservative MP for Rochdale, summed up his party's sense of indebtedness to those men who had fought in the trenches when he spoke at the committee stage of the amendment bill:

> We on this side are deeply sympathetic with the unemployed, and especially with the ex-soldiers. During the course of the Debate it has been suggested there is a special obligation on the nation to make provision for ex-soldiers, and I cannot help thinking it is a national obligation, as these men fought for their country.[46]

Conservatives often supported their claims to defend ex-servicemen's interests by using a gendered discourse, which contrasted men's active service for their country with the supposed laziness of young women who were allegedly abusing the insurance system. While the amendment bill was in committee, the Earl of Midleton, an Irish Unionist, claimed that many girls saw claiming unemployment benefit as preferable to working in domestic service. Midleton asserted that women with experience in this employment were refusing such work 'on all possible grounds, and are leaving on the slightest possible pretext, because they know they will only have to go round the corner and take 15*s.* for doing nothing'.[47] An editorial in *The Times* claimed that at the start of 1921 there were six resident posts in domestic service for every suitable woman that applied. The paper was trenchant in its criticism of unemployed girls, arguing that if they 'refuse employment that lies open to them, because it is not exactly to their taste, they ought not to be paid out of the public purse, and so enabled to live a life of idleness'.[48] It should be emphasised that this language also had a class dimension, with criticism focused on working-class women. Given that young women had been seen as the main abusers of the Out of Work Donation in 1919, a Seeking Work Test was introduced in March 1921. Local employment committees were originally instructed to refuse benefit to women resident with their husbands and the test extended to all claimants who had paid less than twenty weeks of contributions during the previous year, a clause directed mainly at married women.[49]

However, as Marjorie Levine-Clark has shown, government policies of providing preferential treatment for the ex-serviceman came under challenge after 1921. The issue of marital status complicated attitudes towards the perceived worthiness of male unemployment claimants. In some contexts, the married civilian man, who was assumed to act as his family's 'breadwinner', could be seen as having more of a right to participate in relief work than the single ex-serviceman.[50] Furthermore, a Labour campaign to introduce civilian widows' pensions challenged the privileged access which families of deceased ex-servicemen had been given to pension benefits. In promoting the campaign, Rhys Davies, Labour MP for Westhoughton, observed that:

> The conscience of the nation demands that no semblance of 'charity' shall appear in the national treatment of the soldier's widow: that she shall receive in a pension, an entirely honourable recognition of her claim on public funds. The industrial worker, similarly dying from, or disabled by, sickness on equally 'active service' as the soldiers, has surely earned as strong a claim on society. His death is no less a national loss than that of the fighting man.[51]

Labour's bill to provide civilian widows' pensions on the same basis as the benefits enjoyed by war widows was narrowly rejected by the Commons in March 1923. Nonetheless, the Conservatives passed a resolution to support pensions for civilian widows with young children at their party conference the following October.

At the 1924 election civilian widows' pensions formed part of a wide Conservative programme of social reforms, including consumer legislation, higher old age pensions, and an expansion in house building (figure 3.1).

These policies were presented as aiding the family and home life. In the Conservative address to women, designed as a letter from Caroline Bridgeman to

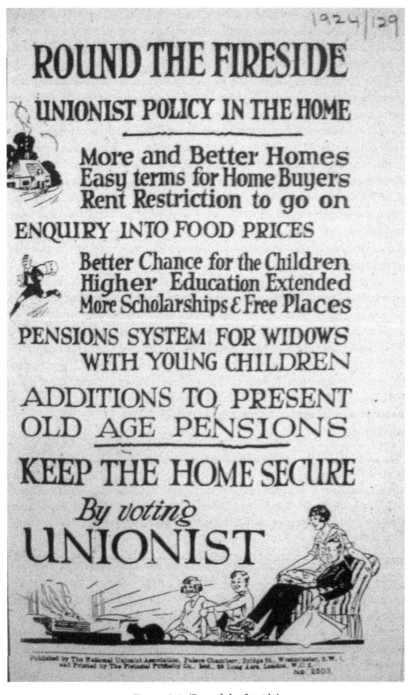

Figure 3.1 'Round the fireside'

party leader Stanley Baldwin, it was claimed that Labour threatened the interests of the female consumer:

> A year ago the country was flooded with promises of cheap food under a Socialist Government. Those who do the family housekeeping know by now how false those promises were. Socialism, when fully carried out ... would compel us to do our household shopping with Government officials in Government shops.[52]

This focus on home issues in appeals to women continued at the 1929 election. Almost three-quarters of Conservative election addresses referred to housing, pensions, welfare and education.[53] Particular attention was paid to a series of social reforms introduced by the Baldwin government: the introduction of civilian widows and orphans pensions, the establishment of a legal procedure for adoption, the introduction of equal guardianship rights over infants, and the Matrimonial Causes Act, under which women no longer needed to prove desertion or cruelty, in addition to adultery as grounds for divorce. Surprisingly few specific appeals were directed towards the new female voters who were enfranchised by the reduction of the voting age for women from 30 to 21. For example, *Women of Today and Tomorrow*, a one-off magazine produced for the election, of which 8.5 million copies were printed, focused on the home with sections on housewifery, better buying and the cost of living.[54] Conservative Central Office justified this strategy by claiming that few young women were likely to identify directly with industrial trade unions. Of the estimated three million women under 30 who were now qualified to vote, it claimed around half did not work for wages, of the remainder fewer than 600,000 were industrial workers.[55] During the Edwardian period WUTRA had encouraged women to play a more active role in politics by claiming that key political issues of the day were vital to their duties in the home. Following the enfranchisements of women in 1918 and 1928 there was remarkably little change in the Conservative Party's broad appeal to women, which continued to focus overwhelmingly on the home, welfare and social reform.

Facing the voters: women in the culture of election addresses

Analysing the depiction of gender roles in election addresses provides us with further insights into the role of women within the Conservative Party and wider electoral culture. The following analysis draws on the records of the National Liberal Club (hereafter NLC), held at Bristol University, and focuses on the appeals that candidates made to female voters, the expectations of women as candidates at parliamentary and local elections, and (more commonly) their role as the wives of candidates. During the early 1920s election addresses were seen as a key element in political campaigning. In 1922 Henry Houston, who had come to public attention as Horatio Bottomley's election agent, produced a large tome on *Modern Electioneering Practice* with Lionel Valdar. For Houston and Valdar the election address was 'the "brief" upon which you have to fight the entire campaign. You cannot run away from it in the middle of the contest. In it you nail your colours to the mast, and by it alone the silent voter will judge you.'[56] The authors also encouraged candidates to pay particular attention to 'the final word', received by voters through the post on the eve of the poll: 'It is desirable, now that women constitute nearly forty per cent of the registered electorate, to have a separate final word to the women voters', ideally signed by the candidate's wife.[57] New voters, it was claimed, would not tolerate the closely typed and verbose printed addresses which had apparently been a common feature of elections before the First World War. Agents were advised to be brief and stick to everyday concerns: 'Tell the electors in plain homely language what your candidate's policy is, and see that the policy bears on the actual facts of workday life. Never mind about the Treaty of Sevres. It is very important, no doubt, but seventy-five per cent, of the electors have never heard of it.'[58] Women, in particular, were deemed to have little time for long-winded and sonorous language:

> You may talk to women electors about 'this great Empire upon which the sun never sets' till you are blue in the face, but if your rival is telling them why ... their daily task as chancellors of the domestic exchequer is so much more difficult, you may depend upon it that you are wasting your breath and he is winning votes.[59]

Despite their very visible presence in public politics through the suffrage and free trade campaigns, women's exclusion from the parliamentary franchise meant that they had rarely featured in Edwardian general election addresses, aside from references to the candidate's attitude to female suffrage. Only two of the printed addresses in the NLC collection for January 1910 contain a photo of the candidate's wife, and one of these (Knutsford) was a lavishly illustrated 16-page booklet.[60] However, on a few occasions the wife of the candidate would write accompanying letters encouraging women to undertake election work, with reference to the effect that tariff reform would have on their duties as housewives.[61] Women also made little impact on the culture of addresses in local elections, in which there were around one million female voters during the Edwardian period. References to specific issues concerning women are noticeably absent from the NLC's collection of addresses for the 1907 London County Council (LCC) elections, apart from references to the candidate's support for women to be allowed to be elected to sit on the LCC and other local authorities. In the next LCC election for which records are held in Bristol, in 1913, the addresses of eight female candidates survive. What is most striking about the language of these texts is the tendency for women to claim that they would devote themselves to traditionally feminine roles if elected. For example, of the two Progressive candidates running in Dulwich it was noted that 'Mr. Phipps will devote himself specially to **Finance and Education**, and Dr. [Sophia] Jevons to questions affecting **women ratepayers** and the medical treatment of school children, housing and public health questions, the care of women lunatics and the mentally deficient.'[62]

In the general election of 1918 some candidates produced separate addresses for male or absent voters and the female electorate such as Harold Glanville, Labour candidate for Bermondsey. In his address to male voters he called for 'just punishment' for the German 'criminals' supposedly responsible for starting the First World War, and noted that two of his sons had fought in France. Glanville also observed that tariff reform would 'have the same effect as the Hun Submarines and give the profiteers a prospect of continuing their gains at your expense'. The address to women was less belligerent in its rhetoric, being almost exclusively focused on the plight of wives and widows of soldiers, and the hardships faced by housewives, with only passing reference to women wage workers.[63] Only five addresses from women candidates survive in the NLC's collection for the 1918 election. However, apart from occasional references to equal pay they suggest that these pioneer women did little to challenge conventional assumptions about the concerns and duties of the female politician.[64] Edith Phipps, Independent candidate for Chelsea, produced a separate appeal to women voters focused on housing, mother's pensions, endowment of motherhood (family allowances), and equal pay. Women candidates, like their male counterparts, devoted much attention to the treatment of discharged servicemen and soldiers' widows.[65] Margery Corbett Ashby (Liberal) even included an image of her husband in the address with the slogan 'A soldier's wife for Ladywood'.[66]

We should be careful not to exaggerate the extent to which electoral culture was 'feminised' after the vote was won. Following the novelty of the 1918 election, few printed addresses had substantial sections directed specifically to women, and by 1929 the separate address to female voters was becoming rare. At that year's election Eric Romilly, Conservative candidate for Hereford claimed: 'I make no special appeal to the women, believing as I do that men and women are equally entitled to the vote, just as they are equally well qualified to use it.'[67] Even during the 1923 election, when the consumer issue of tariff reform was a key concern, only twelve of the seventy addresses sampled from the NLC collection had more than a short paragraph of text directed solely at women.

While there was little new about the rhetorical appeals made to women, male candidates became noticeably keener to depict themselves in family scenes in their election addresses after 1918, although this trend became less common by 1935, when economic pressures limited candidates' use of imagery in addresses.[68] Although it had been common for male candidates to be photographed in military dress for their addresses in the early post-war elections, this trend had become much less common by 1924. This may be surprising given that two hundred Conservative MPs who won seats at the 1924 election had undertaken uniformed service during the First World War, as opposed to only 13 Liberal and 14 Labour MPs.[69]

Throughout the early 1920s Conservative politicians contrasted their records as soldiers with pacifist Labour candidates, who were portrayed as lacking in courage and unable to control trade union militants.[70] For example, Captain Erskine-Bolst,

Coalition candidate for South Hackney at the 1922 by-election, played up his heroic war record and attacked the claims of his Labour opponent Holford Knight, who had been a conscientious objector, to have local support from the British Legion.[71] Erskine-Bolst made much of the apparent rowdyism at his meetings, some of which were broken up to the strains of the 'Red Flag'.[72] Sensationalising the disturbances, one election poster carried the blunt statement: 'Constitution or Revolution? Moderate Men Vote for Erskine-Bolst'.[73] Intriguingly, Conservative publications aimed at women were keen to highlight instances of apparent unruliness and violence by Labour supporters, particularly if it was directed against female politicians.[74] In Leeds the *Conservative Woman* made much of the violence by young men at public meetings in the run up to the 1924 election, publishing an appeal from the wife of Charles Wilson, Conservative MP for Leeds Central. She called the 'Bolshevik' methods of Labour rowdies 'a disgrace to our city'.[75]

However, debates over rowdyism played little part in most contests in 1924 and 1929. The Conservatives' shift away from direct appeals to ex-servicemen's interests at these contests made sense given that this group's privileged access to state benefits and employment opportunities was coming under increasing strain. By the mid-1920s politicians who had seen military service and could claim to represent ex-servicemen, like Clement Attlee and Oswald Mosley, were coming to prominence within the parliamentary Labour Party. Perhaps the repositioning of Conservative politics also reflected a growing cultural fatigue with the First World War as well as an increasing sense that exaggerated tales of Labour rowdyism were beginning to wear thin in their retelling.[76]

For Conservative and Liberal candidates, playing up their family man credentials was an alternative ploy which could be used to imply that their Socialist opponents threatened the safety of the home (although such attacks had become rare by the 1935 election, and Labour also sought to make use of family imagery in election addresses). The two candidates for the North Battersea election in 1923 made remarkably different use of iconography. Whereas Saklatvala, the Labour candidate and Communist Party member, illustrated his address with a depiction of the Peterloo Massacre, his Liberal opponent presented himself as a guardian of family values, which were supposedly threatened by Socialism and Communism (figure 3.2).[77]

Given that the party leadership and individual male candidates were keen to present themselves as the champions of home interests, along the lines propounded by *Home and Politics*, it proved difficult for women candidates to develop a distinct role as Conservative parliamentary candidates. Many of the early Conservative women MPs such as Nancy Astor, Katherine Stewart-Murray (the Duchess of Atholl), and Gwendolen Guinness (Countess of Iveagh) took over seats that had been held by their husbands or other male relatives. As Elizabeth Vallance notes, this meant 'their candidacy was the extension of their acceptable roles as wives' or mothers.[78] Other women struggled to get selected for winnable seats, with less than a third of

TO THE

WOMEN VOTERS of NORTH BATTERSEA.

VOTE FOR

HENRY CAIRN HOGBIN

THE MAN WHO STANDS FOR THE SAFETY OF

WOMEN AND CHILDREN

AND FOR

BETTER HOUSING   FAIR WAGES   CHEAP FOOD.

DO NOT BE INTIMIDATED. **NOBODY** BUT **YOURSELF** NEED KNOW HOW YOU VOTE. THE BALLOT IS **SECRET.**

IF YOU DON'T WANT REVOLUTION AND STARVATION, VOTE AND VOTE **EARLY** FOR **HOGBIN.**

Polling Day—DECEMBER 6th.

Printed by G. W. YOUNG, 84, Bridge Road West, and Published by J. A. WEBSTER, Election Agent, 439, Battersea Park Road, S.W. 11.

Figure 3.2 Hogbin (Liberal), North Battersea election address, 1923 election

female Conservative candidates being elected MPs at each contest between 1918 and 1929, apart from 1923. Even when they succeeded in becoming MPs, women encountered the assumption that their expertise was largely confined to 'women's issues' focused on the home, moral issues and welfare.[79]

After 1918 the growing presence of women in public politics was heralded as offering a challenge to earlier traditions of rowdy street meetings.[80] However, the partial enfranchisement of women in 1918 did not lead to a substantial feminising of wider electoral culture. Assumptions about the appropriate 'women's issues' which female candidates should concern themselves with were already well established within the culture of local elections before the First World War. Early female Conservative parliamentary candidates struggled to develop a distinct space for themselves within the party with their male counterparts often claiming they would act as the guardians of the interests of the home against Socialist intrusions.

Conclusion: the continuities of female Conservatism

In summer 1929 Caroline Bridgeman left her position as leader of the women's Conservative organisation, following her husband's elevation to the House of Lords. This decision to follow her husband's retirement from frontline Conservative politics was indicative of the constrained role that women played within the leadership structure of the party. Bridgeman had been at the forefront of the development of the Women's Tariff Reform League, the forerunner of WUTRA, and the Conservative party women's organisation, entering the political fray following her husband's surprise by-election loss at Oswestry in 1904. And yet, like so many women in the party she placed her own political ambitions as secondary to her husband's career.

Women had been able to take a prominent role within the Conservative grassroots organisation during the Edwardian period through WUTRA's presentation of tariff reform as a housewives' issue. Building on their early lead over Labour in developing a mass-supported women's organisation, after 1918 the women's Conservative organisation continued to focus on issues concerning the home, such as social reform and the cost of living, which it was assumed were the key interest of female voters. With the development of a deflationary political regime after 1920 the Conservative party often valorised the housewife in contrast to its criticism of young working-class women, who it was asserted were claiming unemployment benefit rather than taking low-paid positions within domestic service.

While the women's Conservative organisation attracted significantly more support than its rivals, making the party more accommodating to female activists proved more difficult. The decision after 1918 to focus on building a homosocial branch network along the lines of the pre-war WUTRA meant that women activists at local level had a limited role in party power structures. Women district and constituency agents were excluded from the party's agents association, and the women's branches played little part in the selection of parliamentary candidates. While a small number of women stood as candidates at elections between 1918 and 1929, most of the early female Conservative MPs and senior organisers tended to have male relatives who were prominent within the party. The Conservatives proved more successful than their rivals in winning women into the party in the decade after the 1918 Representation of the People Act. And yet, they did little to give those women a meaningful role in the running of the party both at a local and national level. Tensions between the male and female sections of the party persisted throughout the 1930s and women remained peripheral within the Conservative leadership.[81] The Conservative appeal to female voters remained constrained by assumptions about 'women's issues', which focused on peace, social reform and the home.

Notes

1 Figures from G. E. Maguire, *Conservative Women: A History of Women and the Conservative Party, 1874–1997* (Basingstoke: Palgrave Macmillan, 1998), p. 80; Martin Pugh, *Women and the Women's Movement in Britain, 1914–1999* (2nd edn, Basingstoke: Macmillan, 2000), p. 140.

2 Maguire, *Conservative Women*, chapter 4; Neal McCrillis, *The British Conservative Party in the Age of Universal Suffrage: Popular Conservativism, 1918–1929* (Columbus, OH: Ohio State University Press, 1998), chapter 2; Matthew Hendley, 'Constructing the Citizen: The Primrose League and the Definition of Citizenship in the Age of Mass Democracy in Britain, 1918–1928', *Journal of the Canadian Historical Association*, 7 (1996), 125–51. For a brief but important exception see the analysis of Conservative women's periodical literature in Beatrix Campbell, *The Iron Ladies: Why Do Women Vote Tory?* (London: Virago Press, 1987), chapter 2.

3 David Jarvis, 'Mrs Maggs and Betty: The Conservative Appeal to Women Voters in the 1920s', *Twentieth Century British History*, 5 (1994), 129–52; David Jarvis, 'The Conservative Party and the Politics of Gender, 1900–1939', in Martin Francis and Ina Zweiniger-Bargielowska (eds), *The Conservatives and British Society 1880–1990* (Cardiff: University of Wales Press, 1996), pp. 172–93; David Jarvis, '"Behind Every Party": Women and Conservatism in Twentieth Century Britain', in Amanda Vickery (ed.), *Women, Privilege, and Power: British Politics, 1750 to the Present* (Stanford, CA: Stanford University Press, 2001), pp. 289–314 at pp. 300–2, 308.

4 David Thackeray, 'Home and Politics: Women and Conservative Activism in Early Twentieth-Century Britain', *Journal of British Studies*, 49 (2010), 826–48; David Thackeray, 'From Prudent Housewife to Empire Shopper: Party Appeals to the Female Voter, 1918–1928', in Julie V. Gottlieb and Richard Toye (eds), *The Aftermath of Suffrage: Women, Gender, and Politics in Britain, 1918–1945* (Basingstoke: Palgrave Macmillan, 2013), pp. 37–53; The development of the women's Conservative organisation in Lancashire has subsequently been explored by Neil Fleming. See N. C. Fleming, 'Women and Lancashire Conservatism Between the Wars', *Women's History Review*, 26 (2017), 329–49.

5   Pamela M. Graves, *Labour Women: Women in British Working-Class Politics 1918–1939* (Cambridge: Cambridge University Press, 1994); Cheryl Law, *Suffrage and Power: The Women's Movement, 1918–1928* (London: I. B. Tauris, 1997).

6   Patricia Hollis, *Ladies Elect: Women in English Local Government 1865–1914* (Oxford: Oxford University Press, 1987), pp. 423–8, 431–48.

7   West Sussex Record Office, Chichester, Maxse family MSS, C. Uncatalogued 222, Mary Maxse to Ivor Maxse, 25 May 1918.

8   Tariff Reform League (hereafter TRL), *Monthly Notes*, 19: 1 (July 1913), 68.

9   Thackeray, 'Home and Politics', pp. 830–3.

10 TRL, *Monthly Notes*, 12: 4 (April 1910), 351.

11 Bodleian Library, Oxford, Conservative Party Archive (hereafter CPA), ARE MU29/3, Midland Union notebook 1907–17.

12 See Thackeray, 'Home and Politics', pp. 833–4.

13 CPA, ARE MU29/3, Midland Union notebook 1907–17.

14 *Berrow's Worcester Journal*, 3 May 1913, pp. 3, 7; 23 May 1914, p. 6.

15 Shropshire Archives, Shrewsbury, William Bridgeman MSS, 4629/1/1917/114, Caroline Bridgeman to Mary Maxse, 16 Oct. 1917.

16 David Thackeray, 'Popular Politics and the Making of Modern Conservatism, c.1906–1924' (PhD dissertation, University of Cambridge, 2010), p. 197.

17 CPA, NUCA Executive Committee minutes, Memo 47E, Microfiche, 0.102.23, Notes on a Women's Central Organisation, 16 Jan. 1918.

18 William Bridgeman MSS, 4629/1/1918/16, Caroline Bridgeman to William Bridgeman, 17 Jan. 1918.

19 CPA, NUCA Executive Committee minutes, Memo 47A, Microfiche 0.102.23, Notes on a Women's Organisation under the Representation of the People Bill, 21 Jan. 1918.

20 For the varying responses to the incorporation of women into the local party organisation in north-west England see Fleming, 'Women and Lancashire Conservatism', 333–4.

21 CPA, Microfiche, 0.395.89, Leigh MacLachlan, 'Women's Organisation', *Conservative Agents' Journal*, June 1920, p. 7.

22 By 1923 the affiliated Conservative Clubs had 500,000 members, although many of the clubs were of questionable political value to the Conservative Party, *Conservative Agent's Journal*, Sep. 1923, p. 186.

23 *Conservative Agents' Journal*, Apr. 1922, p. 9.

24 Jarvis, 'Politics of Gender', pp. 174–6, 180–3.

25 CPA, Metropolitan Area, ARE 1/29/1, Herbert Jessel to F. S. Jackson (Party Chairman), 21 Jan. 1924.

26 CPA, Metropolitan Area, ARE 1/29/1, Herbert Jessel, 'Special Difficulties in London in Dealing with the Women', n.d. [*c*.Jan. 1924].

27 CPA, Metropolitan Area, ARE 1/29/1, Herbert Jessel, 'The Women's Organization Generally', n.d. [*c*.1924].

28 Stuart Ball, *Portrait of a Party: The Conservative Party in Britain 1918–1945* (Oxford: Oxford University Press, 2013), p. 180.

29 Pugh, *Women's Movement*, p. 125.

30 For a more detailed discussion of the Unionist Women's Institutes see Thackeray, 'Home and Politics', pp. 842–5.

31 Library of Birmingham, Birmingham Conservative and Unionist Association MSS, Management Committee minutes, 14 Jan. 1927.

32 For a more detailed discussion of Conservative women's activism in Leeds see Thackeray, 'Home and Politics', pp. 840–2.

33 Maguire, *Conservative Women*, p. 79.

34 Parliamentary Archives, London, Davidson MSS, DAV/190, J.C.C. Davidson, Undated memo. [*c*.1930].

35 Campbell, *The Iron Ladies*, p. 50.

36 Marjorie Maxse, 'Women's Organisation', *Conservative Agent's Journal*, Nov. 1927, p. 303.

37 Ball, *Portrait of a Party*, pp. 180–1.

38 In 1937 there were only three women chairmen of Conservative constituency associations in England and Wales. Ball, *Portrait of a Party*, p. 148.

39 NUCA, *Conservative Campaign Guide* (London, 1922), p. 981.

40 For depictions of 'women's issues' in politics in the right-wing press during the 1920s see Adrian Bingham, 'Enfranchisement, Feminism and the Modern Woman: Debates in the British Popular Press, 1918–1939', in Julie V. Gottlieb and Richard Toye (eds), *The Aftermath of Suffrage: Women, Gender and Politics in Britain, 1918–1945* (Basingstoke: Palgrave Macmillan, 2013), pp. 87–104 at pp. 88–95.

41 *Daily Mail*, 23 Feb. 1920, p. 6; 25 Feb. 1920, p. 7; *The Times*, 15 Jan. 1921, p. 8; 16 June 1921, p. 7; 18 June 1921, p. 10.

42 *The Times*, 17 June 1921, p. 10; see also 14 Jan. 1921, p. 11; 15 Jan. 1921, p. 8.

43 *Home and Politics*, Mar. 1920, p. 4; Feb. 1921, p. 3; July 1921, p. 16; Aug. 1921, p. 12.

44 *Scotsman*, 23 Feb. 1921, p. 8; for the government's stated commitment to aid ex-servicemen regardless of the dire economic situation see T. J. MacNamara, 'The Old Year and the New. How Stands the Problem of Unemployed Ex-service Men To-day?', *Comrades' Journal*, Jan. 1921, p. 5.

45 W. R. Garside, *British Unemployment 1919–1939: A Study in Public Policy* (Cambridge: Cambridge University Press, 1990), p. 39.

46 138 H.C. Deb. 5s., 24 Feb. 1921, col. 1234

47 44 H.L. Deb., 5s., 2 Mar. 1921, col. 229; for other examples of Conservative anger at women's refusal to undertake work in domestic service in the early 1920s see Adrian Bingham, *Gender, Modernity, and the Popular Press in Inter-war Britain* (Oxford: Oxford University Press, 2004), pp. 68–9.

48 *The Times*, 3 Mar. 1921, p. 11; See also 24 Feb. 1921, p. 6; 26 Feb. 1921, p. 6.

49 Alan Deacon, *In Search of the Scrounger: The Administration of Unemployment Insurance in Britain, 1920–1931* (London: Social Administration Research Trust, 1976), p. 25.

50 Marjorie Levine-Clark, 'The Politics of Preference: Masculinity, Marital Status and Unemployment Relief in post-First World War Britain', *Cultural and Social History*, 7 (2010), 233–52 at 233–4, 245–6.

51 People's History Museum, Manchester, Labour Party MSS, Microfiche, 1923/11, R. J. Davies, *Widowed Mothers' Pensions*.

52 Shropshire Archives, Shrewsbury, Caroline Bridgeman MSS, 4629/1/4/9, Draft in Pembroke Williams to Caroline Bridgeman, 20 Oct. 1924.
53 David Jarvis, 'Stanley Baldwin and the Ideology of the Conservative Response to Socialism, 1918–1931' (PhD dissertation, University of Lancaster, 1991), p. 419.
54 CPA, CCO170/5/47, A. R. Linforth to Joseph Ball, 20 Mar. 1929; NUCA, *Women of Today and Tomorrow* (London, 1928).
55 CPA, CCO170/5/47, NUCA, 'The New Women Voters', n.d. [1928].
56 Henry James Houston and Lionel Valdar, *Modern Electioneering Practice* (London: C. Knight, 1922), p. 19.
57 *Ibid.*, p. 176.
58 *Ibid.*, p. 20.
59 *Ibid.*, p. 13.
60 Bristol University Special Collections, National Liberal Club (hereafter NLC) MSS, DM668, Crewe (Labour); Knutsford (Liberal).
61 NLC, DM668, Jessie Lupton, 'To the electors of the Sleaford division', Jan. 1910 address; Devon Record Office, Exeter, Morrison-Bell MSS, 2128, Dorothy Buxton, Leaflet letter, 22 Dec. 1909.
62 NLC, DM668, Dulwich Progressive election leaflet; see also South Hackney Progressive election leaflet for a similar gender divide in the concerns of the male and female candidates, both 1913 LCC elections.
63 NLC, DM668, Harold Glanville election addresses.
64 Margaret Corbett Ashby, Emily Phipps, Eunice Murray, Edith How Martyn and Violet Markham.
65 NLC, DM668, Eunice Murray (Independent, Bridgeton); Edith How Martyn (Progressive Independent, Hendon) observed that 'the home is the basis of the nation's welfare; it is the woman's workshop'.
66 NLC, DM668, Margaret Corbett Ashby 1918 election address.
67 NLC, DM668, Eric Romilly (Conservative, Hertford).
68 For politicians using family portraits in their election addresses see for example the following addresses from the 1923 election, Morrison-Bell (Honiton, Conservative); Wedgewood Benn (Leith, Labour), all NLC, DM668.
69 Richard Carr, 'The Phoenix Generation at Westminster: Great War Veterans Turned Tory M.P.s, Democratic Political Culture, and the Path of British Conservatism From the Armistice to the Welfare State' (PhD dissertation, University of East Anglia, 2010), p. 88.
70 Jon Lawrence, 'The Transformation of British Public Politics After the First World War', *Past and Present*, 190 (2006), 185–216 at 197–201; *Home and Politics*, Feb. 1924, p. 5; *Conservative Agents' Journal*, Oct. 1923, p. 222.
71 Erskine-Bolst stood as an independent Coalition candidate, but subsequently joined the Conservative Party. Lancashire Record Office, Preston, Blackpool Conservative Association MSS, C.C. Erskine-Bolst scrapbook, PLC5/14/1, Aug. 1922 election address and 'Another Lie!' handbill.
72 *Hackney and Kingsland Gazette*, 14 Aug. 1922, p. 3; 16 Aug. 1922, p. 3.
73 Blackpool Conservative Association MSS, C. C. Erskine-Bolst scrapbook, handbill.
74 *Home and Politics*, Feb. 1924, p. 5.

75 *The Conservative Woman (Leeds)*, Nov. 1924, pp. 1–2.

76 Jon Lawrence, *Electing Our Masters: The Hustings in British Politics From Hogarth to Blair* (Oxford: Oxford University Press, 2009), pp. 84–5.

77 NLC, DM668, Saklatvala (Labour) and Hogbin (Liberal), North Battersea election addresses, 1923 election.

78 Elizabeth Vallance, *Women in the House: A Study of Women Members of Parliament* (London: Athlone, 1979), p. 27.

79 Brian Harrison, 'Women in a Men's House. The Women MPs, 1919–1945', *Historical Journal*, 29 (1986), 623–54 at 636–44.

80 Lawrence, 'Transformation of British Public Politics', pp. 207–8.

81 Jarvis, 'Politics of Gender', pp. 177, 182.

4

Conservative women and the Primrose League's struggle for survival, 1914–32

Matthew C. Hendley

The Primrose League is usually viewed as a crucial political vehicle for Conservative women during the Victorian and Edwardian eras. Though open to both sexes, the League's true value to the Conservative Party lay in its effective utilisation of female members (who constituted nearly half of its membership) for both canvassing during elections and social functions between elections. Owing to the fact that women lacked the national franchise before 1918, the League has been seen as a vital means for women to interact with national politics.[1] The post-1918 history of this important extra-parliamentary organisation is much less well known than its activities before the First World War.[2] There has been an assumption among historians that the League was superfluous to the Conservative Party once women gained the vote and the Conservative Party began creating a separate organisation for its female members. This chapter challenges this view and focuses on how the League re-made itself for its female members between 1914 and 1932. Despite the challenges of the war and post-war periods, the League avoided the fate of becoming a redundant collection of 'superfluous women' by re-defining itself. In doing so, it revealed the multiplicity of subcultures which existed to support the interwar hegemony of the Conservative Party and the fluidity of strategies utilised in support of the Conservative cause. It also shows how Conservative politics became increasingly feminised during the interwar period.

In its self-transformation, the Primrose League built on two sometimes contradictory processes. During the First World War it created a patriotic associational culture which allowed men and women to work together in a non-confrontational atmosphere.[3] After the war, it helped contribute to building a Conservative culture by becoming an agency of political education for new voters (especially women) and a vehicle for sometimes strident anti-socialist Conservative opinion.[4] It also became a strong voice for a consumption-driven feminised vision of popular imperialism. In these ways, the Primrose League remained a useful weapon for the Conservative cause throughout the 1920s (if reduced from its pre-1914 glory days).

Created to get around the limitations placed on political parties by the Corrupt Practices Act of 1883, the League claimed to be independent but existed for explicitly partisan ends.[5] On the surface, the League was quaintly anachronistic. It had a rigidly hierarchical organisation, a medieval nomenclature and a social calendar filled with fêtes, garden parties and concerts. Its three core principles were the maintenance of religion, the Empire and the Estates of the Realm. Before the war, the League often boasted that it was the 'strongest [political] organisation in the country' with over 800,000 members and 950 local branches called Habitations.[6] From the beginning of the Primrose League, women were excluded from the main leadership positions of Chancellor or Grand Master. Instead, they were segregated into their own Ladies Grand Council which was used as a source of steady donations to help finance the League. Nevertheless, women played an important role in its grassroots activities. In a sense, the League attempted to domesticate politics by merging the private and the public spheres. The result might be said to be the creation of a social sphere – an arena in which politics were never completely absent but were conducted subtly in a non-confrontational atmosphere and absorbed almost unconsciously. During the First World War the Primrose League was able to maintain itself in a challenging political environment by pursuing traditionally 'feminine' activities such as philanthropy and social functions.

In many ways, the League's role in wartime philanthropy was unsurprising. Before the outbreak of war, it had embraced philanthropic work which suited its political agenda, most notably its plan to evacuate the women and children of Ulster in case of civil war.[7] The declaration of the political truce with the coming of the war pushed the League into philanthropic activity to keep its large middle- and upper-class female membership active and to find an outlet for its patriotic energies. Its three main philanthropic wartime initiatives were the War Relief Stamp scheme, the Ambulance Fund and the Needlework Committee.

The War Stamp scheme was not an instant success, though the idea was sound enough. The Primrose League wished to assist the National Relief Fund to help families of soldiers and sailors who were initially left without any means of support.[8] War stamps were to be sold for a penny each and depicted the image of a Tommy and a sailor with the Primrose League emblem. The League initially printed 500,000 stamps and hoped to earn over £3,000 for the National Relief Fund if every member ordered at least one stamp.[9] Unfortunately, by 1917, less than £820 had been raised and nearly 100,000 stamps remained unsold.[10] A scheme to fund a Primrose League ambulance launched in May 1915 was much more successful. In just over a year, over £2,200 was raised and one Primrose League ambulance was at work in France and another in London. Both ambulances had 'Presented by the Primrose League' proudly emblazoned on brass plates.[11]

The most successful philanthropic scheme of all was the Needlework Committee. Set up in October 1914, it comprised many members of the Ladies Grand Council including three women of title.[12] The Committee had two main functions. It collected garments from the Habitations for redistribution to other charities as well as making a number of garments itself. The women of the Committee produced a wide-ranging variety of items including day and night shirts, pyjamas and bed jackets.[13] At the last wartime national meeting (called the Grand Habitation) in 1918, it was noted that over 175,000 items had been sent out with over 80 per cent of the items going to three causes most closely related to British soldiers run through the War Office, English and Foreign Hospitals and the British Red Cross Society.[14]

Fund-raising for philanthropy was not the only preoccupation of the League during the First World War. The League's long-established experience of hosting garden fêtes, whist drives and other social events was put to good use. Hospitality to soldiers and their families could take many forms. The League stand-by of providing teas and entertainments continued to be popular, especially with the wives of soldiers and sailors.[15] In 1916, League habitations in London organised trips for wounded soldiers, which involved entertainments, sports activities and motor outings. In all these cases there seemed to be no overt patriotic or pedagogic element and yet there was no denying their utility for the League and the soldiers. As one piece in the *Gazette* aptly titled 'Smile! Smile! Smile!' explained, 'These social meetings have really a practical value, and *aren't* [*sic*] the lads pleased!'[16]

The League's wartime activities were important because they proved how vital its women members had been to keep the organisation alive. Several patterns emerge from the League's wartime hospitality and philanthropy. First, philanthropy with concrete goals like an ambulance fared best. Second, philanthropy such as needlework which firmly reinforced traditional gender roles was popular both with the League women and positively portrayed in the press.[17] Third, sending knitted goods constituted a personal act of philanthropy which created a link between those on the front lines and those at the Home Front.[18] Fourth, rather than serving as a tepid diversion from the serious business of politics, hospitality served as an extension of it. As most of the organising and hosting of these events was done by women, their importance to the League increased. The ability of the League to create an associational culture in a social sphere away from the direct strains of party politics gave it a distinct advantage. Practically speaking, such events held the League together during the strains of wartime and helped it promote its ideas of social integration. As the *Gazette* reflected in November 1918, the League was 'not only a political but a social society, and one of its main functions is to show people that classes are not antagonistic but that the aim and object of all alike should be to promote the country's good at all costs'. [19]

The Primrose League's raison d'être was shaken by the Representation of the People Act of 1918 (or Fourth Reform Act), which tripled the size of the electorate and enshrined the first significant concession of female suffrage.[20] The issue of enfranchising women had long been a divisive one for the Primrose League. Before 1914, the League had always abstained from taking an entrenched position; it had leading women members on both sides of the suffrage issue. Historians have differed in their interpretations of whether the League was hindered or helped by the suffrage debate.[21] However, once it was obvious that the women's vote was unstoppable, the Primrose League found a new role quickly. A meeting of the Ladies Grand Council in June 1918 strove to unite League members who had been proponents (such as Miss Betty Balfour) and opponents of women's suffrage (such as Lady Jersey).[22] The meeting downplayed past divisions over the issue and framed the question of the women's vote as one of political duty. The Primrose League was praised as the 'first society to organise political education for women' and League members were told to stay committed in order to oppose socialists and pacifists trying to capture women's votes.[23]

It has been suggested by Philippe Vervaecke that the post-war Primrose League was a haven for former anti-suffragists.[24] While such individuals were League members what was more notable is how, once the vote had been granted to female voters, the League quickly began to promote a rhetoric of citizenship explicitly defined in a Conservative manner. A March 1918 article for women pointed out that: 'The vote means a great trust, a great responsibility.'[25] This paternalistic approach indicated both the Primrose League's partisan hopes for women voters and its lack of confidence in their rational abilities. In order for women to be transformed into responsible citizens, special educational efforts were to be launched by the League. In 1918, pamphlets were quickly produced including *The Primrose League and the Women's Vote* and *The Women's Call to Citizenship*. As always, there were calls for canvassing and organisational work in the provinces which included the employment of speakers, though the League was slow to utilise women in this role.[26] Speakers' classes were seen as important in helping neophyte female candidates with voice projection and nervousness. The *Gazette* noted that, in the pre-war period, many (presumably Conservative) women shunned public political work for fear of being tarred as suffragettes.

However, with the arrival of mass democracy, women were now participating openly in politics and assistance was given by the League to help them fulfil their new duties.[27] The *Gazette* also continued to publish advice for speakers on posture, pitch and preparation for speech making.[28] The Grand Council reported to Grand Habitation in 1922 that the Primrose League had to counter the teachings of 'proletarian science'.[29] The League needed to prevent the 'discoveries and truths of science and of historical research' from being perverted and misrepresented.[30] Accordingly, the League launched its lecture series that year at Caxton Hall in Westminster, predominantly devoted to economic issues. Lecture titles included 'Some Economic Definitions', 'Reform versus Revolution', 'Socialism', 'Communism' and 'Britain's Economic Problem'.[31] A year later the Ladies' Grand Council financed a similar course of lectures on economics at Caxton Hall.[32] It also held a summer school which combined social excursions and diversions with the serious business of politics. League worthies from the Grand Council and backbench Conservative MPs gave lectures on topics including housing, the Empire, industrial peace and trade unions. Lectures were mixed with debates, social events and country rambles. The highlight of the session was a model Parliament.[33] Finally, it ran a limited instructional programme of patriotic education for children through its junior branches.[34] None of these efforts were as sophisticated as the educational work undertaken by interwar Conservative institutions like Philip Stott College or the Bonar Law Memorial College. However, the Primrose League's focus on educating women and encouraging them to be political educators showed their desire to play a part in the Conservative battle of ideas.[35]

Clearly the end of the First World War meant that it was not business as usual for the Primrose League. Women in the League were no longer operating solely in the social sphere. In fact, the traditional Primrose League approach would have labelled female members as 'superfluous women' – not in the sense of being unmarriageable women dismissed in the 1920s – but as 'superfluous' to the emerging new world of female Conservative organisations.[36] The major threat to the Primrose League came from the Women's Unionist Associations (WUA), which formed part of the Women's Unionist Organisation (WUO), the Conservative Party organisation for women. The WUO grew to be a major part of the interwar Conservative Party, with approximately one million members by the end of the 1920s, making it the 'largest, most active political organisation in interwar Britain'.[37] The WUA posed a direct threat to the Primrose League since its canvassing, educational work and social activities overlapped considerably. As early as 1919, Habitations were reported to be disbanding to merge their resources with local branches of the WUA. This posed a double threat to the League, which lost branches but also funds and property. The League tried to spell out strict procedures for the dissolution of Habitations.[38] John Ramsden, one of the leading historians of the interwar Conservative Party, has noted that twenty-four Habitations were simply taken over by the party.[39] Competition between the two organisations was often encouraged by party agents seeking the demise of League habitations and their replacement with WUA branches.[40]

The rivalry between the two organisations was so intense that a series of conferences were held from 1921 onwards to iron out differences. The conferences ended amicably with suggestions for future cooperation and mutual representation in each other's organisations. In addition, party agents were issued with circulars from the Central Office urging them to properly respect the League.[41] Chancellors of the Primrose League did their best to foster cooperation and pointed to the harmful effects of organisational rivalry and poaching of members.[42] Ramsden argues that, compared with the men's side of the party, the women's branches and the League had 'established a working relationship ... by the middle 1920s'.[43] Still, frictions continued over such comparatively petty details as the dates of their respective annual meetings.[44] In 1930, a resolution was presented to the National Union Conference to exclude the Primrose League from the Council of the National Union.[45] A year later, the recently elected Chancellor of the League, Douglas

Hacking (1884–1950), pledged to heal the divisions between the two organisations as he held leadership positions in both.[46] It was clear that although relations between the League and corresponding Conservative women's organisations had not erupted into open warfare, there was still considerable sniping. The League had a long tradition of involving women in politics, a nationwide structure and comparatively solid finances in the immediate post-war period. With these advantages in hand, the League re-imagined itself as a political educator of women with a strong anti-socialist tilt and as propagating the acceptable face of British imperialism – which endorsed domestic consumption of imperial goods and increased British settlement in the Dominions.[47]

When considering itself as a political educator of new female voters, it is important to consider the Primrose League's continued ambivalence about female voters. The proposal by Baldwin's Conservative government to equalise the terms of the franchise between men and women in 1928 was greeted by the League with both anticipation and dread.[48] Grassroots opposition to the so-called 'Flapper Franchise' took the form of letters and resolutions from a number of Habitations.[49] The *Gazette* was at pains to counter the popular prejudice that the new voters were young 'flappers' incapable of executing the duties and responsibilities of good citizenship. It earnestly pointed out that the 1928 Act not only gave the vote to over one and a half million women aged 21–25, who might be considered 'flappers', but also that it enfranchised a slightly greater number of women aged 25–30 and nearly two million women over 30.[50] In the run-up to the general election of 1929, Sir Walter Greaves-Lord (1878–1942), the League Chancellor noted the 'special responsibility resting upon the Primrose League in connection with the extension of the Women's Suffrage, for the Primrose League has opportunities and facilities of reaching the women of our day which no other organisation has to the same extent'.[51] Stanley Baldwin in his capacity as the League's Grand Master also expressed confidence in both women voters and the utility of the League in helping instruct such new voters.[52] The League's approaches to women to use their vote wisely varied. Some *Gazette* articles were frankly misogynistic such as 'My New Vote', which compared the pleasure of gaining the vote to buying a new hat.[53] Other articles took a more serious approach while retaining a gendered tone. A special letter composed by Mrs Baldwin to female voters prior to the 1929 election portrayed women as lovers of peace at home and abroad. According to Mrs Baldwin, her husband's government should be supported by women as one that kept the peace.[54] Intriguingly, the Primrose League did not voice any specific concerns about younger working-class women gaining the vote during this time. In fact, the only article which touched on this topic noted a Labour MP's fears that women had a more conservative outlook than men.[55]

For the post-war Primrose League, socialism was a political threat which justified the League's continued existence. Its actions and language against socialism reveals its strongly middle-class view of the world. Working-class men were usually discussed by League publications as being socialised into supporting socialism owing to their involvement in the trade union movement. Rises in strikes after 1918 were attributed to foreign agitators.[56] During the General Strike of 1926, the Primrose League carried on support activities for volunteers attempting to maintain essential services or law and order. The Duke of Sutherland, who was probably the least sensitive of the League Chancellors towards workers' rights and trade unionism, made a successful appeal for volunteers during the strike in response to the government's call for help in maintaining public services. The Grand Council requested League members to put themselves at the disposal of the local volunteer service recruiting committee chairman and to register at local recruiting offices. In addition, a large number of resolutions were passed by Habitations in support of the government during the strike.[57]

Although the League often commented on trade unions and assisted the Government during the General Strike, it felt it had a special role towards women who were seen as particularly vulnerable to socialist wiles. To deal with the socialist threat, the Primrose League launched a multi-tiered counter-attack. To begin with, it offered the rhetoric of social reform and imperialism as constructive alternatives. However, its preferred tactic was to adopt a harsh anti-socialist approach with several facets. The League did its best to portray the British Labour Party as the haven of foreign extremists and linked it as closely as possible to the Communists. It also asserted that socialism threatened traditional ideas of gender and the family.

The Primrose League made little effort to clearly distinguish between socialism, the Labour Party, the Labour Party's allies such as the ILP and the separate Communist Party.[58] Furthermore, the League stressed xenophobic themes and pointed to the failures of the Soviet Union.[59] Unlike many British fascist organisations, the Primrose League was not obsessed with anti-Semitism, but it was not entirely absent. For example, a 1924 article in the *Gazette* noted how the principles of the Labour Party were based on the 'theories of a mid-Victorian German Jew'.[60] Such references were all the more surprising, bearing in mind the Jewish origins of the League's hero Benjamin Disraeli who was frequently praised by League worthies. In addition, the League organised an annual pilgrimage to Disraeli's country home at Hughenden and his grave.[61] Most of the League's post-war xenophobia is found in its critiques of the Soviet Union. In numerous articles and speeches to the Primrose League, the excesses of Bolshevism were luridly paraded, with a special emphasis on the alien origins of its leaders, its poor standard of living for the working class and its attempts to overthrow the twin pillars of family and religion.[62]

The Primrose League's anti-socialist campaign continuously made strong use of domesticated imagery. The prevalence of this imagery reveals the major importance of its female membership. David Jarvis and David Thackeray have shown how the interwar Conservative Party crafted specifically gendered appeals to women.[63] The League was fully aware of such power. League editorials argued that Bolshevik attacks on religion undermined the family.[64] A special effort was made to show that the Soviet Union undertook massive intrusions into the private sphere through the abolition of monogamous marriage and private child-rearing. In its place was free love, 'common ownership' of women and state institutions for the raising and training of children.[65] British women were said to have a special duty to maintain the social fabric and prevent a repetition of the utopian horrors of the Soviet Union.[66]

Throughout all of its arguments, the Primrose League's view of socialism was used as a foil to further justify the League's existence and served as a spur against members' apathy. Instead of being seen as irrelevant to the politics of mass democracy, the League was able to present itself as a non-party cross-class ally of the Conservative Party in the never-ending battle against socialism. It is important to note that despite its anti-socialism, the Primrose League retained five major differences from the marginal fascist organisations of the 1920s such as the British Fascisti. First, the Primrose League never abandoned its support of parliamentary democracy. Second, it never seriously fostered any 'cult' of an all-powerful leader. Third, it was never overtly masculinist and still promoted a place for women in politics. Fourth, it did not recommend an end to trade unionism and its replacement with a corporatist system. Finally, it did not engage in widespread scapegoating of the Jews or any other group (besides the Communists). With these differences in mind, it is unsurprising that the Primrose League did not cultivate political relationships with fascist groups.

As an alternative to the dystopian horrors of socialism, the Primrose League articulated a new ethos of Empire which was distinctly sympathetic to the concerns of female voters. This vision of popular imperialism focused on consumption through Empire shopping and personal ties between Britain and the self-governing Dominions through Empire Settlement. In his address to the League's 1924 Grand Habitation, Baldwin argued that the Empire was not essential for 'glory' or 'boasting' but for 'life'. He called for the League to take its 'part in educating our democracy as to what our Empire stands for'.[67]

Empire shopping, originally the brain child of Leo Amery, was a more politically acceptable method of increasing British purchases of imperial goods than tariffs. The Empire Marketing Board created in 1926, attempted to alter British trade patterns by spending over £1 million through the active promotion of imperial goods. Many of the ads highlighted the female shopper's key role as an imperial consumer.[68] The Primrose League wholeheartedly supported Amery's initiative and helped with its promotion. The League stressed that by giving personal preference to British and imperial goods, British housewives would be participating in a practical form of imperialism which would lessen unemployment in Britain and also help fuel greater imperial purchases of British exports.[69] Assistance for prospective Empire shoppers was offered by the Primrose League in a variety of ways. Recipes for Christmas puddings were given with wholly imperial ingredients; examples of the fruits and produce hailing from different outposts of empire were listed.[70] The Primrose League also recommended publications by the Empire Marketing

Board (such as the *Book of Empire Dinners*) and endorsed EMB posters and maps (on topics such as 'An Indian Rice Field', 'Tea Picking in Ceylon' and 'The Empire Sugar Cane').[71]

Empire shopping privileged the female consumer and reinforced traditional gender hierarchies. In Empire Shopping, the average British woman was unapologetically portrayed as a housewife and controller of the family food budget. It is through her own individual actions in the marketplace that a greater common good was to be achieved. By targeting women for Empire Shopping, the political pitfalls of promoting tariffs were avoided.[72] Empire Shopping also helped re-inforce Conservative gender values by glorifying the role of the housewife and presenting her as an important figure on the world stage. Far from being 'superfluous women', the future of the British Empire and British economic revival lay in the mundane shopping decisions of millions of British women. It made '[b]uying Empire products ... an act of imperial caring, an extension of a mother's caring duty in the home'.[73]

Empire Settlement was another initiative promoted by the Primrose League. The Empire Settlement Act of 1922 devoted up to £3 million per year (for a fifteen-year period) to assisting settlement in the British Empire.[74] Amery had great hopes for Empire Settlement as part of a forward imperial policy to appeal to the British electorate. One of the original goals for the government was the settlement of ex-servicemen on the vast spaces of the Canadian prairie, South African veldt and Australian outback. This would not only reduce the number of citizens competing for scarce employment in Great Britain but would also create prosperity by generating profits overseas which could be channelled back into purchasing British goods. Conservative support for Empire migration also reflected uneasiness over the increasingly urban nature of the British population and their desire 'to restore rural life and values'.[75]

The Primrose League promoted the ideals of Empire settlement. Numerous articles pointed to the unsettled rural areas of Australia, South Africa and Canada and the profits that awaited those willing to work as harvesters and settlers.[76] Readers of the *Gazette* were given regular pictorial glimpses of the Empire in a feature called 'Our Empire Page' in which Canada featured most prominently.[77] Other outposts of Empire fared less well in the *Gazette*. Imperial holdings in Asia, like Malaya, and in Africa, like the Gold Coast, Kenya and the Gambia, were mentioned but accorded much less boosterism than Canada.[78] More volatile parts of the Empire such as India were not given profiles in the 'Our Empire' section at all.[79]

Australia was the subject of a special Primrose League initiative aimed at women. In creating a gendered version of the Empire, personal testimony on settlers' lives written from a female perspective was prominently promoted by the League. In 1926, the *Primrose League Gazette* published a series of articles by Lady Apsley entitled 'Impressions of a Settler's Life in Australia'. Lady Apsley's husband was a minor Conservative politician and former member of the Primrose League's Grand

Council (1923–27). Lady Apsley wished to see if the conditions faced by English emigrants to Australia were as harsh as the Labour Opposition in Parliament implied. Accordingly, under the pseudonyms Mr and Mrs James, the Apsleys settled for one month in a 120-acre allotment in Western Australia near Busselton at the Margaret River.[80] Conditions in Western Australia were fairly primitive but were chronicled cheerfully by Lady Apsley. She noted that though many men were anxious to go on the land, their chief problem was that not 'enough women of the right type [wished] to share a settler's life with them'. Lady Apsley argued that hundreds of settlers' wives lived healthy and contented lives. Her pieces were homilies to Conservative values which stressed the social mobility of English emigrants and the opportunities and egalitarianism which the frontier offered. Her articles, crafted for female readers noted the humble but active socialising that group settlement allowed and the real sense of community it engendered. Lady Apsley wrote of her and her husband's success as settlers despite her unfamiliarity with housework and her husband's with hard physical labour.[81] The chatty style of her articles presented a domestic imperialism in which creating homes for newly married couples to raise families was the key.

In a sense, Lady Apsley's writings echoed the genre of the 'Empire Romance' which was a popular format between the wars.[82] Empire settlement, like Empire shopping was presented as an alternative to both the aridities of a Labour programme of class conflict and the traditional Conservative policies of tariff reform or jingoistic imperialism. With an appeal crafted to female Primrose League members, the presentation of Empire shopping and Empire settlement aimed to further a distinct Conservative sub-culture. The way in which these appeals were gendered towards female Conservatives in addition to the prevalence of domesticated imagery in its anti-socialism campaign also shows how the Primrose League contributed towards the feminisation of interwar Conservative politics.

All in all, the League retained some utility for post-war Conservatives and continued to utilise the work of large numbers of Conservative women. Direct evidence of any electoral impact of the League's work is difficult to determine. Short messages were regularly sent by Conservative MPs and their election agents to the Primrose League after general elections thanking their local Habitations. The general elections of 1918 and 1924 mark the low point and high point of messages of thanks with 35 and 78 received respectively.[83] A more useful snapshot can be taken from ten Habitations profiled in depth by the *Primrose League Gazette* in 1927. Of these ten Habitations, six were in constituencies that were not solidly Conservative. Of these six all were either Labour gains or Labour holds in the 1929 election but all were back in the Conservative fold for the 1931 election, though three (Wednesbury, Rotherham and North Battersea) slipped back to Labour in subsequent by-elections or in the 1935 election.[84] The Primrose League also assisted with local government elections and showed specific interest in elections for the London County Council. However, no specific messages of thanks were sent from any local candidate and coverage given by the League of such elections was limited.[85] The only interwar reference in the *Gazette* for women's participation in local government was a single article encouraging women to serve as Poor Law Guardians.[86] Whether League activity directly affected these election results is impossible to establish. However, what is evident is the persistence with which the League established branches in areas which often seemed to be more natural Labour territory than Conservative territory, as well as the hard work of female League members in the Habitations.

Nationally, League membership numbers though not stellar, held up despite competition from the newly established Women's Unionist Associations. Membership numbers for the post-war League are difficult to determine. The League recorded only new members enrolled and did not publish central statistics for the entire active membership after 1918. The predominant pattern for enrolments seemed to be generally downward, with a temporary surge upwards at key points. A calculation of monthly enrolments shows that new annual membership enrolments climbed rapidly in the aftermath of the war, with the 1923 figure double that of 1919 (26,650 versus 12,578). Post-war enrolments peaked for 1924 with the election of the first-ever Labour government: 28,030 new members were enrolled.[87] After this point, figures steadily declined with 1925 and 1926, the latter the year of the General Strike, being the next highest.[88] The second Labour minority government between 1929 and 1931 did not lead to the same surge in membership as the first.[89] Coupled with concerns over membership were questions about the League's finances. Before the war, the League continually had an annual income of over £8,000, although rising expenses between 1911 and 1914 produced a deficit of nearly £3,000. To help offset the shortfall, the League held a considerable number of capital investments in government bonds and railroads.[90] Although many of the League's Habitations remained active during the war, fewer than half paid their 'tribute' to central League finances for 1918/19, which helped lead to steady post-war deficits.[91]

At the heart of the financial problem was the fact that the Primrose League had traditionally relied on annual subscriptions (or 'tributes') from the social elite who held the highest level of membership in the League – the Knights and Dames. In addition, groups of aristocrats such as the Ladies Grand Council provided large annual infusions of money. The mass membership (or 'Associates') did not pay subscriptions to the Grand Council. This arrangement was inadequate after 1918 and major changes were made. Most notably, all Associates had to pay a tribute of one penny to the Grand Council. In addition, the League launched several special fund-raising efforts and continued its whist drives, dances and bazaars which it had borrowed from the world of female philanthropy.[92] These measures helped stabilise the League although expenditure still exceeded income until 1923/24. When finances were destabilised again by the onset of the Great Depression, the League successfully met the challenge with a special Jubilee Shilling Fund fund-raiser which raised £2,600 by December 1932.[93]

Senior male Conservatives acknowledged the place of the Primrose League and cultivated its leadership positions. From 1918 to 1925, the League's Grand Master was Lord Curzon (who served as Foreign Secretary under Lloyd George and Bonar Law, and Lord President under Baldwin). Perhaps most importantly, Stanley Baldwin, the Conservative party leader from 1923 to 1937, still believed the Primrose League to be a valuable weapon in the Conservatives' political armoury. According to Philip Williamson, Baldwin's earliest political work in the 1880s was founding a rural branch of the Primrose League and 'he continued to attach significance to the League' in the interwar period. To Baldwin, the Primrose League and other related societies were vital for 'social and moral integration, and promotion of self-improvement and good citizenship'.[94] Baldwin spent much time during his political tenure addressing numerous non-political organisations and promoting a sense of associational culture to salve the wounds of wartime. From 1925 onwards, he was the League's Grand Master and addressed its annual Habitations. Of the Primrose League's twelve Chancellors between 1918 and 1932, seven held ministerial office during the interwar period, one held office during the Second World War, one was a Conservative whip and another served as Treasurer of the Conservative Party.[95] The prominence of these figures in the post-war Conservative Party shows that the League still had some practical utility throughout the 1920s. However, it should also be noted that most of the leadership structure (outside of the Ladies Grand Council) was dominated by male aristocratic worthies even if they did also hold ministerial or party positions. Women provided the bulk of the membership, but they lagged in leadership positions. Although women were admitted to the Grand Council after the First World War the main leadership positions were almost always held by males within minimal exceptions.[96] This reliance on male representatives of the old order made the Primrose League increasingly out of touch as the middle class became more important and more meritocratic within interwar British society. It also did not bode well for women who wanted the opportunity to participate in more dynamic leadership positions.

After the Conservative landslide election victory of 1931, the Primrose League's decline accelerated. With a Conservative-dominated coalition in place after 1931 and the continuing growth of Conservative women's organisations, the League seemed less and less relevant. From 1931 to 1939, Labour was not seen by Conservatives as the electoral threat it had been in the 1920s. Neville Chamberlain was not as attuned to the League as his predecessor Stanley Baldwin had been and did not serve as its Grand Master after Baldwin stepped down from that post in 1938.[97] Winston Churchill (whose father Lord Randolph Churchill had helped found the League and whose first ever official political speech was to a Primrose League meeting at Claverton Down, Bath in July 1897) had a soft spot for the League.[98] He was its Grand Master from 1944 to 1965 until he was succeeded by Alec Douglas-Home (Grand Master 1966–83). Churchill gave the annual address at, and presided over, the Grand Habitation meetings until 1957 and continued to send a New Year's Message to the League until 1962. Churchill's addresses regularly had up to 5,000 Primrose Leaguers in attendance at the Royal Albert Hall and he regularly sent out pointed New Year messages to the League.[99] John Ramsden notes that by 1959 it was mostly inactive and reduced to holding a few dinners per year, though 90 MPs claimed still to be members.[100] However, after Churchill's death in 1965 the League continued a steep decline. By 1969, there were fewer than 50 provincial habitations left outside London, which held some 20,000 members (with a much smaller number of London members who paid one guinea versus the usual 5s. membership so they could become Knights of the Imperial Chapter).[101] Although party worthies like Harold Macmillan addressed the League as late as 1981, its membership had been reduced to 'a few hundred' by 1991.[102] It was formally dissolved in 2004 and disbursed its assets (which accounted for £70,000) to the Conservative Party.[103]

All told, the Primrose League did not fade away in the decade after 1918 and it continued to play a role in Conservative popular politics in the 1920s. Female League members had kept the organisation alive during the First World War, particularly through their work in philanthropy and hospitality. Although the post-war world was a rather different one, the Primrose League was able to adjust and contribute towards the Conservative hegemony. Conservative women had a plethora of new and active organisations to join in the 1920s but they did not completely abandon the Primrose League. The League's unique formula of merging partisan rhetoric from a supposedly independent extra-parliamentary organisation with political education for women and a consumption-driven feminised version of popular imperialism gave it a continued place in the world of Conservative organisations. The Primrose League made its own special contribution to the successful feminisation of post-war Conservative politics, which helped ensure interwar Conservative dominance.

Notes

1 Martin Pugh, *The Tories and the People 1880–1935* (Oxford: Basil Blackwell, 1985), p. 49.
2 With the exception of Martin Pugh and myself, most scholars on the Primrose League have focused on the pre-war period, such as: Janet Robb, *The Primrose League 1883–1906* (New York: Columbia University, 1942); Diana Elaine Sheets, 'British Conservatism and the Primrose League: The Changing Nature of Popular Politics 1883–1901' (PhD Dissertation, Columbia University, 1986); Linda Walker, 'Party Political Women: A Comparative Study of Liberal Women and the Primrose League, 1890–1914', in Jane Rendall (ed.), *Equal or Different – Women's Politics 1800–1914* (Oxford: Basil Blackwell, 1987), pp. 165–91. There is some more recent work on the wartime Primrose League but it is only available in French: Philippe Vervaecke, 'Patriotisme philanthropique et citoyenneté féminine: Les femmes et la Primrose

League, 1914–1918', *Revue LISA*, 6 (2008), 57–70 and 'La Politique sans le Parti: La Primrose League et la culture politique britannique, 1883–1919', *Politix*, 81 (2008), 81–104. The post-war Primrose League remains relatively unexamined. An in-house publication by the Conservative Party on the Primrose League has a very brief chapter on the post-1918 Primrose League: Alistair Cooke, *A Gift from the Churchills: The Primrose League, 1883–2004* (London: The Carlton Club, 2010), chapter V, 'Churchillian Twilight'.

3 On the growth of such a non-confrontational associational culture in the inter-war period see: Helen McCarthy, 'Parties, Voluntary Associations and Democratic Politics in Interwar Britain', *The Historical Journal*, L: 4 (2007), 891–912; Helen McCarthy, 'Service Clubs, Citizenship and Equality: Gender Relations and Middle-Class Associations in Britain between the Wars', *Historical Research*, LXXI: 213 (August 2008), 531–52.

4 David Thackeray, *Conservatism for the Democratic Age: Conservative Cultures and the Challenge of Mass Politics in Early Twentieth Century England* (Manchester and New York: Manchester University Press, 2013).

5 On the restrictions placed on British politics by the 1883 Act see Kathryn Rix, '"The Elimination of Corrupt Practices in British Elections?": Reassessing the Impact of the 1883 Corrupt Practices Act', *English Historical Review*, CXXIII: 500 (2000), 65–97.

6 'Annual Meeting of Grand Habitation', *Primrose League Gazette* (hereafter *PLG*), XXII: 56 (May 1914), 4.

7 By August 1914, the League had secured promises of accommodation in Great Britain for 8,000 women and donations of £17,000. Over three hundred of the League's Habitations were involved. This League initiative raised the ire of the Liberals as it was undoubtedly designed to do. The evacuation scheme was also organised with the help of the Women's Unionist and Tariff Reform Association. 'Great Rally at Norwich: Help for Ulster Women', *PLG*, XXI: 51 (December 1913), 8; 'Vice Chancellor's Monthly Letter', *PLG*, XXII: 59 (August 1914), 7; 'A Generous Offer'; 'Will England Help Us?'; 'Help for Ulster Women and Children: Letter from Sir Edward Carson', *PLG*, XXII: 53 (February 1914), 8; Pugh, *Tories and the People*, p. 165.

8 The Fund was launched on 6 August 1914 to alleviate economic distress and raised £5 million by the end of 1915. Arthur Marwick, *The Deluge: British Society and the First World War* (New York: W. W. Norton and Company, 1965), p. 34; Trevor Wilson, *The Myriad Faces of War: Britain and the Great War, 1914–1918* (Cambridge: Polity Press, 1986), p. 775. On problems in receiving these payments see: E. Sylvia Pankhurst, *The Home Front: A Mirror to Life in England during the First World War* (London: The Cresset Library, 1987), p. 25. These problems led to the direct government administration of the scheme by 1916.

9 'The Primrose League and the National Relief Fund', *PLG*, XXII: 61 (November 1914), 20; 'War Relief Stamps', *PLG*, XXII: 60 (October 1914), 2.

10 General Purposes Committee, 'Report to Grand Council', 8 October 1914. Oxford, Bodleian Library. Primrose League Papers, MSS Primrose League 6/1. No. 16. 1914–32, 47; *PLG*, XXII: 61 (November 1914), 4; 'The Editor's Letter', *PLG*, XXII: 62 (December 1914), 5; *PLG*, XXII: 63 (January 1915), 4; *PLG*, XXII: 64 (February 1915), 2; *PLG*, XXII: 66 (April 1915), 4; *PLG*, XXII: 67 (May 1915), 3; 16. 'Untitled

Receipts and Expenditure Sheet', Oxford, Bodleian Library. Primrose League Papers. MSS Primrose League 6/1. No. 16. 1914–32. Leaf 215.

11 'A Primrose League Motor Ambulance', *PLG*, XXIII: 67 (May 1915), 1; 'Report of Grand Council to Grand Habitation, 1916: Primrose League Motor Ambulances', *PLG*, XXIV: 80 (June 1916), 10–12; 'Primrose League Motor Ambulances', *PLG*, XXVI: 110 (December 1918), 6; 'Untitled Receipts and Expenditure Sheet', Oxford, Bodleian Library. Primrose League Papers. MSS Primrose League 6/1. No. 16. 1914–32, Leaf 215.

12 Lady Milman, Lady Borthwick and Lady Parker.

13 'The Needlework Committee at the Head Office', *PLG*, XXII: 60 (October 1914), 4–5.

14 General Purposes Committee, 'Report to the Grand Council', 3 December 1914; Needlework Committee, 'Report to Grand Council', 29 September 1915; Oxford, Bodleian Library. Primrose League Papers. MSS Primrose League 6/1. No. 16. 1914–32. Leafs 63, 113; 'Report of Grand Council to Grand Habitation', *PLG*, XXIV: 80 (June 1916), 10; 'Annual Meeting of Grand Habitation: Comforts for our Fighting Men', *PLG*, XXV: 91 (May 1917), 6; 'Annual Meeting of Grand Habitation: The Primrose League Needlework and War Comforts Fund', *PLG*, XXVI:104 (June 1918), 6.

15 'The Editor's Letter', *PLG*, XXIII: 64 (February 1915), 5.

16 'The Editor's Letter: Hospitality to Soldiers', *PLG*, XXIII: 100 (February 1918), 5; 'Smile! Smile! Smile!' *PLG*, XXV: 92 (June 1917), 5; 'Entertaining Wounded Soldiers', *PLG*, XXIV: 84 (October 1916), 1.

17 John Foster Fraser in the *Standard* as quoted in 'Primrose League Work in War Time', *PLG*, XXIII:73 (November 1915), 6. It also firmly reinforced traditional gender roles by presenting women engaged in a traditionally feminine pursuit which could be performed in the home. Needleworking was a popular wartime philanthropic activity. The Primrose League effort was echoed on a much larger scale by other initiatives such as the Queen Mary's Needlework Guild. Frank Prochaska, *Royal Bounty: The Making of a Welfare Monarchy* (New Haven and London: Yale University Press, 1995), p. 179. The linkage of female patriotism to providing clothing and needlework for the troops had precedents back to the Napoleonic Wars. Linda Colley, *Britons: Forging the Nation, 1707–1837* (London and New York: Yale University Press, 1992), pp. 260–1.

18 On the cultural ramifications of the gap which opened up between those on the front line and those at home see: Paul Fussell, *The Great War and Modern Memory* (London: Oxford University Press, 1975) .This has been well documented in a host of contemporary memoirs by highly literate veterans, most notably in Robert Graves, *Goodbye to All That* (London: Penguin Books, 1986). Recent works like Adrian Gregory, *The Last Great War: British Society and the First World War* (Cambridge: Cambridge University Press, 2008) have shown the strength of links between soldiers and the home front.

19 Agency Committee, 'Report to Grand Council', 7 December 1916. Oxford, Bodleian Library. Primrose League Papers. MSS Primrose League 6/1. No. 16. 1914–32. Leaf 192; 'The Editor's Letter – the Women's Vote', *PLG*, XXVI: 109 (November 1918), 5.

20 The 1918 Act gave the vote to all women over 30 who 'were householders, the wives of householders, occupiers of property of £5 or more annual value or university graduates'. Andrew Rosen, *Rise Up Women! The Militant Campaign of the W.S.P.U.*

1903–1914 (London: Routledge & Kegan Paul, 1974), p. 266; Martin Pugh, *Electoral Reform in War and Peace 1906–1918* (London: Routledge, 1978), pp. 47–164. In numerical terms, the electorate increased from 7.9 million in 1910 to 21.8 million in 1919. Whereas the pre-war franchise represented 28 per cent of the total adult male and female population, the immediate post war franchise represented 78 per cent. David and Gareth Butler, *British Political Facts 1900–1994*, 7th edn (London: Macmillan, 1994), p. 239. The best study of the gendered elements of the wartime suffrage debate is Nicoletta F. Gullace, *'For the Blood of our Sons': Men, Women and the Renegotiation of British Citizenship during the Great War* (Houndmills: Palgrave Macmillan, 2002).

21 Pugh, *The Tories and the People*, p. 66; G. E. Maguire, *Conservative Women: A History of Women and the Conservative Party, 1874–1997* (Basingstoke: Macmillan, 1997), p. 62. Philippe Vervaecke, 'The Primrose League and Women's Suffrage, 1883–1918', in Myriam Boussahba-Bravard (ed.), *Suffrage Outside Suffragism: The Women's Vote in Britain, 1880–1914* (Houndmills: Basingstoke, 2007), pp. 180–201.

22 Julia Bush, *Edwardian Ladies and Imperial Power* (London: Leicester University Press, 2000), p. 174. On the pre-1914 debate between the pro- and anti-women's suffrage groups in the Conservative Party see: Mitzi Auchterlonie, *Conservative Suffragists: The Women's Vote and the Tory Party*. (London and New York: I. B. Tauris, 2007).

23 'Women and the Vote: Socialist Propaganda', *PLG*, XXVI: 104 (June 1918), 5.

24 Philippe Vervaecke, '"Doing Great Public Work Privately": Female Antis in the Interwar Years', in Julie V. Gottlieb and Richard Toye (eds), *The Aftermath of Suffrage: Women, Gender and Politics in Britain, 1918–1945* (Houndmills: Palgrave Macmillan, 2013), pp. 105–23.

25 'The Vote and What it Means', *PLG*, XXVI: 101 (March 1918), 6.

26 I have found reference to the employment of one woman speaker in the rural regions of Northamptonshire, Buckinghamshire, Oxfordshire and Leicestershire and another woman hired to work in Lancashire and Yorkshire. 'Statement by Chairman of the Agency Committee for Grand Council', 4 July 1918; 'Minutes of the Grand Council', 3 October 1918; Agency Committee, 'Report to Grand Council', 3 October 1918; 'Minutes of the Grand Council', 7 November 1918. Oxford, Bodleian Library. Primrose League Papers. MSS Primrose League 6/1. No. 16. 1914–32. Leafs 288, 297–8, 300.

27 'Editorial Notes', *PLG*, XXVII: 113 (March 1919), 3; Mrs Ian Malcolm, 'Speaker's Classes', *PLG*, XXVII: 115 (May 1919), 1. Such attitudes, of course, downplay the efforts of women in the pre-war Primrose League as well as respectable Conservative suffragists. On the latter see: Auchterlonie, *Conservative Suffragists: The Women's Vote and the Tory Party* .

28 'Notes for Speakers: Points for Women Speakers', *PLG*, XXXII: 4 (April 1925), 9.

29 Stuart Macintyre has given his history of interwar British Marxism this same title. Macintyre notes that most of Marx and Engel's works only became available in cheap English language editions in Britain after 1917. Stuart Macintyre, *A Proletarian Science: Marxism in Britain 1917–1933* (Cambridge: Cambridge University Press, 1980), ch. 3.

30 'Report of Grand Council to Grand Habitation 1922', Bodleian Library, Oxford. Primrose League Papers. MSS Primrose League 6/1. No. 16. 1914–32, Leafs 562–3.

31 'A.B.C. of Economics: Simple Lectures on Practical Issues which confront the Nation', *PLG*, XXX: 4 (October 1922), 4.

32 Primrose League, *Ladies Grand Council: Annual Report for year ending December 31st, 1923*. Lady Astor Papers, University of Reading, MSS 1416/1/1/820.

33 'The Summer School at Eastbourne', *PLG*, XXXII: 7 (July 1926), 6.

34 'The Junior Branch Page: The Child and Patriotism', *PLG*, XXXII: 7 (July 1925), 13.

35 For the definitive work on Conservative interwar educational efforts see: Clarisse Berthezene, *Training Minds for the Battle of Ideas: Ashridge College, the Conservative Party and the Cultural Politics of Britain, 1929–54* (Manchester: Manchester University Press, 2015).

36 On the stereotypes of superfluous women and flappers see: Billie Melman, *Women and the Popular Imagination in the Twenties: Flappers and Nymphs* (New York: St Martin's Press, 1988), pp. 17–24.

37 Neal R. McCrillis, 'The Conservative Party in the Age of Universal Suffrage: Popular Conservatism, 1918–1929' (PhD Dissertation, University of Illinois at Chicago, 1993), pp. 111–12; Neal R. McCrillis, *The British Conservative Party in the Age of Universal Suffrage: Popular Conservatism, 1918–1929* (Columbus: Ohio State University Press, 1998), p. 47.

38 'Report of the Finance Committee', 3 April 1919. Bodleian Library, Oxford. Primrose League Papers. MSS Primrose League 6/1. No. 16. 1914–32, Leafs 333–4.

39 John Ramsden, *The Age of Balfour and Baldwin 1902–1940* (London and New York: Longman, 1978), p. 250.

40 'Agency Committee Report to Grand Council', 6 November 1919. Bodleian Library, Oxford. Primrose League Papers. MSS Primrose League 6/1. No. 16. 1914–32, Leaf 386.

41 'Minutes of the Grand Council', 7 July 1921. Bodleian Library, Oxford. Primrose League Papers. MSS Primrose League 6/1. No. 16. 1914–32, Leafs 506, 513; 'Minutes of the Grand Council', 14 July 1921. Bodleian Library, Oxford. Primrose League Papers. MSS Primrose League 6/1. No. 16. 1914–32, Leaf 514.

42 'The Chancellor's Visit to the North', *PLG*, XXXI: 1 (January 1924), 9; 'The Chancellor's Letter: My Northern Tour; Results Anticipated: A Warning', *PLG*, XXXII: 12 (December 1925), 4.

43 Ramsden, *The Age of Balfour and Baldwin*, p. 250.

44 'Minutes of the Grand Council', 20 May 1926. Bodleian Library, Oxford. Primrose League Papers. MSS Primrose League 6/1. No. 16. 1914–32, Leafs 843; 849.

45 'General Purposes Committee Report to Grand Council', 3 July 1930. Bodleian Library, Oxford. Primrose League Papers. MSS Primrose League 6/1. No. 16. 1914–32, Leafs 1154–5.

46 In that year, Hacking was both Chancellor of the League and Vice-Chairman of the National Union. See: Douglas H. Hacking, 'The Chancellor's Letter', *PLG*, XXXVIII: 7 (July 1931), 6.

47 In tying political education so closely to anti-socialism it echoed the pattern found by Veronique Molinari in interwar handbooks created for education of female citizens. Veronique Molinari, 'Educating and Mobilizing the New Voter: Interwar Handbooks

and Female Citizenship in Great Britain, 1918–1931', *Journal of International Women's Studies*, XV: 1 (January 2014), 17–34.

48 The 1928 Equal Franchise Act gave the vote to women aged 21–30 and to those over 30 who had not qualified under the existing property restrictions of the 1918 franchise.

49 Habitations included those at Alsager, Worcester and Abbots Langley, 'Minutes of the General Purposes Committee', 1 June 1927. General Purposes Committee Minute Book 1926–53. Oxford, Bodleian Library. MSS Primrose League 15, Leafs 7–8.

50 All told, the Act gave women a numerical majority of nearly two million over men. 'Pointers for Speakers: Are they Flappers?' *PLG*, XXV: 7 (July 1928), 12.

51 Sir Walter Greaves-Lord, KC, MP, *PLG*, XXXV: 2 (February 1929), 8.

52 'The Grand Master's Message', *PLG*, XXXVI: 1 (January 1929), 3.

53 'My New Vote', *PLG*, XXXVI: 4 (April 1929), 8.

54 'To Women Voters', *PLG*, XXXVI: 6 (June 1929), 1.

55 'The Women's Vote', *PLG*, XXXVI: 3 (February 1929), 6.

56 Matthew Hendley, 'Anti-Alienism and the Primrose League: The Externalization of the Postwar Crisis in Great Britain, 1918–32', *Albion*, XXXIII: 2 (Summer 2001), 243–69.

57 'The Primrose League and the Strike: Splendid Help of Volunteers', *PLG*, XXXIII: 6 (June 1926), p. 6; General Purposes Committee, 'Report to Grand Council', June 3, 1926. Bodleian Library, Oxford. Primrose League Papers. MSS Primrose League 6/1. No. 16. 1914–32, Leaf 852.

58 At the Grand Habitation in 1931, the Chancellor of the League, Douglas Hacking, noted that only two parties existed in the state, one for socialism and the other against. 'Grand Habitation: The Albert Demonstration', *PLG*, XXXVIII: 5 (May 1931), 13.

59 This echoed the Conservative Party's emphases as well. David Anthony Jarvis, 'Stanley Baldwin and the Ideology of the Conservative Response to Socialism, 1918–31', (PhD Dissertation, Lancaster University, 1991), pp. 203–5, 228–34. David Thackeray, ch. 9, *Conservatism for the Democratic Age*; Stuart Ball, *Portrait of a Party: The Conservative Party in Britain, 1918–1945* (Oxford: Oxford University Press, 2013), pp. 57–64.

60 John Buchan, 'Pride and Prejudice', *PLG*, XXXI: 6 (July 1924), 4; Ball, *Portrait of a Party*, 65–6.

61 Annual Report of Grand Council to Grand Habitation 1925–1926', Bodleian Library, Oxford. Primrose League Papers. MSS Primrose League 6/1. No. 16. 1914–32, Leafs 841–2; 'April 19th (Primrose Day): Disraeli Pilgrimage to Hughenden', *PLG*, XXXV: 4 (April 1928), 7; 'A Message from the Grand Master', *PLG*, XXXVIII: 4 (April 1931), 5.

62 In a 1922 address to the League's Grand Habitation, the ultra-right-wing Mrs Nesta Webster claimed that Bolshevism was 'the deliberate plot of a gang of financial speculators' and had been 'worked in Russia by aliens to Russia, and it was being worked in this country by aliens, 'Organisation and Propaganda', *PLG*, XXX: 3 (June 1922), 7. For more on the Primrose League's anti-alienism and link to Soviet Communism see: Matthew Hendley, 'Anti-Alienism and the Primrose League: The Externalization of the Postwar Crisis in Great Britain, 1918–32', *Albion*, XXXIII: 2 (Summer 2001), 243–269.

63 Thackeray, *Conservatism for the Democratic Age*, ch. 8, 'The Peaceable Man and the Prudent Housewife' and ch. 9, David Jarvis, 'Mrs Maggs and Betty: The Conservative

Appeal to Women Voters in the 1920s', *Twentieth Century British History*, V: 2. (1994), pp. 129–52.

64 'The Spiritual Basis of the Home', *PLG*, XXVIII: 2 (February 1920), 4.

65 'Our Letter Box – Bolshevist Laws and Socialist Doctrines', *PLG*, XXVII: 121 (November 1919), 4.

66 Dowager Countess of Jersey, 'A Call to Women', *PLG*, XXXI: 11 (November 1924), 8.

67 'The Albert Hall Demonstration: Address by the Grand Master and Mr. Baldwin – Mr. Baldwin's Speech. Peace and Empire Unity', *PLG*, XXXI: 6 (June 1924), 10–12. Baldwin became Grand Master in 1925 after the death of Lord Curzon.

68 British consumers were urged to purchase imperial products through shop-window displays, documentary films, leaflets, radio broadcasts, hoardings and exhibitions. David Meredith, 'Imperial Images: The Empire Marketing Board, 1926–32', *History Today*, XXXVII (January 1987), 30–36. As Frank Trentmann has shown, this pattern fitted right into the Conservative agenda of transforming the political culture of Britain. Consumer consciousness did not need only be defined by free trade and after female enfranchisement, women's consumerism could be imperial and Conservative. Frank Trentmann, *Free Trade Nation: Commerce, Consumption and Civil Society in Modern Britain* (New York and Oxford: Oxford University Press, 2008), pp. 229–34.

69 One article entitled 'Buy Empire Goods' directly tied the lessening of unemployment to patriotism. 'If in our buying British, we shall be helping to get down our unemployment figures still lower … Let us make the buying of things made by British labour a test of patriotism.' 'Buy Empire Goods', *PLG*, XXXIII: 2 (February 1926), 8. A more specific form reference to female patriotism insisted to British female consumers: 'Let them, as a matter of patriotism, insist on having Empire goods … it is up to the women to see that when they shop they shop with the Empire and keep the money and trade in the Empire'. 'Notes for Speakers and Workers: Empire Shopping', *PLG*, XXXIII:12 (December 1926), 5.

70 'Sparks from other Fires: Christmas Pudding Recipe', *PLG*, XXXIII: 12 (December 1926),13; 'Buy Empire Goods', *PLG*, XXXIII: 2 (February 1926), 8; 'A Mixed Bag: Empire Products', *PLG*, XXXIII: 5 (May 1926), 13; 'Empire Shopping: Buy British!' *PLG*, XXXIX: 11 (November 1932), 13. Trentmann has noted that the Imperial Christmas pudding became the Conservative housewives' version of the 'cheap loaf'. Trentmann, *Free Trade Nation*, p. 232.

71 'The Workers' Note Book: Support Empire Products', *PLG*, XXXV: 2 (February 1929), 10; 'General Purposes Committee Report to Grand Council', 2 June 1927. Oxford, Bodleian Library. Primrose League Papers. MSS Primrose League 6/1. No. 16. 1914–32, Leafs 916–18.

72 David Thackeray, 'From Prudent Housewife to Empire Shopper: Party Appeals to the Female Voter, 1918–1928', in Gottlieb and Toye (eds), *Aftermath of Suffrage*, pp. 47–48. On the origins of the tariff reform campaign for the Conservatives see: E. H. H. Green, *The Crisis of Conservatism: The Politics, Economics and Ideology of the British Conservative Party, 1880–1914.* (London and New York: Routledge, 1995).

73 Trentmann, *Free Trade Nation*, p. 235.

74 Ian M. Drummond, *British Economic Policy and the Empire 1919–1939* (London: George Allen & Unwin, 1972), p. 79; Stephen Constantine, 'Introduction: Empire

Migration and Imperial Harmony', in Stephen Constantine (ed.), *Emigrants and Empire: British Settlement in the Dominions between the Wars* (Manchester and New York: Manchester University Press, 1990).

75 Dennis William Dean, 'The Contrasting Attitudes of the Conservative and Labour Parties to Problems of Empire, 1922–1936' (PhD Dissertation, University of London, 1974), pp. 21–2, 32, 35, 114–15.

76 'Notes for Speakers: Australia's Need', *PLG*, XXXII:.6 (June 1925), 6; 'Looking After the Harvesters: Nearly all 'Working and Satisfied' from 'Empire Page – Canada', *PLG*, XXXV: 11 (December 1928), 7; John S. Done, 'The Call of the Veldt', *PLG*, XXXVIII: 9 (September 1931), 13.

77 Canadian Bridges are featured in 'Our Empire Illustrated', *PLG*, XXXVI: 7 (July 1930), 1; 'Our Empire Illustrated', *PLG*, XXXIX: 5 (May 1932), 1; Ports in 'The Empire Illustrated', *PLG*, XXXV: 11 (November 1929), 1; Trains in 'Our Empire Illustrated', PLG, XXXVIII: 6 (June 1931), 1; Canals in 'The Empire Illustrated', *PLG*, XXXV: 8 (August 1929), 1; Orchards in 'The Empire Illustrated: A Great Apple Country', *PLG*, XXXV: 12 (December 1929), 1; 'Our Empire Illustrated', *PLG*, XXXVIII: 3 (March 1931), 1; Dairy and Grain in 'Our Empire Illustrated', *PLG*, XXXIX: 9 (September 1932), 7; Fish in 'The Empire Illustrated', *PLG*, XXXVI: 6 (June 1930), 11; General agriculture in 'The Empire Illustrated', *PLG*, XXXVIII: 1 (January 1931), 9; 'A Holiday Scene in Canada', *PLG*, XXXIX: 10 (October 1932), 1; 'Canada's Bumper Wheat Harvest', *PLG*, XXXIV: 11 (November 1927), 9.

78 The material prosperity and infrastructure achieved through British rule was mentioned in profiles of Malaya and the Gold Coast but the climate and lack of level of European civilisation was criticised. 'Our Empire Page: Progress in Malaya', *PLG*, XXXV: 3 (March 1928), 10; 'Empire Page: British West Africa: The Gold Coast', *PLG*, XXXV: 8 (August 1928), 6. Colonies in Kenya and the Gambia were even less positively portrayed. 'Our Empire Page: Kenya', *PLG*, XXXV: 4 (April 1928), 9; M. C. Steel, 'Empire Page: The Colony of Gambia', *PLG*, XXXV: 9 (September 1928), 10.

79 'Our Empire Page: Kenya', *PLG*, XXXV: 4 (April 1928), 9; Steel, 'Empire Page: The Colony of Gambia', 10.

80 The Western Australian Government's Group Settlement scheme provided land, houses, roads, materials and a sustenance wage until the land was cleared. Following clearing, the settler repaid the government through a percentage of future income.

81 Lady Apsley, 'Impressions of a Settler's Life in Australia', *PLG*, XXXIII: 7 (July 1926), 8–9; Lady Apsley, 'Impressions of a Settler's Life in Australia', *PLG*, XXXIII: 8 (August 1926), 8–9; 'Lord Apsley as an Emigrant', *PLG*, XXXIII: 8 (August 1926), 10. It is interesting to note that Lady Apsley was also a member of the Victoria League's Executive Committee between 1925 and 1929. The Apsleys wrote a book about their time in Australia entitled, *The Amateur Settlers* (London: Hodder & Stoughton, 1926).

82 Melman, *Women and the Popular Imagination in the Twenties*, chapter 9, 'The Emigrant: Romance and Empire'.

83 The other general election figures were November 1922 election (64 received), December 1923 election (51 received), May 1929 election (65 received) and October 1931 election (46 received). 'Primrose League Work for the Coalition – Letters from Grateful Members of Parliament and election agents', *PLG*, XXVII: 112 (February

1919), 5–6; 'Notes from the Habitations – Letters from Grateful Members of Parliament and Election Agents', *PLG*, XXVII: 113 (March 1919), 5–6; 'The Primrose League and the General Election – Testimony to its Value', *PLG*, XXX: 5 (January 1923), 5–7, 8; 'The Primrose League and the General Election', *PLG*, XXXI: 1 (January 1924), 10–11; 'The New House', *PLG*, XXXI: 2 (February 1924), 5; 'The Primrose League and the General Election – Striking Tributes to its Work', *PLG*, XXXI: 12 (December 1924), 10–11: 'The Primrose League and the General Election – Further Striking Tributes to its Work', *PLG*, XXXII: 1 (January 1925), 12–13; 'The Primrose League and the General Election – Striking Tributes to its Work', *PLG*, XXXVI: 7 (July 1929), 11–13; 'The Primrose League and the General Election – Further Striking Tributes to its Work', *PLG*, XXXVI: 8 (August 1929), 4; 'Incidents of the General Election – Greatest Political Rout in History', *PLG*, XXXVIII: 12 (December 1931), 9–10.

84 The constituencies were Plymouth Drake (Devon), Crewe (Cheshire), Rotherham (South Yorkshire), Darlington (County Durham), Wednesbury (South Staffordshire) North Battersea (London). 'Habitations and their Work IV – Beaconsfield Drake (Plymouth) Habitation', *PLG*, XXXIV: 7 (July 1927), 11; 'Habitations and their Work III – The Crewe Grey-Egerton Habitation', *PLG*, XXXIV: 5 (May 1927), 12; 'Habitations and their Work VI – Rotherham Habitation', *PLG*, XXXIV: 10 (October 1927), 12; 'Habitations and their Work II – Darlington Habitation', *PLG*, XXXIV: 2 (April 1927), 8–9; Habitations and their Work V – Ocker Hill (Dorothy Williams Habitation', *PLG*, XXXIV: 8 (August 1927), 11; 'Habitations and their Work VII – The Battersea and Bolingbroke Habitation', *PLG*, XXXIV: 11 (November 1927), 10.

85 'The Primrose League and the LCC Elections – The Socialist Bait', *PLG*, XXVII: 113 (March 1919), 6; 'The Borough Municipal Elections', *PLG*, XXVII: 120 (October 1919), 4; 'The LCC Elections', *PLG*, XXXII: 2 (February 1925), 3; Duke of Sutherland, 'The Chancellor's Letter: Stern Fight between Municipal Reformers and Socialists', *PLG*, XXXII: 11 (November 1925), 4.

86 'Women as Guardians – Opportunity for Useful Work', *PLG*, XXXII: 2 (February 1925), 11.

87 General Purposes Committee, 'Reports to the Grand Council', Oxford, Bodleian Library. Primrose League Papers. MSS Primrose League 6/1. No. 16. 1914–32; 6 February 1919; 6 March 1919; 3 April 1919; 5 June 1919; 4 December 1919, Leafs 311–13; 319; 331–2; 344–455; 390; Total new enrolment for 1921 was 32,121. General Purposes Committee, 'Reports to the Grand Council', 13 January 1921; 3 November 1921; 1 December 1921. Leafs 465; 521–2; 529–30; Total new enrolment for 1922 was 18 302. General Purposes Committee, 'Reports to Grand Council', 12 January 1922; 2 March 1922; 6 April 1922; 1 June 1922; 6 July 1922; 5 October 1922; 7 December, 1922. Leafs 550–1; 537–8; 544–5; 565–6; 570–1; 582–3; 590–1. Total new enrolment for 1923 was 26,650. General Purposes Committee, 'Reports to the Grand Council', 1 February 1923; 1 March 1923; 12 April 1923; 7 June 1923; 26 July 1923; 4 October 1923; 1 November 1923; 13 December 1923. Leafs 597–8; 604–6; 612–13; 620–2; 636–7; 645–6; 650–1; 664–5. Total new enrolment for 1924 was 28,030. General Purposes Committee, 'Reports to the Grand Council', 17 January 1924; 6 March 1924; 9 October 1924; 6 November 1924; 4 December 1924. Leafs 673–4; 687–8; 719–20; 726; 738–40.

88 From February 1925 to February 1926, 23,839 new members enrolled in the League. For the same period, between 1926 and 1927, 19,432 new members enrolled. General Purposes Committee, 'Reports to the Grand Council', 4 February 1926; 3 February 1927. Oxford, Bodleian Library. Primrose League Papers. MSS Primrose League 6/1. No. 16. 1914–32, Leafs 818–19; 891.

89 In fact, the increase in new members for 1929/30 was slightly less than the previous year (11,425 versus 12,320). 'General Purposes Committee Report to Grand Council', 2 October 1930. Oxford, Bodleian Library. Primrose League Papers. MSS Primrose League 6/1. No. 16. 1914–32, Leafs 1165–6.

90 'Report of Finance Committee', 6 November 1913. Bodleian Library, Oxford. MSS. Primrose League 5/1 No. 15. 1908–14, Leaf 626.

91 Of the 924 Habitations on the organisation's records before the war, 97 went into 'temporary abeyance at the commencement of the war' and only 444 paid their tribute in part or full for 1918–19. 'Report of the Finance Committee', 3 April 1919. Bodleian Library, Oxford. Primrose League Papers. MSS Primrose League 6/1. No. 16. 1914–32, Leafs 333–4. Existing figures show that from 1918 to 1931, annual total expenditure averaged £6,345, while average total revenue was £5,915, leaving an average annual deficit of £430. In the post-war period the League's annual financial picture was brightened by an investment portfolio whose actual value averaged £13,244 during the same period. 'Income Account and Note on Estimates 1919–20'; 'Financial Report for Year 1920–21'. 'Financial Report for Year Ending 31st March 1922'; 'Financial Report for Year Ending 31st March 1927'; 'Report of the Finance Committee, 7 February 1929'; 'Financial Report for Year ending 31st March, 1930'. Bodleian Library, Oxford. Primrose League Papers. MSS Primrose League 6/1. No. 16. 1914–32. Leafs 340–1; 492–4; 560–1; 928; 1050–1; 1136–7. 'Financial Report for the Year ending 31 March 1931'. MSS Primrose League 6/2. Bodleian Library, Oxford University. Leafs 1218–9.

92 Primrose League, 'How You Can Help Our Central Fund', Lady Astor Papers, University of Reading archives. MSS 1416/1/1/820. The tribute of the Knights and Dames was 2/6 and this was to remain the same. 'Draft Scheme', 'Report of Finance Committee', 6 October 1920; General Purposes Committee, 'Report to the Grand Council', April 6, 1922. Bodleian Library, Oxford. Primrose League Papers. MSS Primrose League 6/1. No. 16. 1914–32, Leafs 438, 550–1. On charity bazaars see: F. K. Prochaska, 'Charity Bazaars in Nineteenth Century England', *Journal of British Studies*, XVI: 2 (Spring 1977), 62–84; F. K. Prochaska, *Women and Philanthropy in Nineteenth-Century England* (Oxford: Clarendon Press, 1980), pp. 47–72.

93 'The Jubilee Banquet: The League's Financial Position', *PLG*, XXXIX: 12 (December 1932), 7. Lord Ebbisham [League Treasurer] 'The Jubilee Shilling Fund', *PLG*, XXXIX: 3 (March 1932), 6; 'Gifts to the Shilling Fund', *PLG*, XXXIX: 12 (December 1932), 7.

94 Philip Williamson, *Stanley Baldwin: Conservative Leadership and National Values.* (Cambridge: Cambridge University Press, 1999), pp. 131–3.

95 Primrose League Chancellors during this period who held ministerial office in the inter-war period include the 27th Earl of Crawford and Tenth Earl of Balcarres, the 6th Earl of Clarendon, Sir W. Joynson-Hicks, MP (Later Lord Brentford), the 5th Duke

of Sutherland, the 3rd Lord Strathcona and Mount Royal, and Doug Hacking, MP (later Lord Hacking). Lord Greenwood also served as a minister but was a Coalition Liberal at the time. Sir Henry Page Croft, MP, a Conservative renegade who founded the National Party during the First World War only received office under Churchill during the Second World War. Lord Ebbisham served as Treasurer of the Conservative Party. Lord Titchfield served as a whip of the Conservative Party. The only Primrose League Chancellors holding neither ministerial office nor a prominent party position were Sir Walter Greaves-Lord, MP and the 15th Earl of Pembroke and 12th Earl of Montgomery.

96 Pugh, *The Tories and the People*, p. 50. The Countess of Jersey, a stalwart of the Ladies Grand Council served as a Vice-Chairman [*sic*] of the Grand Council for 1920–21 but other than that the main positions of Grand Master, Vice-Grand Master and trustees, Grand Registrar, Treasurer, Chancellor and Vice-Chairmen were always held by men from 1918 to 1932.

97 Sir Kingsley Wood served as Grand Master during 1938–43. 'Grand Master of the Primrose League', *The Times*, 8 April 1938, 11.

98 Winston S. Churchill, 'First Political Speech – July 26, 1897 – Habitation of the Primrose League, Claverton Down, Bath', in Robert Rhodes James (ed.), *Winston S. Churchill – His Complete Speeches 1897–1963*. vol. 1, 1897–1908 (New York and London: Chelsea House Publishers, 1974), pp. 25–8.

99 On Churchill's speeches to Primrose League meetings and their enthusiastic reception see: 'Mr. Churchill's Belief', *The Times*, 26 April 1952, 3; 'Primrose League Ovation for Sir Winston Churchill', *The Times*, 14 April 1956, 4; 'Welcome for a Grand Master', *The Times*, 5 May 1957, 4. Some of his New Year's messages include 'Mr. Churchill's Call to the Primrose League', *The Times*, 1 January 1947; 'News in Brief – Sir W. Churchill on Great Opportunity', *The Times*, 1 January 1960, 6; 'Sir W. Churchill On 'Stimulus'', *The Times*, 12 May 1962, 5.

100 John Ramsden, *The Winds of Change: Macmillan to Heath, 1957–1975* (London and New York: Longman, 1996), pp. 52–3.

101 Julian Critchley, 'Hard Times for the Primrose League', *The Times*, 8 September 1969, 8.

102 Frank Johnson, 'The Macmillan View', *The Times*, 30 April 1981, 3; Daniel Johnson, 'Disraeli's Primrose Path of Alliance', *The Times*, 20 April 1991, 16.

103 Cooke, *A Gift from the Churchills*, 84.

5

Modes and models of Conservative women's leadership in the 1930s

Julie V. Gottlieb

In the aftermath of suffrage, women came into their own in the Conservative Party as party workers, as communal and national leaders, as MPs, and as part of a notional women's bloc of voters that Conservatives believed they could rely upon at election time. The valuable work performed by Conservative women at grass roots has been acknowledged in the scholarship, as have the strategies developed by the party to mobilise women as both party workers and voters. However, much less attention has been conferred on those Conservative women who became, on the one hand, virtual national celebrities, and on the other, to the instrumental roles these and other Conservative women played in framing Britain's foreign policy. Yet these two tendencies were intrinsically linked, and it is by writing Conservative women into (rather than back into) the story that we can rethink the relationship between gender, war and peace on the eve of the Second World War.

By the late 1930s two Conservative women MPs in particular achieved celebrity and notoriety. Lady Nancy Astor, a self-styled feminist, was the first woman MP to take her seat, rising to prominence in the sphere of foreign relations when she was identified as the hostess of the so-called Cliveden set. The other Conservative MP to devote herself to international issues, and in her case as an outspoken critic of appeasement, was Katherine the Duchess of Atholl, the first woman MP from Scotland, an avowed anti-(non)feminist, and Chamberlain scourge. Both defied stereotypes of Tory femininity in their own personal styles, by taking an abiding interest in international affairs when most Conservative women were expected to be focused on the local and parochial, and by engaging with women across party lines to advance their passionately held policies. Contrasting Astor's and Atholl's careers with that of Irene Ward MP highlights how these early Tory women MPs could carve out their own gendered political identities within the party. Arguably, Ward came closer to fulfilling the expectations of the role of a woman Conservative MP, although it is also striking how she too held important positions in international relations. Therefore, this tryptic biographical case study provides the opportunity to explore the institutional and cultural obstacles faced by Conservative women to emerge as power-brokers and policy-makers; it probes the complex and sometimes paradoxical relationship between feminism and Conservatism; and it considers why, despite a long line of spirited and formidable women Conservative leaders, both Margaret Thatcher's and now Theresa May's respective ascension to the role of party leader and PM has too often been seen as unprecedented.

Despite the considerable political success of the Conservative Party, its Conservative Women's Association (CWA), and Tory women's scoring many significant 'firsts' in the aftermath of suffrage, there is a noticeable under-representation of Conservative and especially centre-right women in the historiography, by historians of women and historians of the party. How and why have scholars, and especially feminist scholars, been reluctant to study Conservative women? Under the expanding shadow of the American New Right and Thatcherism in Britain in the 1970s and even more so in the 1980s – both of which were interpreted as a direct or causal reaction to the Women's Liberation Movement – feminists established a relationship of polar opposition between the Right and feminism. Feminists started to identify a new menace to democracy, to liberal ideals and to feminism, in the form of 'Right-Wing Women'. This was most vividly portrayed in Andrea Dworkin's American-focused *Right-Wing Women* ([1978]1983 British edition). In the radical feminist counter-attack against the American New Right, Dworkin made a passionate case against these reactionaries who, she deemed, had 'succeeded in getting women to act effectively against their own democratic inclusion in the political process, against their own civil equality, against any egalitarian conceptions of their own worth'.[1] Similarly concerned by the neo-liberal turn and the backlash against feminism it entailed, Beatrix Campbell's *Iron Ladies: Why Do Women Vote Tory?* (1987) took a more empirical and journalistic approach as she tried to account for the 'endurance of a formidable phalanx of Tory women',[2] and ascertain how British Conservativism had enabled women to make sense of themselves and their world since the late nineteenth century.

Dworkin characterised the American Right at the time she was writing as 'a social and political movement controlled almost totally by men but built largely on the fear and ignorance of women'.[3] It was at this point of collision between an increasingly self-defensive Second Wave Feminism and correspondingly more self-assured and uncompromising New Right in both the American and British contexts that the stark polarisation between women and the Right was inscribed. This seething adversity was very much the product of its time and place, and of that specific historical moment. Radical and not so radical feminists were reacting to immediate threats, and went on the counter-attack by constructing a stigmatised female other, the enemy within the women's community, the traitor to female solidarity. The Dworkin Right-wing woman suffers from false consciousness; she does not possess agency; she is oppressed without knowing it, or worse, she takes masochistic pleasure from patriarchal dominance and aggression.

All this makes sense at these junctures in American and British history. However, this paradigm forged in the political firestorms of the late 1970s and 1980s suffocated reasoned discussion of the relationship between women and Conservatism. In particular, it served as a blocking mechanism to balanced reflection on the relationship between conservatism and feminism – broadly defined as the belief in the equality of the sexes and political activity in the service of the expansion of women's opportunities in social, political, and cultural life in the national and international spheres.

The relationship between conservatism and women, and conservative women and feminism is in the process of being recalibrated by historians and political scientist. David Cameron's stated ambition to feminise the Tory Party when he took on the leadership in 2006, the prominence of feminist-identified figures like Theresa May when she was the Home Secretary and Louise Bagshawe in government, two Tory election victories and the post-Brexit party system that strongly suggest that in Britain we are living in the 'long Conservative century', and the installation of Britain's second Tory woman Prime Minster provide a different context in which to interrogate the history of women in the party. This contemporary context has led Bryson and Heppell to argue that 'because conservatism and feminism are rich, complex, evolving and at times self-contradictory bodies of thought that continue to develop in interaction with both 'real world' experiences and other ideologies, they are likely to have some elements in common and share some centre ground'.[4]

How does this backdrop change our expectations and the way we formulate our questions about (centre) Right-wing women in the 1920s and 1930? What does seem clear is that the absolute adversarial relationship between feminists and conservatives that we see in the Thatcherite 1980s does not exist between the two world wars. Starting with the suffrage movement, Conservative affiliation and feminist fervour were not mutually exclusive, and there was little sense that it was the 'Right-wing woman' *per se* who was the enemy – of course, the very terminology and ideological labelling is atavistic, and in the early to mid-twentieth century it was not common to refer to the Conservative Party as 'the right'. A number of Tory women were prominent suffragists, and Louisa Knightley founded the Conservative and Unionist Women's Franchise Association in 1908.[5] Conservatives were represented among the suffragettes as well, with Lady Constance Lytton as one example, and WSPU-donor Lady Lucy Houston, simultaneously a diehard feminist and ultra-Tory imperialist and defence-ist. Edith Lady Londonderry and Thelma Cazalet were two Tory suffragists who became important figures within the party between the wars. This is not to deny the dominant strains of anti-feminism within the Tory party, many of whose members provided the leadership and personnel for the Anti-Suffrage League, for instance.[6] However, Balfour, Lord Robert Cecil, Victor 2nd Earl of Lytton and the 2nd Earl of Selborne all supported women's suffrage. Nor should we forget that the anti-suffragists were not all Tories, and there were also Liberal and even a smattering of Labour enemies of women's suffrage.

It is also true that Conservatives remained opponents to women's suffrage through-out the war, but when partial women's suffrage became a legislative *fait accompli* in March 1918, much of that oppositional energy evaporated. Even more so, 'for all the railings against the Equalization Bill which appeared in the *Daily Mail*, the last anti-suffragist campaign of 1927–28 was a low-key, almost an exclusively male affair, with only a smattering of Tory backbenchers ready to obstruct the principle of franchise equalization'.[7] Indeed, what might have been a neat narrative of Tory anti-progressivism on gender issues is disrupted when we look at the period after suffrage, and when a number of former suffragettes found their political home in the Conservative Party and even further to the Right, from Emmeline and Christabel Pankhurst, to Flora Drummond, to Norah Elam and Mary Allen, the latter two ending their political days as members of the Mosley's British Union of Fascists.

In the aftermath of suffrage, was the Tory feminist self-contradictory or a plausi-ble cross-sectional identity? It is important not to exaggerate the accommodation that the Conservative Party and its women members made with what they defined as feminism, and illuminating research on the 1920s has demonstrated that the construction of the Tory woman remained conventional. While the women's sphere expanded on becoming enfranchised citizens and valued party workers (as party member, in the CWA, as women organiser, and agent) this was only to mobilise women as mothers, imperialists, consumers, and anti-Socialists – but not feminist.[8] In 1929 when J. C. C. Davidson MP was asked to explain why the majority of women would vote Conservative in the coming General Election, he explained that

> In the first place, women, by nature, are inherently conservative. From their youth up they love to 'conserve'. Hence the 'bottom drawer', their household goods and their savings. Woe betide anyone who seeks to deprive them of their belongings! Women know that the Conservative policy safeguards the possessions and rights of citizens, both individually and collectively.[9]

In 1930 the new Conservative Training Centre at Ashridge, the founding of which was to 'make the party a more congenial home for women',[10] designed a special course for MPs' wives, with the Countess of Iveagh MP talking about 'some trials of a Member's wife', and male MPs filling out the syllabus with sessions on industry insurance and national taxation, foreign relations (Captain Eden MC MP), the moral effects of unemployment (Hon. Mary Pickford CBE), general party organisation (Miss Maxse), women and local government, public speaking at political meetings and at bazaars and so on, the economic causes of unemployment, and Conservative principles (Mr A. Bryant).[11] A search through local newspapers where the activities and areas of interest of the Conservative Women's Associations were well represented has revealed little if any use of the term 'feminism', and scarce attention to the main issues that preoccupied interwar welfare or equalitarian femi-nists. Instead, the party framed its appeal to women in these terms:

In city, town, village and hamlet women can do much to assist the Conservative Party – a Party who have in the past shown how earnestly they desire to improve the conditions of the people and who have legislated in a wonderfully successful manner on behalf of women and children … And it was this Party who, in accordance with their pledges, removed the remaining political disabilities of women and enabled them to exercise the franchise on exactly the same terms as men. Conservatives have worked for, and welcomed, the full co-operation of women in political life. They believe that the share which women can contribute to the common endeavour will help to bring about the earlier and fuller realization of the Party's ideals – the greater happiness, well-being, and security of the people of these islands.[12]

This confirms J. Lovenduski *et al.*'s assessment that 'Conservative women were wary of feminist strategies and reluctant to be thought of as feminists.'[13] In the 1920s, 'that not all women were or sought in any way to be connected with feminist issues was thus made only too clear, as was the problem of seeing feminism as inseparable from social welfare'.[14] Women's issues were identified as home, children, education, domestic service (and the servants crisis of the post-war years) and, increasingly in the course of the 1930s, defining the party's position on and women's investment in peace/security and the appeasement of the dictatorships.[15] Indeed, the Conservatives addressed women on defence policy and sought to demonstrate their own support for disarmament – a heavily woman-identified issue – through the language and figures of home economics, as in this example.

Another point which exercises a disheartening effect on the Socialist propagandists in this constituencies is their discovery that all their attempts to alarm working women on the question of armaments are rendered futile when Unionist canvassers quote two facts only. Not every housewife has a 'head for figures,' but no arithmetical ability is required to enable her to see what the Conservative Government has done for disarmament when she is told that £5½ millions a year less is being spent on Defence than when the Socialist Government was in power. When she learns also that the total personnel of all our armed forces of the Crown (including Reserves and auxiliary forces) is only 674,000 to-day, as compared with 940,000 in 1914, she does not forget the figures – much to the chagrin of the 'Red critics,' who are so fond of picturing the policy of their political opponents as that of the 'mailed' fist.

A commitment to 'peace' could be framed as both anti-Socialist and women-oriented.

Nonetheless, between the wars it is within the Conservative Party and by a number of women Conservatives that women's firsts were scored. And this is even before we remember that the 1928 Equal Franchise legislation, more commonly known as the Flapper Vote, was passed by a Conservative government. It is misleading to understand interwar Conservatism as a break on women's citizenship aspirations in some specific areas of endeavour, such as local and parliamentary representation, sport and leisure pursuits (flying was especially popular with 'nationalist feminists'), and even in the sphere of international affairs and diplomacy, which may well come as a surprise, given the party's and the CWA's ambivalence about the League of Nations and the very popular and successful League of Nations Union.

Women MPs of all parties, including Tories Lady Astor, Thelma Cazalet, Florence Horsbrugh, Mavis Tate and Irene Ward, served on the Executive Committee of the National Council of Women, whose two principal objectives were to increase the representation of women in local and national government and to campaign for legislative reforms to elevate the status of women.[16] We need to be able to draw out these points without trumpeting these achievements, and in the final analysis it is not tenable to argue that feminists or feminism (even in the diluted interwar variants) could flourish within the sphere of Conservative politics. However, some Conservative women could also be Tory feminists, and pursue their liberationist agendas from the right of the political spectrum. Nor was this something that seemed to trouble interwar feminists too much, as it would incense Radical Feminists in the 1970s. British feminists and feminist organisations *did* reach out to Conservative women, and vice versa.

Where issues about sexual equality did arise was in terms of women's representation among candidates, and the achievements of the women MPs who sat on the Conservative benches. These women MPs were embraced by the party and by the press, and there was a plethora of news items about this new and curious species and the habits of women in the House, and peppered with anecdotal detail about their dress, demeanour and their interaction in the 'Boudoir', the one female-only space in Westminster. Women MPs were portrayed as fashion models as well as role models, and as political celebrities.[17] Where they themselves drew the line, or at least this was the case with many women candidates, was at standing up as a candidates exclusively for women and even less so for feminism. For example, when Mrs Gerald Beaumont (Conservative) launched her campaign for the Yorkshire constituency of Rothwell in the 1935 general election, she made this point: 'This is not an outbreak of ardent feminism on my part – and, anyway, we are all agreed nowadays that women in Parliament to deal with questions affecting women and the home are very necessary – but simply local patriotism; I dislike seeing Yorkshire out of the running when Lancashire can produce a woman candidate for the Bury division – Dr Edith Summerskill.'[18]

While the rank and file in the CWA avoided overtly feminist issues, a number of women leaders did consider themselves feminists. Tory hostess Lady Londonderry was a self-proclaimed sex warrior, developing a distinctive brand of ultra-patriotic feminism. By the eve of war, in October 1938, she dreamed of a nation that would, within a decade, be laughing at itself for 'her pink thoughts and her pink boys', and instead reignite the spirit of Britannia in 'women Territorials as well as men – airwomen as well as airmen – vanguards and airguards [*sic*] – as virile a race again as ever existed, and confessedly proud of being citizens of British birth'.[19] Thelma Cazalet-Keir's feminism was less chauvinistic. As the Conservative MP for Islington from 1931, Cazalet was proud that her mother had been a keen supporter of the

Pankhursts in suffrage days, she had had the honour of doing the obituary broadcast on Mrs Pankhurst, and she described herself as 'an avowed feminist', but qualified this by saying: 'I never thought there is any special virtue in being the first woman to do this or that – unless this or that is of outstanding importance.' [20] Further, she was 'the only woman who appears to be on the steps of the throne of office' in Chamberlain's new administration, appointed Parliamentary Private Secretary to Kenneth Lindsay, the Under-Secretary for Education, and, as such 'she is the only woman, too, who has a seat behind the Government bench'. [21]

These women can then be contrasted with the Duchess of Atholl, an avowed anti-suffragist before the war, but who nonetheless fulfilled so many equalitarian feminist aspirations in practice as the first woman Conservative to be appointed to ministerial office (Parliamentary Secretary to the Board of Education in 1924, while the first Conservative woman appointed Cabinet minister was Florence Horsbrugh in 1953), in her anti-fascist humanitarian work and as a formidable critic of her own party and Prime Minister on foreign affairs. Atholl forged vital working partnerships and friendships with leaders of the interwar feminist movement in the context of her anti-appeasement politics – Eleanor Rathbone and Ellen Wilkinson.

It is interesting how Atholl's anti-feminism became a liability, even within the Conservative Party. She had angered feminists by opposing the equal franchise bill, and she voted against a bill for equal pay in the civil service. Indeed, 'Nancy Astor warned the party leadership against appointing her on the grounds that she was not a feminist.' [22] Yet Atholl took a progressive view on the ordination of women in the Presbyterian Church, and she wrote *Women and Politics* (1931), which, while unapologetically Conservative in its tone, encouraged women to embrace their citizenship. Her aversion to feminism aside, she was independent-minded and courageous, taking a heroic stand against fascism in Spain and Germany by the mid-1930s. While in so doing her anti-Communism hardly wavered, she was nevertheless dubbed the 'Red Duchess'. She then went on to stake and ultimately jettison her parliamentary career by forcing a by-election over the Munich Agreement in December, 1938.[23] She lost this much-publicised by-election, and never returned to Parliament despite the support she had mustered from the British Popular Front and her effective anti-Nazi working relationship with Winston Churchill.

It is Lady Nancy Astor who stands out as a vivid example of the paradoxical relationship between Conservatism and feminism. Astor has received a great deal of attention, scholarly and less so, but discussion of her feminism has focused on the 1920s and especially her efforts in organising the Consultative Committee of Women's Organisations (of which she was president), her energetic support for the Equal Franchise Bill, and her enthusiastic and publicity-minded embodiment of the role of first woman MP. However, her commitment to feminist principles and her loyalty to party became more problematic – and more compelling – in the 1930s.

Astor was a feminist on the domestic front and champion of women's causes. Her overriding concern was with women's status in the labour market and the right to work. She was an Old Feminist in this regard, and her interest in the progressive feminist Six Point Group (founded my Lady Rhondda), of which she was a Vice-President, stemmed from these concerns. She emerged as a national figure, and women victims of sexism in employment from all over the country wrote to her for advice and aid, to which she was deeply sympathetic.

Her interests extended into the international sphere, and Astor was an internationalist feminist campaigner, with a connected concern with the worldwide profusion of women's suffrage and world peace. In the 1920s she was associated with the Women's Peace Crusade, a great advocate of disarmament, and the campaign for women's admission to the consular and diplomatic service. She provided a focal point at home for women pacifists who regularly turned to her for leadership in the hope that she might realise their vision of a women's peace movement on national and international lines. But Astor's status in both the international peace and suffrage movements must be put in context, and she was involved with middle-of-the road organisations but conspicuously absent from her affiliations was the Women's International League for Peace and Freedom (WILPF). Although she was a Vice-President of the Six Point Group, she did become more and more uncomfortable with what she diagnosed as its leftist anti-fascist positioning, exemplified by her half-hearted work on behalf of individual women victims in Nazi Germany. By 1936 when she was already hosting the German ambassador at her parties, a conflict of interests emerged between her feminism, which she admitted had to be premised on a rejection of fascism, and her work for Anglo-German understanding. The German Embassy tried to win her over to the Nazi nationalisation of womanhood by sending her the speeches of Gertrud Scholtz-Klink, the Nazi woman leader, but these appear to have fallen on deaf ears. In fact, when Scholtz-Klink visited London at a particularly portentous moment, in early March 1939 – after Munich, after Kristallnacht, and just days before Hitler's troops marched into Prague and put paid to the Munich Agreement – Astor was the only woman MP who made her views on the visit of the so-called woman fuehrer known. Astor refused to meet her, judging that her activities 'give no recognition to the rights of women in any sphere but the home'.[24]

Astor's feminism and anti-fascism were inherent, and she was the first to draw attention to this. She was a passionate defender of women's rights, and from the very start of the Nazi regime she reacted with alarm at its attack on women as a collective, and especially in the labour market, and to cases of individual women who were imprisoned on political grounds. As an international suffragist she repeatedly made the point that democracy and a 'woman-made' peace was impossible as so many countries failed to enfranchise women, and however ideal an international women's peace movement may be, composed of the mothers of the world, the hope was futile as long as women remained disenfranchised. She articulated this formula of feminism/democracy/anti-Nazism throughout the 1930s, and evoked it with greater purpose in her bid to contest the Cliveden set conspiracy theory. As she put it: 'I have never been one of those feminists who wanted rights for women because they dislike men. If the dictators realized what women are, they would be far more frightened of us than they are of the politicians.'[25]

But in more private correspondence she could also admit how she used her connections in high places to work behind the scenes, and it is easy to see how for much of the public, especially on the Left, she was always no more and no less than a patrician exercising undue influence. Paradoxically, her sex was used against her by her notionally progressive leftist opponents, and all her efforts in the feminist cause were as good as forgotten when she was portrayed in popular lyrics, political cartoons and national jokes as a Jezebel, Cleopatra, femme fatale, or schoolmarm.

The cabal of pro-German arch-appeasers included *Times* editor Geoffrey Dawson, Foreign Secretary Lord Halifax, and Lord Lothian, and was directed by and from the Cliveden seat of the Astors. The Cliveden set story is well known, and even if contemporaries and historians came to understand it to be not fact but more fairy tale in the Left's search for villains, it remains central to the narrative of appeasement.[26] But in both popular and scholarly treatments of the story, historians have failed to see the importance of gender, both in the sense that its most recognisable protagonist was a woman – while others were identified as part of the entourage as well, most prominently Lady Londonderry and Lady Austen Chamberlain – and in the way that, in part, its illegitimacy and nefarious character was because within the set women were given free reign and, as it was figured, exercising power without responsibility.[27] Even though Astor was an elected MP of some eighteen years standing at the time the story broke, this was beside the point and the propagators of the myth and the world-wide press that ran with the story delighted in characterising her as a string puller, and a great manipulator of powerful men. She was a foreign influence most obviously because she was a Virginian, and also because she was a woman in a man's world of diplomatic affairs. In the press it was represented as the conspiracy of the women, as a women's cabal.

Astor herself was increasingly anxious to distance herself from the Cliveden set story. She certainly held anti-Semitic beliefs but she did make a number of gestures to demonstrate sympathy for the Jews by, for instance, giving a fair hearing to Zionism and lending her support to refugee relief efforts later in the 1930s. Further, as already suggested, Astor called on her feminist credentials to try to rescue her reputation from the Cliveden set taint. In May 1939, she told a Rotary International Association for Great Britain and Ireland at Brighton: 'Twenty years in the House of Commons have taught me it is nonsense to talk about the complete man or the complete woman … I don't know why they always say women are the weaker sex,' she commented. 'Eve with only one rib was stronger than Adam who was the first to shout that he had been tempted. I have never been one of those feminists who wanted rights for women because they disliked men. If the dictators realized what women are, they would be far more frightened of us than they are of the politicians.'[28]

It is important to emphasise the significant points of contrast between Atholl and Astor on women's issues and feminism, on foreign policy and in terms of personal style and status within the Conservative Party. In all these respects they were the antithesis to the other. In terms of gender politics, Astor was progressive and committed to fulfilling her role as the first woman MP, and she was an active member of feminist organisations like the Six Point Group and the International Alliance of Women. Her feminism fed her pacifism, a very gendered pacifism based on biologically determined constructions of women as nurturers and therefore the world's natural pacifists. This then followed to her conspicuous engagement with foreign policy, and her identification as the hostess-leader of the Cliveden set, and a supporter of Chamberlain and appeasement throughout 1938 and 1939. In contrast, Atholl was widely known to have been anti-women's suffrage, and she would never make common cause with feminist organisations to advance gender-specific concerns. However, she led by example, and provided a striking model of women's leadership, collaborating closely with some of the great feminist politicians of the day, namely Eleanor Rathbone and Ellen Wilkinson, in anti-appeasement and anti-fascist campaigns. Despite this, Labour women were warned off lending their support during her famous and ultimately frustrated by-election fight in December 1938.

There was a total of seven women Conservative MPs in the House from the 1935 general election until the outbreak of the Second World War (thirteen Conservative women had been elected in 1931 while all the women candidates standing for other parties failed to win seats; in the 1935 general election nine women were elected, seven of whom were Conservatives). Each brought different experiences, interests and dynamics and rather eccentric personalities to the Conservative benches, and one could just as easily contrast Astor and Atholl with Florence Horsbrugh, Mavis Tate, Thelma Cazalet or Lady Davidson. But the focus here is on Miss Irene Ward because she 'knows more than any woman, and perhaps most MPs. Some believe that she is the best type of Conservative woman member, and she does not waste an opportunity to raise the question of coal and miners.'[29] She would be complimented for working 'at her Parliamentary job far harder than most men. Grit has carried her through.'[30] Ward represented the middle ground, both in terms of Tory policies and as a new breed of woman MP who personified consensus. She was described and admired for being forthright, unpretentious, accessible and well informed about issues many might only expect men to know much about:

> It was she who put out the redoubtable 'Maggie' Bondfield at Wallsend-on-Tyne, where she talks like a Dutch aunt to her dour miner constituents. When her meetings are dull, which isn't often, she says: 'For heaven's sake ask me something.' She is tall, fair and active physically and mentally. Swims and plays tennis well. She knows a good deal about mining, and has just introduced a Bill to stop the sale of British ships abroad; a first-class subject which any one of the several hundred Conservative men might have taken up. The measure looks like going through ... The range of knowledge and activity among the women MPs is extraordinary.[31]

Further, she dodged the 'f-word', and she does not seem to have used the term feminism to define herself nor was it used to define her position by others, although Maguire does recognise her as one of a triumvirate comprising herself, Tate and Cazalet who tried to force the Conservative Party to take a more progressive stand on women's issues.[32]

In stark contrast to her patrician colleagues, Ward had made her own way in politics. In 1931 she won her seat in a rare woman-against-woman race in Wallsend-upon-Tyne, defeating Labour's Margaret Bondfield, the first woman to be appointed to Cabinet as Minister of Labour. Ward convinced voters in this industrial and distressed area – that was also the base of the Londonderry family – that she could best represent their interests. Perhaps that explains why she leaned but never lurched towards the progressive side of the party, and, while she did not take high-profile roles in any of the following cross-party campaigns, she still lent her name and support to causes that were not in keeping with traditional conservatism. Her mother had already been a keen suffragist, and she joined with Astor, Cazalet, Ida Copeland and Eleanor Rathbone (Independent) in objecting to the gross under-representation of enfranchised women in the proposed reformed Indian constitution.[33] She readily joined other cross-party initiatives, for example, coming to the aid of Basque children through the National Joint Committee for Spanish Relief and supporting the British Nationality and Status of Aliens (Amendment) Bill (1937), which sought to give women the same control over their nationality as possessed by men.

Although she devoted most of her energy to domestic and welfare issues that had particular salience to her Wallsend mining and shipping constituents, she was also well travelled on the Continent and overseas. As her pocket diaries reveal, in the 1930s she travelled to Hungary, Austria, Finland, Romania, Germany and Czechoslovakia, and she was a frequent visitor to France both on official business and for leisure. Her passport, valid from 1933 to July 1938, reveals that she travelled to Turkey, France, Finland, Poland, Russia (1933 and again 1934), Germany (May 1934), Hungary (1935), Austria (August and September 1935), Argentina, USA (1936) and Italy. She was not entirely unlike another Labour rival, 'Red' Ellen Wilkinson, in her preoccupations with the wider world and as a 'transnationalist', in practice, if not also by principle. Ward made a number of lecture tours to the Continent, and when she was preparing to embark on another one to the Baltic states under the auspices of the British Council, she explained: 'I have been invited to give these lectures in the Baltic States because we are very anxious to make contact with European countries, particularly just now in view of international relations.'[34] She was acknowledged to be one of three of the women MPs who were 'diligent lecturers. The most versatile in her choice of subjects is Miss Ellen Wilkinson; the most "highbrow" is Miss Eleanor Rathbone. Between the two comes Miss Irene Ward, who prefers to concentrate her attention on the popular representation of systems of government and the part woman has in them.'[35]

On a lecture tour of the USA in 1936 Ward's chief interests were identified as 'industrial problems and foreign policy',[36] and her American audiences were only disappointed that she exercised discretion and was 'mum on the Wally incident' (just before the Abdication). She was reported to have denied 'that the British lion has ceased to growl and is beginning to look kindly on the Nazi swastika. "We feel sorry for the German people, and are inclined to think that they were treated rather harshly after the war. But there is a great distinction between the German people and the Nazi regime. England is neither friendly nor unfriendly to the Nazi government. We do not express ourselves either way. One must mind one's own business."'[37] In foreign policy she represented the National Government's position, and she was loyal to Neville Chamberlain. Indeed, that explains why she was invited by Eden to be substitute delegate to the League of Nations in 1937.[38] Again in the autumn of 1938, at the zenith of the policy of appeasement, she was appointed assistant delegate, the only woman and the only member of the British delegation who did not hold Cabinet rank. She was invited to go to Geneva a third time as substitute delegate in 1939, for the League Assembly that was scheduled to open on 11 September, as recognition of her 'experience of Geneva' and 'her excellent work ... over the last two years.'[39]

Logically, the entry of women into the consular service was one of her causes, and as chairman of the Woman Power Committee during the war it was Ward who Foreign Secretary Anthony Eden informed that Miss Craig McGeachy, attached to Harold Butler's staff in Washington, had been granted local diplomatic status. This was a highly important item of news for women MPs as McGeachy was the first British woman to receive such status.[40] Ward would spend 38 years in the Commons before being elevated to the Lords as Baroness Ward upon her retirement, and she was credited as 'probably the best constituency member Westminster has known'.[41] When Ward died in 1980, Prime Minister Margaret Thatcher's characterisation provided her with a fitting epitaph: 'a doughty fighter without being a blue-stocking'.[42]

In conclusion, it seems immediately clear that the Conservative women leadership figures of the interwar years do not fulfil the stereotype promoted by Dworkin, who argued that 'the Right offers women a simple, fixed, predetermined social, biological, and sexual order'.[43] The Conservative women leaders who carved out their roles and their political identities between the wars were much abler at making accommodations with feminism, or at least an interpretation of that creed in which women's rights were earned through the performance of women's duties. In the aftermath of First Wave Feminism, Astor could say: 'I am a natural born feminist. I find women honest, practical, disinterested and sometimes really gifted with vision.'[44] As Tory icon and equally as demon of the Left, Margaret Thatcher has cast a long shadow, making it difficult to imagine modes and models of women's Conservative leadership without Britain's first woman prime minister as their logical culmination. However, the post-1975 vantage point is inevitably distorting, and there were various models of feminine and even feminist Tory leadership that did not prefigure Thatcher. All roads do not lead to Margaret Thatcher. We have yet to see what kind of shadow Theresa May will cast, and there can be little doubt that the very different way in which she situates herself on gender issues and opportunities for women in the Tory Party will establish different models and modes of female leadership.

Notes

1 Andrea Dworkin, *Right-wing Women: The Politics of Domesticated Females* (London: Women's Press, 1983), pp. xii–xiii.
2 Beatrix Campbell, *Iron Ladies: Why Do Women Vote Tory* (London: Virago, 1987), p. 2.
3 Dworkin, *Right-wing Women*, p. 34.
4 Valerie Bryson and Timothy Heppell, 'Conservatism and Feminism: The Case of the British Conservative Party', *Journal of Political* Ideologies, 15: 1 (February 2010), 31–50.
5 See Mitzi Auchterlonie, *Conservative Suffragists: The Women's Vote and the Tory Party* (London: I. B. Tauris, 2007) and Julia Bush, *Edwardian Ladies and Imperial Power* (Leicester: Leicester University Press, 2000), esp. chapter 10 'Imperialism, the Women's Movement and the Vote'.
6 See Brian Harrison, *Separate Spheres: The Opposition to Women's Suffrage in Britain* (London: Croom Helm, 1978).
7 Philippe Vervaecke, '"Doing Great Public Work Privately": Female Antis in the Interwar Years', in Julie V. Gottlieb and Richard Toye, (eds), *The Aftermath of Suffrage* (Basingstoke: Palgrave, 2013), p. 105.
8 See David Jarvis, 'Mrs Maggs and Betty: The Conservative Appeal to Women Voters in the 1920s', *Twentieth Century British History*, 5: 2 (1994), 129–52; and Neal McCrillis, *The British Conservative Party in the Age of Universal Suffrage: Popular Conservatism, 1918–1929* (Columbus: Ohio University Press, 1998).
9 PUB 254/1 'Woman of To-Day and To-Morrow: The Paper Every Woman Should Read' (Pub by the National Union of Conservative and Unionist Associations), Vol. 1, No. 1 (1929), CPA, Bodleian, Oxford.
10 Clarisse Berthezène, *Training Minds for the War of Ideas: Ashridge College, the Conservative Party and the cultural politics of Britain, 1929–54* (Manchester: Manchester University Press, 2015), p. 35.
11 'Lessons for MPs Wives: Syllabus of Conservative Training Centre', *Lancashire Evening Post*, 8 Feb., 1930. 'It is a sign of the times that many MPs who were necessarily kept at Westminster during the Parliamentary Session rely on their wives to maintain that personal contact with voters which, to-day, is regarded as essential, whilst at election times they are frequently called upon to address afternoon meetings of women, in addition to doing a considerable amount of canvassing of "doubtful" electors. [Lady Iveagh MP is chairman of the Women's Unionist organisation] In city, town, village and hamlet women can do much to assist the Conservative Party – a Party who have in the past shown how earnestly they desire to improve the conditions of the people and who have legislated in a wonderfully successful manner on behalf of women and children ... And it was this Party who, in accordance with their pledges, removed the remaining political

disabilities of women an enabled them to exercise the franchise on exactly the same terms as men. Conservatives have worked for, and welcomed, the full co-operation of women in political life. They believe that the share which women can contribute to the common endeavour will help to bring about the earlier and fuller realisation of the Party's ideals – the greater happiness, well-being, and security of the people of these islands.' 'Women's Activities', *Exeter and Plymouth Gazette*, 5 February 1930.

12 'Women's Activities', *Exeter and Plymouth Gazette*, 5 February 1930.

13 J. Lovenduski, P. Norris and C. Burness, 'The Party and Women', in Anthony Seldon and Stuart Ball (eds), *Conservative Century: The Conservative Party since 1900* (Oxford: Oxford University Press, 1994), p. 612.

14 Barbara Caine, *English Feminism, 1780–1980* (Oxford: Oxford University Press, 1997), p. 207.

15 'Women Voters: Why they Should Support the Conservatives', *Exeter and Plymouth Gazette*, 27 November 1928.

16 Caitriona Beaumont, *Housewives and Citizens: Domesticity and the Women's Movement in England, 1928–64* (Manchester: Manchester University Press, 2013), p. 23.

17 See Laura Beers, 'Model MP? Ellen Wilkinson, Gender, Politics and Celebrity Culture in Interwar Britain', *Cultural and Social History*, 10: 2 (June 2013), 231–50.

18 'A Woman's Week-End Musings',' *Yorkshire Evening Post*, 28 October 1935.

19 The Marchioness of Londonderry, *Retrospect* (London: Frederick Muller Ltd, 1938), p. 256.

20 Thelma Cazalet-Keir, *From the Wings* (London: Bodley Head, 1967), p. 127.

21 'Men, Women and London', *Gloucestershire Echo*, 13 July 1938.

22 DNB entry, Murray, Katharine Marjory Stewart, Duchess of Atholl.

23 See Stuart Ball, 'The Politics of Appeasement: the Fall of the Duchess of Atholl and the Kinross and West Perth By-election, December 1938', *Scottish Historical Review*, LXIX: 187 (April 1990), 49–83.

24 'Nazi Woman's Visit: Lady Astor has no Sympathy with her Activities', *Western Morning News*, 9 March 1939. See Julie V. Gottlieb and Matthew Stibbe, 'Peace at any Price: The Visit of Nazi Women's Leader Gertrud Scholtz-Klink to London in March 1939 and the Response of British Women Activists', *Women's History Review* 26: 2 (2016), 173–94.

25 'Hint by Lady Astor', *Cornishman*, 11 May 1939.

26 See Norman Rose, *The Cliveden Set: Portrait of an Exclusive Fraternity* (London: Pimlico, 2001).

27 See Julie V. Gottlieb, *'Guilty Women', Foreign Policy and Appeasement in Interwar Britain* (Basingstoke: Palgrave, 2015).

28 'Hint by Lady Astor', *Cornishman*, 11 May 1939.

29 'Do you Know About these Twelve Women MPs?' *Daily Mail*, 12 April 1938.

30 'Young Men of To-Morrow in the New Parliament', *Sunday Referee*, 17 November 1935.

31 'Women MPs Have Done Their Work Well', *Gloucester Citizen*, 16 June 1939.

32 G. E. Maguire, *Conservative Women: The History of Women in the Conservative Party, 1874–1997* (Basingstoke: Macmillan, 1998), p. 100.

33 'Indian Women Voters: To the Editor of the Times', *The Times*, 28 July 1933.

34 'Wallsend MPs Baltic Tour', *Evening Chronicle and Evening World*, 17 January 1936.

35 'Women Lecturers', *Birmingham Daily Mail*, 20 January 1936.

36 'Miss Irene Ward MP Mum on Wally Incident', *Boston Traveler*, 30 October 1936.

37 *Ibid.*

38 22 July 1937 from Anthony Eden, Foreign Office, to Irene Ward MP, MS. Eng.c. 6968 Irene Ward Papers, Correspondence 18 November 1935–20 September 1941.

39 8 July 1939, Lord Halifax, Foreign Office to Irene Ward MP, MS. Eng.c. 6968 Irene Ward Papers, Correspondence 18 November 1935–20 September 1941.

40 'Women as Diplomats: First Appointment', *Liverpool Daily Post*, 2 October 1942.

41 David Wood, 'Will a Woman Leader get the Women's Vote', *The Times*, 15 August 1977.

42 'Baroness Ward', *The Times*, 28 April 1985.

43 Dworkin, *Right-wing Women*, p. 22.

44 'Women', Speech for America (1934), Nancy Astor Papers, MS 1416/1/1/1434 'Lady Astor, MP. Speaking at the Bachelor Girls Exhibition in London yesterday, said she was an unrepentant feminist, and after many years of public life could say, with her hand on her heart, she was a more convinced feminist than ever. The days for women were coming.' ('Lady Astor on Woman's Progress', *Western Morning News*, 13 November 1930).

6

The middlebrow and the making of a 'new common sense': women's voluntarism, Conservative politics and representations of womanhood

Clarisse Berthezène

The historiography on interwar Conservatism has stressed the success of the Conservative Party's mobilisation of women and the stability of the female vote in this period. Historians have shown how the interwar Conservative Party developed specific tactics of targeted electioneering, and how very much alive it was to the plurality of the new electorate – especially women – with shifting appeals and strategies directed towards them according to their age, class and region.[1] Indeed, the franchise extensions of 1918 and 1928, which quadrupled the Edwardian electorate, presented political parties with new challenges to expand their appeals in what became a contest to shape the political character of the electorate and a battle of ideas.[2] An intense competition to win women's support and mobilise women as party workers ensued and, in this process, the meaning of gender roles and the definition of this new citizenry and of the nation as a whole were at stake. This was to do less with gender equality or women's equal capacity for politics, but rather with sound political strategy and constructing an efficient anti-socialist alliance.

Historians have had a tendency to oppose what is seen as Conservatism's *positive* appeal, that is its historic capacity to construct political identities and assimilate diverse constituencies of support with the Conservative Party's more *negative* anti-socialist strategy. Its positive appeal has been interpreted as producing cultures of democracy,[3] while its more negative tactics produced disparaging stereotypes of Labour and the unionised working class as nihilist Bolsheviks set on destroying the family and Englishness. The latter sheds light on the Conservatives as redoubtable class warriors.[4] This chapter shows that both appeals were part and parcel of the same overall Conservative response to the political challenges of the interwar period, and it explores the contested nature of a feminine 'conservative modernity' and the manufacturing of a 'new common sense'.[5]

In Chapter 5, David Thackeray shows that the Conservative Party leadership and individual male candidates were keen to present themselves as the champions of home interests, playing up their family-man credentials against what they presented as the rowdy electoral culture of Labour. Domestic and private, feminine and 'English', conservative modernity challenged an older narrative of Conservatism as masculine, aggressive and imperial.[6] From the early 1920s most new members of the Conservative Party were women and by the 1930s it seems the majority of members of the party were women.[7] The 'disproportionate' success and political hegemony of the Conservative Party in the 1930s was due to the fact that, 'In *every* social class the majority of women voted Tory ... a large majority of working-class women voted Conservative – a much higher proportion than men – and it is on this that the Tory electoral hegemony of the 1930s was ultimately based.'[8] While middle-class women's electoral support for the Tories can perhaps be explained by their class solidarity and belonging to the Anglican Church,[9] working-class women's vote has been understood as a failure of the trade unions to mobilise them and/or as the result of 'politics of envy'.[10] Of course, these interpretations are not mutually exclusive.

This chapter aims to offer another perspective on this issue by examining the contribution women made to the Conservative Party, to Conservatism, to the formulation of Conservative principles and to the changing language of the nation in the 1930s and 1940s. How did they carve out a place for themselves in a party that still held deeply rooted prejudices against women? What were the strategies they used to claim power? How did they recast the 'public sphere' as legitimate for female activity? Understanding why women voted Tory and how they contributed to Toryism entails exploring the relationship between Conservatism as a party poli-tics as well as conservatism as a set of attitudes and beliefs; it implies understanding the meaning of what can be referred to as a middlebrow culture with its insistence on common sense and the way it seemed after 1918 to link women and conserva-tism. Indeed, the traditional stereotypes of women thinking with their hearts rather than their brains chimed with a specifically Baldwinian concern about the middle-brow and 'ordinary' conservatism, and helped to produce a distinct understanding of 'common sense'. This chapter examines how the deliberate choice of middlebrow rhetoric as well as the language of citizenship enabled Conservative women to con-struct a cross-class language of democracy. This language was particularly instru-mental in mobilising and indeed, in their own terms, 'infiltrating' the voluntary sector and gaining large constituencies of support.

A language of caution: defending 'women's interests' but not 'feminism'

Incrementally, since the end of the nineteenth century, the rhetoric of Conservatism's appeal changed forms of expression and shifted from anti-radicalism to anti-socialism as the values of 'home and hearth' came to dominate the language of popular Toryism.[11] The success of the more family-centred Primrose League and the waning of working men's clubs were constitutive of this evolution towards a more explicit cult of domesticity.[12] By the 1920s, Conservative men acknowledged that women had become essential to the party in terms of canvassing, propaganda and fund-raising. By 1928, women were seen as indispensable to the party's very existence through the party's vibrant associational life, which they were responsible for, and which explained much of its success in responding to the new mass electorate.

Although their importance was fully recognised, there was still much concern that they might excessively 'feminise' the party and promote 'the ephemeral, the superficial and the decorative'.[13] On the one hand, the party was keen to present itself as the party of domesticity, reliability and quietude fighting against Socialism and its alleged destruction of the family. 'The family' in its idealised form was seen as the essential unit of society and, as such, stood in for the nation. It needed to be preserved and this was the most powerful argument in the anti-Socialist fight. Lady Astor insisted that Conservative women present themselves as a 'great bulwark against Bolshevism'.[14] On the other hand, the continual alarm at the possibly contested nature of gender roles meant that women needed to be particularly cautious in their dealings with men, and, while Astor self-identified as a feminist, most women within the Conservative Party would not use that word.

Adopting a language of citizenship rather than feminism was one way women advanced their interests without causing unnecessary alarm among the men of the party.[15] Marjorie Maxse, the first administrator of the Women's Unionist Organisation (WUO) in 1923, explained that her aim was 'to teach women to be voters and Conservative voters, not to create a feminist movement within the Conservative party'.[16] Throughout the 1920s and 1930s, the WUO and the Conservative Central Women's Advisory Committee (CWAC) sought to utilise the power base that political citizenship had granted women in 1918 and 1928 to encourage their members to show they were responsible and active citizens. Combating 'political apathy',[17] having 'better-informed canvassers',[18] urging women 'to take a keener interest and a more active part in Local Government Elections'[19] were priorities. Indeed, acknowledging the status of women as equal citizens and focusing on education in citizenship was key to reassuring men while still encouraging women to participate in local and national politics. It enabled them to distance themselves from feminism, which was seen as closely associated to the destruction of traditional family values, while nonetheless providing a public voice for women.[20] The term 'feminism' also seemed to imply the defence of sectional interests rather than the defence of the nation as a whole, and the rhetoric of the party was based on unity against the alleged sectionalism of the Labour party.[21] However, while the term 'feminism' was willingly abandoned to what they saw as 'the Left', even if some Conservative women self-identified as feminists, the term 'citizenship', it was felt, should not be ceded to the Socialists. Citizenship was to be defined in terms of rights and duties, with an emphasis on duty and service.

The Conservative staff college, Ashridge College, aimed to provide classes in citizenship for both women and men and to teach 'a sane and traditional view of citizenship without bias or propaganda'.[22] The Conservative obsession with the promotion of 'good citizens of sound constitutional views'[23] gave an opportunity to women of an expanding middle class to act as missionaries of this type of citizenship and to take an active part in constructing the narrative of Conservatism. The Conservative MP for Lancaster and parliamentary secretary to Lord Halifax when he was President of the Board of Education, Herwald Ramsbotham explained in 1934: 'If citizenship is, as I suppose it is, a combination of intellectual, moral and social qualities, it is a big job to have to "teach" it, particularly by the direct method as a school subject.'[24] Prime Minister Stanley Baldwin, who came to epitomise a Conservative leadership of quietude, offered a rhetoric of citizenship as service and duty which spoke to the traditional role of women as carers offering service:

> The assertion of people's rights has never yet provided that people with bread. The performance of their duties, and that alone, can lead to the successful issue of those experiments in government which we have carried further than any other people in this world.[25]

Citizenship was less a status than a means of engagement in the life of the nation.[26] Citizens should 'have a sense of social responsibility and the will to sink [their] own immediate interests, and the interests of [their] class, in the common good'.[27] While the Left was seen as emphasising citizens' rights, the Conservatives laid stress on their duties.

In this quest to involve women at the local and national level and to teach them how to be citizens, the language of domesticity was seen by the WUO as the most efficient one. It meant tapping into a pre-existing reservoir of themes used by the Conservative Party since at least the creation of the Primrose League in 1883. The Conservative Party had been keen on presenting women as 'Chancellors of the Exchequer of the home', valuing them for their own qualities that were different from that of men. Building on this 'domestic feminism' rather than opposing it meant that it was possible for women never to openly or explicitly challenge existing gender roles and what was seen as acceptable for men and women, while actually demanding, in the name of their citizenship, the right to work in the occupation of their choice, with equal pay, equal status for married women and equal moral standard. It enabled them to become political actors without challenging the gender hierarchy in any direct way.

Pat Thane points out that between 1928 and 1964, the majority of British women married and had children. These years represent a 'golden age ... of the near universal, stable, long-lasting marriage'.[28] Addressing the female electorate through the lens of domesticity therefore also made sense from the point of view of the female electorate. The novelty was to address them not simply as *wives* but as *housewives*, a term which had taken on a professional and a modern connotation, associated with efficiency and management.[29] Although the WUO did not support demands for family allowances payable to mothers, it called for low food prices and lower-cost housing.[30] Enabling women to build on their domestic expertise to demand social rights made it possible for them to carve a place for themselves in the public sphere and to contribute to local and national politics, while apparently maintaining the status quo. Although it is easy to understand why the aftermath of suffrage years, from 1928 to 1964, have been portrayed as a moment of backlash against the women's movement, a retreat into domesticity, what David Doughan called 'this apparently grey and amorphous half-century of feminism',[31] it is also important to see the strategies that lay behind this apparent endorsement of gender hierarchies.[32]

The WUO and the Central Women's Advisory Committee (CWAC) both called for more courses for women in political education and requested speakers from Central Office, encouraging women to engage in local and national politics. Foregrounding gender difference and domesticity by no means involved being stifled by domestic duties but rather playing a political role that complemented their domestic role.[33] The Mothers' Union explicitly stated that 'for a woman to give up all outside interests, to entirely merge her personality in that of another, is to help in producing husbands and fathers of a wrong type; the bully, the autocrat, the dictator. We have no use for that type [of mother] today',[34] which shows how distant the discourse was from Victorianism. The Conservative Women's Advisory Committee strongly encouraged wives and mothers to fulfil their duties as citizens by being elected to local government, for instance. In order to do so, it was recommended they take up classes, particularly in speaking, but also in areas such as economics. Women travelled to Ashridge College, which had opened in 1929 for training, and study groups formed throughout the country, offering courses on subjects ranging from canvassing to foreign policy.

While, officially, the objective at Ashridge was 'to offer to adult British citizens of both sexes and all classes education in democratic citizenship on traditional and constitutional lines',[35] in effect, age and class were deemed crucial as the Conservatives were under the impression that younger women were particularly ignorant of politics and susceptible to the influence of more progressive forces. There were many complaints at Ashridge from 'women of middle age, who went desiring to gain experience as branch chairmen, anxious to have an opportunity of improving their powers of speech and to imbibe suitable propaganda to circulate among the members of their Association on their return' but felt 'older students were not welcome'. The Speakers' Class '[they] were told was intended for those students under thirty'.[36]

In 1935, 20 per cent of scholarships were granted to young women, one of the requirements being that they were between the ages of 17 and 27. More women than men attended the classes every year and the targets of the courses were 'the right stamp of working girls and women' and 'girls of the more or less leisured classes – those, for example, who having left school or university were intending to take up secretarial or political work'.[37] The grants offered were for the 12-week course in citizenship in which the curriculum included reading, tutorials, debates, essay writing and lectures and the main subjects were economics, constitutional history, political theory, foreign relations and British imperial development. Women were encouraged to take up economics, not simply general economic questions, but also economic theory. The rhetoric of the home made it possible to take classes that were previously seen as the preserve of men, thus redefining what was acceptable for women, without directly challenging gender roles. Women were also taught to be 'missionaries' and to impart their political knowledge to others within their communities. Playing on the long-standing role of transmission by women, on their maternal role of guidance and moral leadership, they were encouraged to teach to others what they had been taught.

Anti-intellectualism and the middlebrow

Tapping into the Conservative Party's self-identified anti-intellectualism was another strategy for women to appropriate a specific place for themselves within the Party. One of the important characteristics of interwar Conservatism was its simultaneous apparent obsession with and abhorrence for intellectuals, and in particular highbrow intellectuals.[38] What Stefan Collini describes as the 'war of the brows'[39] was effectively a discursive war of electoral politics. Conservative women's self-description as 'practical, common sense, in service of others' was not only part of this war of the brows but also an attempt to gain recognition within their own party. This description was thus interwoven into a broader stereotype of Conservatives as essentially pragmatic, abstraction-avoiding and un-intellectual. By positioning themselves as the embodiment of a middlebrow culture that Stanley Baldwin did so much to promote and to present as the essence of the national character, they spoke to the widespread representation of womanhood that privileged the heart over the head, character over reason. It was on the reiteration of the well-worked idea that 'character' was more important than 'brains' that they initially positioned themselves within the Conservative Party. It had the double effect of presenting them in a reassuring light and giving them tools to move forward and promote what they saw as women's interests. They used the stereotypes of women being more down to earth than men, more aware of the realities of daily life as a badge of their Conservatism.

The middlebrow language used by Conservative women drew on an older language, that of philanthropy, and the idea that women 'have very little interest in doctrines, arguments or serious speculations of any kind … women's concern is not with ideas or principles, but with persons and things',[40] setting a familiar and comforting light on their new positions within the Conservative Party. It is useful to trace the development of ideas of heart versus brain to show the intellectual recasting of philanthropy as a strategic language for women in politics because it conflated with the Conservative self-definition as anti-intellectual, against abstract ideas and principles. The Conservative critique of rationalism and its emphasis on feeling rather than theorising echoed particularly with women, who were seen as the 'feeling sex'.[41] Ernest Barker, a Liberal who crossed over to the Conservatives because he felt 'bothered … by the abstract intellectualism' of the Liberal Party, wrote to Arthur Bryant in 1938: 'I admit more and more the practical wisdom of the good ordinary Englishman, facing the facts and "feeling" the right way through them – as a good countryman feels his way through a new countryside.'[42] The emphasis on 'feeling' and instinct chimed with many women who considered the Conservative Party offered a more congenial home than the Labour Party, which did not seem to recognise the demands of 'home and hearth'.

This battle of the brows was taken on not only by women within the Conservative Party but also by many women within the numerous non-partisan associations with which the party had links. They identified with a glorification of English culture as practical, common sense and middle-of-the-road. It was also an efficient response to the common accusation that they were irrational and emotional. The emphasis Conservatism laid on inner strength and moral steadfastness was precisely how many women understood their womanhood and their femininity.[43] The rhetoric of 'responsible womanhood' was at the heart of an attempt to construct a specifically female citizenship and its aim was to 'arouse a sense of civic responsibility, provide them [women] with knowledge on which to base sound and considered opinion, and prompt them to take a part in national or local self-government'.[44] The qualities associated with 'responsible womanhood' were *empathy* – much of Marjorie Maxse's success within the Conservative Party was almost invariably attributed to her ability to empathise with the views of others, being *sensible*,[45] being *practical*,[46] being full of *common sense* and ready to be of *service* to others. It was deemed safe to deploy these traditionally feminine skills outside the home and as long as women's actions were presented as extensions of their domestic virtues, they were seen as acceptable. Stanley Baldwin's statement that we should 'dedicate ourselves … to the service of our fellows, a service in widening circles, service to the home, service to our neighbourhood, to our county, our province, to our country, to the Empire, and to the world. No mere service of our lips, service of our lives',[47] describes very accurately how Conservative women understood their citizenship. They felt they were articulating the specificities of the local and the national. Classes at Ashridge taught women speakers to associate Conservatism with 'national values' while at the same time being alive to the parochialism of constituents. They found a place for themselves by putting to the fore the very qualities that were, allegedly, historically those of the nation and which the Conservative Party meant to represent.

Naturally, the 'middlebrow' was not confined to one party and was in fact very much cross-party, but the Conservatives were quick to recognise this trend, presenting themselves as the true representatives of national values. Conservative women in particular became instrumental in developing a middlebrow, as opposed to highbrow, paradigm and portraying their Labour counterparts as 'cerebral' and 'speculative', all very un-English qualities, which smacked of foreign political extremism.[48] Building on the prejudicial attitudes about gender roles and turning these 'heart versus brain' stereotypes into assets, or more, badges of Conservatism and patriotism, was the tour de force played by Conservative women. Their domestic expertise could be made to resonate with the Baldwinian ideal of Conservative citizenship and its emphasis on duty and on the local. In so doing, Conservative women developed a different kind of common sense about the national character. They represented a form of modernity, which was middlebrow and which identified the national with the domestic and the private. Alison Light evokes 'a nation of gardeners and housewives', as opposed to, earlier in the century, a nation of aggressive imperialists.[49] What Light refers to as the feminisation of the idea of the nation contributed to bringing to the fore an image of the English as a peaceable, tolerant and moderate people.[50] Baldwin's political success, which has been attributed to his ability to articulate and embody a vision of the nation as 'uniquely peaceable'[51] that resonated with a substantial constituency of voters, was in no small part due to Conservative women's contribution to this language, which carried a form of optimism and a belief in British exceptionalism: Conservative women contributed to defining English national character as 'common sense, good temper, ordered freedom, progress'.[52]

A democratic language

The discourse of the middlebrow offered an ideal language to discuss and embrace the process of mass democratisation and female citizenship that many Conservatives identified as the main challenge of the day. Its 'apparent artlessness'[53] made it an ideal tool to reach across social classes. The Conservative Women's Organisation was very much alive to the opportunity this language offered to appeal to female voters who might have had little interest in party politics. In this respect, voluntary associations were seen as essential mechanisms in party propaganda precisely because they were non-party political, yet played an important role in civic training.

During the interwar period, the Conservative Party had strongly encouraged middle-class women's non-partisan social commitment to voluntary action and their being 'missionaries', in order to create an associational culture apart from the direct rough and tumble of party politics.[54] While Baldwin liked to say that, 'The whole spirit of the [voluntary] movement is service for others ... By teaching our own people the spirit of service which the friendly societies inculcate, we are playing our part in making our democracy fitter and nobler,'[55] Conservatives came to see voluntary associations as part of the new rules of the political game. Politics were no longer simply the art of government by a few men in a cigar room but required a broader knowledge of, and approach to, social life.

Women within the Conservative Party were aware of the immense reservoir of good will and votes those associations represented. They saw it as their duty to 'infiltrate' them. Conservative women's links with charitable local organisations had always contributed greatly towards integrating the party into the life of communities.[56] On 30 September 1936, at a meeting of the National Society of Women Organisers, it was stated that

> More efforts should be made to get Conservatives to attend meetings of the Co-Operative Society, and to vote. Several members gave instances where a drive had been made and Conservatives had been able to out-vote Labour. Other members stated that the Labour members would pack the hall in advance, and the difficulties were almost insuperable ... It was stressed that representatives should be formed to attend meetings of the League of Nations Union, and Peace Council. Miss Ferguson felt that such representatives must be 100% Conservatives, with strong Conservative Principles and prejudice, as otherwise if weaker representatives are sent to such meetings, they sometimes get impressed with the views of the other side. The meeting unanimously agreed that a strong propaganda campaign was necessary.[57]

The CWAC had correspondence with and members on the committees of the Over-thirty Association, Women's Freedom League, National Council for Equal Citizenship, London and National Society for Women's Service, Wayfarers' Sunday Association, Open Door Council, Six Point Group, National Council of Women and Women's Guild of Empire.[58] Yet, at a CWAC meeting on 22 March 1937, one of the Resolutions was: 'That this Conference whilst fully appreciating the importance of maintaining membership and activities of organisations connected with the Party would urge all members of Constituency Associations to interest themselves to a far greater extent in the local branches of Non-Party Organisations.'[59] It also urged 'members of Trade Unions and Co-operative Societies to increase their activities in order to free these Societies from Party Politics, thereby gaining for the worker the best industrial benefits possible and maintaining the principles for which each was formed'.[60] In a similar vein, Dame Regina Evans explained at a CWAC meeting in March 1936 that 'there was a need to obtain a panel of women throughout the Areas who would be prepared to attend meetings of other societies and was sure this could be done especially if they were coached beforehand and knew that there were others there to support them'.[61] Lady Bridgeman confirmed that 'putting suitable women on Government Committees and Commission' was a priority. The voluntary sector was seen as both an observatory and an antechamber of politics where different tensions worked themselves out.

A recurring problem was the shortage of trained women organisers. One of the difficulties, the North Area Women Organisers Society explained, was that 'the hours of work of women organisers compare[d] unfavourably with other professions'. In order 'to attract the best recruits more leisure should be available'.[62] At another meeting a month later, it was stressed that there was a 'need for leisure to keep up outside interests': this enabled the organisers 'to keep in touch with people who would not attend Political Meetings'.[63]

There were debates about the training of women organisers and some were of the view that 'organisers had no time for intellectual pursuits' and classes.[64] Simple language was needed in order to bond with female workers. However, it was also argued that 'Educational lectures and Speakers' Classes' were necessary 'in order to gain political knowledge and confidence in speaking'.[65] Confidence in speaking to male audiences was indeed a crucial issue. Another problem was that of the salary which depended on the constituency. Poor constituencies found it difficult to raise salaries as 'to poor people the salary of agents and women organisers were so much higher than their own'.[66] But it was pointed out in a later meeting that there was a 'danger of women being engaged at a lower salary than men'.[67]

Conservative women played an important role in developing and sustaining a variety of non-party organisations in the interwar and wartime period. One in particular, the Women's Voluntary Services (WVS), set up in 1938 by Lady Reading at the request of the Home Office, had over a million volunteers at the height of the war and was crucial in supporting the war effort. The government wished to draw on the existing and extensive voluntary work by women to assist in dealing with the problems they foresaw in the war that was shortly expected, in particular with regard to the anticipated severe bombing and evacuation. Marjorie Maxse who had become chief organisation officer of the Conservative Party was appointed in 1940, along with Lady Iris Capell and Mary Agnes Hamilton, one of the three vice-chairs of the WVS.

Although officially non-political, the WVS was very much a Conservative organisation, with much overlap in personnel.[68] The WVS saw itself as an association of 'practical women', who were at the same time 'caring, no-nonsense' and eager to 'get the job done', as opposed to those who wasted their time on 'speculative theorizing', which was seen as characteristic of their Labour and Liberal counterparts.[69] Lady Reading very much understood the advantages of this anti-intellectual creed: it spoke to all classes and served to distinguish those she referred to as 'us', the simple, common-sense women, from 'them', the left-wing highbrows, cut off from the real world. The WVS were 'a local housekeeping service on a national scale'.[70] Her remark to Sir Wyndham Deedes of the National Council of Social Service (NCSS) that a memo of his was 'drafted by far more intelligent people than we were' and 'perhaps misunderstood by people who were more practical'[71] is relevant in this structural anti-intellectualism, which was interpreted as the democratic language par excellence because it was not highbrow, that is to say not elitist. Despite the conspicuous hierarchical class structure of the WVS, this middlebrow language carried the in-built assumption that class identities were fluid.[72]

One reading of the increasing presence of women within the Conservative Party has been that they were held in a 'primarily exploitative relationship'[73] wherein political work easily elided into active support for voluntary associations. However, the WVS provides a different example. After the war, the Labour government developed innovative social policies and also engaged in an active debate about the role of voluntary action in what became known as the 'welfare state'. The WVS's work became more oriented to general social relief. It was a community-based, independent organisation, which recruited volunteers to assist government departments, local authorities and voluntary bodies in a range of activities. Lady Reading argued that the WVS represented a new kind of volunteering adapted to the needs of the modern welfare state, providing an effective intermediary body to transform central objectives into local action. She thought of the WVS not as 'a voluntary organisation financed by the State, but [as] a State service furnished by volunteers'.[74] As a government-funded organisation that relied on volunteer workers, the WVS brought together women from other organisations, most notably the Women's Institutes, Townswomen's Guilds and the Girl Guides movement. Local leadership was largely drawn from women who were already leaders of other organisations and a clear hierarchy of command was established from the central offices in Tothill Street, London.

While the WVS had made itself useful to both local authorities and national state, it had many detractors within other voluntary associations that had supported it during the war only on the assurance that it would close down after the war. At the end of the war, many members of the WVS resigned, expecting the organisation to close down: the Women's Institute (WI) withdrew its members from the WVS advisory committee; the National Union of Townswomen's Guilds withdrew as well. Several voluntary bodies such as St John Ambulance, Red Cross, stayed on.[75] In September 1945, the Attlee government took the decision to extend the life of the WVS, which was seen as indispensable in the transition from war to peace. The Home Office provided funding on the wartime basis, and departments making regular use of the WVS services were required to contribute to the costs. This arrangement was renewed in 1947 and again in 1951 and the financial responsibility for local WVS offices was transferred from local authorities to central government. But this was not a seamless process: in 1948 Home Office civil servants debating the future of the WVS proposed to merge the WVS and the NCSS which had been established in 1918 to foster cooperation between the voluntary sector and the state (but was seen as unsuccessful), in order to create an infrastructure body for the voluntary sector that would recruit volunteers directly and coordinate volunteer work for statutory services. Herbert Morrison, as Lord President of the Council, was in charge of the relationship between the Government and the voluntary sector and he agreed with Lady Reading that 'there was a good case for singling the WVS out from other organisations as regards continuing Government financial assistance'.[76]

However, in 1948, the Women's Group on Public Welfare (WGPW)[77] became a major focus of opposition to WVS. They stated their demands as follows:

(a) That the difference between a genuine voluntary organisation and one acting on behalf of a Government department should be clearly defined.

(b) If the WVS is to be regarded as a voluntary organisation it should have a constitution of a democratic nature as to other such voluntary organisations. If in fact it is to be an auxiliary Government Service then its work should be clearly defined, so as to in no way overlap with, or undermine, that of the free voluntary organisations.

(c) If public funds are to be used to subsidise the Service the cost should be made known publicly.

(d) If it is to be in fact an auxiliary Government Service a new title should be adopted as the present one is misleading.

(e) That it should be recognised that the WVS is not a co-ordinating body and is therefore not in a position to act as a representative women's organisation since it has no democratic machinery through which it can achieve this.

(f) If the WVS desires to be recognised as a voluntary social organisation the scope and limits of its activities should be clearly defined to avoid over-lapping.[78]

The WVS's response to the accusation of lack of democratic control was that they were efficient and modern: they had no committees because it was the best way to get things done quickly. The WVS was more modern than 'the hit-and-miss old-world charitable voluntary service conception'; it was a transmission belt for the 'translation of central objectives to the lowest level in order that the central idea can be carried through to local action'.[79] Lady Reading claimed to have found the solution to save voluntary action from disappearing for lack of funding: 'people should give of their muscle, their sweat and their thought, rather than their purse'.[80] The days of charity and patronage were over.[81] The important point of course was to foster 'a national welfare consciousness … in the individual',[82] which was so important to the Conservative idea of national character. Lady Reading reiterated that working with organisations which were 'entirely theoretical in outlook' would undermine the WVS' chief virtue: its capacity to make rapid and innovative responses to unanticipated demands, 'a more practical approach to life'.[83]

While the WI was very outspoken against 'intermediary women's service likely to overlap and undermine the strength of long-established voluntary and independent women's organisations',[84] several articles from *Social Service* defended the WVS and emphasised the need for 'a partnership in social effort between voluntary organisations and central and local government' and the need for positive involvement on the part of the voluntary organisations.[85] The vice-chair of the Conservative Party Organisation, Marjorie Maxse, accused the WGPW of being 'an assembly of impractical theorists', who have 'a definite antagonism against us because we want things to be done on a practical basis'.[86]

While the Home Office put pressure on the NCSS to negotiate a merger with the WVS, the WGPW hoped the local Standing Committees of Women's Organisations would be the natural successor to the WVS. There was much agreement at the Home Office, but also at NCSS that the WVS 'performed efficiently a number of peacetime tasks which would be much more costly if they were carried out by public authorities'. On 22 June 1949, a debate took place at the House of Lords on 'Voluntary Action for Social Progress' initiated by Lord Samuel. The merging scheme between the NCSS and the WVS did not take place, but in the autumn of 1951, the permanence of the WVS through central government funding was finally settled.

Interpretations of the WVS have focused on it being an expression of middle-class social leadership and essentially an anti-democratic controlling organisation or, on the contrary, part of the 'cultures of democracy' at work in Britain through-out the interwar period and the aftermath of the Second World War.[87] While it has been seen as 'an intriguing moment of convergence between middle-class female associationalism and the planning state',[88] it can also be interpreted as an intriguing moment when women within the Conservative Party reassured men that the wel-fare state was not destroying voluntary action and the prominence of Conservative activism through non-partisan voluntary associations. They convinced the gov-ernment that WVS was a model of peacetime voluntary action and served as an example of how to foster constructive engagement with the social and legislative transformations of the post-war era.

The WVS's presence nationwide and its outreach to working-class women via the Housewives Service, for example, meant it had a lot to offer to the Conservative Party's strategy of 'infiltration' of the associational world, which had been so suc-cessful in the interwar period. The Conservative Party very much saw the advan-tages of cultivating the involvement of its members in the non-partisan world of women's organisations. Lady Reading may have been successful in adapting middle-class social leadership to the process of state expansion, but the WVS was also successful in diffusing Conservative values and language.

While James Hinton sees the WVS as an extension of the social maternalism of late Victorian philanthropy, it may have more to do with the 'Conservative femi-nism' of the interwar period, upholding gender hierarchies and celebrating domes-ticity while fighting for the advancement of women's interests. Many of the women within the WVS were also equal rights activists, defending

1 Economic Equality – equal pay –; Equal opportunities; Equality in Social insurance;
2 Equal Status for the Married women; Nationality of Married Women; Income Tax of Married Persons; Purchase of Women: Marriage Contracts;
3 Equal Moral Responsibility;
4 Women Police;
5 Women Peers.[89]

Evelyn Emmet, Marjorie Maxse and Lady Davidson, who had been active mem-bers of the WVS, were all part of the committee that wrote up the Women's Charter in 1948 and they felt they were building on a gendered vision of society, emphasis-ing the notion of character-building, practical womanhood and common sense. In 1941, Evelyn Emmet had explained:

I think one of the lasting effects of WVS up and down the breadth of the country will be the lesson in Local Government to the women of this country. Some of us had the privilege of serving on Local Authorities before the war but the big mass of the people in this country neither knew or cared in who represented them on the local council nor were in the least interested in what they did or how the rates were spent. Education, Housing, Sanitation, Food, all matters which concern the home we are fighting to help are a matter of supreme interest to women. It will be our duty from now on to see to these things in our immediate neighbourhood ... Lastly I look upon WVS as a practical form of Christianity. We serve without favour or reward for the most part anonymously ... without Freedom, Justice, and Charity life is not worth living and they [the people of this country] are ready to die to the last man and woman in this simple belief.[90]

There is a middle ground between interpretations of the WVS as the expression of middle-class imperialism and views of the WVS as embodying cultures of democracy and British exceptionalism. There is a political angle to the WVS as an efficient instrument of diffusion of Conservative values and language and 'conservative modernity'. This shows there were varied versions of Conservative womanhood, different from the British Housewives' League for instance, which can be interpreted as part of a reform tradition that had as one of its main goals the public advancement of women. Conservatism offered a language for the demands of the home and the family, which Conservative women used to defend their own interests, but also to contribute to what they saw as an innovative, socially engaged and modern Conservatism. The WVS is one example of how they invented new forms of cooperation between statutory and voluntary agencies and acted as a spearhead for peacetime voluntary work. While they maintained social hierarchies and principles of mutuality rather than equality as social dynamics,[91] they contributed to reinventing Conservative appeals and redefining what was acceptable for women.

Notes

1 David Jarvis, Adrian Bingham, Stuart Ball, Ina Zweiniger-Bargielowska among others.
2 Clarisse Berthezène, *Training Minds for the War of Ideas: The Conservative Party, Ashridge College and the Cultural Politics of Britain, 1929–54* (Manchester: Manchester University Press, 2015).
3 Helen McCarthy, 'Whose Democracy? Histories of British Political Culture Between the Wars', *The Historical Journal*, 55: 1 (March 2012), 221–38; Kit Kowol, 'Ford County: Henry Ford's British Farms and an Experiment in Conservative Modernity', *Journal of British Studies* (forthcoming).
4 Ross McKibbin, *The Ideologies of Class. Social Relations in Britain 1880–1950* (Oxford, Clarendon Press, 1990); David Jarvis, '"Behind Every Great Party": Women and Conservatism in Twentieth Century Britain', in Amanda Vickery, *Women, Privilege, and Power: British Politics, 1750 to the Present* (Stanford, CA: Stanford University Press, 2002), p. 306.
5 Alison Light, *Forever England: Femininity, Literature and Conservatism between the Wars* (London: Routledge, 1991), p. 10.

6 *Ibid.*; Jon Lawrence, 'Forging a Peaceable Kingdom: War, Violence, and Fear of Brutalization In Post-First World War Britain', *The Journal of Modern History*, 75: 3 (September 2003), 557–89; Kowol, 'Ford County'.

7 J. W. B. Bates, 'The Conservative Party in the Constituencies', Unpublished thesis, University of Oxford, 1994, p. 82, in Ross McKibbin, *Parties and People. England: 1914–1951* (Oxford: Oxford University Press, 2010), p. 98.

8 McKibbin, *Parties and People*, p. 97.

9 *Ibid.*

10 Selina Todd, *Young Women, Work and Family in England, 1880–1950* (Oxford: Oxford University Press, 2005). Carolyn Steedman, *Landscape for a Good Woman: A Story of Two Lives* (London: Virago, 1986).

11 Jon Lawrence, 'Class and Gender in the Making of Urban Toryism, 1880–1914, *English Historical Review*, 108 (1993), 630–52; Jarvis, 'Behind Every Great Party', p. 306.

12 Jarvis, 'Behind Every Great Party'.

13 David Jarvis, 'British Conservatism and Class Politics in the 1920s', *English Historical Review*, 110 (1996), p. 182.

14 Lady Astor, minutes of the 1921 Conservative Party Conference, NUA 2/1/37.

15 See Caitriona Beaumont, *Housewives and Citizens. Domesticity and the Women's Movement in England, 1928–64* (Manchester: Manchester University Press, 2013), p. 3.

16 Marjorie Maxse, *Conservative Agents Journal*, May 1924.

17 CWAC Minute Book, 26 March 1936, CCO 170/1/1/1.

18 CWAC Minute Book, 11 December 1935, CCO 170/1/1/1.

19 CWAC Minute Book, 10 February 1937, CCO 170/1/1/1.

20 Caitriona Beaumont, 'Citizens, not Feminists: The Boundary Negotiated Between Citizenship and Feminism by Mainstream Women's Organisations in England, 1928–39', *Women's History Review*, ix (2000), 411–29.

21 Stanley Baldwin insisted the Conservative and Unionist Party stood for 'Unionist in the sense that we stand for the union of those two nations of which Disraeli spoke two generations ago; union among our own people at home which, if secured, nothing else matters in the world.' S. Baldwin at the Albert Hall, 4 December 1924, in Stanley Baldwin, *On England And Other Addresses* (London: Philip Allen & Co., 1926), p. 73.

22 Reginald Hoskins, Undated memorandum, January 1934, Education Committee Minutes 1934, Ashridge Papers.

23 Reginald Hoskins, Report on the 1933 session, no date, March 1934, Education Committee Minutes 1934, Ashridge Papers.

24 Herwald Ramsbotham to Ernest Simon, 3 December 1934, Bryant papers, C 28.

25 Stanley Baldwin, 'Democracy and the Spirit of Service', London, 4 December 1924, in *On England and Other Addresses* (London: Philip Allan & Co., 1926), p. 71.

26 Beaumont, *Housewives and Citizens*, p. 42.

27 Sir E. Simon and E. M. Hubback, *Training For Citizenship* (London, 1935), p. 14.

28 Pat Thane, 'Family Life and "Normality" in Post-War British Culture', in R. Bessel and D. Schumann (eds), *Life After Death: Approaches to a Cultural and Social History of Europe during the 1940s and 1950s* (Cambridge: Cambridge University Press, 2003), quoted in C. Beaumont, *Housewives and Citizens*, p. 8.

29 Light, *Forever England*, p. 218.

30 See Ina Zweiniger-Bargielowska, *Women in Twentieth-Century Britain: Social, Cultural and Political Change* (Routledge, 2014), pp. 321–34.

31 David Doughan, *Lobbying for Liberation: British Feminism 1918–1968* (London: City of London Polytechnic, 1980), quoted in Linda Perriton, 'Forgotten Feminists: The Federation of British Professional and Business Women, 1933–69', *Women's History Review*, 16: 1 (2007), 81.

32 Julie V. Gottlieb and Richard Toye (eds), *The Aftermath of Suffrage. Women, Gender and Politics in Britain, 1918–1945* (Palgrave Macmillan, 2013); Adrian Bingham, 'An Era of Domesticity? Histories of Gender and Women in the Interwar Period', *Cultural and Social History*, 1 (2004), 225–33.

33 Beaumont, *Housewives and Citizens*; Maggie Andrews, *The Acceptable Face of Feminism: The Women's Institute as a Social Movement* (London: Lawrence & Wishart, 1998).

34 *The Mothers' Union Journal*, 158 (September 1934), quoted in Beaumont, *Housewives and Citizens*, p. 53.

35 3 July 1934, draft of a memo of the purposes of the college by A. Bryant.

36 Private report sent to Lady Newton, 16/2/1931, Ashridge Papers.

37 *Ibid.*

38 Berthezène, *Training Minds for the War of Ideas.*

39 Stefan Collini, *Absent Minds: Intellectuals in Britain* (Oxford: Oxford University Press, 2006).

40 Looking at the interwar popular press, R. C. K. Ensor believed this was what editors had concluded. R. C. K. Ensor, 'The Press', in Sir Ernest Barker (ed.), *The Character of England* (Oxford: Clarendon Press, 1947), quoted in Adrian Bingham, *Gender, Modernity, and the Popular Press in Interwar Britain* (Oxford Historical Monographs, 2004), p. 118.

41 Light, *Forever England*, p. 14.

42 Ernest Barker to Arthur Bryant, 7 October 1938, Bryant papers, E1.

43 Light, *Forever England.*

44 Draft of a memorandum on the purposes of the college by Arthur Bryant, 3 July 1934, Ashridge papers.

45 When Conservative women were described, they were very often presented as sensible. Being 'sensible' justifies their appointment to a job: 'Three sensible women were appointed', Lady Emmet papers, WVS, 27 April 1939, Ms. Eng. c. 5722.

46 CWAC minutes are full of memos on the fact that 'practical women are needed'. CCO 170/1/1/1.

47 Stanley Baldwin, *Service of Our Lives: Last Speeches as Prime Minister* (London: Hodder & Stoughton Ltd, 1937), p. 144.

48 Julie V. Gottlieb, *'Guilty Women', Foreign Policy and Appeasement in Inter-War Britain* (Palgrave Macmillan, 2015).

49 Light, *Forever England*, p. 211.

50 *Ibid.*

51 Lawrence, 'Forging a Peaceable Kingdom', 588. Lawrence describes the advent of the notion of a 'peaceable' nation as a return to the myths of 1914 and the war to end all wars.

52 Peter Mandler, *The English National Character. The History and Idea from Edmund Burke to Tony Blair* (Yale University Press, 2006), p. 151.

53 Light, *Forever England*, p. 11.

54 Ken Young, *Local Politics and the Rise of Party: The London Municipal Society and the Conservative Intervention in Local Elections, 1894–1963* (Leicester University Press, 1975); Ken Young, 'The Party and English Local Government' in Anthony Seldon and Stuart Ball, *Conservative Century: The Conservative Party since 1900* (Oxford: Oxford University Press, 1994); J. W. B. Bates, 'The Conservative Party in the Constituencies', Oxford, DPhil, 1994.

55 Stanley Baldwin, *On England And other Addresses* (Philip Allen & Co., 1926), pp. 263–4.

56 Jarvis, 'Behind Every Great Party', p. 305.

57 National Society of Women Organisers Minutes, 30 September 1936, CCO 170/2/1/1.

58 National Society of Women Organisers Minutes, 10 February 1937, CCO 170/1/1/1.

59 Central Women's Advisory Committee Minute Book, 26 March 1937, CCO 170/1/1/1.

60 *Ibid.*

61 Central Women's Advisory Committee Minute Book, 26 March 1936, CCO 170/1/1/1.

62 National Society of Women Organisers Minutes, 16 April 1937, CCO 170/2/1/1.

63 National Society of Women Organisers Minutes, 28 May 1937, CCO 170/2/1/1.

64 *Ibid.*

65 National Society of Women Organisers Minutes, 10 September 1937, CCO 170/2/1/1.

66 National Society of Women Organisers Minutes, 28 May 1937, CCO 170/2/1/1.

67 National Society of Women Organisers Minutes, 4 April 1938, CCO 170/2/1/1.

68 There was much overlap in personnel between the Conservative party and WVS: Marjorie Maxse, Lady Lloyd (Brecon), Evelyn Emmet, Mrs Weston (Chelmsford) Huxley, Lady Davidson, etc.

69 James Hinton, 'Voluntarism and the Welfare/Warfare State. Women's Voluntary Services in the 1940s', *Twentieth Century British History*, 9: 2 (1998), 283.

70 Lady Reading, 15 May 1947 in Hinton, 'Voluntarism and the Welfare/Warfare State', p. 280.

71 Lady Reading, note on meeting with Sir Wyndham Deedes, 3 September 1947, WRVS Al/38 File, in Hinton, 'Voluntarism and the Welfare/Warfare State', p. 283.

72 On WVS, see James Hinton, *Women, Social Leadership and the Second World War: Continuities of Class* (Oxford: Oxford University Press, 2002).

73 Jarvis, 'Behind Every Great Party', p. 303.

74 Hinton, *Women, Social Leadership, and the Second World War*, p. 217.

75 *Ibid.*, pp. 218–19.

76 *Ibid.*, p. 219.

77 Created in September 1939 as the Women's Group on Problems arising from Evacuation, under the chairmanship of Margaret Bondfield (Labour) and Priscilla Norman (Cons) with the NCSS providing secretariat and accommodation. In 1940, it changed its name to WGPW.

78 Meeting of the Women's Group on Public Welfare (in association with the NCSS), May 11, 1948, WGPW/27/4/48/70, CPA.

79 Memo by Lady Reading, 11 October 1946, in Hinton, *Women, Social Leadership and the Second World War*, p. 216.

80 *Ibid.*

81 *Ibid.*, p. 217.

82 *Ibid.*

83 *Ibid.*
84 *Ibid.*, p. 215.
85 A. M. Watson, 'Social Service and Civic Responsibility', *Social Service*, XXII: 1 (June–Aug. 1948), 7.
86 *Ibid.*, p. 216.
87 Hinton, *Women, Social Leadership and the Second World War*; McCarthy, 'Whose Democracy?'
88 Hinton, *Women, Social Leadership and the Second World War*, p. 232.
89 Women's Organisations. April 1945–November 1947, CCO3/1/24.
90 Speech by Emmet at Marlborough, 17 March 1941, Ms Eng. c. 5723 1944–45, Emmet papers.
91 Jon Lawrence, 'Paternalism, Class, and the British Path to Modernity', in Beers and Thomas, *Brave New World*, p. 46.

7

Churchill, women and the politics of gender

Richard Toye

In 1953, Lady Violet Bonham Carter was approached to contribute a chapter to a book that was to be published as a tribute to Prime Minister Winston Churchill on his eightieth birthday. Bonham Carter, the daughter of H. H. Asquith, was a formidable Liberal politician in her own right, and was also one of Churchill's few close female friends. She was happy to be included in the volume but she vigorously rejected the suggestion of the editor, Sir James Marchant, and the publisher, Desmond Flower of Cassell and Company, that her contribution be entitled 'Churchill – a woman's point of view'.[1] She told Marchant: 'Your other contributors might just as well be asked to write of him from a "man's point of view" and I cannot imagine anything more boring and limiting than either approach. He is a great human being and must be approached as such.' Moreover:

> I have never heard him generalise about women; his attitude to Suffragettes was, I imagine (very much like that of my father and most other politicians who disliked being hit over the head with dog-whips and other implements), irritated and defensive; his attitude towards votes for women is a matter of history. There was nothing particularly characteristic or individual about it.[2]

And as she pointed out to Flower: 'I am afraid I could not express "a woman's point of view" about Mr. Churchill because such a view does not exist! [...] Even on the suffrage, as you will remember, there were differences of "view" among women.'[3]

This little episode is revealing of the state of gender politics at the end of the Churchill era. On the one hand, there was the sweeping sexist assumption that, as Bonham Carter was 'the only woman who has been asked to contribute to the volume', it should fall to her 'to express the woman's point of view'.[4] On the other, there was, at least, a dim awareness on the part of some Establishment men that women's perspectives were in some sense important, even if the overall approach to them remained tokenistic and patronising. The House of Commons in these years remained 'a very masculine place', and something similar could be said about politics in general.[5] However, some women politicians, although considerably isolated and operating within a man's world, were able to carve out prominent positions for themselves. It was understandable if some of them, like Bonham Carter, tried to avoid being pigeonholed as the representatives of 'women's issues'.[6] There might not have been much progress in the years since Churchill's first (1899) election campaign, when the would-be statesman had declared himself 'the most uncompromising enemy' of votes for women; but there had been some.[7]

Where, however, did Churchill himself stand in relation to these changes? And if indeed there was 'nothing particularly characteristic' about his attitudes and public statements in relation to women, is the topic even worth studying? Arguably, in fact, it is the very conventionality of his views that lend them their interest; close to the centre of British politics for multiple decades he reflected prevailing gender assumptions more than he changed or challenged them. But perhaps, too, his approach was a little more distinctive than Bonham Carter acknowledged. There were some significant differences between his rhetoric and that of other leading Conservatives. And, at the very least, he did make some critical interventions (for example over the issue of equal pay) that had significant repercussions at the time. The degree to which his attitudes played a part in the Conservative election defeats of 1945 and 1950, and the victory of 1951, are worthy of investigation. It is also interesting to consider his relative neglect of woman-oriented rhetoric, in contrast with his predecessors as Tory leader. His silences could themselves be rather telling.

A certain amount of work on Churchill and women has already been done. Paul Addison has written a useful general essay, which includes discussion of Churchill's personal relationships.[8] His earlier book on Churchill's domestic policies also includes helpful material on the women's suffrage question as well as some brief comments on his approach to women's wages and working conditions and equal pay.[9] Quite a lot has also been published on Clementine Churchill, notably the biography by her daughter Mary Soames.[10] Furthermore, in her book on women and appeasement, Julie V. Gottlieb devotes a chapter to the 'women Churchillians' who emerged as vocal and prominent anti-appeasers during the 1930s.[11] There is much other relevant literature too, such as David Jarvis's analysis of the Conservative appeal to women in the 1920s, and Ina Zweiniger-Bargielowska's work on the impact of austerity on women voters in the 1940s and 1950s.[12] Martin Francis, for his part, has explored Churchill's 'emotional economy' in relation to developing post-Second World War codes of masculinity, concluding that 'Churchill's extravagant patrician personality fitted uneasily into a political culture that prioritized self-restraint'.[13]

In order to fit in with the theme of the volume, a substantial part of this chapter considers the period after 1924, when Churchill returned to the Conservative fold after twenty years in the Liberal Party. By this point, unlike during his previous (pre-1904) Tory phase, some women were able to vote. It is, however, also important to reflect on his earlier attitudes and experiences, which informed his later ones. Thus, after reviewing Churchill's early attitudes and actions with respect to female suffrage, the chapter analyses Churchill's attitude to the extension of the franchise in the late 1920s, his record on social and taxation policy as Chancellor of the Exchequer, and his attitude to women's issues as both Prime Minister and Leader of the Opposition in the 1940s and 1950s. It also examines how far Churchill constructed his public appeals in gendered terms. To what extent did he specifically attempt to appeal to women voters and to women as wartime citizens – and how did his efforts (or the lack of them) fit into the context of the Conservative Party's parallel efforts?

Churchill did, of course, come from a strongly Conservative aristocratic background, but his family was by no means wholly conventional. His father, Lord Randolph Churchill, was a self-styled 'Tory Democrat' whose meteoric ascent to the chancellorship was quickly followed by personal and political disaster when he was outsmarted by the Prime Minister, Lord Salisbury. After his 1886 resignation he never held office again and he died young in 1895, when Winston was not yet twenty-one. Lord Randolph's American wife Jennie was an energetic figure who, in spite of the tensions in her marriage, made efforts to further her husband's career. During the 1885 general election she campaigned on his behalf in his Woodstock constituency.[14] One of Lord Randolph's biographers notes that although Jennie was 'never a political manipulator ... she was fully prepared to speak on platforms and give interviews; she was prominent in Birmingham later in the year [after Lord Randolph switched constituency], organizing "phalanxes of lady canvassers" and giving interviews in the press; she remained one of the chief organizers of the Primrose League, and appeared at provincial meetings with [Lord Randolph] Churchill in the campaigns of 1886'.[15]

Although the League – which Lord Randolph had helped to found – was a very hierarchical (one might say snobbish) organisation it was notable for its inclusion of all classes and both genders in its activities. Winston Churchill joined it at age 13, became 'a knight of the Primrose League' three years later, and gave his first political speech to the Bath Habitation in 1897.[16] Thus, Winston was raised in an atmosphere in which women's political activity was not uncommon, albeit heavily circumscribed.

Much responsibility for Churchill's upbringing was entrusted to his beloved nurse, Elizabeth Everest, from whom he undoubtedly absorbed certain views at the time, notably her anxieties about the Fenians.[17] (Churchill spent part of his childhood in Dublin.) After Lord Randolph's death, Winston and his mother became closer. As a young man in the army, trying simultaneously to make his way as a journalist, author and putative politician, she used her Establishment connections to further his prospects. Lady Randolph has been cited as an opponent of female suffrage (as was Lord Randolph).[18] However, shortly before the First World War she wrote a play, *The Bill*, that appeared to look forward optimistically to the dawn of universal suffrage (including women) but it is extremely unlikely that it had any impact on her son's views, which developed independently.[19]

As we have seen, Winston Churchill started his career as a determined opponent of votes for women, at a time when the issue was not high on the political agenda. However, he modified his position around the time that he switched from the Conservatives to the Liberal Party in 1904. In that year he recorded a vote in the Commons in favour of female suffrage. However, when the Women's Social and Political Union (WSPU) adopted militant tactics, Churchill became one of their particular targets. During the 1906 election campaign Sylvia Pankhurst disrupted one of his meetings, demanding to know if the Liberal government would give women the vote.[20] Churchill responded: 'On the only occasion when I have voted I have voted for giving votes to women. Now, having regard to the treatment I have received, and to the destruction of great public meetings which I have witnessed time after time, nothing will induce me to vote for giving votes to women.' For this he was cheered loudly, but he nonetheless rowed back from this emphatic declaration: 'I am not so hostile to the proposal as I thought it right to say just now – (laughter), but I am not going to be hen-pecked – (much laughter) – on a question of such grave public importance. – (Hear, hear.)'[21]

Over the next few years, Churchill continued to blow hot and cold. During the Manchester by-election which he was obliged to fight (and which he lost) upon his promotion to the Cabinet in 1908, he promised to do his best to help get women the vote, 'because I do think sincerely that the women have always had a logical case, and they have now got behind them a great popular demand among women'. Now that the movement was no longer restricted to 'a few extravagant and excitable people', it was becoming more like previous movements for the extension of the (male) franchise. Churchill also referred to the government's struggles over its Licensing Bill, a cause which it is hard to believe was particularly close to his heart. He said: 'When I see the great forces of prejudice and monopoly with which we are confronted, I am ready to say that the women must come into the fighting line and do their share in fighting for the cause of progress.'[22] The following year, however, he told a deputation from the Women's Freedom League (which had split from the WSPU) that their cause had gone backwards on account of the adoption of militant tactics. Although he said that he still supported the cause, he made clear that he was not going to do much to assist it whilst militancy continued.[23]

In 1910 he gave some encouragement to the proponents of the compromise Conciliation Bill – put forward at a point when the WSPU had temporarily suspended militancy – but then backed away at the last minute. The bill would have given the vote to women on the basis of a household franchise, thereby creating a limited number of mainly prosperous new electors and thus probably damaging the Liberal Party. Churchill regarded this as 'a capricious and one-sided addition' to the electorate. However, he did acknowledge 'that there is a proportion of women capable of exercising the Parliamentary franchise, not merely for their own satisfaction, but to the public advantage'. His proposed solution was to 'give a vote to a comparatively small number of women of all classes by means of a series of special franchises ... arising from considerations of property, arising from considerations of wage-earning capacity, or arising from considerations of education'. Alternatively, he was prepared to consider 'a broad measure of adult suffrage, or practically adult suffrage, by which every person should have a vote over the age of twenty-five years'.[24] Churchill had married Clementine Hozier in 1908. On this occasion, reportedly, 'Mrs Winston Churchill was very angry and disappointed in her husband's attitude [as] she understood from him until 2 or 3 days previously that he was going to vote for the Bill.'[25]

There is no need to trace here all the twists and turns of Churchill's subsequent involvement in the Edwardian franchise debate – which did not, of course, result in women getting the parliamentary vote before 1914. Nor is it necessary to review in detail the harsh and abusive treatment meted out to suffragette prisoners, including during Churchill's period as Home Secretary (1910–11).[26] A number of factors are worth noting, however. The suffrage question did not fall out on straightforward party lines. A majority of MPs could happily have agreed in principle that at least some women should get the vote. The issue was, which ones, and on what terms. As we have seen, the answer to that question had implications for the outcome of future elections: a narrow measure of enfranchisement would probably benefit the Conservatives, whereas a wider one would probably help the Liberals. Churchill thereby looked at the problem from the perspective of party advantage just as he would later, from a different point of view, when resisting franchise equality in the 1920s. One the other hand, there was probably more to it than that. He certainly resented his treatment at the hands of the militants.[27] Moreover, Churchill's colleague Charles Masterman may have got it right when he suggested that he was intellectually in favour of votes for women but was instinctively against it.[28] Hence Churchill's repeated payment of lip service to the principle combined with practical resistance to such pre-war schemes of reform as actually wound up on the table.

Churchill was not indifferent to women's welfare. For example, as President of the Board of Trade (1908–10) he legislated to improve conditions in the 'sweated trades', such as tailoring, in which the majority of employees were female. As Minister of Munitions during the latter stages of the First World War he boasted of the Ministry's role as 'pioneers of women's employment in the industrial and even the military field'.[29] However, his view was that social progress for women did not depend on them having the vote. At the time of the 1910 Conciliation Bill he argued: 'The greatest measure of social reform and social benefaction which has ever passed from the point of view of expense to the State is the Old Age Pensions Act [of 1908], passed by a man-made Parliament, who at the very least considered the cause of woman as fully as that of man.'[30] Churchill raised no objection to the Representation of the People Act (1918), which brought about full manhood suffrage and also extended the vote to a substantial group of (mainly propertied) women over 30. But at the general election that same year he made little effort to make a specific appeal to the new female voters. The exception came when he addressed a meeting of 2,500 women electors in his Dundee constituency. According to the *Manchester Guardian*:

> When the heckling began the women fired at Mr. Churchill scores of questions with a volubility, persistence, and skill which far out-distanced anything of the kind their men folk had been accustomed to indulge in at election times [...] Mr. Churchill was evidently not quite equal on all occasions to giving a direct answer to the scores of questions put to him. 'I am only a man, not an encyclopaedia,' he said once, when a demand was made that an answer should be given immediately to some intricate question.

Nevertheless, the meeting passed a resolution in his favour by a huge majority, and he went on to win re-election easily.[31] In spite of the extension of the franchise, he clearly hoped that the House of Commons would remain a male redoubt. When Nancy Astor became the first woman MP to take her seat, in 1919, he did not speak to her for two years, although he knew her well. When she asked him why, he replied that he had hoped to freeze her out: 'When you entered the House of Commons I felt like a woman had entered my bathroom and I'd nothing to protect myself with except a sponge.'[32] He was, of course, by no means the only male parliamentarian to feel that way.

At the elections of 1922 and 1923 Churchill stood as a Liberal and was on both occasions defeated. The advent of the first Labour government presaged his transition back to the Conservative Party, which occurred step by step. The first stage was his candidature for a by-election in the Abbey Division of Westminster, as an independent anti-socialist in opposition to an official Conservative. Churchill later recalled: 'When I fought the Westminster election in the spring of 1924, I declared flatly against any further extension for at least ten years without being conscious of any appreciable loss of support.'[33] He did, however, encounter vocal opposition from some women, not all of them ardent suffragists. At one meeting he 'met with considerable interruption from a rather noisy congregation of Socialists in the gallery of the theatre, from a group of orthodox Conservative women at the back of the stalls, who were insistent on a demand that he should outline his policy as well as denounce Socialism, and from a few feminine enthusiasts for the grant of the franchise to women on the same terms that it is held by men'.[34] According to *The Times*, 'The independent candidate is meeting with definite hostility from women, who attack his record on the extension of the franchise to their sex and distrust his attitude to the grant of the vote to men and women.'[35]

During his final campaign meeting he faced a great deal of interruption, 'the main burden of which consisted of remarks on Gallipoli and taunts by women about "murders in Ireland"'.[36] (The claims about Ireland are explained by Churchill's role, as a minister in the Lloyd George coalition, in the bloody attempts to secure victory in the Anglo-Irish War of 1919–21. At the time, the independent, or Asquithian, Liberal Party had deplored the violence, and its criticisms included appeals directed specifically at women).[37] As Churchill lost to the official Tory by less than fifty votes, it is impossible to help wondering if the women's vote did in fact play some part in his defeat. He might never have won over the suffragists, but he might have done more to woo those Tory women who were being encouraged to regard him as 'a schoolboy playing truant from the Liberal Party'.[38]

It is striking that Churchill made no attempt to couch his anti-socialist appeal in terms of the threat allegedly posed to the family by Labour, a standard Conservative trope.[39] There was an obvious contrast here with Stanley Baldwin, who couched his appeal to women partly in terms of the danger socialism posed to children's religious education and to Christianity in general.[40] (Churchill's religious views were unconventional. In spite of occasional pre-1940 usages, he adopted the language of 'Christian civilization' generally quite late on and to only a limited extent).[41] Philip Williamson has argued that Baldwin, 'In contrast to the often patronising attitudes of other leading politicians […] did not speak to female audiences largely on "women's issues", but assumed that their politics were as serious and wide-ranging as those of men.'[42] Be that as it may, Baldwin nonetheless did talk about women in condescending terms. Justifying the equalisation of the franchise in 1927 (in the presence of Emmeline Pankhurst, no less), he remarked: 'I have perhaps not a complete and profound confidence in any feminine logic, but I have it in feminine instinct.'[43] For his part, Churchill rarely made broad, normative statements about women's capacities.[44] Nor did he indulge in platitudes about women's 'natural conservatism'. Yet he resisted the extension of women's rights. He was thus both less patronising and less progressive than Baldwin, whose leadership he was about to accept.

At the general election of 1924, Churchill stood in the Epping constituency as a 'Constitutionalist', unopposed by any official Conservative. (He formally rejoined the Tory party the following year.) During the election, Baldwin issued the following statement: 'The Unionist Party are in favour of equal political rights for men and women, and desire that the question of the extension of the franchise should, if possible, be settled by agreement. With this in view they would, if returned to power, propose that the matter be referred to a conference of all political parties on the lines of the Ullswater Committee.'[45] According to Churchill's recollection, this had very little impact at the time:

> In the General Election so little was the matter in the public mind that I do not remember having referred to the declaration of the Leader of the Conservative Party and I certainly continued to answer the routine questions of the women's societies by general statements to the effect that 'while the principle of an equal franchise for both sexes was indisputable it was too soon to make a new large expansion of the electorate'. No one seemed the least upset at this.[46]

Churchill's declarations certainly don't appear to have had any adverse effect on his own prospects in Epping (where there were 22,752 male voters and 18,652 female ones).[47] He secured a majority of nearly 10,000. Baldwin offered him the position of Chancellor, which he accepted with alacrity. The question of franchise equality could not be avoided, however, even though Churchill would clearly have liked it to be put into abeyance.

In February 1925, the Cabinet was obliged to consider its attitude, when a Labour MP introduced a private member's bill which would have equalised the franchise for men and women at age 21. Its response was to sidestep the matter for the time being by promising future action. However, in the Commons the Home Secretary, Sir William Joynson-Hicks, appeared to go somewhat beyond the authority granted to him by his colleagues. He promised not merely a conference (in line with Baldwin's pledge) but to definitely legislate for equal voting rights before the end of the Parliament, so that at the next election there would be no difference in the age at which men and women went to the polls. Churchill, however, did not protest at the discrepancy at that time, nor did any other ministers. It was only two years later, when the government began to ponder concrete steps to make good on its promises, that he began to raise difficulties. In a lengthy Cabinet memorandum Churchill conceded that 'the principle of equal rights for men and women […] is bound to come'. He made no argument that the currently un-enfranchised women were not capable of exercising the vote. Nevertheless, he argued that their enfranchisement would be damaging to the Conservative Party's electoral prospects, especially if unaccompanied by Redistribution Bill. Because there was (he said) no great popular demand for an equal franchise the government might, in effect, be able to wriggle out of the commitment that Joynson-Hicks had made.

Churchill put forward a series of complex alternatives to full adult suffrage, including 'the compromise proposal of an equal residential qualification at 25 and an equal occupational qualification at 21 for both sexes'. However, he also raised the possibility of a more positive course: 'to throw ourselves boldly and with as much confidence as we can muster, into universal suffrage with the consequent inseparable Redistribution Bill, both to be made effective before the General Election'.[48] That said, there was no doubt about his basic attitude. The diary of the Conservative MP Victor Cazalet records a visit with Churchill. 'We talked of "Votes for Flappers". He is very strong against it, but fears it will be carried.'[49]

Viscount Cecil, Chancellor of the Duchy of Lancaster, drafted an effective reply to Churchill's memorandum. Part of this was couched in terms of gender assumptions that Churchill had eschewed: 'generally speaking a woman is more conservative than a man because she is less adventurous and more religious, both of which characteristics make against revolution and Bolshevism'. Yet Cecil also deployed some rather more powerful objections to Churchill's arguments. On the one hand, 'the newly enfranchised voter has a tendency to vote for the Party which has bestowed the vote … if we refuse to extend the franchise now and the

Labour Government come in next time and extend it, the majority of the new voters will vote Labour.' On the other, 'in spite of the very ingenious reasoning of the Chancellor, I feel sure that we should suffer greatly in public estimation if we were to go back from the pledge given on the 18th February, 1925'. Furthermore, if there was no great agitation for franchise equality, as Churchill claimed, this was probably partly because the government had promised to enact it: 'the women might urge with some truth that in consequence of that pledge they abstained from agitation and that it is partly due to that abstention that there is now no serious movement of opinion on the question'.[50] Cecil was not a particularly influential minister but on this occasion, at any rate, his views were in line with those of the majority. The Cabinet reaffirmed its policy of an equal franchise at 21.[51]

Churchill's opposition, though undoubtedly sincerely felt, needs to be kept in perspective. True, he was one of nearly 150 Conservative MPs who abstained on the Second Reading of the Representation of the People (Equal Franchise) Bill in 1928.[52] But he had not actually expected a division to take place, and he distanced himself from the 'idiotic' fulminations of Lord Rothermere's *Daily Mail*, which did its best to talk up the significance of the abstentions.[53] Although Churchill, like Rothermere, justified his stance on the franchise more in terms of anti-socialism than anti-feminism, we can also see that the latter placed a much higher priority on the issue than the former did.[54] Compared to many of Churchill's other campaigns – over the Russian civil war, over India, and over appeasement, for example – the Chancellor's actions with respect to the franchise were small beer. It may well be that his arguments about the electoral consequences of equalisation were in fact a blind for a deeper-seated dislike of the advance of women's rights that he did not feel able to articulate openly. Either way, though, he stopped well short of launching a crusade.

When it came to devising his financial plans as Chancellor, there is not much evidence that Churchill thought deeply about how to court the new female elector-ate. An exception was his successful efforts to extend the pre-war system of National Insurance to widows and orphans. Arguably, though, this was the anomaly that demonstrated the rule, insofar as the scheme was the product of a collaboration with Neville Chamberlain, the rather more female-friendly Minister of Health.[55] Further evidence that Churchill did take some account of female voters is his obser-vation, when devising his plans for the reform of local government taxation, that: 'A reduction of the Beer Duty, which would carry far-reaching benefits to the economy of a great number of working-class homes, is not attractive to an electorate which for the first time in world history will comprise a majority of women.'[56] On the other hand, his 1925 budget imposed a duty on imported silk, and he shrugged off accusations that he 'had committed an ineffable meanness in taxing the finery of poor working girls.'[57]

Although the gender dimension of the 1929 election should not be overstated, both main parties did make some attempt to exploit the female vote. One cricket-themed Labour poster portrayed the woman voter as 'The New Umpire' calling batsman Baldwin 'Out!' The well-known 'Conservative Sun-Ray Treatment' poster featured the equal franchise and widows' pensions as two of the warming sunbeams beating down on an appreciative population. Conservative Central Office issued a document to candidates outlining some cautious but mildly progressive suggested replies to questions on women's rights: a copy survives in Churchill's papers.[58] Churchill's election speeches, though, focused mainly on attacking Lloyd George's plans for public works to cure unemployment. He made little attempt to appeal to the (female) domestic consumer, failing even to boast about the abolition of the tea duty in his final budget.[59]

During his 1930s 'wilderness years' Churchill made no particular effort to appeal to women's opinion over questions of appeasement and rearmament. As Gottlieb has noted with respect to the Munich crisis, Churchill appeared to set no great store by the letters (both critical and approving) he received from women voters. She argues: 'We have ample evidence to show that Chamberlain was inspired by the tens of thousands of messages of support, and uniquely moved by those sent by women, whereas Churchill does not appear to have been inordinately flattered by women's adulation or moved to action by their entreaties.'[60] Nevertheless, he was very happy to make use of women contacts if they were able to assist his campaign. The young journalist Shiela Grant Duff recalled meeting him at Chartwell: 'He wanted to see me simply and solely because I had lived for a year in Czechoslovakia and could perhaps give him useful information.'[61]

Churchill was by no means a strict believer in equal opportunities. He did, though, have strong views on gender roles even if he did not often express them. In 1938 he did so in an article on 'Women in War' written at the behest of Emery Reves, his journalistic agent.[62] Churchill began by stating that: 'The idea of women entering the line of battle and fighting in war is revolting to us.' He argued, however, that the tradition of chivalry was under threat, and that inroads were being made upon 'the immunity of women from violence' from two different directions:

> The first is the feminist movement, which claims equal rights for women, and in its course prides itself in stripping them of their privileges. Secondly, the mud-rush of barbarism which is breaking out in so many parts of the world owns no principle but that of lethal force. Thus we see both progressive and reactionary forces luring woman nearer to danger, and exposing them to the retaliation of the enemy.

Interestingly (or perhaps bizarrely) Churchill had no objection to individual women disguising themselves as men in order to fight, because they would not be seen to be doing so *as women*. He was also 'thrilled by the spectacle of a weak woman' (such as Joan of Arc) 'leading and encouraging strong men'. But, even though he conceded that technology had rendered redundant the practical arguments against women fighting, he held a strong, visceral objection to it. By contrast, their participation in munitions work and such-like was acceptable. This line of reasoning drew him into some rare words of praise for Nazi Germany:

> It is very remarkable that the most virile and militaristic nation at the present time – the Germans – have set their faces like flint against using women as fighters. They hold to the broad human principle that the woman's place is in the home and that the male protects her. Their arrangements are perfected to give women plenty to do in making war-stores and munitions.

Churchill concluded the article by observing that the ascendancy of feminist ideas in Britain and the habit of treating men and women equally was an artefact of the circumstance that the country was at peace, was 'highly civilized', and was an island: 'The tests of war would very soon show that the stronger sex would have to do the fighting and the weaker the suffering and weeping'.[63]

Andrew Roberts has argued that 'by the time of the Second World War, Churchill had embraced sexual equality with fervour. [...] far from being a male chauvinist, Winston Churchill should be seen in his proper light, as a doughty proponent of sexual equality so long as there was a war to win'.[64] It is true that, having been appointed to Chamberlain's War Cabinet as First Lord of the Admiralty, he called for 'more than a million women' to 'come boldly forward into our war industry'.[65] Nevertheless, Roberts puts the case much too strongly. As we have seen, Churchill's support for women's involvement in the war effort did not imply a belief in sexual equality. Churchill was willing to pay tribute to women's wartime achievements, and he claimed that 'the bounds of women's activities have been definitely, vastly and permanently enlarged'.[66] At the end of the war, though, he was extremely eager to see women released from Service roles as soon as possible: 'the sooner they are back at their homes the better'.[67] He was pragmatic enough to know that the contribution of women was essential – indeed his daughter Mary served in the Auxiliary Territorial Service – but it seems that he was not wholly comfortable with it.

A Mass-Observation (MO) spot poll of 75 people carried out just before the fall of Chamberlain's government found that Eden was the most popular candidate to replace him as Prime Minister (33 votes) with Churchill as the only other serious contender (22 votes). MO found that 'Eden gains on the women's votes, Churchill being much less popular among women than among men'.[68] Unfortunately, the sample size was too small to be meaningful. Nor, in spite of the wealth of evidence of ordinary people's reactions to Churchill as war-time Prime Minister, is it possible to say with any precision whether responses to him varied on gender lines. Nevertheless, there are some significant clues regarding the popular reaction to Churchill's one significant wartime statement on an issue relating to gender. This was his insistence, in March 1944, that the Commons reverse a vote in favour of equal pay for women teachers. This had come about as a result of an amendment to the Education Bill put down by the Conservative MP Thelma Cazalet-Keir. This was the wartime coalition's only parliamentary defeat – by one vote. Churchill, without discussing the merits of the issue, was adamant that the matter be treated as an issue of confidence. He thus succeeded in persuading (or browbeating) the House into deleting the clause in question, by an overwhelming majority.[69] The Prime Minister was motivated by what he saw as an opportunity for squashing opposition to his government in general, not by any great concern about the matter at hand: 'He was sorry that the issue raised had been on equal pay for women, but the issue in these cases did not much matter and he proposed to rub their noses in it.'[70] Churchill later forgave Cazalet-Keir to the extent of appointing her as Parliamentary Secretary for Education in his short-lived caretaker government. As he did so he told her, chuckling, 'Now, Thelma, no more of that equal pay business.'[71]

According to the Ministry of Information's Home Intelligence Report, the equal pay debate 'stimulated widespread discussion of the question of equal pay [...] Though opinion is divided, support for the principle of equal pay appears to outweigh opposition. Objections are raised on the fear that it might mean either smaller salaries for men or, alternatively, less chance of a job for women.'[72] One MO diarist, staying with her husband in Bishop Auckland, where he was stationed, recorded an argument with a fellow lodger: 'We had a long argument with the Yorkshireman about Parliament & Churchill's dictatorial attitude [...] My husband and I are both furious about it and even my husband's mess, who are on the whole very Conservative, agree that Churchill's conduct over the whole business has amounted to sharp practice. But everyone in this house keeps emphasising that Churchill is the only man who can run the war and what a splendid record he has.'[73] Adelaide Poole, a retired nurse, took a similar view of Churchill's handling of the Commons: 'I hate such bullying, and I find the people I have spoken to round here agree with me.'[74] J. B. Gregory was disturbed by his discussion with a fellow (male) teacher who 'supported Churchill and was against equality in any respect for women'.[75] So views were clearly mixed; although where there was anger with Churchill it seems to have been a result of his high-handed political tactics rather than of strong feelings about the principle of equality.

In July 1945, during the period when the country was awaiting the results of the general election, Churchill remarked: 'I hear the women are for me, but that the men have turned against me.' (When Clementine 'reminded him how bitterly he had opposed the vote being given to women' he acknowledged this was 'Quite true'.)[76] Yet neither he, nor the Conservative Party in general, had made a strong conscious effort to appeal to the female vote. The same, in fact, was true of the Labour Party. The Liberal Party, by contrast, demanded that women receive 'equality of opportunity and status', and Communist candidates emphasised both 'safer motherhood' and equal pay.[77] A further sense of Churchill's thinking at this time can be found in his posthumously published essay *The Dream*. Written in 1947–48, it contains an imagined exchange with his father on the topic of female suffrage. Winston concedes that it has not turned out as badly as he had expected:

> 'You don't allow them in the House of Commons?' he [Lord Randolph] inquired.
> 'Oh, yes. Some of them have even been Ministers. There are not many of them. They have found their level.'
>   'So Female Suffrage has not made much difference?'
>   'Well it has made politicians more mealy-mouthed than in your day. And public meetings are much less fun. You can't say the things you used to'.[78]

Even making allowance for the Churchill's use of irony throughout the piece, this was clearly patronising. Whereas he certainly did tolerate and even encourage the political participation of women he regarded as exceptional, such as Bonham Carter, it seems he expected female MPs to remain few in numbers and circumscribed in their roles. He could tolerate formal equality but did not welcome the notion of substantive equality. In this, of course, he was in line with many of his contemporaries.

Zweiniger-Bargielowska has rightly emphasised that gendered appeals to housewives struggling with post-war austerity played a significant part in the Conservative recovery that led to the party's return to office in 1951.[79] However, it is important not to overstate the ubiquity of this type of discourse within the party's rhetoric. It is also necessary to recognise that Churchill was not the driving force behind it. For example, at the 1950 party conference, Mrs F. Poynter, a delegate from Cardiff, made an impassioned plea on behalf of her fellow housewives about the rising cost of living. Churchill referenced her speech in his: 'there is no doubt that Mrs Poynter made her point'.[80] But, in spite of his general deprecation of rationing and restrictions he dwelt little throughout these years on the disproportionate impact that these phenomena had on women. Certainly, there were exceptions, but his brief remarks on these lines have to be weighed against the enormous mass of his overall output of words.[81] Similarly, the 1950 conference committed itself to the principle of equal pay. (Cazalet-Keir, now outside Parliament, continued to campaign on the issue.) Churchill's final government did make modest progress on this score – but again this was done without obvious input or enthusiasm from Churchill himself.[82]

In conclusion: Bonham Carter's belief that there was 'nothing particularly characteristic or individual' about Churchill's attitude was understandable. She was quite right that he did not often generalise about women. However, this reluctance to 'to roam into the abstract question of the relations between the sexes, their relative capacities and capabilities' was itself noteworthy.[83] It marked him out from many other politicians who wanted to do exactly that. To that extent it reminds us that we should be cautious when generalising about Conservative gender attitudes. Just as there were 'multiple identities of anti-socialism' so there were substantial variations in Tory views of women, reflecting, in part, the wide variety of influences on the party (including Liberal ones).[84] More speculatively, one might suggest that Churchill's disinclination to make normative statements about what he referred to as an 'entire race of women' was partly a product of a collision between his intellectual beliefs and his gut instincts. Arguably, he dressed up his objections to women's suffrage (and its extension) in terms of party calculation precisely because he wanted to avoid revealing the inner convictions about female capacity that fuelled the bitterness of his opposition. In fairness, when his opinions did at times slip out (as in his 'Women in War' article) they were not especially deplorable by the standards of the time, however oddly they may read today. And if he generally kept his views to himself, perhaps he deserves some credit for doing so. The contrast with his racial attitudes is striking. He showed no diffidence whatsoever in asserting white superiority.[85] In comparison, although no gender progressive, Churchill appears to have been conscious that arguments based on male–female biological differences were unlikely to cut much political mustard. He was undoubtedly an anti-feminist, but a semi-closeted one. It is not particularly surprising that his attitude was antediluvian. What is more interesting is that he did not openly glory in it being so.

Notes

1 James Marchant to Violet Bonham Carter, 27 Jan. 1953, MS Bonham Carter 290, Bodleian Library, Oxford.
2 Bonham Carter to Marchant, 28 Jan. 1953, MS Bonham Carter 290.
3 Bonham Carter to Desmond Flower, 5 Feb. 1953, MS Bonham Carter 290. As published, Bonham Carter's chapter carried the title 'Winston Churchill – As I Know Him'. James Marchant (ed.), *Winston Spencer Churchill: Servant of Crown and Commonwealth* (London: Cassell and Co. Ltd, 1954), pp. 147–61.
4 Flower to Bonham Carter, 3 Feb. 1953, MS Bonham Carter 290.
5 Margaret Thatcher, *The Path to Power* (London: HarperCollins, 1995), p. 108.
6 See, notably, Patricia Hollis, *Jennie Lee: A Life* (Oxford: Oxford University Press, 1997), pp. 140–1.
7 'Comedy of Manners', *Daily Mail*, 4 July 1899.
8 Paul Addison, 'Churchill and Women', in Richard Toye (ed.), *Winston Churchill: Politics, Strategy and Statecraft* (London: Bloomsbury, 2017).
9 Paul Addison, *Churchill on the Home Front, 1900–1955* (London: Pimlico, 1993).
10 Mary Soames, *Clementine Churchill* (London: Cassell, 1979). See also Joan Hardwick, *Clementine Churchill: The Private Life of a Public Person* (London: John Murray, 1997), and Helen Jones, '"Let us go Forward Together": Clementine Churchill and the Role of the Personality in Wartime Britain', in Richard Toye and Julie V. Gottlieb (eds), *Making Reputations: Power, Persuasion and the Individual in Modern British Politics* (London: I. B. Tauris, 2005), pp. 109–17.
11 Julie V. Gottlieb, *'Guilty Women', Foreign Policy and Appeasement in Inter-war Britain*, (Basingstoke: Palgrave Macmillan, 2015), chapter 9.
12 David Jarvis, 'Mrs Maggs and Betty: The Conservative Appeal to Women Voters in

the 1920s', *Twentieth Century British History*, 5: 2 (1994), 129–52; Ina Zweiniger-Bargielowska, *Austerity in Britain: Rationing, Controls, and Consumption, 1939–1955* (Oxford: Oxford University Press, 2000).

13 Martin Francis, 'Tears, Tantrums, and Bared Teeth: The Emotional Economy of Three Conservative Prime Ministers, 1951–1963', *Journal of British Studies*, 41 (2002), 354–87. At 358.

14 'The Election Contest at Woodstock', *Birmingham Daily Post*, 1 July 1885.

15 Roy Foster, *Lord Randolph Churchill: A Political Life* (Oxford: Clarendon Press, 1981), p. 216.

16 WSC to Lady Randolph Churchill 23 March 1887 and J.W. Spedding to WSC 10 July 1890, in Randolph S. Churchill (ed.), *Winston S. Churchill Volume I Companion Part I, 1874–1896* (London: Heinemann, 1967), pp. 131, 205; Speech of 26 July 1897. Unless otherwise stated, all Churchill's speeches, statements and radio broadcasts cited are from Robert Rhodes James (ed.), *Winston S. Churchill: His Complete Speeches, 1897–1963* (New York: Chelsea House Publishers/R. R. Bowker Company, 1974).

17 Winston Churchill, *My Early Life: A Roving Commission* (London: Macmillan, 1941 [1930]), p. 16.

18 Addison, *Churchill on the Home Front*, p. 48.

19 A copy of the paly can be found at the Churchill Archives Centre. See also '"The Bill", *The Observer*, 28 June 1914.

20 Addison, *Churchill on the Home Front*, p. 48; HC Deb 16 March 1904 vol 131 cols 1331–68. *Pace* Addison, it was a Resolution, not a Bill, which lay before the House. It passed by 182 to 68.

21 Speech of 5 Jan. 1906.

22 'Women's Suffrage: Mr. Churchill and Progress', *Manchester Guardian*, 16 April 1908.

23 Speech of 18 October 1909.

24 Speech of 12 July 1910.

25 J. H. Lewis diary 16 July 1910, J. H. Lewis Papers, D31, National Library of Wales.

26 See Addison, *Churchill on the Home Front*, pp. 129–39, 161–2; Richard Toye, *Lloyd George and Churchill: Rivals for Greatness* (London: Macmillan, 2007), pp. 76–84.

27 Lord Riddell diary, 6 Feb. 1912, Riddell Papers, MS 62956, f. 79, British Library.

28 Lucy Masterman, *C. F. G. Masterman: A Biography* (London: Nicholson and Watson, 1939), p. 166.

29 Addison, *Churchill on the Home Front*, pp. 77–8, 193.

30 Speech of 12 July 1910.

31 'Mr. Churchill and Women Electors', *Manchester Guardian*, 6 Dec. 1918. 'Heckling', in this context, simply meant a question-and-answer session.

32 BBC radio interview with Nancy Astor, 1956, www.bbc.co.uk/programmes/p01lfw2p (accessed 17 April 2015).

33 Winston Churchill, 'The Franchise Question: Memorandum by the Chancellor of the Exchequer', CP 80 (27), 8 March 1927, The National Archives, Kew, London (henceforth TNA), CAB 24/185.

34 'Abbey Election', *The Times*, 12 March 1924.

35 'Abbey Election', *The Times*, 13 March 1924.

36 'Abbey Election Campaign', *The Times*, 19 March 1924.

37 'An Irish "Reprisal"', (London: Liberal Publication Department, Oct. 1920); 'To Every Woman: Do you like Violence?' (London: Liberal Publication Department, 1921).

38 'Abbey Contest', *The Times*, 14 March 1924.

39 Stuart Ball, *Portrait of a Party: The Conservative Party in Britain 1918–1945* (Oxford: Oxford University Press, 2013), p. 92. It may be noted that Churchill took a liberal attitude to divorce. See his article, 'Marriage and Divorce', *Sunday Dispatch*, 28 Sept. 1941.

40 'Mr. Baldwin's Appeal to Women', *Manchester Guardian*, 27 Oct. 1924.

41 Paul Addison, 'Destiny, History and Providence: The Religion of Winston Churchill', in Michael Bentley (ed.), *Private and Public Doctrine: Essays in British History Presented to Maurice Cowling*, Cambridge; Cambridge University Press, 1993), pp. 236–50; Philip Williamson, 'Christian Conservatives and the Totalitarian Challenge, 1933–40', *English Historical Review*, 115 (2000), 607–42; Richard Toye, *The Roar of the Lion: The Untold Story of Churchill's World War II Speeches* (Oxford: Oxford University Press, 2013), pp. 23, 46.

42 Philip Williamson, *Stanley Baldwin: Conservative Leadership and National Values*, (Cambridge: Cambridge University Press, 1999), p. 221.

43 'Unionist Policy', *The Times*, 28 May 1927.

44 He had, however, done so during his Oldham by-election fight, when he spoke in conventional anti-suffragist terms 'of the charming influence which women were able to indirectly exercise in public affairs'. 'Comedy of Manners', *Daily Mail*, 4 July 1899.

45 The Election', *The Times*, 18 Oct. 1924. As Speaker of the House of Commons, James Lowther (later Viscount Ullswater) chaired the cross-party committee that resulted in the Representation of the People Act (1918).

46 Churchill, 'The Franchise Question', CP 80 (27), 8 March 1927, TNA, CAB 24/185.

47 'Election Campaign', *The Times*, 20 Oct. 1924.

48 Churchill, 'The Franchise Question', CP 80 (27), 8 March 1927, TNA, CAB 24/185.

49 Victor Cazalet diary, 3 April 1927, quoted in Robert Rhodes James, *Victor Cazalet: A Portrait* (London: Hamish Hamilton, 1976), p. 118.

50 Lord Cecil, 'The Franchise Question', CP 85 (27), 11 March 1927, TNA, CAB 24/185.

51 Cabinet meeting of 13 Apr. 1927, Cabinet 27 (27), TNA, CAB 23/54.

52 Clementine told him: 'really as it was bound to go thro' it was naughty of you not to vote – I fear it may cool off some of the Epping Women – young and old'. Clementine Churchill to Winston Churchill, 4 Apr. 1928, in Mary Soames (ed.), *Speaking for Themselves: The Personal Letters of Winston and Clementine Churchill* (London: Doubleday, 1998), p. 318.

53 Winston Churchill to Clementine Churchill, 5 Apr. 1928, in Soames, *Speaking for Themselves*, pp. 319–20.

54 See Adrian Bingham, '"Stop the Flapper Vote Folly": Lord Rothermere, the Daily Mail and the Equalization of the Franchise 1927–8', *Twentieth Century British History*, 13: 1 (2002), 17–37.

55 Graham Stewart, *Burying Caesar: Churchill, Chamberlain and the Battle for the Tory Party* (London: Phoenix, 2000), p. 37.

56 Winston S Churchill, 'Rating Relief. A Plan to Aid Manufacturing and Agricultural producers, and Especially the Basic Producer', CP 8 (28), 20 Jan. 1928, TNA, CAB 24/192/8.

57 Speech of 25 June 1925.

58 'Questions to Parliamentary Candidates General Election, 1929: Women's Rights', Churchill Papers, CHAR 2/166/67–69, Churchill Archives Centre, Cambridge.

59 Another Tory poster, which portrayed a youngish woman drinking tea, urged: 'The Tea-Duty has Gone! Your Duty Remains! Vote Conservative!'

60 Gottlieb, *Guilty Women?*, chapter 9.

61 Shiela Grant Duff, *The Parting of Ways: A Personal Account of the Thirties* (London: Peter Owen, 1982), p. 158.

62 Emery Reves to Winston Churchill, 4 Oct. 1937, Churchill Papers, CHAR 8/554/6.

63 Winston Churchill, 'Women in War', *Strand Magazine*, Feb. 1938, in Michael Wolff (ed.), *The Collected Essays of Sir Winston Churchill Vol. I: Churchill and War* (London: Library of Imperial History, 1976), pp. 380–7.

64 Andrew Roberts, 'Churchill the Wartime Feminist', *Chartwell Bulletin*, No. 48, June 2012, www.winstonchurchill.org/publications/chartwell-bulletin/bulletin-48–jun-2012/churchill-the-wartime-feminist (accessed 21 Apr. 2015).

65 Speech of 27 Jan. 1940.

66 Speech of 28 Sept. 1943.

67 Winston Churchill, 'Man-Power: Note by the Prime Minister', 5 July, 1945, CP (45) 62, TNA, CAB 66/67/12.

68 'Political Crisis Report', Report No. 99, 10 May 1940, Mass-Observation Archive.

69 Speeches of 29 and 30 March 1944.

70 R. A. Butler, note of Apr. 1944, quoted in Addison, *Churchill on the Home Front*, p. 376.

71 Thelma Cazalet-Keir, *From the Wings* (London: The Bodley Head, 1967), p. 123.

72 'Home Intelligence Weekly Report No. 183', 6 April 1944, TNA, INF 1/292.

73 E. Murray diary, 30 March 1944 (MO diarist no. 5380), Mass-Observation Archive.

74 A. R. Poole diary, 2 Apr. 1944 (MO diarist no. 5399), Mass-Observation Archive.

75 J. B. Gregory diary, 31 March 1944 (MO diarist no. 5089), Mass-Observation Archive.

76 Lord Moran, *Winston Churchill: The Struggle for Survival, 1940–1965* (London: Sphere Books, 1968), p. 283.

77 F. W. S. Craig (ed.), British General Election Manifestos 1918–1966, Political Reference Publications, Chichester, 1970, p. 110; R. B. McCallum and Alison Readman, *The British General Election of 1945* (London: Geoffrey Cumberlege/Oxford University Press, 1947), p. 108.

78 Winston S. Churchill, 'The Dream', reproduced in Martin Gilbert, *Winston S. Churchill Vol. VIII: 'Never Despair', 1945–1965* (London: Heinemann, 1988), p. 368.

79 Zweiniger-Bargielowska, *Austerity in Britain*, chapter 5. Interestingly, however, Conservative officials believed that they had 'lost heavily amongst women sympathisers' at the time of the party's narrow defeat in 1950. Public Opinion Research Department, 'Confidential Supplement to Public Opinion Summary No. 14', 13 April 1950, Conservative Party Archive, Bodleian Library, Oxford, CCO 4/3/249.

80 *71st Annual Conference: Blackpool 12–14th October, 1950* (London: National Union of Conservative and Unionist Associations, 1950), pp. 47, 111.

81 Speeches of 21 Apr. 1948 and 7 June 1950.

82 Joni Lovenduski, Pippa Norris and Catriona Burness, 'The Party and Women', in Anthony Seldon and Stuart Ball (eds), *Conservative Century: The Conservative Party Since 1900* (Oxford: Oxford University Press, 1994), pp. 611–35, at 632.

83 Speech of 12 July 1910.

84 On anti-socialism, see David Thackeray, *Conservatism for the Democratic Age: Conservative Cultures and the Challenge of Mass Politics in Early Twentieth Century England* (Manchester: Manchester University Press, 2013), chapter 9.

85 Richard Toye, *Churchill's Empire: The World That Made Him and the World He Made,* (London: Macmillan, 2010).

8

'The statutory woman whose main task was to explore what women … were likely to think': Margaret Thatcher and women's politics in the 1950s and 1960s

Krista Cowman

A prominent question that emerged in the many appraisals of Margaret Thatcher's life that appeared shortly after her death was how to position the United Kingdom's first woman Prime Minister in relation to the women's movement and to feminism. In some ways the question may have seemed unnecessary, given Thatcher's own ambivalent attitude towards both on assuming office. John Campbell's 2003 biography observed how Thatcher had 'determinedly played down the feminist aspects of her victory' on her arrival in Downing Street in May 1979 when, on being asked what both Mrs Pankhurst and her own father would have made of her election, she ignored the invitation to position herself at the end of a century of feminist campaigns to access Parliament and opted only to speak of her father and his influence on her political career, privileging her patriarchal legacy above any broader genealogy of the women's movement.[1]

On other occasions she could be directly hostile to feminism and the women's movement, and many of her contemporaries who offered posthumous assessments of her life made much of her antipathy to both. Douglas Hurd, who served under Thatcher as both Foreign and Home Secretary, told reporters at the *Daily Telegraph* that she 'wasn't a feminist. All that line of argument left her cold.'[2] A number of Thatcher's own later comments, which expressed contempt for the women's movement of the 1960s and 1970s, were invoked in support of an interpretation of her character that emphasised her individualism over any need to make common cause with other women. One phrase in particular, 'I owe nothing to Women's Lib', which the *Observer* quoted her as saying in December 1974, was widely repeated.[3] Equally popular were the words more recently attributed to her by Paul Johnson in *The Spectator* in 2011, 'The feminists hate me, don't they. And I don't blame them. For I hate feminism, it is poison.'[4] Consequently, many feminist commentators who had consistently distanced themselves from Thatcher and Thatcherism were quick to point out the lack of fit between the woman PM and the women's movement. Suggesting that any aspect of Margaret Thatcher's life or career might be read as feminist, concluded Julie Bindel, was 'an insult to the many women who sacrificed their lives to make things better for women, when she was responsible for making them worse'.[5]

Nevertheless, despite the seeming clarity of Thatcher's own words on the subject and the condemnation of prominent feminist writers, other summaries of her life were more concerned with attempting to reclaim the legacy of Britain's first woman prime minister for women more generally, although they found it to be, at best, an uncomfortable fit. 'Margaret Thatcher was a real feminist', the novelist Lionel Shriver declared, before adding somewhat confusingly: 'She did not pursue justice for her gender; women's rights … was clearly a low priority for her. She was out for herself and what she believed in.'[6] Natasha Walter, who was one of the first writers to attempt to define Thatcher as 'a feminist icon' in her book *The New Feminism*, published some fifteen years before the politician's death, said in 2012 that 'nothing I have ever written before or since has brought so much fury on my head', but stood by her original statement based on a belief that a woman prime minister gave all women a sense of possibility while continuing to condemn the politics of Thatcherism.

It is not my intention here to enter into the controversy of whether Margaret Thatcher ought to be viewed as either 'feminist' or 'anti-feminist' on behalf of either side of the argument. Rather, this chapter explores some of the ways in which she chose to engage with women's politics in the earlier part of her career from her election to Parliament in 1959 until the mid-1960s, at a time before post-war British feminism took on a coherent identity through the Women's Liberation Movement and when the younger politician was possibly less careful of her public image. It considers some of the occasions where, in her early years as a candidate and a junior MP, Thatcher could be seen aligning herself with women's issues, taking up women's questions and working with women's groups outside Parliament and the Conservative Party. The chapter concentrates on three distinct but overlapping areas: her pre-election activity and early work in Parliament, her alignment with broader women's politics in the 1960s and her engagement with public feminist commemorations both in the 1960s and surrounding the fiftieth anniversary of the Equal Franchise Act in 1978. Looking at examples of her activity in these three areas reveals a more complex positioning of Margaret Thatcher as a political woman both in terms of her activity and in the way that she chose to position herself within the trajectory of twentieth-century British feminism.

Party political climate

It ought not to be surprising that the twentieth-century Conservative Party provided Britain's first female Prime Minister, given that the party could lay claim to a number of other 'firsts' in its attitude to women members and supporters. The party had relied heavily on the work of its women supporters since the nineteenth century when the Primrose League, a mixed-sex group of Tory supporters, proudly declared itself to be 'the first body to recognise the usefulness of women in politics' and made much of the role played by its women canvassers and speakers.[7] In the early twentieth century a number of other Conservative organisations, affiliated to the party, or broadly aligned with it, built on the precedents set by the League in the nineteenth century to offer further opportunities for political participation by Conservative women. These bodies, which included Conservative and Unionist Women's Franchise Association and the Women's Tariff Reform Association, offered a broad range of experiences for those who wished to carry out political work under a Conservative banner.

This legacy continued after the First World War. The Party first admitted women as equal members in 1918 whereupon it developed a strong internal women's organisation with a large women's department and its Central Women's Advisory Committee (set up in 1919 and incorporated into formal party structures in 1928), which later became the Women's National Advisory Committee. Another separate body for women organisers was wound up after the war when Conservative women were able to become constituency agents on the same terms as men. The national bodies oversaw a network of local organisations for Conservative women through-out the country.[8] The members of these local organisations were more likely to be workers and supporters than candidates, however, and although the Conservative Party did quite well for the number of women MPs it sent to Westminster com-pared to other parties, the number of candidates was often lower than those fielded by the Labour Party.

In keeping with this picture, Margaret Thatcher's early political activism was channelled through the mixed-sex environment of the Oxford University Conservative Association rather than the party's women's organisation. Yet while this initial immersion in mixed-sex student politics may have made the young Thatcher less aware of her gender than some of her political contemporaries, her search for a safe seat quickly brought her personal experience of the problems facing women in politics in the 1950s. At this point she evidently believed in – and valued – the support of other Conservative women. In her the first volume of her autobiography she described Marjorie Maxse, the party's Women's Chairman and Beryl Cook her area agent as 'strong supporters', although Maxse initially described Thatcher in more muted terms, saying that she was 'quite a good candidate' after her selection at Dartford.[9] Sex-based solidarity between Conservative women could not be taken for granted and Thatcher herself found that women were often harder than men to impress at selection committees, especially when it came to asking potential candidates awkward questions about combining personal and political life. Her autobiography, written when her views on the women's movement were more firmly fixed, noted how she

> used to describe how I had found it possible to be a professional woman and a mother by organizing my time properly. What I resented, however, was that beneath some of

the criticism I detected a feeling that the House of Commons was not really the right place for a woman anyway. Perhaps some of the men … entertained this prejudice, but I found then and later that it was the women who came nearest to expressing it openly. Not for the first time the simplistic left-wing concept of 'sex discrimination' had got it all wrong.[10]

This lack of obvious support from a broader Conservative women's organisation may have discouraged the young candidate from identifying herself too closely with it, but it did not preclude her from attempting to create specific appeals based on gender rather than party concerns. Before she was elected in 1955 coverage of her two campaigns at Dartford then Finchley drew attention to both her youth and her gender. By her own admission, being 'the youngest woman candidate fighting the 1950 campaign' made her 'an obvious subject for comment' and she was 'asked to write about the role of women in politics'.[11] At this point in her career she was more than happy to do so, albeit with a somewhat ambiguous approach to the issue. In an article 'The Youngest Woman Candidate Calls to Women' published in *The Evening Post* in January 1950 she confusingly warned against separating 'political affairs into those that concerned men and those that concern women' but at the same time called for 'more women in the House … to see that women's rights are adequately defended'. In the article, Thatcher offered a Conservative slant on a number of issues identified as being of particular concern to women including housing, shopping and rationing and closed by noting that as there were a million more women voters than men, women had a 'special responsibility' at the ballot box and that 'all parties are wanting to attract more women'. Nevertheless, the piece also singled out Labour's Edith Summerskill at the Ministry of Food for particular attack, suggesting that sexual solidarity ought not to overcome political differences.

Two years later, Thatcher wrote a further piece about women's role in public life couched in more general terms. In this article, which appeared in the *Sunday Graphic*, published as a series to mark the accession of Queen Elizabeth II in 1952, Thatcher cited the achievements of a number of notable women including Caroline Haslett, Rose Heilbron and Barbara Ward before calling for 'more and more women at Westminster, and in the highest places too … Why not a woman Chancellor – or Foreign Secretary?'[12] Party made less appearance here, with the focus being entirely on women's abilities and the need for them to be greater evidenced in public life, regardless of their political affiliation.

Conditions in Parliament

Such vacillations between applauding the presence of women as women and privileging party above gender were commonplace in the writing and work of early women MPs. Women were few in number in the House of Commons, although it is important to remember that they were not entirely alone. In *The Iron Lady,*

Phyllida Law's cinematographic portrayal of Margaret Thatcher's life, much is made of her first experiences of the House of Commons. In early scenes, Law emphasises her subject's physical isolation in that environment as a means of suggesting her exceptionalism in the world of public politics. Thus we see Thatcher entering the House as a tiny figure, physically overwhelmed by the vaulted Pugin interior, being denied entry to the bustling, clubbable male spaces and directed instead to the Lady Members' Room, a dark space, empty save for a chair and ironing board. The next two scenes show her in the lobby and debating chamber, a sole (and small) woman in a blue hat, overwhelmed by a sea of men in dark suits. While these images play to good dramatic effect in the film, they nevertheless sit somewhat at odds with the reality. In her own account of this time, Thatcher described the Palace of Westminster as 'a bewildering labyrinth of corridors to the uninitiated. It was some time before I could find my way with ease around it', but she also recalled some 'modestly appointed rooms set apart for the twenty-five women Members – the "Lady Members' Rooms" – where I would find a desk to work at'.[13] The precise figure for women MPs that she mentions here is significant.

The number of women in the House of Commons had grown at a slow pace since Nancy Astor took her seat, rising from one in 1919 to fifteen in 1931, falling back to nine in 1935 then up to twenty-four in 1945, twenty-one in 1950, twenty-four in 1955 and twenty-five in 1959.[14] So, while the number of women who were elected remained extremely small in comparison to the numbers of men, and the general election of 1959 saw a slight fall in the number of women candidates – eighty-one down from ninety-two in 1955 – the slight rise in their success with twenty-five women (twelve Conservative and thirteen Labour) elected, one more than at the previous election, meant that when Margaret Thatcher entered the House she did so alongside the largest intake of women MPs to date. Some of the women returned in 1959 were highly knowledgeable parliamentarians whose experiences dated back to an era when women MPs were extremely rare and still seen as daringly novel. Megan Lloyd George and Jennie Lee were both returned to Parliament in 1929 at the first general election in which women could vote on equal terms to men, although they had not served continuously. Irene Ward and Edith Summerskill had both been in Parliament since before the Second World War, elected in 1931 and 1938 respectively. Only three of the women who were returned in 1959, Margaret Thatcher, her fellow Conservative Betty Harvie Anderson and Labour MP Judith Hart were entirely new to the House of Commons.

The comparatively small number of new women MPs in the 1959 intake, and the larger number of women in the House in comparison with previous Parliaments are significant in that they offered the young Margaret Thatcher a different political network from those with which she was familiar outside of Westminster. It is true that there was never a clear consensus among mid-twentieth-century women MPs as to how far their loyalties to each other lay – if indeed they admitted to having them. Some women MPs such as Nancy Astor were sympathetic to cross-party work by women and attempted to form a solid gender-based block on certain issues. Most, however, were more inclined to agree with Eleanor Rathbone's summary that 'a woman's party is not possible because of politics'.[15] Nevertheless, as Brian Harrison's study of the work of women MPs up to 1945 has pointed out, the gendered spatial arrangements of the Palace of Westminster which continued to exclude women from a number of its bars and many other common areas long after they had been admitted as elected Members of Parliament combined to promote a certain level of solidarity among the numbers of women who shared the facilities of the Lady Members' Room, regardless of party.[16] By the 1950s the space provided for women in Parliament had not grown significantly since the moment when a partition was hastily put up to make a space for Nancy Astor, the first woman to take up her seat, in 1919. The Lady Members' room – described by Labour MP Leah Manning as 'a dank dark dungeon without even a toilet of our own, and a wash-basin with a jug of water and a pail underneath' also contained desks and a telephone and served as both work and social space for all women MPs.[17] Slightly improved accommodation was provided in 1945, which – as shown in Phyllida Law's film to somewhat comic effect – did contain an ironing board, an essential piece of equipment for women who often rushed straight to political functions after lengthy Commons sittings and had nowhere else to change.

For many women MPs the shared space of the Lady Members' Room gave rise to some surprising alliances. Shirley Williams's autobiography, while highly critical of the policies, activities and personal style of Margaret Thatcher, recorded one unexpected incident that took place there. During one debate when she found herself in the middle of extremely hostile questioning during her tenure as Secretary of State for Prices and Consumer Protection, Williams turned and noticed out of the corner of her eye

> a figure behind the Speakers' Chair intently watching my performance. It was Margaret Thatcher … When my ordeal was finished, I retreated to the Lady Members' Room where she was ironing a dress. 'You did well', she said. 'After all, we can't let them get the better of us'.[18]

Even Barbara Castle, another co-inhabitant of the Lady Members Room whose politics were consistently at odds with Margaret Thatcher's managed some words of praise in her own autobiography for the latter's 'genuine … charm and courtesy' with her Parliamentary colleagues.[19] Squeezed out of the broader spaces of Westminster and still partly defined by their novelty, women MPs would often end up supporting each other despite their well-articulated party differences.

Broader cross-party campaigning

The comparatively small numbers of women in Parliament, and their forced reliance on shared provisions such as the Lady Members' Room encouraged limited gender-based solidarities across party lines in Parliament. However, in the 1950s and early 1960s, such gender-based solidarities could spread beyond the boundaries of Westminster. Although these decades came before the emergence and cohesion of the so-called 'second wave' of British feminism characterised by the Women's Liberation Movement (WLM), numerous studies have now demonstrated that the mid-twentieth-century period separating women's franchise campaigns from the first stirrings of the WLM in the 1960s were not devoid of feminist activity. Work by Caitriona Beaumont, Pat Thane, Cheryl Law, Maggie Andrews and others attests to the statement of veteran feminist Hazel Hunkins Hallinan that there had 'always been a woman's movement this century', and that the two highly visible peaks of the suffrage and Women's Liberation movements were not separated by a moribund trough of feminist lethargy. [20]

Sometimes activism had to be looked for in different places, however, and a good deal of work was done by organisations that did not necessarily self-identify as feminist. Groups such as the Women's Institute, Mothers' Union and Townswomen's Guild were among those actively campaigning to improve women's day-to-day lives in a number of ways, while not acknowledging their activity either as feminist or as part of a wider campaign.[21] There was also activity beyond the formal boundaries of national organisations and their regional branches. Recent work – much of it still ongoing – in urban history has begun to recognise the important – and sometimes dominant – role played by women in a number of local campaigns concerned with control over the immediate environment, especially those in relation to play spaces and local traffic control.[22] This is not entirely surprising – decades of research into women's participation in late nineteenth-and early twentieth-century politics has emphasised importance of the neighbourhood & the local to this.[23] In the mid-twentieth century as the urban landscape changed, women's involvement in creating this – in issues such as housing, play and child safety – now become highly political.

It is through the overlapping areas of better housing and improved play provision that Margaret Thatcher can first be seen to be connecting her work as an MP to a wider women's movement after her election in the 1950s. These were issues that had long preoccupied a number of women's groups. Indeed, as far back as the immediate aftermath of the First World War, the Women's Housing Sub-Committee, a group set up by the Ministry of Reconstruction to consider what the best form of new housing might look like when seen 'from a housewife's point of view', considered the provision of play space in its report which also called for a number of improvements in housing to enable women to achieve their full potential as new citizens.[24] After the Second World War the question of play and its impact on women's lives was again associated with new housing provision, particularly with a newer trend to high-rise living, which saw families moved out of traditional terraced streets to larger estates, often situated some way from existing parks and playgrounds. A Government report on the issue in 1952 noted that 'the need most keenly felt by mothers in blocks of flats is 'somewhere safe for the children to play', and recommended that playgrounds should be 'a first call on the available space round flats'.[25]

Margaret Willis, a sociologist employed by the London County Council Architect's Department, published a report on *Living in High Flats* in 1955. Although the report noted that many residents were appreciative of the height, space and views that high flats offered, it went on to query their suitability as an environment for young children.[26] As local authorities throughout the country increasingly looked to high-rise building as the solution to the post-war housing crisis, worry about the impact of such environments on children increased. In 1961, the Joseph Rowntree Trust responded to concerns raised by the Women Public Health Officers' Association regarding 'the well-being of the children and of their harassed mothers' living in high flats.[27] High flats here were defined as being of five or more storeys, although some commentators considered that three should be the limit.[28] The sociologist Joan Maizels was commissioned to undertake research in London supplemented by some investigations in Liverpool and Birmingham.[29] Interviews were carried out with residents living on the fifth floor and above and focused on families with children aged between 2 and 5 (i.e. pre-school children). Maizels's work was overseen by a small voluntary committee of politicians and experts. Eirene White, Labour MP for East Flint, was chosen to chair the committee. She invited Lady Allen of Hurtwood, widow of Independent Labour Party leader Clifford Allen, who was a landscape architect and prominent campaigner for radical children's play spaces such as adventure playgrounds, to join in.[30] Other members were Dr David Morris, a paediatrician, Miss Swift from the Women Public Health Officers' Association, Mary Sutherland (recently retired as the Labour Party's Chief Woman Officer) and Margaret Thatcher. Hence most of the committee members had a long-standing interest in the welfare of women, or children, or both, and many approached this from an avowedly feminist perspective. The committee oversaw production of the final project report, *Two to Five in High Flats*, which was published by the Housing Centre in 1961, a decade before the publication of Pearl Jephcott's better-known survey of Glasgow estate life, *Homes in High Flats*, work for which was also funded by Rowntree.[31]

The tone and findings of the report, with which Margaret Thatcher was closely involved, reflected those of a number of similar inquiries from the 1950s and 1960s. *Two to Five* was highly woman-centred in both its approach and its conclusion. A total of 206 mothers were interviewed about their general theme of raising children in flats, with only seven fathers contributing. Consequently, the report gave a large proportion of space to the voices of its female interviewees. It expressed concern about the impact of high living, not just on young children, but also on their mothers. Unlike other contemporary studies (for example Lindy Burton's investigations into child safety which posited maternal stress and the early end of breastfeeding as key factors rendering children more susceptible to road accidents) mothers were not blamed for the situation or for their children's problems.[32] Rather they were described as being in urgent need of help from local authorities and national government. The report's recommendations were broad. There were specific suggestions for the design of flats and their location, organisation and arrangement of play facilities but also wider observations such as the statement that, 'Enlightened social policies should make efforts to discover human needs rather than to assume that the absence of demand reflects the absence of need.' The committee recommended that the official standards set by the Ministry of Housing and local government should be amended in include 'standards of play space and equipment' for young children in high flats, and that the ministry should pay special attention to such provision when approving planning applications.

Margaret Thatcher and Eirene White launched the report together at a joint press conference at the House of Commons in May 1961. This event emphasised the needs of children and the anxiety of their mothers, which increased, according to Eirene White, 'the higher you go in flats'. Children had 'insufficient exercise ... insufficient air, and ... lacked a vital factor in their development, that of mixing with other children'. Mrs Thatcher added that currently '94 local authorities were building high flats, and once the flats were up there was often nothing they could do', suggesting the need for intervention at the planning stage. The report was subsequently sent to the Ministers of Housing, Education and Health.

Margaret Thatcher did not pursue the matter of prioritising women's needs in urban design after the report was launched, although the question of safe play became an increasingly pressing one for women into the 1960s. Indeed, her autobiography says little about her choice to involve herself with the project initially or about the work of the committee beyond recalling her participation at the launch of the report, with a retrospective summary of post-war housing. 'I have a press conference with Eirene White, the Labour MP for East Flint, on the lack of provision being made for the needs of pre-school children in high-rise flats, a topic of growing concern at this time when so many of these badly designed monstrosities were being erected.' [33] Nevertheless, her participation on the committee offers one instance in which her politics can be seen to demonstrate a motivation that rested more closely on gender than on party politics and a rare instance of her working directly on an issue with other women across party lines.

Although much more attention has subsequently been given to Pearl Jephcott's work on this subject, the earlier inquiry carried out by Maizels was by no means insignificant.[34] Its largely female team of researchers and project committee had come together to produce what the architectural historian Roy Kozlovsky classed as one of the first challenges to the popular post-war modernist approaches to housing 'by female critics who were more attuned to the everyday experiences of women and children'.[35] *Two to Five in High Flats* was positively received by a number of radical groups, and featured in two consecutive issues of *Anarchy* although the journal made no explicit mention of the contributions of either Thatcher or White.[36]

Margaret Thatcher's own brief description of her involvement in *The Path to Power* offered little by way of explanation for her involvement other than noting that it was one way in which she 'had remained to a modest degree in the public eye' in her early parliamentary career.[37] Yet this committee, with its predominantly leftward-leaning membership and its strong 'condemnation of the architects, and planners, and … the local authorities' was not an obviously uncontroversial choice, in that it went against much of the prevalent planning orthodoxies of its time.[38]

Feminist genealogies

Despite her later dismissal of the women's movement, in her work towards *Two to Five in High Flats*, Margaret Thatcher had herself joined with other women across party lines in a campaign that was specifically aimed at improving the lives of working-class women and their children. At the same time, there were occasions when Margaret Thatcher was happy to align herself with the public legacy of the suffragette movement in ways which make her later unwillingness to connect herself to Mrs Pankhurst appear a less obvious course of action for her to take.

In 1961, she accepted an invitation to address a meeting of Finchley Women Citizens' Association as it celebrated its 50th anniversary. The first Women Citizens' Association had been established by Eleanor Rathbone in Liverpool in 1911. Rathbone, a strong believer in party political independence who was herself later elected as an independent woman MP, hoped that her Municipal Women's Association would interest municipal women voters in demanding the parliamentary vote and at the same time would provide a forum where women might become educated in questions of politics and the responsibilities of citizenship.[39] The associations flourished across Britain after the First World War and many remained active through the 1950s and early 1960s, crediting themselves with influencing a number of legislative changes including cervical screening, the appointment of women police and the right of married women to retain their own nationality.[40] Thus they were clearly identified as feminist bodies, with a legacy stretching back to the suffrage movement. Margaret Thatcher's speech acknowledged the importance of several key figures in feminist history (including John Stuart Mill and Frederick Pethick-Lawrence) and paid tribute to earlier women MPs, recognising that those of the 1960s owed 'a tremendous lot to those women who first got into the House. They were not a docile lot.[41] She then went on to speak of her hopes for more women (and especially married women) in prominent positions in the future, and how this might be achieved through improving education and thus bringing 'an end to the deplorable phrase "why educate her? – she's going to get married anyway."' [42] Accepting an invitation from the WCA branch in her constituency as it celebrated a key anniversary may have been a pragmatic move on the part of an ambitious woman MP. Nevertheless, in the content of her speech, Margaret Thatcher chose to place herself firmly within a feminist trajectory where non-'docile' (e.g. direct) action by women had led to the earlier gains on which her generation built.

Other connections made by Margaret Thatcher in the 1960s were potentially more controversial, and less easily explained away through constituency connections. One example is her support for the Suffragette Fellowship, made all the more surprising by her later attempts to publicly distance herself from attempts to place her within a suffragette legacy. The Suffragette Fellowship was formed in 1926 with the specific aim of preserving and perpetuating knowledge of the contribution of the militant wing of the suffrage movement towards winning the vote.[43] As a report in its second newsletter in December 1936 explained, it aimed to 'correct all false or damaging stories which may be circulated, not only about the Militant Movement, but of the women who took part in the Militant Movement. In this way the Fellowship hopes to hand down to posterity a true and accurate account of the Militant Movement and its leaders.'[44] The Fellowship feared that what it saw as the direct connection between militancy and the achievement of the vote might be lost in public memory and worked tirelessly to prevent this. The Fellowship's later aim to expand its membership to a new generation of women without first-hand experience of the militant campaign, and thus to develop more of a campaigning edge, was not ultimately successful, but it did involve itself in a number of campaigns in the 1940s and 1950s, including controversially heading up public condemnation of the then Princess Elizabeth's decision to use the word 'obey' in her marriage to Philip Mountbatten.[45]

The Fellowship led on numerous commemorations of key feminist anniversaries such as the granting of equal votes for women (1958, 1968 and 1978) Prisoners' Day (commemorating the first arrests of Annie Kenney and Christabel Pankhurst in October 1905) and Mrs Pankhurst's birthday in July. These all received press attention, especially during the decadal commemorations when prominent suffragettes were in demand by newspapers, television and radio. In 1966, Margaret Thatcher aligned herself directly with the Fellowship issuing invitations to a memorial meeting for one of its members, Theresa Garnett, who died in May. Although Garnett had eventually left the Women's Social and Political Union (WSPU) as militancy escalated from 1911, it was as the suffragette who had attacked Winston Churchill with a dog-whip in Bristol that she was best remembered, an incident which was recalled with irony at the memorial meeting as Churchill himself later signed an approbatory mention in dispatches for Garnett's work as a nurse during the First World War.[46] The memorial was held in June at the House of Commons, where members of the Suffragette Fellowship and the International Alliance of Women with which Garnett had worked in her later years, joined together to pay 'tribute to her work and memory'.[47]

Margaret Thatcher made no mention of her role in putting together this event in her autobiography, and no record of what she may have said there is currently available in the catalogue of her archives. Although she had been a key figure during the militant campaign and remained active in the Suffragette Fellowship and the Women's Freedom League into the 1960s, Garnett was not sufficiently well known in later years for her death to attract much by way of press attention. Nonetheless, it is difficult to see Thatcher's participation in this event as naive or accidental, especially given that she aligned herself with the Fellowship again in the much higher-profile events arranged to celebrate the fiftieth anniversary of the Equal Franchise Act in July 1978. Although the Fellowship had by this point largely ceased its operations following the death of many of its members, it was the militant memory it originated which predominated in public events. Members of the *Spare Rib* collective who joined the official celebrations attended the first part of the official celebrations at Victoria Gardens dressed in Suffragette (i.e. [WSPU]) colours.[48] The few surviving suffragette prisoners who attended, including Connie Lewcock and Leonora Cohen, proudly displayed their prison medals. Margaret Thatcher, as leader of the Opposition, was one of the speakers at a Gala Dinner at Westminster Hall, opening an exhibition commemorating the equal franchise jubilee.[49] David Doughan, who as the librarian of the (then) Fawcett Library had been a key figure in organising the exhibition, took a somewhat cynical view of Thatcher's participation, saying that in following Prime Minister Jim Callaghan she 'demonstrated that she had at least heard of Elizabeth Garrett Anderson, Emily Davies and Elizabeth Garrett Fawcett' unlike the first speaker.[50]

The fiftieth anniversary celebrations took place within the context of a wider feminist movement in Britain than those of previous years. They were not without controversy. Speeches at Victorian Gardens (where Margaret Thatcher did not participate) were interrupted by hecklers including the group from *Spare Rib* who felt that the celebrations overlooked the large amount of work still to be done before women gained equality.[51] Special anger was unleashed on Conservative MP Sally Oppenheim who reminded the crowd that suffragettes had been noted for their dignity.[52] (*Spare Rib* later reported that one ex-militant, Jessie Stephens, recalled being pelted with 'a handful of dried mackerel – so much for respect, Sally!', suggesting that the irony of these remarks were not lost on all of the audience). Margaret Thatcher avoided such direct confrontation with protesters in the evening (although there were pickets outside, the formal ticketing arrangements made for a more sedate gathering) but did not avoid all controversy, noting in her speech her personal regret that Winston Churchill had been provided such consistently strong opposition to women's votes.[53] Commenting on the event, the *Daily Mail* described the participation of the woman 'whom many hope to see as the first woman Prime Minister' was 'a proper celebration of 50 years'.[54] Thatcher herself drew an oblique parallel with her own situation, noting that while 'at the height of the Suffragette movement women chained themselves to the railings outside Number Ten Downing Street' they were no longer 'content to be outside looking in', thus placing herself firmly within the history of the suffragette movement and its direct actions.[55]

Conclusions

As the introduction to this chapter suggests it has not been my intention to add to attempts to position Margaret Thatcher awkwardly within the women's movement as a feminist, iconographic or otherwise. Nevertheless, when the activities of her early decades in politics, particularly before her election as Leader of the Opposition are examined it is not difficult to find instances of her working in some unexpected places, or presenting general arguments about the need for more women, regardless of party, in public life. These appear surprising when viewed through the prism of her later career when she was less keen to promote women, notably to her own Cabinet. The recent biographical representation of her earlier political work in *The Iron Lady* has been less than helpful in encouraging a more complex approach to her politics, as it has played up the individualistic aspects of her career against any attempts at collaboration with other women across party lines. Yet this chapter offers some examples of instances where Thatcher did work collectively with other women, often on unexpected causes, such as the campaign for playground provision in high flats that was seen as extremely radical in its time.

There are also examples where Mrs Thatcher can be seen as clearly opting to place herself within a trajectory of events that could be described as comprising a feminist genealogy, linking with the Suffragette Fellowship or participating in celebrations of women's votes. Such celebrations were always cross-party affairs with women MPs from all sides of the House of Commons joining together to mark their achievements to date.[56] Many of those who wrote appraisals of Thatcher's political career in the immediate aftermath of her death were quick to note her tendency to 'pull the ladder of equal opportunity up behind her' after becoming Prime Minister.[57] This may well have been true. Shirley Williams recalled being told by Lynda Walker, Minister for Overseas Development, how her failure to be appointed to a Cabinet position was best explained by the fact that she didn't believe 'Margaret much cares for girls around her', which suggested that the first woman Prime Minister very quickly forgot her concern at the lack of support she had received from other political women during her search for a safe seat.[58] Nonetheless, while in opposition her occasional public alignment with suffrage campaigners and commemorations demonstrates a level of awareness on her part that there *was* a ladder, and one that others had scaled before her.

In the political context of the 1950s and early 1960s, Margaret Thatcher's attitudes to women's organisations and to political questions that could be defined as women's issues were complex and sometimes contradictory. They are also more difficult to trace than some of her other political interests. Much of her very early career is unrecorded in her own archive, and her memoirs are much more forthcoming on internal party struggles than on broader movements. Her involvement in external women's campaigns or with groups such as the Suffragette Fellowship is more likely to be recorded in the archives of particular campaigns or organisations rather than in her own papers, with much potential for further research on these issues. Nevertheless, such instances of a more woman-centred approach to her political work as can currently be traced suggest that a simplistic division of her politics into 'pro' or 'anti' feminist is no longer sufficient. In the much less equal world of 1950s politics alliances with other women were arguably more necessary and certainly more apparent among her interests than in later years.

Notes

1 John Campbell, *Margaret Thatcher: The Iron Lady* (London: Jonathan Cape, 2003), p. 1.
2 Matthew Holehouse, 'A Pioneering Woman with No Time for Feminists', *Daily Telegraph*, 8 April 2013.
3 'Sayings of the Week', *The Observer*, 1 December 1974. The occasion and circumstances under which Margaret Thatcher spoke these words have not been traced although the quotation appeared in numerous commentaries on her life, for example, Jessica Elgot, 'Margaret Thatcher Dead: Was the Iron Lady A Feminist?' *Huffington Post UK*, 8 April 2013; Helen Lewis, 'Margaret Thatcher: Feminist Icon?' *New Statesman*, 8 April 2013.
4 Paul Johnson, 'Failure of the Feminists', *Spectator*, 12 March 2011.
5 Julie Bindel, 'To Call Margaret Thatcher a Feminist is an Insult', ITV news report 9 April 2013, www.itv.com/news/2013–04–09/to-call-margaret-thatcher-a-feminist-is-an-insult (accessed 8 January 2016). See also Beatrix Campbell, 'Margaret Thatcher is Dead', www.beatrixcampbell.co.uk 9 April 2013 (accessed 10 January 2016).
6 Lionel Shriver, 'Muscular Feminism', www.slate.com 8 April 2013 (accessed 12 January 2016).
7 The phrase appears repeatedly in the League's paper *The Primrose League Gazette*. On its history see Janet Robb, *The Primrose League* (New York: Columbia University Press, 1942); Martin Pugh, *The Tories and the People, 1880–1935* (Oxford: Blackwell, 1985).
8 These changes are summarised in Krista Cowman, *Women in British Politics 1689–1979* (London: Palgrave 2010), pp. 134–7.
9 Margaret Thatcher, *The Path To Power* (London: HarperCollins, 1985), p. 65; Note of Interview with Miss Maxse, 1 February 1949, Margaret Thatcher Foundation1949 February 1.
10 Thatcher, *The Path To Power*, p. 94.
11 *Ibid.*, p. 72.
12 Margaret Thatcher, 'Wake up Women!' *Sunday Graphic*, 17 February 1952.
13 Thatcher, *The Path to Power*, p. 108.
14 Figures from Pamela Brookes, *Women at Westminster* (London: Peter Davis, 1967).
15 Elizabeth Vallance, *Women in the House* (London: Athlone Press, 1979), p. 83.
16 Harrison, 'Women in a Men's House: The Women MPs, 1919–1945', *Historical Journal*, 29: 3 (1986), 623–54, p. 634.
17 Leah Manning, *A Life for Education, an Autobiography* (London: Victor Gollancz, 1970), p. 91.
18 Shirley Williams, *Climbing the Bookshelves* (London: Virago, 2009), p. 148.
19 Barbara Castle, *Fighting All the Way* (London: Macmillan, 1993), p. 442.
20 Caitriona Beaumont, *Housewives and Citizens: Domesticity and the Women's Movement*

in England, 1928–1964 (Manchester: Manchester University Press, 2013); Pat Thane, 'Women in Public Life in Britain since 1918', *Historical Research* 76: 192 (2003), 268–85; Cheryl Law, *Suffrage and Power* (London: I. B. Tauris, 1997); Johanna Alberti, *Beyond Suffrage: Feminists in War and Peace* (Basingstoke: Macmillan, 1989).

21 See in particular Catriona Beaumont, 'Where to Park the Pram? Voluntary Women's Organisations, Citizenship and the Campaign for Better Housing in England, 1928–1945', *Women's History Review*, 22: 1 (2013), 75–96; Judy Giles, *The Parlour and the Suburb: Domestic Identity, Femininity and the Suburb* (Oxford: Berg, 2004).

22 See for example Krista Cowman, 'Play Streets: Women, Children and the Problem of Urban Traffic, 1930–1970', *Social History*, 42 (2017), 233–56; Simon Gunn, 'Ring Road: Birmingham and the Collapse of the Motor City Ideal in the 1970s', *Historical Journal* (2017).

23 This connection is explored in June Hannam, 'Making Areas Strong for Socialism and Peace: Labour Women and Radical Politics in Bristol, 1906–1939', in K. Cowman and I. Packer (eds), *Radical Cultures and Local Identities* (Newcastle: Cambridge Scholars Press, 2010), pp. 71–94.

24 Krista Cowman, 'From the Housewife's Point of View: Female Citizenship and the Gendered Domestic Interior in Post-First World War Britain, 1918–1928', *English Historical Review*, 130 (2015), 352–83.

25 *Living in Flats: Report of the Sub-Committee of the Central Housing Advisory Committee on Social Needs and Problems of Families Living in Large Blocks of Flats* (London: HMSO, 1952).

26 Margaret Willis, *Living in High Flats*, London County Council Architects' Department, 1955. For different interpretations of her findings see Roy Kozlovsky, *The Architectures of Childhood* (Aldershot: Ashgate, 2013), p. 208; Gavin Weightman, Stephen Huphries, Joanna Mack and John Taylor, *The Making of Modern London* (London: Ebury Press, 2007), p. 461.

27 Joan Maizels, *Two to Five in High Flats: An Enquiry into Play Provision for Children aged Two to Five Years living in High Flats* (London: The Housing Centre, 1961), p. 1.

28 A. Ravetz and R. Turkington, *The Place of Home: English Domestic Environments 1914–2000* (London: Taylor & Francis, 1995), p. 50.

29 A smaller pilot project linked to Maizels's investigation was simultaneously carried out at the London School of Economics under the direction of Peter Townsend.

30 Lady Allen of Hurtwood, *Memoirs of an Uneducated Lady* (London: Thames & Hudson, 1975), p. 246.

31 Pearl Jephcott, *Homes in High Flats: Some of the Human Problems Involve in Multi-Storey Housing* (Edinburgh: Oliver & Boyd, 1971).

32 Lindy Burton, *Vulnerable Children: Three Studies of Children in Conflict* (London: Routledge, 1968), p. 117.

33 Thatcher, *The Path to Power*, p. 117.

34 See, for example, the Leverhulme Trust project 'Housing, Everyday Life & Wellbeing in Glasgow c.1950–1975', led by Professor Lynn Abrams at the University of Glasgow. www.gla.ac.uk/schools/humanities/research/historyresearch/researchprojects/hous-ingandwellbeing (accessed 10 January 2017).

35 Kozlovsky, *Architectures of Childhood*, p. 208.

36 *Anarchy* 7, September 1981, p. 14; *Anarchy* 9, November 1961, pp. 287–8.

37 Thatcher, *Path to Power*, p. 117.

38 Allen, *Memoirs of an Uneducated Lady*, p. 246.

39 See Krista Cowman, *Mrs Brown is a Man and a Brother! Women in Merseyside's Political Organizations, 1890–1920* (Liverpool: Liverpool University Press, 2004), pp. 74–6.

40 National Women Citizens' Association, *National Women Citizens' Association 1918–1968* (London: NWCA, 1968).

41 *Finchley Times*, 17 February 1961.

42 *Ibid.*

43 For the Fellowship's importance in creating – and perpetuating – a particular view of suffrage history see L. E. N. Mayhall, 'Creating the Suffragette Spirit: British Feminism and the Historical Imagination', *Women's History Review* 4 (1995), 319–44.

44 *Calling All Women*, December 1936.

45 *Daily Mail*, 10 October 1947, p. 1.

46 *Daily Mail*, 15 November 1909, p. 9; *Calling All Women*, February 1967.

47 Obituary, 'Theresa Garnett', *International Women's News*, 1967.

48 Editorial, 'Spare Rib looks at 50 Years of Woman's Suffrage', *Spare Rib* 73 (August 1978), pp. 3–4.

49 On this and other celebrations see David Doughan, 'Celebrating 50 Years of Equal Franchise in the United Kingdom: Personal Recollections of the Celebrations in 1978', *Women's History Review* 7: 3 (1998), pp. 419–24.

50 Doughan, 'Celebrating 50 Years', p. 421.

51 See *The Times*, 'Protestors Speak Out at Suffrage Ceremony', 3 July 1978, p. 2; *Daily Mail*, 'Angry Women's Libbers Turn on the Suffragettes', 3 July 1978, p. 3; *Spare Rib*, '50 years [c]on', August 1978, p. 11.

52 Doughan, 'Celebrating 50 Years', p. 423.

53 Margaret Thatcher, 'Speech Celebrating 50th Anniversary of Women's Suffrage', Margaret Thatcher Foundation 1978 July 3 MO.

54 'Fifty Years of Female Voting', *Daily Mail*, 3 July 1978, p. 6.

55 Thatcher, 'Speech Celebrating 50th Anniversary'.

56 See Jean Mann, *Woman in Parliament* (London: Odham, 1962), pp. 50–4.

57 Jenni Murray, 'What did Margaret Thatcher do for Women?' *Guardian*, 9 April 2013.

58 Williams, *Climbing the Bookshelves*, p. 159.

9

Conservatism, gender and the politics of everyday life, 1950s–1980s

Adrian Bingham

In 1967, Eric Nordlinger, a young, well-connected American political scientist, published *The Working Class Tories*, a detailed study of 'English manual workers who vote for the Conservative Party'.[1] Intrigued that one in three working class adults voted against their 'natural' class interests, he explored the place of hierarchy, social status and deference in English political culture, and argued that these voters could be grouped into two categories, 'deferentials' and 'pragmatists'. Explaining the design of his research, Nordlinger admitted that an 'important decision' had to be taken early on 'whether or not to include women in the sample'. Given the relatively modest sample size of 717 working-class respondents, 'it was thought best not to include women', for by doing so, 'the reliability of many of the findings would have been markedly reduced, having had to rely upon half the number of respondents for generalizations about men and women separately'. The author was little troubled by this exclusion, though, because 'there is good reason to suppose that in many instances the women's political attitudes are simply those of their husbands' as reflected in a female mirror'. If women had been included, he concluded, 'the data would probably be much the same as that of the male workers except for a higher frequency of conservative and politically passive attitudes'.[2]

It says much about the political science of the 1960s that such a substantial research project, grounded firmly in the contemporary methodologies of the American academy, could have so complacently ignored half of the working-class population. By that point, a considerable amount of data had been accumulated, both in Britain and in other Western countries, which suggested that women inclined to the right politically.[3] The esteemed American political scientist Seymour Lipset had observed in 1960, for example, that in 'practically every country for which we have data ... women tend to support the conservative parties more than do men'.[4] Gabriel Almond and Sidney Verba likewise noted in their influential 1963 comparative study *Civic Culture* that 'it would appear that women differ from men in their political behaviour only in being somewhat more frequently apathetic, parochial, conservative, and sensitive to the personality, emotional and aesthetic aspects of political life and electoral campaigns'.[5] These political inclinations were frequently assumed to be rooted in innate female character traits and, as such, further study seemed to many to be largely redundant. Such attitudes were not restricted to scholarly circles, of course, but were widely shared by politicians, political commentators and journalists. 'It is a generally accepted fact', wrote a 'special correspondent' of *The Times* during the 1964 election campaign, 'that women tend to vote for the status quo, and a female majority would therefore tend to favour the Conservatives.'[6]

By the 1970s, though, such assumptions were under attack from at least two fronts. First, the resurgence of feminism, and the growing influence of feminist ideas in the academy, led to a more critical approach to the techniques and findings of political science. In 1975 Murray Goot and Elizabeth Reid, two scholars working in Australia, published a devastating critique of existing studies of women's political activity. 'Too often,' they concluded, 'where voting studies have actually looked at women voters, prejudice has posed as analysis and ideology as science.'[7] Generalisations about women, in both political science and political journalism, increasingly had to be substantiated, defended and qualified. Second, from the mid-1970s, polling evidence suggested that the 'gender gap' was narrowing or closing – indeed, it increasingly seemed that younger women were leaning to the Left.[8] Precisely at the time that the Conservative Party elected Margaret Thatcher to be its first female leader, the conventional equation of women with conservatism no longer seemed valid.

The exposure of the methodological limitations and gender-blindness of postwar political and social scientific surveys has led, understandably, to a scholarly reluctance to use their findings to explain the political culture of the period. Nevertheless, there remain distinctive patterns of gendered political behaviour to explain. Data from Gallup polls and the British Election Surveys indicate that between 1945 and the 1970s a significantly higher percentage of women than men voted for the Conservatives, with the gender gap (calculated as the percentage Conservative–Labour lead for women minus the Conservative–Labour lead for men) opening up to as much as 17 per cent at times in 1951 and 1955; it averaged 14 per cent between 1945 and 1955, and 8 per cent between 1959 and 1974.[9] Even when more women voted Labour than Conservative, as in the elections of 1945 and 1966, they remained notably less likely to do so than men. These gender gaps were of real importance, giving, for example, the Conservative Party in the 1951 general election an advantage, distributed evenly across marginal and safe constituencies, of around 1.2 million women's votes when the overall difference between the parties was less than a quarter of a million votes.[10] Without female voters in the electorate, Pippa Norris has observed, it is likely that the Labour Party would have won every general election from 1945 to 1979.[11]

Since the mid-1990s, political scientists and sociologists have tended to draw on later – and apparently more rigorous – data to explain voting trends, highlighting the impact of a variety of demographic, social and cultural factors, including women's greater longevity, differences in workforce participation, educational attainment or religious affiliation and the supposed transition from material to post-material values.[12] Historians such as Ina Zweiniger-Bargielowska and G. E. Maguire, meanwhile, have focused on the strengths of the Conservative machine and the appeal of the party's policies, noting, for example, the integration of large numbers of women into the party organisation, the success of its central communications, particularly on the issue of consumption and living standards, and the attraction of the party's 'feminist agenda', which promised action on matters such as equal pay to improve the position of women.[13] This work has significantly deepened our understanding of the post-war gender gap and the dynamics of Conservative support. Nevertheless, both approaches remain rather distant from, and make numerous assumptions about, the political attitudes and behaviour of ordinary female voters. If the political science literature often pays insufficient attention to the changing historical context, the historical research rarely explores in detail how Conservative policies and political communications were actually received by the public. As Lawrence Black has pointed out, 'Party utterances were rarely known to many voters in such detail as historians can excavate'; we therefore need to do more to understand how political messages resonated with the realities and experiences of everyday life.[14]

This chapter offers a critical analysis of the political and social scientific surveys of the post-war decades to provide some fresh perspectives on the rise and fall of the gender gap in voting patterns. As Mike Savage has argued, early sociological research can provide a useful resource in understanding social change, as long as we take into account some of its assumptions about class, gender and ethnicity, or are prepared to read it against the grain; a number of historians, including Selina Todd, Angela Davis, Jon Lawrence and Laura King and have demonstrated the value of this approach for topics such as affluence, marriage and parenting.[15] It was in 1950 that political scientists in Britain first conducted a sustained study of a specific constituency during a general election campaign, building on the earlier, more anecdotal, research of the survey organisation Mass-Observation in the 1940s.[16]

A number of similar surveys followed, and although they lacked the scale and rigour of the national studies conducted under the auspices of the British Election Survey from 1963, they do provide plenty of suggestive quantitative and qualitative detail for the period in which the gender gap was at its largest. The public prestige of political and social science in these decades ensured, moreover, that these surveys were also important contributions to, and interventions in, contemporary debates about political and social change. As Jon Lawrence has shown, for example, post-war notions of 'affluence' were heavily shaped by sociological research.[17] In the same way, the political science of the 1950s and 1960s had a significant role in informing politicians, activists, pollsters and journalists about the place of gender in political culture.

This chapter aims, therefore, to contribute to the wider project of 'rethinking right-wing women' by examining the period in which female voters in Britain were most inclined to support the Conservative Party, namely the 1950s and 1960s, and then offering reasons why this alignment started to break down in the 1970s and 1980s. It also seeks to further our understanding of the political career of Margaret Thatcher, one of the 'right-wing women' who skilfully adopted, and benefited from, a gendered political language as she rose through the ranks, before finding its power fading when she became leader. The first part of the chapter analyses a number of key surveys into post-war political culture, highlighting in particular the common findings that high politics remained distant from the everyday lives of most voters, and that women, in particular, often felt alienated by, or impatient with, a politics that was still dominated and defined by men. Politics tended to engage voters most directly where it dealt with, and spoke in the language of, everyday life.

The second part of the chapter then examines how the Conservative Party adapted its policy and communications to the key social and cultural changes of the 1950s and 1960s. It suggests that one of the main reasons for the Conservative appeal to women was a plausible and sincere rhetorical invocation of the hard-working, ambitious and consumerist, but still traditionally minded, housewife or part-time worker. This approach helped the party to speak to the aspirations and anxieties of lower middle-class and upper working-class women. This was a rhetoric that Thatcher, in particular, mastered, and used to her advantage. By the 1970s, however, the impact of social change, the emergence of a more pluralistic society, and the impact of feminism, undermined the coherence and plausibility of this unifying language of the housewife. Just as Callum Brown has noted the weakening discursive appeal of traditional Anglican ideas to young women in the 1960s and 1970s, so too the gendered political message of the Conservatives lost much of its resonance.[18] By the time that Margaret Thatcher became Prime Minister in 1979, the language of the housewife often seemed artificial or outdated, and Thatcher's own policies helped to further undermine its purchase.

Before proceeding with the substantive analysis, it is worth offering some cautions and caveats. Any study of gendered differences in political activity or voting behaviour runs the risk of lapsing into rather crude generalisation, if not reproductions of the sorts of stereotypes that were deployed in the period in question. It was, indeed, the tendency to generalise about women, in a way that would have been considered inappropriate or unacceptable with regard to men, that was one of the main markers of the gendered power relations of the era. We must always bear in mind both the many – and, across this period, increasing – similarities in men and women's political attitudes and behaviour, as well as the numerous other identities – class, age, region, occupation, ethnicity – that shaped political responses. Millions of women voted Labour, and in the 1945 and 1966 elections, more did so than vote Conservative; there were, moreover, occasional surveys – such as Trenamen and McQuail's study of a constituency in Leeds in 1959 – that argued that in some places women inclined to the Left rather than the Right.[19] Nevertheless, surveying the evidence as a whole, the extent and consistency of the political disparities between men and women in these post-war decades, as well as the energy with which parties developed specifically gendered approaches, means that we cannot fully understand the political dynamics of the period without attending to them; and it is to this task that the chapter turns.

A gendered political culture? Political and social survey evidence

The limitations of explanations of the 'gender gap' that rely solely on examining policy making and political communication are revealed by even the most cursory look at social survey research. One of the dominant themes of surveys across this period is what David Butler and Donald Stokes in 1969 called 'the remoteness of politics': even if turnout at general elections was fairly high, large swathes of the population did not feel deeply or consistently interested in, engaged with, or knowledgeable about Westminster politics and the machinations of the party struggle.[20] Policy initiatives or shifts in political positioning often took a long time to be recognised by many electors, if they were noticed at all, and the fine details of speeches and manifestos were often lost.

The widespread lack of interest in politics was highlighted by the first sustained social scientific study of a British general election, Mark Benney, A. P. Gray and R. H. Pear's survey *How People Vote*, which focused on the constituency of Greenwich in February 1950.[21] Almost half the respondents described themselves as 'not very interested' in politics (despite the interviewers' expectation that such a response might be avoided as 'self-condemnatory'), a little over a third were 'moderately interested', and about 10 per cent 'very interested'.[22] There were strikingly similar findings in subsequent surveys. A. H. Birch's examination of 'political life' in the Derbyshire town of Glossop, conducted in 1953–54, devoted a whole chapter to the 'politics of the unpolitical' – that is, 'the great majority of the citizens, who do not belong to a party, do not attend political meetings, and rarely make any public declaration of their political beliefs'.[23] Birch found that 56 per cent of his respondents had 'no interest' in politics; 33 per cent were 'moderately interested', and 11 per cent were 'very interested'.[24] Indeed, for Birch, even members of the constituency parties were not necessarily deeply politically engaged: the local parties were 'essentially social organizations whose members turn to political activities only when this is forced on them by national or local elections … The great majority do nothing for their party save pay a subscription, vote for its candidates, and drink an occasional glass of beer in the local club.'[25] Surveys in the 1960s reached similar conclusions. In 1964, Mark Abrams found 15 per cent of respondents to be 'very interested in politics', 37 per cent to be 'fairly interested', and the remaining 48 per cent having only the 'most ephemeral interest'; Bealey, Blondel and McCann, investigating Newcastle in 1964, suggested that: 'Three-quarters of the electors both vote and do not seem to participate otherwise in political activities.'[26]

These results should be interpreted carefully. 'Politics' was defined fairly narrowly, and was taken to refer to the battle of the parties at Westminster, and the related skirmishes in the constituencies, rather than more expansive debates about the distribution of power or resources. Many held firm views about social and economic inequalities, the behaviour of 'bosses', and the operation of the law, but these were not necessarily construed as an 'interest in politics'. The evidence that 'high politics' left many people cold is compelling, however. Politicians were often viewed suspiciously as 'them' rather than us, and party communications were treated with considerable scepticism. A Mass-Observation study of election literature in 1946 observed that the 'overwhelming majority dislike or at least disregard it'; the most common opinion 'is that it is nonsense and not to be taken seriously, that it is just not worth bothering about, a waste of paper'.[27] Mass-Observation reached similar conclusions after the 1950 election, noting that 'those for whom the propaganda is basically prepared are the least likely to come into contact with it, let alone be influenced by it'.[28] Party support, numerous surveys noted, depended on 'deeper feelings than an intellectual appreciation of policy', and were based far more on long-term social and economic factors such as class, age, region and employment status than short-term responses to policy announcements.[29]

These surveys consistently found that women were less interested in, and less knowledgeable, about politics than men. As Goot and Reid highlighted in their 1975 study, such findings were often viewed rather uncritically, and any contrary evidence downplayed. When one survey found that the 'number of wives who reported political conversations with their husbands was very much larger than the number of husbands who reported talking to their wives', the conclusion drawn was that 'men do not feel that they are discussing politics with their wives; they feel they are telling them'.[30] That men and women may have defined politics differently, or discussed it with a different language or register, does not seem to have been considered. In individual households, moreover, gender dynamics could vary significantly. When asked by Mass-Observation in 1950 about his voting preference, one man admitted: 'I really don't know what I am going to vote. It's my wife that tells me all about that, and she isn't in at the moment.'[31]

Nevertheless, the consistent and repeated discovery of different levels of interest between men and women, which, as the political scientist Rosie Campbell notes, is still found in contemporary studies, surely illustrates an actual, rather than imagined, tendency: namely that many women were alienated from, and intimidated by, a political world that had so long been dominated and defined by men, in which female candidates, MPs and leaders remained thin on the ground, and where so-called 'women's issues' were often stereotyped, mocked or marginalised. Even where men and women vote the same way, moreover, there may be what Campbell describes as a 'motivational gender gap', with support being given for different reasons.[32]

A Mass-Observation 'post-mortem', on the 1945 election, for example, found that, 'Large numbers of working women consider politics to be a man's affair and vote as their husbands tell them.'[33] Benney, Grey and Pear, studying the general election campaign five years later, found that while 64 per cent of men were interested in politics, only 38 per cent of women were; this disparity was particularly evident in working-class families. Women were also significantly less likely to know the party or the name of the local MP.[34] The surveys of the 1960s, again, identified similar patterns. In 1964, Mark Abrams found that only 8 per cent of women claimed to be 'very interested' in politics, compared to 21 per cent of men; Bealey, Blondel and McCann likewise observed that, 'Women discuss politics rather less than men … and they are less aware than men of the issues of the General Election.' They noted a difference in political interest between the sexes was 'an assertion which is commonly made on the basis of casual impressions', and concluded that this difference was indeed based in reality. Women, they argued, had 'attitudes of spectators more than that of actors'.[35] In this context, the survey evidence suggests that it was those political issues that connected most with ordinary experience, and which were framed in the language of everyday life, that resonated most with women. Housing, the availability of food and household items, and prices, were repeatedly found to be the most important issues for female respondents in the late 1940s and early 1950s, for example; men were preoccupied with housing and wages too, but rated nationalisation and international affairs highly as well.[36] Other evidence suggest that women, as the primary carers of children, gave a higher priority to educational issues than men.[37]

There was a similar consensus about women's conservatism, which was often situated within a broader framework of social conventionality. Writing in 1956, Benney, Grey and Pear could argue that female voters' inclination to the political right was as widely accepted as their relative lack of interest in politics more broadly: 'That women are more conservative than men, not only in political affiliation and on specific issues, but also in their views on a wide range of social customs, has become a commonplace among survey findings.'[38] Margaret Stacey, in her detailed study of the Oxfordshire town of Banbury, published in 1960, noted: 'The tendency for women to be traditionally minded is one which recurs', and explained this in broad patterns of female socialization:

> A concept of what is appropriate to the female runs from the nursery through education to employment … it is the wife-mother role that stamps women's attitudes above other sectional interests … They are more religious and more conservative in politics. Maintenance of the institution of the family apparently leads them to show more concern about maintaining established institutions generally.[39]

In Glossop, Birch pointed to the role of the Anglican Church as a significant influence on female voters, with 41 per cent of women declaring themselves to be active church members, compared to 27 per cent of men – a striking finding given that men participated more extensively in all other forms of associational culture.[40] The perceived strength of female conservatism was such that Benney, Grey and Pear suggested that the Labour stronghold of Newcastle would become a marginal seat if the electorate were entirely comprised of women.[41] Robert McKenzie and Allan Silver, surveying working-class constituencies in urban England in the late 1960s, found that women over 45 were significantly more likely to vote Conservative than men (with a gender disparity as wide as 17 per cent for those over 65); this was attributed to a greater tendency to be deferential, although the study did offer some of the first evidence that this was less than case for younger women.[42]

Such findings certainly did not go unnoticed within the Conservative Party, which was increasingly attuned to the value of opinion polling in helping to develop strategy. The party's Public Opinion Research Department, established by Central Office in 1947 to enable the party to have better information about the attitudes of the electorate, recognised that women disproportionately voted Conservative, and the reliance on the female vote was still being highlighted internally at the end of the 1960s.[43] Surveying the post-war electoral battles, a Conservative Research Department report observed in 1969 that 'it is only because women have the vote and are both more numerous and more likely to vote Conservative that we have been able to win a General Election during this time'.[44] The acceptance of the belief that these crucial female voters were less politically educated than their male equivalents led to the Women's National Advisory Committee's sub-committee on Party Literature for Women warning Central Office that its propaganda was too complicated for ordinary housewives, and suggested that a female officer be appointed to consider 'how questions would strike women electors'.[45] Given the prejudices that many in the party held, however, such advice risked the party adopting a rather patronising approach. One female activist, writing in the *Conservative Agents' Journal* in January 1966, complained that assumptions about women's lack of political curiosity had become too firmly entrenched, and had not taken account of shifts in the wider culture:

> For a long time it was believed that women were fundamentally uninterested in politics. However true it may have been when women first entered political organisation, it is certainly not true today. Better education and television have combined to make women, particularly the younger ones, comparatively well informed, politically. They are less inclined to enjoy being a captive audience, listening to words of wisdom expounded from the platform of a draughty hall.[46]

The strength of the stereotypes about female voters ensured, however, that it took a long time for such advice to be heeded within the party.

The near unanimity of the findings of these post-war surveys, and the repetition of their judgements and interpretations, made it very easy for politicians, journalists and political scientists to assume, consciously or not, that women's perceived lack of interest in politics, and their support for the Conservatives, were natural or innate tendencies that were unlikely to change significantly in the near future. Until the 1970s, there was little discussion about how women might be attracted or mobilised by a different political language or approach, and similarly little appreciation that women might be alienated by the male-dominated and defined structures, hierarchies and performances of politics. Indeed, the historian should perhaps ask not why were the Conservatives more successful than Labour in attracting female voters, but rather why they were less ineffective. Part of the answer, of course, involves the weaknesses of the Labour Party's organisation and communications, as well as the male domination of the trade union movement. As Amy Black and Stephen Brooke have noted, the Labour movement 'took little notice of the activities of its women's organisations' in the post-war period'.[47] The remainder of this chapter focuses, however, on Conservative communications, and how they were able, with some degree of persuasiveness, to connect with the common experiences of everyday life.

Conservative political communication: the appeal to the housewife

The Conservative party's political communications of the post-war period were strongly shaped by traditions established in earlier decades. During the interwar years, both the Conservative press and the party propaganda machine expended considerable effort in trying to integrate the new female voters into the political system and explaining why politics was important and relevant for them, rather than being solely a male domain. These appeals tended to celebrate women's domestic roles as chief consumer, guardian of the family purse, and prime defender of the household. Party propaganda warned that under the Labour Party, the state and the unions would intervene in the private sphere and reduce individual and family freedoms.[48] As Caitriona Beaumont and James Hinton have noted, too, popular women's organisations such as the Mothers' Union, the Women's Institute and the Townswomen's guilds, and during the war the Women's Voluntary Services, often encouraged and consolidated conservative thinking in apparently non-political and sociable environments.[49] In the late-1940s, as Ina Zweiniger-Bargielowska has shown, the party was able to use these traditional appeals to make a powerful critique of the Labour government's austerity and controls, and to build, in particular, on the discontent of suburban housewives in the midlands and south east.[50] In the 1951 general election there was a significant gendered disparity in Conservative support, of approximately 17 per cent.[51]

In the three decades from the mid-1950s, however, new political and social issues emerged which forced the party to rework its appeals to women. Four key developments were particularly important in reshaping the 'politics of everyday life'. First, increasing material prosperity – 'affluence' – and the intensification of consumerism upon which the Macmillan government of 1957–63, in particular, based its appeal; second, changes in the social and economic position of women, notably the movement of many married women into part-time work, and the increasingly insistent calls for gender equality made by feminist campaigners in the 1970s; third, the constellation of developments labelled 'permissiveness', namely challenges to conventional sexual morality, changes to the regulation of sexuality (such as divorce and abortion reform), the liberalisation of the censorship regime, and the introduction of the contraceptive pill; and fourth, immigration, particularly from the West Indies and Asia, which changed the ethnic make-up of Britain and hastened the emergence of a pluralistic society. These political and social changes ensured that the party had to do more than resurrect the themes that had served them well in the interwar years: it needed to adapt to new opportunities and challenges. This section explores how the party sought coherent and persuasive ways of addressing different groups of female voters, trying to appeal to aspirational and socially mobile upper working-class and lower middle-class voters while also channelling the unease at social and cultural change felt by many of the older and more rural voters.

One Conservative politician who was conspicuously successful in adapting to these changes was Margaret Thatcher, not just because she rose to lead the party, but because she had a particularly compelling way of connecting political issues to the experiences of everyday life, and had a distinctive stance on so many of the themes identified here. Thatcher's political career spans the period examined here: she stood unsuccessfully as a candidate for Dartford in the 1950 and 1951 general elections, before being elected in Finchley in 1959. She gradually climbed up the ranks, entering the Shadow Cabinet in 1967, and becoming Secretary of State for Education and Science on Edward Heath's victory in 1970. After Heath led the party to defeat in 1974, she became party leader.[52]

A key reason for her rise to power was the deftness with which she negotiated the gendered cultures and languages of politics. She unashamedly celebrated individualism and material improvement; she enthusiastically praised the shrewdness of the ordinary housewife and the ambition of the professional women, while conveying a distaste for organised feminism; she pragmatically accepted certain social reforms while maintaining a religiously based defence of conventional moral values; and she understood the anxieties generated by immigration while avoiding the excesses of the Powellite rhetoric. Thatcher herself repeatedly extolled the plain common sense of ordinary women: 'Don't be scared of the high language of economists and Cabinet ministers, but think of politics at our own household level', she told voters in the 1940s.[53] She frequently suggested that women, through work, motherhood and marriage, had a better understanding of the realities of taxation and inflation than the politicians running the economy. During the 1960s, she attacked Labour by adopting the perspective of the housewife: 'So once more the married woman who goes to the butcher, grocer and dry cleaner and then, when she is finished and wishes for a little pleasure, to the hairdressers, will find that prices are going up', she lamented in 1966.[54] To a questioner who complained about the 1966 World

Cup taking up too much attention, she answered that those thus distracted were mainly men and so 'the women can get on and do the job in their absence'.[55] And despite the wealthy lifestyle she obtained on marrying Denis Thatcher, she repeatedly emphasised that politics had not distanced her from the mundane activities of domestic life, telling the feminist Jill Tweedie in the late 1960s, for example, that: 'I've got a housekeeper but I still do the cooking myself ... rush in, peel the vegetables, put the roast in ... all before I take off my hat.'[56] She offered a model of how the party could create a persuasive and modern popular Conservatism for women.

Of the four developments identified, the Conservative party's presentation of itself as the creators and defenders of affluence was perhaps its strongest suit, and certainly seems to have resonated with many suburban women in the late 1940s and 1950s, in particular. The sociologist Mark Abrams found that 'it is mainly in the area of consumption and leisure that conversation and argument acquire a lively and widespread reality', observing that 'rather than discuss politics the average citizen greatly prefers to discuss a new car model or clothes styles'.[57] By connecting to the keenly felt and widely debated aspirations of everyday life, politicians could erode some of the gulf between themselves and voters.

The Conservatives were generally more confident and persuasive than Labour in this area, with many on the Left uncomfortable about what they saw as the empty materialism of modern affluent society.[58] The Tories played on the anxieties of the aspirational about high levels of taxation, state intervention and economic controls, and also on the fears of the growing power of the sectional, male-dominated trade unions. As Matthew Hilton has noted, the consumer was increasingly reconfigured in the mid-twentieth century in the form of the middle-class housewife, and this helped the Conservative party, and a range of other social conservative women's organisations, to pose as champions of her interests.[59] Linked to this was the defence of home owners and home ownership, which was one of the main elements of the 'creative and positive side' of Conservatism, from Macmillan's pledge in 1950s to build 300,000 houses a year, up to Thatcher's right to buy scheme in the 1980s.[60]

Macmillan's celebration of a population who had 'never had it so good' led naturally to the 1959 general election campaign run on the slogan 'Life is better with the Conservatives – Don't let Labour ruin it'. Sir Michael Fraser, Chairman of the Conservative Party Research Department between 1951 and 1964, noted in the wake of the resounding election victory in 1959 that 'the growth of a high-consumption economy since 1955 has been remarkable', and had made a 'particularly strong influence on the younger people and the new voters'. Whereas Labour had warned about returning to the unemployment and poverty of the past, the Conservatives had embraced, and were associated with, 'the improvement in the conditions of life'.[61] The Conservatives were most vulnerable, a memo surveying a less favourable position four years later concluded, when the party was 'seen as remote from the aspirations of ordinary people' – such as when there was a focus on the wealth and social exclusiveness of its leaders and supporters.[62] This was a particular problem when Sir Alec Douglas-Home took over leadership against the more savvy and modern figure of Harold Wilson.

The party played not just to aspiration, but also to envy. Carolyn Steedman, writing about her upbringing in the 1950s, observed that her mother's economic and social disappointments turned her away from a Labour background into Conservative supporter: 'she came away wanting: fine clothes, glamour, money; to be what she wasn't … When the world didn't deliver the goods, she held the world to blame" The story that she told her children about her life, Steedman noted, 'was a form of political analysis', and underpinned her support of the Conservative party, 'the only political form that allowed her to reveal the politics of envy'.[63]

The changing position of women, by contrast, generated far more tensions and difficulties for the Conservative Party. Suspicion of gender equality and the belief that women were better suited to the private sphere were both very deeply rooted in Conservative circles, and this would increasingly become a problem, especially with younger voters, towards the end of the period. Nevertheless, the Conservatives did have some success in adapting their messages on affluence to target the many married women who were working part time, partly to earn enough to buy the new consumer commodities and to improve the lot of their family.[64] Margaret Thatcher, for one, was a firm advocate of value of combining marriage and career, writing in 1952 that she 'should like to see married women carrying on with their jobs, if so inclined, after their children are born'; it was, she observed, 'possible to carry on working, taking a short leave of absence when families arrive, and returning later', and in that way 'gifts and talents that would otherwise be wasted are developed to the benefit of the community'.[65] Returning to her theme two years later, she argued that 'there is much to be said for being away from the family for part of the day', because it was difficult for the stay-at-home mother 'not to get a little impatient and very easy only to give part of one's attention to their incessant demands'.[66]

Thatcher also criticised Britain's tax system for discriminating against married women because it simply added their income to that of their husbands rather than taxing them separately. There were other progressive elements to the Conservative message, too. Zweiniger-Bargielowska has emphasised the acceptance of feminist demands about equal pay and citizenship in the party's 1949 women's charter, *A True Balance: In the Home, in Employment and as Citizens*. With women such as Irene Ward leading the campaign for equal pay, it was adopted as party policy at the 1950 party conference and enacted by the government for the public sector in 1955. Macmillan's administration also passed the legislation that enabled women to enter the House of Lords in 1958. During the 1950s and 1960s, moreover, women's issues were not consistently high on the agenda of the Labour Party, and they did little to outflank the Conservatives here.[67]

Permissiveness was another development that threatened to create splits along generational lines. From the mid-1960s, Conservative MPs, and newspapers such as the *Daily Express* and the *Daily Mail*, developed a persuasive and influential set of arguments that presented an urbane liberal metropolitan elite, personified by Labour's Roy Jenkins, as instituting well-meaning but wrong-headed reforms – liberalisation of the censorship regime, removal of the death penalty, changes to the law regarding abortion, homosexuality and divorce, a shift away from traditional education techniques – which threatened to sacrifice traditional moral standards and might potentially lead to rising crime, loss of discipline in schools, a sexualised culture and a selfish and materialistic younger generation.[68] Several surveys suggested that many of these developments, particularly the greater availability of sexually explicit content for a largely male market, were of greater concern to women than men. A major study for *New Society* magazine in November 1969 found that 84 per cent of women believed that there was 'too much publicity given to sex', compared with 70 per cent of men.[69]

A National Opinion Poll (NOP) survey the following year similarly found that only 26 per cent of women approved of 'Changing sexual attitudes in the 1960s', compared with 39 per cent of men, and 68 per cent of women believed that there was too much sex on television, as opposed to 47 per cent of men.[70] A number of campaigners, notably Mary Whitehouse, developed a distinctively gendered rhetoric that focused on the threat to the family and the traditional moral virtues of young women.[71] The Conservative Party maintained a certain distance from Whitehouse while using similar rhetorical tropes; indeed, female activists had consistently raised issues of morality and law and order at party conferences since the 1930s, and often used a gendered language of female anxiety and male (sexual) violence.[72] Thatcher, too, drew on this language, declaring that it was her experience as a mother that made her 'instinctively hostile' to the permissive society, and claiming that the 'average woman' feared sexual licence and drugs for her children. Thatcher also opposed divorce law reforms allowing automatic divorce after five years' separation, on the grounds that it would make it too easy to desert a woman.[73] It was not difficult, moreover, to expose Labour divisions in this area. Although Jenkins and his supporters were keen to hasten the arrival of a 'civilised society', most of these controversial legislative reforms were passed as private members' bills owing to the caution of Wilson and Callaghan on issues of sexual morality. While Labour could easily be attacked for enabling a damaging permissiveness, it conversely could not convincingly claim the credit with more progressive opinion.

During the 1960s, immigration became another issue that resonated strongly with 'ordinary' voters and featured in visions of how everyday life in Britain was changing. A Gallup poll conducted in June 1961 found that 76 per cent of the population were in favour of restrictions on Commonwealth immigration, with only 21 per cent in favour of maintaining freedom of entry. After Enoch Powell's 'Rivers of blood' speech in March 1968, opinion polls found between 67 and 82 per cent of respondents to be supportive of his views.[74] These anxieties were clearly shared by significant numbers of women and men, although the limited evidence we have, including a major survey of prejudice conducted by Mark Abrams for the Institute of Race Relations in 1969, indicates that a slightly higher percentage of men than women were concerned by this issue.[75] This was an area where the Conservative Party reached out to ordinary voters of both sexes with carefully crafted populist rhetoric, based on a long tradition of custodians of the 'national interest'.[76] If Powell's speech put him beyond the pale and led to him being sacked from the Conservative shadow cabinet, Thatcher was able to exploit the same anxieties using what Stuart Hall has described as the 'magical connections and short-circuits which Powellism was able to establish between the themes of race and immigration control and the images of the nation, the British people and the destruction of "our culture, our way of life"'.[77] As Ewen Green has noted, the immigration legislation introduced by the Thatcher administrations (the Nationality Acts of 1981 and 1984) were 'essentially Powellite' in their manner of defining Britishness 'by narrow boundaries of geographical origin and kinship'.[78]

By looking briefly at these four different areas, therefore, it is possible to iden- tify plausible reasons why Conservative appeals to female voters in the post-war decades would have reached a receptive audience, while at the same time sowing seeds for later difficulties. By the early 1980s, the voting gender gap had narrowed significantly, and there is some evidence that younger women were starting to move disproportionately to the Left. There are a number of reasons for this, but of central importance was the diminishing persuasiveness of the rhetoric of the 'ordinary housewife' that had been deployed so successfully by the Conservatives for several decades. A combination of the social and economic changes which significantly increased the numbers of women in the workforce, and saw many professions being transformed by female entrants, with the influence of the resurgent feminist move- ment of the 1970s, rendered the roles of housewife and mother far less appealing to younger women, and left the language of domesticity looking decidedly old- fashioned to younger generations. Callum Brown has noted that during the 1960s, 'women cancelled their mass subscription to the discursive domain of Christianity'. This was significant not only in the narrow sense that the Anglican Church was a key recruiter of women into the Conservative Party, but more broadly, the weakening of feminine discourses of respectability and piety helped to erode the notions of duty and sacrifice on which the image of the traditional housewife had been built.[79] At the same time, the popular Conservatism of the traditional Tory papers, the *Daily Mail* and the *Daily Express*, in which the housewife had a central rhetorical role, was challenged by the brasher and more masculine right-wing appeal of Kelvin MacKenzie's *Sun*.

The Conservative positions on permissiveness, gender equality and immigra- tion, while still appealing to many older women, were sometimes positively alienat- ing to younger women, and the messages about economic competence, aspiration and material improvement were increasingly complicated by the economic divi- sions and dislocations of 1980s Britain. Thatcher's achievement of being the first female prime minister, moreover, was compromised by her obvious distaste for feminism and by her reluctance to promote other women to leading positions in the party; she was frequently portrayed as an entirely exceptional, and indeed often masculine, figure. As Laura Beers demonstrates in Chapter 10, moreover, feminists in the late 1970s and early 1980s started to find a more conducive environment in an evolving Labour Party, and used this platform to appeal directly to young female voters.

Only twenty years after it was written, Nordlinger's complacent assumption that 'in many instances the women's political attitudes are simply those of their husbands', seemed to come from a very different era. By the 1980s, it had become clear that the political, social and cultural shifts of the 1960s and 1970s had gravely weakened many of the conventional assumptions about femininity, and this left Conservatives struggling to find a unifying language with which to attract women who had grown up in this period of change. If women did indeed lean to the Right in the immediate post-war period, it was often not for the reasons that the political scientists gave. The Conservative Party benefited from a political culture that they too, misunderstood; and just as the party congratulated itself that it had enabled a woman to rise to the top, that culture started rapidly slipping away.

Notes

1 The book originated in a doctoral dissertation written at Princeton University, under the supervision of Harry Eckstein. In the book's acknowledgements, Nordlinger thanked Sidney Verba, who had recently co-authored the influential study *The Civic Culture* (see note 5 below), as well Samuel Beer, Seymour Lipset and Richard Rose, all noted authorities on political culture. See Eric A. Nordlinger, *The Working-Class Tories: Authority, Deference and Stable Democracy* (Berkeley and Los Angeles: University of California Press, 1967), p. 7.

2 Nordlinger, *The Working-Class Tories*, pp. 13, 58.

3 The most important early comparative study was Maurice Duverger, *The Political Role of Women* (Paris: UNESCO, 1955).

4 M. Goot and E. Reid, *Women and Voting Studies: Mindless Matrons or Sexist Scientism?* (London: Sage, 1975), p. 18.

5 Gabriel Almond and Sidney Verba, *The Civic Culture: Political Attitudes and Democracy in Five Nations* (Princeton: Princeton University Press, 1963), p. 388.

6 *The Times*, 17 Sept. 1964, p. 9.

7 Goot and Reid, *Women and Voting Studies*, p. 9.

8 P. Norris, 'Gender: A Gender-Generation Gap?' in G. Evans and P. Norris (eds), *Critical Elections: British Parties and Voters in Long-Term Perspective* (London: Sage, 1999); Rosie Campbell, *Gender and the Vote in Britain: Beyond the Gender Gap?* (Colchester: ECPR Press, 2006); Rosie Campbell, 'What do we Really Know About Women Voters? Gender, Elections and Public Opinion', *The Political Quarterly*, 83: 4 (2012), 703–10.

9 In 1955, for example, 55 per cent of women said they voted Conservative, and 42 per cent

Labour (+13 per cent gap), whereas 47 per cent of men said they voted Conservative, and 51 per cent Labour (−4 per cent gap), producing an overall gap of 17 per cent. See Norris, 'Gender: A Gender-Generation Gap?', pp. 151–4; Joni Lovenduski, Pippa Norris and Catriona Burness, 'The Party and Women', in Anthony Seldon and Stuart Ball (eds), *Conservative Century: The Conservative Party Since 1900* (Oxford: Oxford University Press, 1994), 615; Ina Zweiniger-Bargielowska, 'Explaining the Gender Gap: The Conservative Party and the Women's Vote, 1945–1964', in M. Francis and I. Zweiniger-Bargielowska (eds), *The Conservatives and British Society 1880–1990* (1996), pp. 194–223; Amy Black and Stephen Brooke, 'The Labour Party, Women and the Problem of Gender', *Journal of British Studies*, 36 (1997), 419–52.

10 Black and Brooke, 'The Labour Party, Women and the Problem of Gender', 420.

11 Norris, 'Gender: A Gender-Generation Gap?', pp. 151; Campbell, 'What do we Really Know About Women Voters?'

12 Norris, 'Gender: A Gender-Generation Gap?, pp. 154–5; Lovenduski, Norris and Burness, 'The Party and Women', in David Denver, Christopher Carman and Robert Johns, *Elections and Voters in Britain* (Basingstoke: Palgrave Macmillan, 2012), p. 61.

13 Zweiniger-Bargielowska, 'Explaining the Gender Gap', 'feminist agenda' p. 210; G. E. McGuire, *Conservative Women: A History of Women and the Conservative Party, 1874–1997* (Basingstoke: Macmillan, 1998).

14 Lawrence Black, *Redefining British Politics: Culture, Consumerism and Participation, 1954–70* (Basingstoke: Palgrave Macmillan, 2010), p. 6.

15 Mike Savage, *Identities and Social Change in Britain Since 1940: The Politics of Method* (Oxford: Oxford University Press, 2010); Selina Todd, 'Affluence, Class and Crown Street: Reinvestigating the Post-War Working Class', *Contemporary British History*, 22: 4 (2008); Angela Davis, 'A Critical Perspective on British Social Surveys and Community Studies and their accounts of Married Life, *c.*1945–70', *Cultural and Social History*, 6: 1 (2009), 47–64; Jon Lawrence, 'Social-Science Encounters and the Negotiation of Difference in early 1960s England', *History Workshop Journal*, 77: 1 (2014), 215–39; Laura King, *Family Men: Fatherhood and Masculinity in Britain, c.*1914–1960 (Oxford: Oxford University Press, 2015).

16 Denver, Carman and Johns, *Elections and Voters in Britain*, chapter 1.

17 Jon Lawrence, 'Class, "Affluence" and the Study of Everyday Life in Britain, *c.*1930–64', *Cultural and Social History*, 10: 2 (2013), 273–99.

18 Callum Brown, *The Death of Christian Britain* (Abingdon: Routledge: 2001).

19 J. Trenamen and D. McQuail, *Television and the Political Image* (London: Methuen, 1961).

20 David Butler and Donald Stokes, *Political Change in Britain: Forces Shaping Electoral Choice* (London: Palgrave Macmillan, 1971), p. 40.

21 A. Mark Benney, P. Gray and R. H. Pear, *How People Vote: A Study of Electoral Behaviour in Greenwich* (London: Routledge & Kegan Paul, 1956).

22 *Ibid.*, p. 125.

23 A. H. Birch, *Small-Town Politics: A Study of Political Life in Glossop* (Oxford: Oxford University Press, 1959), p. 95.

24 *Ibid.*

25 *Ibid.*, 92–3.

26 Mark Abrams, *The Newspaper Reading Public of Tomorrow* (London: Odhams Press, 1964), p. 40; Frank Bealey, J. Blondel and W. P. McCann, *Constituency Politics: A Study of Newcastle-under-Lyme* (London: Faber & Faber, 1965), p. 187.

27 Mass-Observation File Report 2410 'Battersea By-Election', July 1946.

28 Mass-Observation, *Voter's Choice: A Mass-Observation Report on the General Election of 1950* (London: Art and Technics, 1950), p. 5.

29 Mass-Observation File Report 2282 'Post-Mortem on Voting at the Election', Sept. 1945, p. 5.

30 Benney, Gray and Pear, *How People Vote*, p. 109.

31 Mass-Observation, *Voter's Choice*, p. 3.

32 Campbell, 'What do we Really Know About Women Voters?'; Campbell, *Gender and the Vote in Britain*, p. 21.

33 Mass-Observation, 'Post-Mortem on Voting at the Election', p. 2.

34 Benney, Grey and Pear, *How People Vote*, pp. 125, 129.

35 Abrams, *The Newspaper Reading Public*, p. 41; Bealey, Blondel and McCann, *Constituency Politics*, pp. 198–9.

36 For example, Mass-Observation, *Voter's Choice*, p. 8.

37 Laura Beers, 'Thatcher and the Women's Vote', in Ben Jackson and Robert Saunders (eds), *Making Thatcher's Britain* (Cambridge: Cambridge University Press, 2012), pp. 127–8.

38 Benney, Grey and Pear, *How People Vote*, p. 108.

39 Margaret Stacey, *Tradition and Change: A Study of Banbury* (Oxford: Oxford University Press, 1960), pp. 47, 136.

40 Birch, *Small-Town Politics*, p. 194.

41 Bealey, Blondel and McCann, *Constituency Politics*, p. 170.

42 Robert McKenzie and Allan Silver, *Angels in Marble: Working Class Conservatives in Urban England* (London: Heinemann, 1968), pp. 86–7, 187, 190.

43 McGuire, *Conservative Women*, p. 120. On the Conservative Party's use of polling, see Andrew Taylor, 'The Conservative Party, Electoral Strategy and Public Opinion Polling, 1945–64, *British Elections & Parties Review*, 7: 1 (1997), 207–25; Andrew Taylor, 'Speaking to Democracy: The Conservative Party and Mass Opinion from the 1920s to the 1950s', in Stuart Ball and Ian Holliday (eds), *Mass Conservatism: The Conservatives and the Public Since the 1880s* (Abingdon: Routledge, 2002).

44 McGuire, *Conservative Women*, p. 121.

45 *Ibid.*, p. 122.

46 Joan Varley, 'No "Lady Bountifuls": The Way to an Efficient Women's Organisation', Conservative Agents' Journal, Jan. 1966, in Stuart Ball, *The Conservative Party since 1945* (Manchester: Manchester University Press, 1998), pp. 85–6.

47 Black and Brooke, 'The Labour Party, Women and the Problem of Gender'.

48 D. Jarvis, 'Mrs Maggs and Betty: The Conservative Appeal to Women Voters in the 1920s', *Twentieth Century British History*, 5: 2 (1994), 129–52; Adrian Bingham, 'Enfranchisement, Feminism and the Modern Woman: Debates in the British Popular Press, 1918–1939', in J. V. Gottlieb and R. Toye, *The Aftermath of Suffrage* (Basingstoke: Palgrave Macmillan, 2013), pp. 87–104.

49 Caitriona Beaumont, *Housewives and Citizens: Domesticity and the Women's Movement*

in England, 1928–64 (Manchester: Manchester University Press, 2013); James Hinton, *Women, Social Leadership, and the Second World War: Continuities of Class* (Oxford: Oxford University Press, 2003).

50 Ina Zweiniger-Bargielowska, 'Rationing, Austerity and the Conservative Party Recovery after 1945', *Historical Journal*, 37: 1 (1994).

51 Norris, 'Gender: A Gender-Generation Gap?, p. 152.

52 On Thatcher's early career, see Charles Moore, *Margaret Thatcher: The Authorized Biography, Volume One: Not For Turning* (London: Penguin, 2013).

53 Moore, *Margaret Thatcher*, p. 87.

54 *Ibid.*, p. 182.

55 *Ibid.*, pp. 183–4.

56 *Ibid.*, p. 186.

57 Abrams, *Newspaper Readership of Tomorrow*, p. 41.

58 Lawrence Black, *The Political Culture of the Left in Affluent Britain, 1951–64* (Basingstoke: Palgrave, 2002).

59 Matthew Hilton, 'The Female Consumer and the Politics of Consumption in Twentieth-Century Britain', *Historical Journal*, 45: 1 (2002), 103–28.

60 Martin Pugh, 'Popular Conservatism in Britain: Continuity and Change, 1880–1987', *Journal of British Studies*, 27: 3 (1988), 254–82; Matthew Francis, 'A Crusade to Enfranchise the Many': Thatcherism and the 'Property-Owning Democracy', *Twentieth Century British History*, 23: 2 (2012), 275–97.

61 Sir Michael Fraser [Chairman of CRD 1951–64], 'Some reflections on the general election campaign, 1959', memo 1 December 1959, CPA/ ACP/3/(59) 76, cited in Ball, *The Conservative Party since 1945*, p. 112.

62 Fraser and J. Douglas, 'Public opinion since 1959', memo 11 Dec. 1963, CPA, SC/63/14, cited in Ball, *The Conservative Party since 1945*, p. 113.

63 Carolyn Steedman, *Landscape for a Good Woman: A Story of Two Lives* (London: Virago, 1986).

64 Dolly Smith Wilson, 'A New Look at the Affluent Worker: The Good Working Mother in Post-War Britain', *Twentieth Century British History*, 17: 2 (2006), 206–29.

65 *Sunday Graphic*, 17 February 1952.

66 McGuire, *Conservative Women*, p. 124.

67 Black and Brooke, 'The Labour Party, Women and the Problem of Gender'.

68 Stuart Hall, Chas Critcher *et al.*, *Policing the Crisis: Mugging, the State and Law and Order* (London: Macmillan, 1978), chapter 8, 'The Law-and-Order Society: the Exhaustion of "Consent"'; Mark Donnelly, *Sixties Britain: Culture, Society and Politics* (Harlow: Pearson, 2005), chapter 10, '1968, Cultural Crisis and Women's Liberation'.

69 *New Society*, 27 November 1969, p. 849.

70 Marcus Collins, 'Introduction', in Collins (ed.), *The Permissive Society and its Enemies: Sixties British Culture* (London: Rivers Oram Press, 2006), p. 19.

71 Lawrence Black, *Redefining British Politics* (Basingstoke: Palgrave, 2010), chapter 5.

72 Beatrix Campbell, *The Iron Ladies: Why Do Women Vote Tory?* (London: Virago, 1987).

73 Moore, *Margaret Thatcher*, p. 185.

74 N. Deakin (ed.), *Colour and the British Electorate 1964* (London: Institute of Race Relations, 1965), p. 5; Donnelly, *Sixties Britain*, p. 168.

75 N. Deakin (ed.), *Colour, Citizenship and British Society* (London: Panther, 1970), p. 320. The British Social Attitudes survey of 1984 found no gender difference.
76 McKenzie and Silver, *Angels in Marble*, chapter 2.
77 Stuart Hall, 'The Great Moving Right Show', *Marxism Today*, Jan. 1979, p. 19.
78 E. H. H. Green, *Thatcher* (London: Hodder Arnold, 2006), p. 138.
79 Brown, *The Death of Christian Britain*, pp. 195–6.

10

Feminist responses to Thatcher and Thatcherism

Laura Beers

The self-described 'feminist stand-up comic' Bridget Christie published *A Book for Her*, in which the author attempts to make the politics and precepts of the modern women's movement accessible – and funny – to women. The book includes a riff on 'Tory feminism'. Christie's point of departure is the phenomenon of Conservative women, including the Prime Minister Theresa May (then the Home Secretary and former Minister for Women and Equalities), wearing a T-shirt with 'This is what a feminist looks like' emblazoned across the chest. In her rendering, the shirt's back reads, 'Not really, I'm a Tory, you gullible dick.' She continues the joke: 'underneath that it says, "I axed the Health in Pregnancy Grant. I closed Sure Start Centres … I cut child benefit and slashed tax credits. I shut down shelters for battered wives and children. I cut rape counselling and Legal Aid … I cut funding for CCTV cameras and street lighting, making women much more vulnerable. I closed down all twenty-three Specialist Domestic Violence Courts. I cut benefits for disabled children … I tried to amend the Abortion Act so that women receive one-to-one abortion counselling from the Pope before they go ahead with it." … The back is much longer than the front, by the way. It's a tailcoat, basically. They're wearing tailcoats.'[1]

The specific policies which Christie highlights were all implemented during Conservative Prime Minister David Cameron's first government. However, her broader anti-Tory tone highlights a crucial transformation in feminist attitudes towards party politics that began under Thatcher. In the 1970s, the Women's Liberation Movement (WLM) viewed both Labour and the Tories as part of the mainstream political establishment, dominated by men and largely indifferent to women's concerns. Thatcher's free market ethos and her emphasis on traditional family values, which she articulated from the late 1970s onwards, compounded by the cuts to social welfare programs and the marginalisation of the Equal Opportunities Commission during her first government, convinced many feminists that the two 'establishment' parties were not, in fact, interchangeable.[2]

This chapter makes use of the socialist feminist journal *Feminist Review*, the Marxist *New Left Review*, and *Spare Rib*, the monthly magazine of the WLM, which included contributions from socialists, radicals and other members of the diffuse and fragmentary women's movement. The chapter uses these sources to advance the argument that the entrance of militant feminists into the Labour Party in the 1980s should be understood principally as a response to the perceived radicalisation of right-wing women, and particularly to the perceived threat of Thatcherism to feminism. It challenges narratives which have argued that Thatcherism in practice was not unambiguously hostile to the goals of the WLM, and that the influx of feminists into the Labour movement is better understood as a response to the positive reforms within the Labour organisation and leadership than as a negative response to Thatcherism. As such, it adds to our understanding of the history of right-wing women by highlighting the extent to which Thatcherism was *perceived* by feminists to be incompatible with feminism, even if the practical record of Thatcher's administrations was more nuanced. Further, in emphasising the extent to which militant feminists' embrace of Labour politics was a grudging and contested phenomenon, it underscores the uniqueness of the WLM as predominantly a social movement which sought to operate outside formal party-political channels. In this respect, Second Wave Feminism in 1970s Britain was distinct both from its American counterpart, which was much more integrated into networks of political lobbying and party politics, and from First Wave Feminism in Britain which (excepting the pre-First World War Women's Social and Political Union) was similarly closely tied to the party-political establishment.[3]

The irony of women's liberation feminists being pushed into the arms of the Labour Party as a consequence of the ascendancy of the first female leader of the Conservative Party was not lost. Thatcher's 'occupation of the supreme political office, and ... the confidence and authority with which she carried out its duties ... made it seem more possible for women to be powerful, to succeed in a man's world'.[4] At the same time, women, as child bearers, mothers, and frequently part-time often low-skilled workers, suffered disproportionately through her governments' reforms 'aimed directly at freeing up the economy – most importantly, deregulation, but to some extent privatization as well – and measures to reduce public spending and dependence on the Welfare State'. Such policies 'increased hardship and struggle, especially for mothers either working or wanting to work, single mothers, "carers", the elderly, and the poor'.[5]

In a May 1979 leader, the *Spare Rib* editorial team dismissed the question of whether a victory for Thatcher would be regarded 'as a victory for women's liberation, proof of what-the-modern woman-can-achieve'. This question was, they argued, misleading: 'For us as feminists, the issue is not the success or failure of one individual woman, but whether the actual policies of Thatcher, and of the party which she leads, can promote the interests of women in general.'[6] As it became apparent that Thatcher's governments would not promote what WLM feminists deemed to be the interests of women in general, many determined that the paradox of Thatcher's gender identity was easier ignored. As Heather Nunn has written, 'Thatcher's political presence highlighted a taboo area of feminist analyses ... Thatcher constituted a problem ... [in that h]er authority seemed to derive from both her movement across gender identities, troubling the binaries of sexual difference, and also through the way she endorsed an unequal gender divide by locating women within the domestic and moral sphere and placing men as active political subjects.'[7]

Thatcher too largely eschewed engagement with feminist discourse. She famously proclaimed in a 1978 interview, 'No, I am not a feminist', and left it at that.[8] She justified her government's policies through a rhetoric of choice and competition, on the one hand, and through an emphasis on reducing the deficit, on the other. She prioritised the commitment to 'fiscal responsibility' over full employment and the safeguarding of the social minimum in language intended to appeal to the female electorate. She asserted, speciously, that, 'international economics work just the same as home economics', and argued that, just as a family could not spend more than it took it, neither could a nation.[9] Justifying her policies in November 1982, she noted: 'Some say I preach merely the homilies of housekeeping or the parables of the parlour. But I do not repent. Those parables would have saved many a financier from failure and many a country from crisis.'[10] Such language was intended to appeal principally to women, who retained primary control over household spending, even in families where both parents worked full time. And, there was evidence that such language was effective. Although support for the Conservative Party among women fell during the 1980s, more women than men continued to support the Tories, with women more inclined than men to disapprove of deficit spending.[11] (Women's comparative preference for Thatcher was not anomalous. While the 1980s arguably saw the beginnings of gender dealignment in voting patterns, women had traditionally shown a greater inclination to vote Conservative.[12])

A quarter of a century on from Thatcher's resignation, David Cameron and his Chancellor of the Exchequer George Osborne not only embraced the Thatcherite logic of deficit reduction, but went a step further in committing to achieve a budget surplus by the end of the current Parliament. (After taking over the premiership, May quickly abandoned this pledge.)[13] The Ipsos-MORI 2015 public opinion almanac (which did not disaggregate its findings by gender) reported that, 'the government has succeeded in setting a narrative for the majority of the public that we need continuing cuts to balance the budget. If that means services can do less, we have to live with that'.[14] Notably, however, an earlier poll conducted in advance of the 2011 budget showed a greater conviction amongt women than amongt men that the government was 'cutting spending too much' (46 per cent of women v. 40 per cent of men).[15] While these figures show only minority dissatisfaction with fiscal austerity, they perhaps reflect a growing acceptance of the feminist line, espoused consistently since the late 1970s, that Conservative policies directed at cutting the welfare state are in practice anti-women.

This critique of Conservative social and economic politics was more clearly articulated by so-called 'socialist feminists', who, unlike radical feminists, identified themselves as on the far-left fringes of the political spectrum. (Radical feminists, in contrast, tended to reject the entire left–right spectrum of male-dominated party politics as patriarchal and inimical to the goals of the women's liberation movement.) Yet, despite their disillusionment with Thatcherite economics, it took time for militant socialist feminists to reach the conclusion that the best way to combat Thatcherism was through the Labour movement. Even at the 1983 election, social-ist feminists remained divided over whether or not to support Labour, and many members of the movement never reconciled themselves to participation in main-stream party politics. However, the growing entrance of women's libbers into local Labour women's sections from the early 1980s, and their increased prominence on, and ultimate dominance of, the National Labour Women's Committee and the London-centred Women's Action Committee are a direct result of the impact of Thatcherism on the WLM.

Both women's liberation activists and some historians of the movement have argued that there was comparatively little difference between Labour and Conservative attitudes towards feminist demands in the 1960s and 1970s. Looking at this purported similarity from a more positive perspective, the historian Elizabeth Homans has argued that both parties in this period were relatively open to reforms that benefited women's material and social position, as long as these did not threaten the post-Second World War Beveridge consensus based around assump-tions of the gendered household and the family wage. In this context, she has exam-ined the process of collaboration between feminists (including some members of the WLM) and party politicians from both sides of the aisle to enact the Equal Pay, Sex Discrimination, and Child Benefit acts.[16] While Homans emphasises points of engagement between feminists and the principal political parties, Sarah Perrigo, a political scientist who was active in the WLM in the 1970s and became a member of the Labour Party shortly before the 1979 election, has argued that: 'Until the late 1970s there was neither significant pressure nor any real incentive for the Labour Party to take gender issues seriously. There was no competition from other political parties on women's issues. Further, despite the widespread mobilisation of women in the feminist movement, there was little attempt by women influenced by femi-nism to exert pressure directly on the political system.'[17]

Her retrospective analysis closely echoes the contemporary scepticism of the WLM towards the idea that the Labour Party was substantially more receptive to feminism than the Tories. Members of the WLM in the 1970s were inclined to present both parties as almost equally out of touch with women's demands. This double-edged hostility towards mainstream party politics was expressed most strongly by radical feminists. Whereas socialist feminists saw the economic superstructure as the driving force behind both class and gender oppression, radical feminists identified male patriarchal oppression as the dominant explanation for women's marginalisation.[18] Thus, as Joni Lovenduski and Vicky Randall argued in 1993, 'Radical feminists in particular have been wary of participation in the public politics of political parties, the state, or other organizations. They have theorized public political institutions as part of the apparatus of male dominance or patriarchy. Such institutions are organized on male hierarchical principles and around masculine interests.'[19] The radical/socialist divide within the WLM led to increased tensions over issues including cooperation with male activists, and participation in mixed-sex political and pressure groups. The tension between the two branches of the movement became so acute that the WLM annual conference, first held at Ruskin College, Oxford, in 1970, ultimately became dysfunctional. The last conference was held in Birmingham in 1978, and the discontinuation of the movement's annual conferences is often pointed to as symbolic of its decline.[20] In their 1993 survey history of contemporary feminist politics, Lovenduski and Randall admit to their own greater sympathies for socialist and opposed to radical feminist analysis and state their strong belief 'that feminists *should* be prepared to engage in public politics'.[21] Their commitment to public political engagement was not uncommon among socialist feminists in the 1990s; yet this subsequent rapprochement should not disguise the fact that, in the 1970s and early 1980s, socialist feminists were almost as hostile towards mainstream politics as their radical sisters.

More than any other WLM document, *Beyond the Fragments*, the 1979 manifesto co-authored by Sheila Rowbotham, Lynne Segal and Hilary Wainwright, underscores the extent of this hostility. Looking back on the 1970s from the perspective of the early 2000s, Segal characterized *Beyond the Fragments* as an effort 'to build upon what we saw as the strengths of the autonomous, loosely networked women's movement of the 1970s to unite the various factions of the left and Labour movement through grass-roots solidarity and activism'.[22] Yet, while Segal later wrote of the threesome's ambition to bring together factions of the 'Labour movement', there is little discussion of engagement with the Labour Party (as distinct from with trade unionism). While the authors write of moving beyond the fragments towards a more constructive socialist activism, none is advocating that feminists attempt to make that revolution through the Labour Party. Of the three authors, Wainwright engages most directly with the relationship between the Labour Party and the feminist movement, but even she shows significant scepticism about the possibility of Labour advancing either a feminist or a socialist agenda. She notes that, 'everyone's bleedin' disgusted with [Labour] … It's strongly felt that there's little worth in fighting for the Labour Party. So people take the easy way out and grab what they can; ignoring the wider fight for a society in which we can all have the opportunity to live a more fulfilled life.' While she mused that: 'Perhaps things will get revitalized now that we are forced to fight the Tories', her prescriptions at the end of her chapter are for 'socialist alliances' forged through greater cooperation between fringe socialist parties.[23]

Writing in the *New Left Review* in 1984, the socialist feminists Angela Weir and Elizabeth Wilson noted that although, 'In its early years the British women's movement sought to create a relationship with, and exert an influence on, the trade unions ... the relationship of feminists to the left was nonetheless always ambivalent. In the early 1970s the Labour Party hardly seemed an option for the new generation of revolutionaries.'[24] While rejecting the radical feminists' essentialist dismissal of the Labour Party, the socialist-feminist historian Barbara Taylor's 1983 study *Eve and the New Jerusalem* appeared to offer a historically deterministic reading of the masculine culture of the modern-day Labour Party and trade union movement.[25]

This scepticism of the Labour party as any more supportive of women's interests than its Conservative opponents was fuelled by the autonomous culture of the WLM.[26] As Nicolas Owen has highlighted, this culture extended to a separatist approach that excluded not only engagement in mainstream politics, but acceptance of cooperation with male supporters of feminists' goals.[27] This scepticism was not lessened after Thatcher's election as Conservative Party leader in 1976, when increasing numbers of socialist-feminist women found their way into the Labour Party in reaction to the perceived threat to women's interests posed by Thatcher's Conservative Party. Lovenduski and Randall have argued that 'the most important' change to British political culture in the 1980s 'was the fact that the Labour Party and the trade unions, in their hour of need, became much more receptive to feminist arguments'.[28] In their view, it was principally the changing attitude of the party which facilitated the influx of women into the Labour movement. There was, thus, a positive *pull* towards Labour, not simply a negative *push* into the arms of Thatcher's opponents. This argument is bolstered by their even-handed assessment of the impacts of Thatcher's agenda on women, which concludes by saying: 'Thatcherism was not a complete disaster for women. It brought new opportunities, and it was not inspired by any consistent anti-feminist animus.'[29]

While this analysis is based primarily on an assessment of the economic impacts of Thatcherism, Lovenduski and Randall also note that: 'Mrs Thatcher's government adopt[ed] a similarly equivocal stance on questions of female sexuality and fertility ... Despite the regular imprecations of Mrs Thatcher, Rhodes Boyson, Norman Tebbit, and others against the permissive 1960s and their legacy ... it is difficult to point to any concrete victories in this area for the moral conservatives.'[30] This assessment discounts the 1988 legislation forbidding local authorities from teaching about homosexuality in schools, as well as legislation on television standards, but otherwise is broadly accurate, particularly when the Thatcher governments' legacy is contrasted to the policy agenda put forth by the moral conservatives in this period.

Thatcher's government did not come out behind the 1979 private member's bill put forth by John Corrie, Conservative MP for Bute and North Ayrshire, which would have curtailed the period during which a woman could obtain an abortion to the first twenty weeks of pregnancy, and put other restrictions on access to counselling and abortion provision. Thatcher similarly abstained in the vote on the 'Alton Bill', a 1988 private member's bill which would have reduced the legal period for obtaining an abortion to eighteen weeks.[31] Beatrix Campbell has argued that Thatcher's hands-off attitude towards moral legislation reflected the changing views of right-wing women over the course of the previous two decades. Campbell began her discussion of Conservative women and sexuality by stating: 'Part of the problem about deciphering the attitudes of Conservative women to permissiveness and sexuality is that they are *assumed* to be represented by the anti-permissive crusades of the moral right. But are they?'[32] Her answer was a resounding no. Over the next few pages, she quoted interview after interview with Tory women who expressed disapproval for proposed limitations on abortion access and discontent at the way in which their lack of sexual knowledge had impacted on their own personal and marital fulfilment. In contrast, Lawrence Black has been quicker to accept that the moralising rhetoric of activists such as Mary Whitehouse had a wide purchase within broader culture. He endorses Jeffrey Weeks's assessment that, 'far from being a crank … there was something deeply representative about Mrs. Whitehouse'. However, in Black's reading, Thatcher was unwilling to push the moral right's agenda, not because of any fundamental disagreement in principle, but because 'Thatcher saw the state as a cause of Britain's crisis and was chary of turning to it to remedy the nation's moral welfare'.[33] While the reasons for the Thatcher governments' reluctance to take issues on of moral reform remain contested, it is clear that women's liberation feminists did not perceive Thatcher to be a particular threat to women's sexual emancipation. While cooperation between the WLM and the trade unions in opposition to the Corrie Bill in 1979 is frequently seen as a model for women's political mobilisation, critiques of Thatcherism within the WLM press rarely reference issues of female sexuality, and instead focus on the socio-economic impact of Thatcher's policies on women in the workforce and the home.

The following discussion does not discount Lovenduski and Randall's conclusion that 'some women have benefitted from the whole ethos of self-help and enterprise' of Thatcherism.[34] Certainly, despite a narrowing gender gap, women of all ages and socio-economic demographics, except young working women, continued to prefer Thatcher's party to the Labour alternative throughout her premiership.[35] Instead, what follows focuses on the perception of Thatcher within the WLM and argues that it was vehement opposition to Thatcher's economic policies, much more than an enthusiasm for a reforming Labour Party, which fuelled the influx of militant women into mainstream party politics in the 1980s.

In the run-up to the 1979 election, *Spare Rib* ran an editorial entitled 'Is Margaret Thatcher for Women?" Over two full columns, the editors made their case that: 'The Tories' attempt to appeal to women across class-lines, via the common factor of being housewives, is calculated and very skilful. Providing praise for the housewife, however, comes cheap; providing nurseries, housing, social security benefits, and adequate health care does not. Labour has massively reduced public spending, but the Tories plan heavier cuts.' On the issue of law and order, they conceded that: 'Thatcher's vision of a vastly increased police force, with added powers, may seem very appealing to those many people – particularly women – who *do* now live in fear.' But, could it be trusted? 'The Women's Liberation Movement – which has led the fight on crimes against women – is already suffering police harassment and surveillance (Special Branch at conferences, raids on women's centres and benefits, beatings and arrest on the November Reclaim the Night demonstration) and, under a Conservative government, we can doubtless expect worse.' In case anyone should miss the point that their censure of the Tory programme was not an endorsement of Callaghan's government, the editors concluded: 'While we at *Spare Rib* have no illusions in Labour, those of us who are voting intend to vote for them – for the simple reason that we want to keep the Tories out.'[36] (Notably, embedded in the final sentence was the message that some of the editorial staff were too disenchanted with party politics to bother registering a vote.)

While the editorial team of the socialist-feminist journal *Feminist Review* did not state their views in advance of the 1979 election, they subsequently expressed their anxiety at the result, noting that, 'We might view [the election of "the first-ever woman premier in an advanced capitalist country"] more positively were it not for Margaret Thatcher's reactionary and anti-feminist views.' Thatcher's victory would force the WLM to revisit 'the question of the political strategy of the women's movement, and in particular its relationship to the labour movement'. However, while socialist feminists might be drawn towards cooperation with the Labour Party in order to combat Thatcher's economic policies and the presumed coming assault on welfare programmes, the editors warned that 'this may be double-edged for women if we are encouraged by the left parties to see our feminist demands as peripheral to an orthodox conception of the class struggle. We must defend our right to organize autonomously and resist attempts to define our interests as diversionary frills.'[37]

Despite scepticism, a growing number of socialist feminists made the move into Labour Party politics in the early 1980s. The WLM had always been a numerically small movement, and the influx of WLM women into the party did not profoundly reshape its demographics. The Labour Party had been around 40 per cent female in the 1970s, and remained so in the early 1990s.[38] However, the comparatively small number of WLM women made their presence felt, particularly in the party's local women's sections, institutions created in the party's early years that had largely fallen dormant in the post-1945 era and which saw a renaissance in the 1980s as spaces for discussion of women's issues. Alongside came the renaissance of Labour's annual women's conference. WLM women were also active in the Labour Women's Advisory Committee (WAC), which after 1980 emerged as a major voice for constitutional reform, demanding that the annual party conference be required to take up resolutions passed by the annual women's conference, and that the women's conference directly elect the female representatives to the National Executive Committee (NEC). In addition, women became active in local government, and particularly in the Greater London Council (GLC), controlled by the left wing of the Labour Party from 1981 to 1986. Notably, Hilary Wainwright joined the Labour Party in the early 1980s and became vocal within the women's sections, while Sheila Rowbotham worked as a research officer for the Labour-led GLC's Industry and Employment Department, producing a newspaper, 'Jobs for a Change', and contributing to the London Industrial Strategy between 1983 and the GLC's dissolution in 1986.

Yet, while WLM women viewed the post-1979 Labour Party, which was strongly influenced by left-wing activists (pejoratively dubbed the 'loony left'), as a more promising site for engagement than the Callaghan-led party of the 1970s, the WLM remained deeply sceptical of the party. The push of Thatcherism, more than the pull of the Labour left, remained the party's principal allure. During the 1983 general election, the various organs of the WLM largely refrained from intervention in the campaign. While the internationalist-feminist legal organisation Rights of Women organised a press conference urging women not to vote Tory, it refrained from openly endorsing the Labour Party or taking sides between Labour and the newly formed Social Democratic Party (SDP). The feminist journal *Outwrite* ultimately endorsed Labour on its cover, but *Spare Rib* stood remarkably aloof from the campaign.[39] After Thatcher's re-election, Valerie Coultas, a journalist for *Socialist Action* and member of the Vauxhall Labour Party, wrote to *Spare Rib*'s letters column. There, she argued:

> *Spare Rib* cannot allow itself to become so internalized that it fails to reach out to the issues that thousands of women are concerned about ... Silence on such an event also means that you are failing to bring women's issues to the fore when women – particularly uncommitted women – are most likely to be thinking about politics.[40]

That same issue contained an article by Coultas on the outcome of the general election, in which she noted that a plurality of women (43 per cent) had voted for Thatcher, but that, according to exit polls, the remainder had been almost evenly split between Labour and the SDP. In explaining the outcome, she pointed to the 'big battle' which Labour feminists had fought and largely lost to get the party to focus on issues of interest to women, including the promotion of women within the party and abortion rights.[41] Despite her support for Labour, Coultas had little faith in the party's commitment to feminism. (Notably, Coultas herself had only joined the Labour Party as a response to the perceived threat of Thatcherism, having previously been active in the far-left International Marxist Group.)

The other intervention in the September 1983 issue was by Sarah Roelefs, a self-described lesbian-feminist and member of the Islington South branch of the Labour Party. In 'Can Feminism Win?', she took a more optimistic view of the effect that feminists' entry into the Labour Party over the previous few years had already had, citing the influence of the feminist-dominated Women's Action Committee on the 1983 Labour manifesto, and its section on a 'Better Deal for Women', which promised strong interventions on equal pay and right to work, nursery provision, social care, and support for rape victims and battered women. Yet, Roelefs lamented that many candidates and local parties buried the manifesto promises on women in a misguided obsession with vote-catching. 'Worse has followed the election. Concern with "credibility" in order to win the all-important votes next time has led many sections of the party to wholesale abandonment of many manifesto promises.' However, she did not take from this that it was futile to attempt to work with, or through, the Labour Party. Instead, she argued, 'the Labour party, as theoretically the party that fights for social justice, provides unique opportunities for us. We see no reason why the Labour party should be left to get on with its own sexist, heterosexist and racist ways.'[42]

Roelofs had joined the party in 1980, after the election of the Thatcher government. In an interview with the *Feminist Review*, she presented her decision primarily in terms of the perceived 'radicalisation within the left wing of the Labour Party around the question of internal democracy. The demands of the Campaign for Labour Party Democracy (CLPD) were beginning to have an effect and the left-wing current around Tony Benn strengthened its influence: these two developments democratized the party to the extent that a lot of women like myself thought there was the possibility of using it to achieve some of the aims of the women's liberation movement.' *Feminist Review* interviewed Roelofs alongside two other Labour women, one of whom had been a party member for over thirty years, and one who had joined in 1977, and endured what she termed a few 'lonely years' before other feminists began flooding into the party in the early 1980s. Mildred Gordon, the oldest of the three women, argued that the influx of women in the 1980s could be explained by the fact that 'women nowadays recognize that Thatcher is an anti-feminist woman'. Roelofs supported this assessment, and offered an observation that painted a much less optimistic picture of the Labour Party than that which she had used to justify her decision to join: 'given how bad the Tories were for women ... I think it's important that we vote Labour not because of what a Labour government may do for us as women – I don't think we can rest our trust in a Labour government – but because it gives us a better chance to do things for ourselves.'

Kate Allen, a Camden borough councillor, echoed the concerns of many who were sceptical about the party's seeming embrace of feminists after 1979: 'I think the Labour Party has to be careful not to appear engaged in a cynical attempt to co-opt women to a struggle which is not in all cases theirs, as if women were just being drawn in for the purpose of winning elections and nothing else.'[43] This scepticism was reinforced at the party's 1983 annual conference when the WAC's demands for constitutional changes to give women a greater voice on the NEC were dismissed after a half hour's debate. *Spare Rib* ran an article on the conference titled 'Labour

Women Left in the Cold', which tellingly began by asking, 'Will the Labour Party ever change?'[44]

That socialist feminists' engagement with Labour was principally about combating Thatcherism is perhaps most evident in Beatrix Campbell's 1987 classic, *The Iron Ladies: Why Do Women Vote Conservative?* Unlike other socialist feminists, Campbell remained a member of the Communist Party of Great Britain (albeit an increasingly disillusioned one), and did not enter the Labour Party ranks in the 1980s. *Iron Ladies*, however, reads almost like a 'how to' manual advising Labour on how to court disaffected Tory women. She identifies employment policies, particularly the Thatcher government's hostility towards European directives on equal pay and family leave, and its promotion of women's part-time work without securing benefits to part-time workers, as crucial in alienating the female electorate. She also points to women's – particularly younger women's – greater opposition to the government's Trident cruise missile programme, as compared to their male counterparts, as a reason for the narrowing of the gender gap. Her analysis of the reasons for women's disaffection from the Conservative Party are more astute than her analyses for why women vote Tory, which rely heavily on arguments about law and order and hang 'em and flog 'em Toryism, which have been shown by polling data to be largely peripheral to most women's political agendas. Yet, what is most telling about her book is its engagement with issues of mainstream electoral politics and its clear support for Labour.[45]

Campbell was not the only prominent member of the WLM to have taken a greater interest in electoral politics by 1987. Whereas, in 1983, *Spare Rib* had dismissed the general election as largely irrelevant to feminism, in May–June 1987 it ran extensive coverage of the campaign. In 'What's in a Vote?', Melissa Benn, Tony Benn's daughter, began by stating that:

> the first priority of most feminists in this country this General Election will be to vote Thatcher out … Her policies on jobs, nuclear weaponry, the National Health Service, privatization of health, transport and council services, race and immigration, law and 'order' … all these are enough to show why it is not a credible choice. And, on women's rights, although the Tories have a tradition of strong women working within and for the party, there is precious little feminism among Tory women. 'Strong women' are either a political resource for the power of men or they are women who have made it into the world of men, like Thatcher or Currie. While there are Tory women who want to eliminate discrimination in the tax system, for example, or have better child care facilities, Tory women don't know what to do in general with the language of feminism. Feminism to them seems to make concrete a form of female powerlessness it is their explicit role to deny.

Toryism, she argued, was antithetical to feminism. So, what about Labour and the SDP-Alliance? 'On women, Labour's position is more complicated, because more elusive. The Labour leadership's attitude to women is one defined by negatives or absence, rather than hostility and repudiation. Labour women have built up a set of excellent policies on women: Jo Richardson has been working hard on getting support for the idea of a Ministry of Women, and examining its possible structures.' She claimed that, 'The virtually all male, all white leadership of the party – and singularly uninspiring they are at that – simply do not grasp either the politics, or the potential popular appeal, of presenting and cohering Labour's policy around women: making women central.' Nonetheless, Melissa Benn declared her intention to support Labour and encouraged other feminists to engage with the election. 'The mistake, I think, of radicals who do not vote at all or who make a protest vote against Labour is that they both take the general election too seriously, and yet not seriously enough. Voting has not much to do with politics when you get right down to it, as most politics is extra parliamentary. Yet, a general election clearly does make some difference to our own and others' lives. It is a time when we have a responsibility to make our symbolic mark, and then get on with politics as usual.'[46]

Benn's advocacy for Labour elicited an angry letter from Gillian Wilson of the Cambridge University Conservative Association in the following month's issue. Wilson argued that feminists could come in all political shades and denounced *Spare Rib*'s partisanship in running the piece. Francesca Ashurst's article in the June 1987 issue echoed Wilson's hostility to Benn's pro-Labour message, but from the opposite end of the political spectrum. Ashurst argued that 'we should be more critical of the ways "Women's Issues" are packaged for us' by the Labour party. Nonetheless, if the Labour party was found wanting, it could no longer be equated with the Conservatives. 'The left' might be failing to embrace the opportunity to 'promise to rebuild a better' welfare system, but it was 'the right' which had 'dismantle[d] the welfare state' over the past seven and a half years, with disastrous consequences for women.[47] It was less that the Labour Party had done anything positive for women since 1979 than that Thatcher's Conservative Party had become so much worse.

Some still saw both mainstream parties as irredeemable, and, over the course of the 1980s, feminists continued to debate whether women should work with Labour or remain aloof from party politics altogether. In a March 1981 article in the *Feminist Review*, Val Coultas clearly outlined the terms of the debate. Coultas's article began by urging her fellow feminists to face the tough reality that 'We cannot look back forever', and to accept that, 'In facing the future feminists in Britain must take a long, hard look at two crucial problems, how to build a women's movement and how to work out our relationship to political parties, particularly the Labour Party.' While she expressed little confidence in Labour, she underscored that, 'led by Margaret Thatcher the Tory government has brought us down to earth with a jolt. Liberties that we took for granted in the past decade are increasingly under attack – the right to work, to strike and picket, the right to a basic level of social security, the right to live in a council house. For women, who rely so heavily on the facilities of the welfare state, the blows are particularly crushing because our independence from men (however limited) is at stake. Anger and militancy about this state of affairs is not lacking. But opposition … has been rather fragmented.' (Here Coultas, intentionally, alluded to *Beyond the Fragments*.) While it was true that Labour 'has yet to' show much interest in 'feminist demands', 'the Labour Party has the support of millions of people' and thus 'makes it possible to reach a far broader constituency of women if we can get their backing for our campaigns. We should work with all social groups, but particularly the Labour Party.'

Coultas ended her essay by posing a series of questions for her fellow socialist feminists, including:

- Is such an alliance [between the WLM and Labour] possible given the traditionalist attitudes of the Labour Party and the trade unions?
- But would such an alliance not threaten the 'autonomy' of the women's movement?
- Why should we bother with the Labour Party though? Surely it is the trade unions that are more important because they are the only real weapon working people have to fight with? Anyway the Labour Party has lost its active working-class base since the war.
- What about the style of the Labour Party?
- But the Labour Party is utterly reformist and orientated only to Parliament. It never keeps its election promises and it always ends up managing the economy for big business.
- What about the other political parties? Are their ideas not closer to feminism than the Labour Party's? Is it not more important to work with them?[48]

These questions, as much as the answers, reveal the extent of WLM ambiguity towards the Labour party, even as large numbers of formerly militant feminists were flocking to its ranks. Over the course of the 1980s, former WLM members became accustomed to their new identities as Labour Party activists, but few felt fully comfortable within the party. In the early 1990s, Sylvia Bashevkin interviewed 43 women's movement activists. By the time that the interviews were conducted, most of the activists she interviewed professed to be 'Labour Party voters or members'. However, 'doubts about the intentions of Labour in power were shared by virtually all activists, whether pragmatists or radicals. Many recalled the beginnings of public service cutbacks under the last Callaghan government, arguing that Labour had largely set the stage for Thatcher's subsequent efforts.' Their suspicion of Labour reflected the WLM's long-held aversion to party politics: 'Parallel with their distrust of Labour, pragmatists and protesters also shared a cynical interpretation of the larger party system.'[49]

This cynicism resurfaced quickly after the initial flood of optimism among both feminists and members of the far left about the future direction of Labour between 1979 and 1983. After the 1983 election defeat, the party began to turn against its left wing and to re-impose order and discipline within its ranks – a reorientation which left many feminists activists feeling marginalised and disenchanted.[50] In September 1987, Loretta Loach, the daughter of Labour activists who became a socialist feminist with a healthy dose of scepticism for her parents' politics, asked:, 'Can

Feminism Survive a Third Term [of Margaret Thatcher]?" Loach admitted that she was anxious. In response to Thatcherism, the Labour party had gradually fallen into the hands of reformists such as Neil Kinnock who held to 'a very traditional agenda for power in which the state rather than political will disposes of our desire ... All of this bodes ill for the future of socialist feminism. It is not that our fortunes are entirely bound up with the Labour Party ... but our ability to intervene in various political ways has recently focused and drawn hope from the party's changing complexion. This is now moving into decline.' Kinnock's focus on unifying the party and 'prevent[ing] criticism of any kind' should compel feminists 'to question the nature and value of our connection with it'. Perhaps, 'a renewed, autonomous alliance of left feminists might be required to meet the challenge Thatcher will be making'.[51]

Hilary Wainwright too reflected that the reformist turn within the Labour party from the mid-1980s might ultimately push feminists and other radicals out of the fold. The radical left, she wrote, 'has different views from the leadership on how Thatcherism can be most effectively challenged, and sees electoral change as only one part of a socialist transformation. Since 1983 the space for the left to put forward these differences has steadily diminished and is likely to contract still further ... Some on the left will simply go along with the leadership in the hope of influencing the occasional policy; others will find themselves in an increasingly defensive corner unless they strike out on a more independent path.'[52] Yet, for all of the talk of forging a new brand of independent politics, feminists for the most part remained inside the Labour Party, and did their best to change policies from within. The determination of feminists to weather the 'tough times' of the Thatcher years, pushed them irreversibly in an 'increasingly credible, legitimate, and system-oriented direction'.[53]

In certain respects, the above discussion sits awkwardly in a volume on right-wing women, in that it is principally a discussion of the ways in which far-left-wing women responded to the changing face of the political right, and specifically to the rise of Margaret Thatcher. Politics, however, is inherently a story of relationships. Part of the story of what it meant to be a right-wing woman in the 1980s was how that identity, with its emphasis on economic liberalism, family values and self-help, impacted on those women who did not share her values. We cannot understand why so many militant feminists found their way into the Labour Party in the early 1980s without appreciating the extent to which they perceived Thatcherism as an existential threat to feminism. And finally, to return to Bridget Christie's comic riff with which this chapter opened, we cannot understand how and why a new generation of female Conservative leaders have sought to reclaim feminism for the right without appreciating the extent to which feminist politics became associated (albeit uneasily) with the Labour party from the 1980s.

Notes

1 Bridget Christie, *A Book for Her* (London: Arrow Books, 2016), pp. 81–2.
2 While 'Women's Liberation' terminology is more commonly associated with Second Wave Feminism in the United States, both radical and socialist feminists in 1970s Britain embraced the term, which was widely used in the publications which form the primary source base for this chapter. See, inter alia, Sheila Rowbotham, *Women's Liberation and the New Politics* (Spokesman pamphlet, no. 17) (London: Bertrand Russell Peace Foundation, 1971).
3 For a comparative discussion of second wave feminist groups and party politics in Britain, Canada and the USA see Sylvia Baskevkin, 'Tough Times in Review: The British Women's Movement during the Thatcher Years', *Comparative Political* Studies, 28: 4 (January 1996), 525–52, and her *Women on the Defensive: Living through Conservative Times* (Chicago: University of Chicago Press, 1998). On British first wave feminists' party political identities see Laura Beers, '"Women for Westminster", feminism, and the limits of non-partisan associational culture', in Julie V. Gottlieb and Richard Toye (eds), *The Aftermath of Suffrage* (London: Palgrave Macmillan, 2013), pp. 224–42.
4 Joni Lovenduski and Vicky Randall, *Contemporary Feminist Politics: Women and Power in Britain* (Oxford: Oxford University Press, 1993), p. 53.
5 *Ibid.*, p. 47.
6 *Spare Rib*, May 1979, pp. 3–4.
7 Heather Nunn, *Thatcher, Politics and Fantasy: The Political Culture of Gender and Nation* (London: Lawrence & Wishart, 2002), p. 17.
8 Interview with *Hornsey Journal*, 21 April 1978, Margaret Thatcher Foundation Website (MTFW) Item 103662. Available at www.margaretthatcher.org/document/103662 (accessed 2 June 2016).
9 Radio Interview for IRN, 28 Nov 1980, MTFW Item 104452. Available at www.margaretthatcher.org/document/104452 (accessed 29 March 2016).
10 Patrick Cosgrave, *Thatcher: The First Term* (London: Bodley Head, 1985), p. 6.
11 Bob Worcester, memorandum, 26 May 1983, in *Red Book 1983* (the collated collection of privately commissioned polls and memoranda prepared by MORI for the Labour party in the aftermath of the 1983 election). Held at the Labour Party Archive, People's History Museum, Manchester.
12 Pippa Norris and Joni Lovenduski, 'Gender and Party Politics in Britain', in Pippa Norris and Joni Lovenduski, *Gender and Party Politics* (London: Sage, 1993), p. 39.
13 At her first Prime Minister's Question Time, May said: 'We have not abandoned the intention to move to a surplus; what I have said is that we will not be targeting that at the end of this Parliament.' See report in *Financial Times*, 20 July 2016.
14 *The Ipsos-MORI Almanac 2015.* Available at www.ipsos-mori.com/Assets/Docs/Publications/ipsos_mori_almanac_2015_lowres.pdf (accessed 22 March 2016).
15 Ipsos MORI Political, 'Budget Poll for The Economist', March 2011. Available at www.ipsos-mori.com/Assets/Docs/Polls/mar2011econom_web.pdf (accessed 22 March 2016).
16 Elizabeth Homans, 'Visions of Equality: Women's Rights and Political Change in 1970s Britain' (PhD thesis submitted to Bangor University, December 2014).

17 Sarah Perrigo, 'Women and Change in the Labour Party 1979–1995', in *Parliamentary Affairs* 49: 1 (1996), 117.

18 Angela Weir and Elizabeth Wilson, 'The British Women's Movement', *New Left Review*, 148 (1984), 74–103, offers a succinct discussion of the radical/socialist divide within the WLM, albeit one written from the biases of socialist feminism.

19 Lovenduski and Randall, *Contemporary Feminist Politics*, p. 6.

20 For an example of this narrative of late-1970s decline, see Anna Coote and Beatrix Campbell, *Sweet Freedom: The Struggle for Women's Liberation* (Oxford: Blackwell, 1982), p. vii.

21 Lovenduski and Randall, *Contemporary Feminist Politics*, p. 9.

22 Lynne Segal, 'Jam Today: Feminist Impacts and Transformations in the 1970s', Lawrence Black, Hugh Pemberton and Pat Thane, *Reassessing 1970s Britain* (Manchester: Manchester University Press, 2013), p. 149.

23 Sheila Rowbotham, Lynne Segal and Hilary Wainwright, *Beyond the Fragments: Feminism and the Making of Socialism* (London: Merlin Press 1979), pp. 214, 237ff.

24 Weir and Wilson, "The British Women's Movement", p. 76.

25 Barbara Taylor, *Eve and the New Jerusalem: Socialism and Feminism in the Nineteenth Century* (Cambridge, MA: Harvard, 1993).

26 Norris and Lovenduski, in 'Gender and Party Politics in Britain', p. 35, note that 'Second Wave feminism in Britain was characterized by a desire for autonomy and offered a wide-ranging critique of party politics'.

27 Nicholas Owen, 'Men and the 1970s British Women's Liberation Movement', *Historical Journal* 56: 3 (2013), 801–26.

28 Lovenduski and Randall, *Contemporary Feminist Politics*, p. 15.

29 *Ibid.*, p. 53.

30 *Ibid.*, p. 44.

31 Martin Durham, 'The Thatcher Government and the "Moral Right"', *Parliamentary Affairs* 42: 1 (1989), 58–71.

32 Campbell, *Iron Ladies.*

33 Lawrence Black, '1968 and all That(cher): Cultures of Conservatism and the New Right in Britain', in Anna von der Goltz and Britta Waldschmidt-Nelson (eds), *Inventing the Silent Majority: The Emergence of the New Right in the USA and Western Europe* (Cambridge: Cambridge University Press, 2017).

34 *Ibid.*, p. 46.

35 Laura Beers, 'Thatcher and the Women's Vote', in Ben Jackson and Robert Saunders, (eds), *Making Thatcher's Britain* (Cambridge: Cambridge University Press, 2011), pp. 113–31.

36 *Spare Rib*, May 1979, 3–4.

37 *Feminist Review*, 3 (1979).

38 Norris and Lovenduski, 'Gender and Party Politics in Britain', p. 42.

39 "The Women's Movement and the Labour Party: An Interview with Labour Party Feminists," *Feminist Review*, 16 (Summer 1984), 75–87, 80.

40 *Spare Rib*, September 1983, 4.

41 *Ibid.*, 13.

42 *Ibid.*, 30.

43 'The Women's Movement and the Labour Party'.

44 Melissa Benn, 'Labour Women Left in the Cold', *Spare Rib*, 16.

45 Beatrix Campbell, *Iron Ladies: Why Do Women Vote Tory?* (London: Virago, 1987). On women and polling data, see Beers, 'Thatcher and the Women's Vote'.

46 Melissa Benn, 'What's in a Vote?', *Spare Rib*, May 1987, 18–22.

47 *Spare Rib*, June 1987, 4–5.

48 Val Coultas, 'Feminists Must Face the Future', *Feminist Review*, 7 (Spring 1981), 35–48.

49 Sylvia Bashevkin, 'Tough Times in Review: The British Women's Movement during the Thatcher Years', *Comparative Political Studies*, 28 (January 1996), 525–52; 542–4.

50 Perrigo, 'Women and Change in the Labour Party'.

51 Loretta Loach, 'Can Feminism Survive a Third Term?', *Feminist Review*, 27 (September 1987), 23–35, 32–3. On the Loach family's political background see Mandy Merck and Lynne Segal, 'Loretta Loach Obituary', *Guardian*, 6 December 2011.

52 Hilary Wainwright, 'The Limits of Labourism: 1987 and Beyond', *New Left Review*, 164 (July/August 1987), 34–50, 48.

53 Bashevkin, 'Tough Times', 547.

11

The (feminised) contemporary Conservative Party

Rosie Campbell and Sarah Childs

Introduction

The UK Conservative Party, since 2005, is undoubtedly a more feminised institution. The party saw significant increases in the number of Conservative women MPs returned to Westminster at the 2010 and 2015 general elections. It had established new women's forums for policy debate among its women members, and participated in inter-party competition for women's votes, reflecting the interventions of key women party and parliamentary actors over the last three elections. And of course, in 2016 the Conservative Party had its second woman leader and the UK's second woman Prime Minister, the Rt Hon. Theresa May. May had publicly supported the feminisation of the party, speaking out on women's descriptive representation pre-Cameron, and was a co-founder of Women2Win with Baroness Anne Jenkin, as the latter's contribution to this book outlines. May was also supportive of the party addressing what are commonly considered to be women's issues in the 2005 period onwards. That said, the 2010–15 Conservative/Liberal Democrat coalition government faced vocal feminist criticism from the outset; suggestions that anonymity would be given to men accused of rape were met with the accusation that the unit of the Coalition was 'sealed' over women's bodies. Economic austerity was also loudly and continuously criticised as having a disproportionate and negative impact on women. The assessment from the women's movement was clear: Cameron's commitment to feminisation had been mere electoral opportunism masking both a neo-liberalism that fails to see how gender structures society, and a social conservatism that valorises the traditional gendered division of labour.

However, Cameron remained publicly committed to gender equality and Conservative women will argue that public expenditure cuts are not intended to have a disproportionate impact on women and, furthermore, that they are necessary to stimulate growth in the economy that in the median term will benefit both men and women. Clearly any assessment of the feminisation of the contemporary

Conservative Party will vary according to the variety of feminist thought that is used to make the appraisal. In this chapter we argue that feminisation – the integration of women and women's issues in politics[1] – is best understood as a process rather than an end point; as such we explore continuity and change in the extent to which the UK Conservative Party has incorporated women's bodies and concerns into the party hierarchy and policy in the 2010–15 period.

In respect of descriptive representation at the parliamentary level, the Conservative Party has continued the upward trend in the proportion of Conservative women in the parliamentary party but the rate of change slowed – as a result of dropping the 'A list' equality promotion strategy (employed in the 2010 election but not in 2015). Despite improvements in the representation of Conservative women in the House of Commons the party remains significantly behind the Labour Party, largely because of the Conservatives' continuing rejection of quotas or compulsory all-women shortlists. In 2015 the party increased the number of Conservative women MPs from 49 to 68, which resulted in the party achieving a parliamentary party that is now over 20 per cent female. The proportion of Conservative women MPs remains, however, comparatively small.

Women make up more than 40 per cent of the parliamentary Labour Party (with a total of 99 Labour women MPs). And note that Labour delivered this historic representation of women in an election where it saw a net loss of 26 seats. In addition, the Conservative success relied on a rather 'last minute' effort to select women candidates in winnable seats in the final year ahead of the election, when the portents were not looking good for women's representation on the party's benches. In fact, one year before the election, key gender equality insiders were very worried that the number of Conservative women MPs would decrease rather than increase. Considerable persuasive energy had to be expended to ensure that more Conservative women MPs were elected the following May. Indeed, some party insiders were so worried that a good number of senior women suggested that 'all options would need to be on the table' (code for all-women shortlists, AWS) if the number of Conservative women in Parliament declined in 2015. Given the increases in the number of Conservative women elected on polling day, what appetite there was within the Conservative party for equality guarantees looks to have passed – at least for the time being. Although the Conservative Party has made improvements in terms of women's descriptive representation, the mechanism for delivery (internal party negotiations and persuasion) remains largely invisible. As such there is a danger that this somewhat informal approach might lead to the perception in the wider party that the numbers of women elected is increasing 'naturally', which may, in turn, lead to complacency and the risk that hard won gains could be eroded in future elections.

Turning to substantive (acting for) representation the Conservative Party in 2015 was very much in alignment with the other major parties in terms of the women's issues it addressed in its election manifesto.[2] Policy offerings 'for women' were notable in respect of childcare, violence against women and girls (VAWAG), and women and development. That said, attention to such women's issues, and indeed the 'liberal feminist' position adopted in respect of these, remain subject to considerable leftist-feminist criticism in light of what can be called the 'gendered austerity critique'. Widely held among leftist-feminist commentators, academics and activities, this critique claims that despite the party advocating individual policies 'for women' that can be considered feminist, its underpinning governing economic strategy was one that damages women.[3] In other words, the impact that austerity politics has on women cannot be mitigated by discrete 'women friendly' policies. Critics might also consider these women's policies 'safe' issues, such as rhetoric condemning violence against women and promoting the role of women in international development. Such policies cost relatively little in economic terms and Fit with wider conservative ideologies. The tensions here surrounding what constitutes feminist policy feeds into debates concerning how to evaluate parties' and politicians' claims to be acting 'for women'.[4]

A feminised political party: a framework for analysis

A definition of a 'feminised party' is necessary in order to evaluate the extent to which the Conservative Party under Cameron was feminised. This chapter argues that a feminised party must at its core have women participating within its structures, and must address women's issues, concerns and perspectives. In practice, these two dimensions are likely to overlap. A party's possible response to the twin demands of feminisation can be distinguished on the basis of whether it makes positive (feminist), neutral or negative (anti-feminist) responses to both dimensions of feminisation. For example, a political party may choose to integrate women but not to address their concerns. Alternatively, they may integrate women and their concerns but not do so in a feminist fashion on either dimension – refusing to see women as a group with representational needs and adopting a neutral or anti-feminist ideological position. This description of feminised parties suggests empirical research should investigate:

1 The level of women's participation in party structures, including, but importantly not limited to, the parliamentary party; whether the party employs specific mechanisms in both party structures and the parliamentary party to guarantee women's descriptive representation;
2 Whether women's participation is substantive across the party's various structures and activities or symbolic and limited to certain forms or places;
3 The nature of the role, remit and ideology of women's organisations and, in particular, whether these are integrated formally into the wider party structure and policy making bodies, and to whom they are accountable, both upwards and downwards (with bearings on notions of intra-party democracy);
4 Whether a party regards women as a corporate entity capable of being represented

(both descriptively and substantively) and if so, whether the party is susceptible to feminist arguments for this. This might include whether the party makes gender-based and or feminist claims rather than non-gendered, neutral or anti-feminist claims; and finally

5 The extent to which party policies are gendered and in what ways.

Feminised change in the Conservative Party 2001–15[5]

The feminisation of the Conservative Party across both dimensions since the early to mid-2000s is mapped in Table 11.1. Note how this process of feminisation post-dates the premiership of Margaret Thatcher (1979–90).[6] Despite being the first woman Prime Minister, Thatcher's Cabinet was for nearly all of her time in office all male, and she did little actively to recruit more women parliamentary candidates. It is notable that the party in the 1990s was one in which women's group identities were effectively side-lined. The years 2001–5 saw the emergence of feminisation demands from both the voluntary and the parliamentary party, but for the most part this was behind the scenes. There was talk among some women that it would be better if the party had more women MPs, for example, but this rarely generated stronger calls for the party to intervene in selection processes.

Labour's quota policy of all-women shortlists (AWS) was explicitly criticised, not least, for offending against the principle of merit – which was not regarded as a gendered concept. The 'catch up' years occurred during 2005–10. Women activists in the party self-consciously gendered the leadership election that ultimately saw David Cameron elected party leader. A critical actor – Anne Jenkin – was, already noted, moved to establish, working with Theresa May MP and others, a new ginger Group Women2Win in order to press the case for women's descriptive representation. She was persuaded by the argument that the best opportunity was prior to, rather than after, the election of a new leader. And under Cameron, feminisation became a key pillar – albeit not always so acknowledged by party scholars – of the party's modernisation strategy. Women's bodies would symbolise that the Tories were no longer the 'nasty' party that May had talked about at the 2002 party conference.

The context post-2005 was conducive to feminisation: the party had lost three successive general elections, and there was concern over the 'loss' of the female vote to Blair's New Labour. Cameron's support among party members gave him a mandate for reform too. Ultimately, the party would fight an election in 2010 with a competitive manifesto on women's issues, for example, relating to work/life balance: the gender pay gap, flexible working, and maternity and paternity leave.[7] They more than doubled the number of Conservative women MPs in 2010 to 49, but Conservative women MPs still constituted just 16 per cent of the parliamentary party. This figure was far short of the Labour Party and the party leadership arguably failed to maximise potential feminisation gains at this critical moment.[8]

Table 11.1 Feminisation of the Conservative Party

1990s–early 2000s Women, and women's parts of the party side-lined	Conservative women were of two distinct types (Maguire 1998): (1) the traditional woman member infamous for making sandwiches and stuffing envelopes, and (2) the 'career' Conservative woman who was seeking political office. The latter was few in number. The former under threat: the CWO's existence was questioned: the Hague Reforms downgraded its role; pressure is put on women constituency committees to close down; the CWO 'may' but did not have to be included on all mainstream voluntary committees at regional and constituency levels.
2001–5 'behind the scenes' feminisation demands	Conservative Party leadership fails to recognise that British society has changed: 2005 GE manifesto constitutes women as victims of crime (a woman's handbag is stolen), matrons (who will keep hospital wards clean) for example (Childs *et al.* 2010)
2005–10 The 'politics of catch up'	Establishment of Women2Win by among others Anne Jenkin and Theresa May; post of Vice-Chair for Women revived; May calls for the establishment of an 'A' list of candidates; 2005 CWO fringe meeting at party conference witnesses call for positive discrimination; Women2Win undertake sustained activities to train, mentor and support women parliamentary candidates; sell out CWO annual conferences (2006–7). CWO publish post-election critique of party vis-à-vis women – picked up by the media. Establishment of women's overview group and women's policy review group, chaired by May and Laing, respectively. *Women's Policy Group Report*, 'Women in the World Today', fed directly into the 2010 general election manifesto, even as it was not accorded the same status as six policy review groups. General election manifesto more competitive on women's terrain than previously. Establishment of Conservative Women's Forums; the party Convention Strategy Committee includes the CWO. All the regional chairmen were instructed to include the CWO on their committees and, within their regions, to ask the area and constituency committees to do likewise.
2010–15 Feminisation downgraded	As Home Secretary and Women's Minister, May plays less of a role as a critical actor; other senior women active pre-2010 similarly play lesser roles at least until late in the parliament; the CWO has a much lower profile and there is a failure to institutionalise feminisation the 'women's parts of the party'; the VC for women post is abolished (re-established in 2014); Women2Win continue to provide training etc. for candidates; 'priority list' candidate selection measures are dropped – the party relies on equality promotion and rhetoric. Legislative activity on 'safe women's issues', not least violence against women, is high profile, but critics question funding for this, as well as the Coalition's austerity politics. Cameron's personal commitment questioned following decision not to wear the Fawcett T-shirt.

During 2010–15, feminisation was less a party leitmotif with gender somewhat side-lined once again. In terms of the integration of women in the party, strong equality promotion measures were dropped for candidate selection at the 2015 general election. The party's women's organisations appear to have suffered from a failure of institutionalisation, and previous gains proved precarious (a potential problem previously identified).[9] In policy terms, despite high-profile campaigns to draw attention to austerity's deleterious gendered impact, the effects on women were defended as unfortunate collateral damage.[10] In sum, the 2010–15 Parliament turned out to be a less than favourable context for Conservative Party feminisation. In the first instance, extant critical actors, not least Theresa May MP, were much less active; as Home Secretary she was preoccupied with her ministerial portfolio.[11] The gender gap in voting – whether perceived or real – also appeared to resonate less with the party leadership.[12] The party's grass roots were less favourably disposed vis-à-vis modernisation as, among other reasons, the party faced the United Kingdom Independence Party (UKIP) threat from the right. And there was a retreat from modernisation in the context of the economic crisis and greater ideological purity (see special issue of *British Politics* 2015). Finally, the personnel of the Coalition government was also very male.[13]

Table 11.2 outlines in more detail the party's reforms to its selection processes between 2005 and 2010, showing how the party leadership sought to change who did the selecting, and how the party relied on – at its most progressive – a 'priority' or 'A' list of candidates, from whom selectorates were expected, but not required, to select: this list would be 50 per cent female, at least at its outset.

The parliamentary party and the descriptive representation of women

In 2015 there was an increase in the percentage of women in the House of Commons from 22 per cent to 29 per cent (see Table 11.3). Much of this overall increase was driven by the Labour Party and the Scottish National Party (SNP) who increased the percentage of women among their MPs from 35 to 43 per cent, and 17 to 36 per cent respectively. The increase on the Conservative benches was from 16 to 21 per cent. Labour's success relied once again (its fourth time) on its use of party quotas – AWS. The SNP success likely resulted from a combination of a feminisation of the party that had taken place since the 1990s and the fact that the party won many seats that they did not expect to gain at the time that the candidate selections were made.

Table 11.4 reinforces these observations, by showing the placement of women candidates by seat safety. This captures the likelihood of each party translating women candidates into MPs at the election; there is little point selecting large numbers of women candidates in those seats that the party will be unlikely to win. Here, the Labour Party was considerably ahead of the other parties: 54 per cent compared with 33 per cent overall. This is again the positive result of using AWS precisely

Table 11.2 Conservative Party selection reforms 2005–10[1]

Date	Reforms
May 2006	(1) The creation of a 'priority list' of candidates, of whom at least 50% would be women, with a 'significant' percentage from black/minority ethnicity and disabled communities; (2) A three-month progress review; (3) The use of headhunting, mentoring and guidance of local associations; and (4) The option of holding primaries (either open or closed) or 'community panels' to select candidates. Associations in vacant Conservative-held and target seats would be 'expected' to select from among the priority list candidates.
August 2006	(1) Constituency associations with fewer than 300 members were expected to hold a primary. (2) Where associations choose not to employ a primary model, members would draw up a shortlist of three or four candidates from a list of 12–15. The shortlist would be sex balanced: 2 women and 2 men; the final decision would be made by the EC on the basis of in-depth interviews; and (3) If the EC shortlists an AWS (by default), the existing model of selection could be retained.
Jan. 2007	(1) Associations were permitted to choose from the full list of approved candidates with a requirement that at each stage of the selection process at least 50% of the candidates would have to be women; (2) Associations could still choose to select solely from the priority list.
Sept. 2009[2]	(1) All applications were to be sifted by Association Officers along with the Party Chairman and a representative from the Candidates' Department; (2) Six candidates were to go before (ideally) a Special General Meeting or Open Primary; (3) The Association Executive could meet to remove the 'completely unsuitable' and add a reserve in 'exceptional' circumstances; the final field could be reduced to four; (4) Any seats where the sitting MP announces his or her retirement after 1 January 2010 would be selected by 'by-election rules'; Associations would simply be presented with a list of three candidates by the party from which to choose.[3]
2010–15	Abolition of the A list; 2014 onwards, additional persuasion efforts amid fears of decline in the numbers of women MPs.

1 Source: J. Ashe, R. Campbell, S. Childs and E. Evans, 'Stand by your Man', *British Politics*, 5: 4 (2010).
2 In November 2009 Cameron announced that the candidate list would be reopened.

Table 11.2 *Continued*

Jeremy Middleton, Chairman of the National Conservative Convention
(Conservativehome, accessed 7 August 2009), stressed that the Association picks the
shortlist, does the interviews and runs the selection process and, moreover, that the
rules were agreed 'collectively' by 'all members' of the Board, presumably to pre-empt
accusations that representatives of the voluntary party were excluded.

3 The Party Chairman preferred that sitting MPs announce their retirement pre-Christmas
(Conservativehome, accessed 30 July 2009). Jonathon Isaby of Conservativehome
makes the same appeal to avoid 'the scenario where the members who have loyally
worked for them over the years have that restrictive shortlist foisted upon them' (Times
online, 19 November 2009).

Table 11.3 Women MPs by party 2015

Party	Number	Percentage
Conservative	68	21
Labour	99	43
SNP	20	36
Lib Dem	0	0
Green	1	100
UKIP	0	0
Other	3	15
Total	191	29%

Source: Parliamentary Candidates UK; percentages are rounded www.parliamentary
candidates.org funded by the Leverhulme Trust and the ESRC.

Table 11.4 Women candidates by party and seat type 2015

	All seats		Target seats	
	Women candidates %	**Men candidates %**	**Women candidates %**	**Men candidates %**
Conservative	32.2	67.8	28.2	71.8
Labour	33.2	66.8	52.8	47.2
SNP	37.7	62.3		
Liberal Democrat	27.6	72.4	35	65
UKIP	13.5	86.5	20	80
Green	37.6	62.4	36.4	63.6
Plaid Cymru	28.9	71.1		
Total	28.2	71.8		

Source: Parliamentary Candidates UK.

in the seats the party was likely to win. In contrast, the Conservative Party placed women in only 28 per cent of their target seats. This is an improvement on their historic record, but still far behind the other main parties. It is worth recalling that the percentage of women MPs on the Conservative benches was 3.3 per cent in 1983, 4.5 per cent in 1987, 6 per cent in 1992, 8 per cent in 1997, 8.6 per cent in 2001 and 15.7 per cent in 2005; the figures for Labour were 4.8 per cent, 9.2 per cent, 13.7 per cent, 24.2 per cent, 23 per cent, 27.7 per cent and 31.6 per cent. These differences are not, as stated above, the result purely of the supply of women candidates but rather reflect the demand for women candidates created by the Labour Party, and institutionalised via AWS.

That the Conservative Party managed to increase its women MPs at all in 2015 was in very large part due to the efforts in the final year of the Parliament. There was considerable concern among a handful of key gender equality activists within the party, who noted the failure of the party to select women in the party's target seats. As of December 2014 the pattern of parliamentary selections by party revealed that the Conservatives were behind the other two main parties: in each of the three largest parties' retirement seats – those seats they hope, if not expect to hold, at the election – 35 per cent of Tory candidates were women; 75 per cent of Labour candidates were women; and 40 per cent of Lib Dem candidates were women. It appears that the gender activists efforts to make the leadership face up to its problem of selecting women paid off.

Understanding Conservative attitudes towards quotas

The Conservative Party has maintained its equality promotion measures associated with Women2Win, and the party centre has continued to push the message of women's representation, and continues to train selectorates. That said, the amount of equality rhetoric looks much reduced, at least publicly. And the party's strongest equality promotion measure, the 'Priority' or 'A' list, used for 2010, was 'quietly dropped' for 2015. Party gender equality insiders were clear from summer 2014 that the leadership would not be adopting any new interventionist measures.

How has this situation come about? A number of the 2010 intake women MPs had been publicly critical of AWS, not least in the 2012 and 2014 parliamentary debates on the Speaker's Conference. While Home Secretary, Theresa May was less the high-profile party spokesperson on this issue in the 2010–15 Parliament compared to previous years. Yet it would not be fair to present women's descriptive representation outcomes as a failure of commitment by those women who were active on women's representation prior to 2010. If anything, some of these women have become more politicised on this issue over time. Halfway through the 2010 Parliament there was an emergent realisation that too many 'good' women potential candidates were failing to 'click' with constituency selectors; unable to 'swagger', women aspirants were falling to selectorate bias.[14]

Consciousness of these practices felt all the more real to those Conservative women who had been long seeking women's presence. There was a strong sense that the male party leadership was not taking women's under-representation sufficiently seriously and that it had walked away from its strong equality promotion measures of 2010.[15] In short, political will at the very top was felt to be lacking, at least until quite close to the election. Public gender equality voices included senior Cabinet and ex-Cabinet women MPs such as Maria Miller, Caroline Spelman and Nicky Morgan alongside peers such as Baroness Jenkin, one of the co-founders of Women2Win. Their response to the selection figures was to demand that post-2015 'all options' including AWS must be 'on the table'.[16] However, this demand appeared linked to a decline in the numbers of women MPs in 2015. Had the number of Conservative women MPs decreased we might have expected a group of senior Conservative women, supported by a few of their male allies, to collectively come out of the quota closet and demand all-women shortlists.[17] With the decline in the numbers of Conservative women MPs (from 70 to 67) following the snap 2017 general election reaction from party gender activists is anticipated.

In order for full AWS to be implemented by the Tories, three factors would need to be addressed.[18] First, the party leader would need to counter membership hostility. When Cameron talked of AWS in 2010 it was felt that they might just constitute the metaphorical back-breaking 'straw' for unhappy members.[19] And if there was reluctance previously to interfere with local party autonomy how much harder might this be when the number of women MPs had just increased? Second, there is the ideological consideration; Conservatives have hitherto lacked a language that supports quotas.[20] Third is the need for more extensive elite Conservative support. The recently appointed Education Minister was one of the women seen 'kite-flying' quotas alongside Baroness Jenkin. Although immediately 'slapped down' by the then leadership,[21] this group of Conservative women could be a leader's Praetorian Guard if quotas are ever advocated. Indeed, if the Conservatives shifted to advocating legislative rather than party quotas then intra-party hostility might well be moderated: internally, it could be presented as a constitutional reform rather than a top–down party reform critical of the party's grass roots.

There has been little sign of any such move since 2015. The appointment of Theresa May as PM means that the Conservative Party is now led by a woman who has a good record on descriptive representation. Indeed, she has, as PM, continued her support for Women2Win. Nevertheless, the Party Chairman's evidence to the Women and Equalities Committee inquiry in 2016[22] offered little reassurance that the party would revisit more interventionist measures; and in the debate on *The Good Parliament*,[23] a report which included a recommendation to commence Section 106 of the Equality Act 2010, which requires political parties to provide candidate diversity data, the government maintained its preference for the voluntary provision of this data.[24]

One development which speaks to the feminisation at the parliamentary level if not within the party qua party is the post-election establishment of a Women and Equality Select Committee (WEC) in the House of Commons.[25] If quotas were not yet palatable, clearly the setting up of the WEC was. Chaired by the ex-Cabinet minister, the Conservative Maria Miller, the proposal for such a committee had had cross-party support during 2014/15. The proposal itself was contained within a report by the All Party Parliamentary Women in Parliament Group (WIP APPG) chaired by the ex-MP and Conservative Mary Macleod. This new institution 'was appointed by the House of Commons on 3 June 2015 to examine the expenditure, administration and policy of the Government Equalities Office (GEO)'. That MPs from all parties, along with the support of some senior men, were prepared to ensure, in the run up to and the immediate aftermath of the election, that the committee was established shows a certain commitment to the institutionalisation of gender and equalities within the House of Commons. Conservative women MPs championed this publicly too. Margot James MP, for example, cited this as one of her top three gender aims at the WOW cultural festival on London's Southbank.[26] In its first year the WEC has undertaken inquiries into: transgender equality; the Equality and Human Rights Commission; the Gender Pay Gap; employment opportunities for Muslims; Women in Executive Management; Pregnancy and maternity discrimination; sexual harassment and sexual violence in schools.[27] In the aforementioned debate on *The Good Parliament* the 2016 government announced its support for making the WEC a permanent committee.[28]

'Acting for' women

There is little evidence that the UK Conservative Party is socially conservative or anti-feminist, compared with the US Republican, for example.[29] Instead, there is evidence of liberally feminist attitudes. British Conservative women MPs are overwhelmingly socially liberal.[30] Indeed, Conservative women are, on average, more economically wet, more centrist, less post-materialist, and more one-nation than Conservative men.[31] Women members are also more predisposed to feminism, whether in terms of equal opportunities, women's suitability for politics, the impact of women's paid work on family life and childcare. The issue of equal pay polarises members' views further.

The post-2005 Conservative Party leadership under Cameron accepted that British society was no longer that of the 1950s, with its bifurcated and romanticised sexual division of labour. Here, belatedly, was acceptance of the triumph of liberal feminism.[32] The 2010 Conservative manifesto, accordingly – and seeking to compete on the women's terrain – offered a series of policies for women that addressed, most notably, the balancing of work and family life, violence against women, and women and development concerns.[33] Many of these Conservative pledges for women reflected, moreover, feminist analysis in so far as gender relations are recognised to be bifurcated, hierarchical and problematic.[34] That said, alongside these liberal feminist policies there were also some more socially conservative ones (marriage tax allowance (MTA), in particular), and an overarching economic framework that would turn out to be highly gendered in its effects..[35]

Reviewing the five years of the Conservative-led Coalition, a series of policies and legislative interventions can be identified that extended opportunities for women. These include greater flexibility in parental leave; the right to request flexible working, now available to all employees;[36] greater state support in the tax system for childcare; and various measures taken, domestically and internationally, to address women's health;[37] and violence against women. The commitment to protect NHS funding and overseas aid also had a significant gender dimension.[38] More in-depth analysis[39] of the Coalition's actions regarding VAWAG concluded that this policy area has become widely accepted as a legitimate political concern across the political spectrum. The Coalition's efforts in the area of VAWAG frequently built upon New Labour's legacy. Coalition interventions included making stalking a specific offence;[40] the enactment of the 2010 EU Commission's anti-trafficking directive, in the Protection of Freedoms Act 2012;[41] the development of a modern slavery Bill in 2014–15; and the introduction of an action plan regarding female genital mutilation (FGM) (it was first made illegal in 1985).[42] One notable development was the criminalisation of FGM, an approach over which there are differences of opinion among women's civil society and third-sector groups.[43] It has to be noted too that criticism of the amount of money tied to VAWAG – and whether it was ring-fenced – was loudly made by feminist activists.

Childcare, another key cross-party women's issue, saw intra-Coalition division in the 2010 Parliament, particularly over Conservative Party attempts to relax the children:childcarer ratios, which was resisted by the Liberal Democrats. Coalition policy on childcare was multi-faceted, and reflected acknowledgement that governments of all hues should address the issue of women's work/life balance, whether on the grounds that many mothers work; single mothers should work; or on the basis of an economic imperative to boost GDP. Table 11.5 shows that some childcare provisions introduced by the Coalition were positively received by feminists – not least, more free childcare, and subsidies for the cost of childcare – even as others were highly criticised – the preference for non-working single parents to work and for their children to receive professional childcare.[44]

Whether a government acts 'for women' is not just about its policies on what are widely or commonly regarded as women's issues; it is also about its wider policies. And it is in respect of the Coalition's austerity economic policy that attracted sustained leftist-feminist criticism.[45] Prioritising spending cuts over tax rises would always – and inevitably – disproportionately disadvantage women facing the 'triple jeopardy' of greater reliance on welfare state services, benefits and employment. The Women's Budget Group, the Fawcett Society and the Labour Party all sought to lay bare the economic costs for women.[46] As stated, criticism of the Conservative

Table 11.5 Evaluating coalition childcare policies

Positive measures	Critique	Preferred policy
• Increases in childcare support • Tax free childcare under 12s worth 20% • 15 hours free childcare under 2s	• Sure start no longer ring-fenced • Query emphasis on lone parents working • Critical of the reduction in childcare element in working tax credit • Subsidies unlikely reduce costs; worsen quality • Marketplace is uncompetitive • Early years premium – is this a 'one off' expenditure • Queries parents with income of 300K need childcare assistance	• Childcare is an end in itself • Extend and increase free entitlement to childcare • Direct public provision of childcare by highly qualified and well paid staff • Fund childcare at source; • Increase spending on SureStart • Abolish high income tax on child benefit for those families earning more than 50K

Sources: www.wbg.org and MacLeavy, *A 'New Politics'*.

Party's preference on spending cuts resides in a suspicion that these have an ideological as well as an economic underpinning.[47] Theoretical comparison of feminism and neo-liberal economics[48] suggest that such an economic settlement presupposes what many – particularly feminist economists and political scientists, social policy experts and feminist activists – would depict as an anti-feminist economic policy. Defenders admittedly will have little truck with much criticism that austerity is a feminist issue, arguing that the policies are not designed to disproportionately affect women – the 'collateral damage' defence. Instead, they will argue that ultimately women will benefit from deficit reduction.

The 2015 Conservative manifesto can be analysed to document party differences, and in particular, the Conservative Party's differentiation from its 2010 Coalition partner. Six main 'women's issues' were identifiable across the main seven parties' manifestos:[49] (1) women and paid work; (2) mothers and childcare; (3) carers and the 'cared for'; (4) VAWAG; (5) public life; and (6) human rights, development and immigration. As in 2010 there was a broad consensus about what constitutes the main terrain of women's issues in the UK, or more precisely, what parties consider should be addressed in their general election manifestos. Women's work and the work/life balance, and childcare[50] issues were again the battleground, cementing their centrality in UK politics, and is analysed in more depth here.[51]

All of the parties (bar UKIP) were in agreement that large companies (250+ employees) should be required to publish their gender pay gap data. Table 11.6 outlines each party's pledges that address the component parts of the gender pay gap. The Conservatives' pledges were minimal here compared to the other main parties, with only one additional pledge on top of its commitment to the publica-

Table 11.6 Party pledges and the gender pay gap

Components of the gender pay gap	Pledge	Parties
Gender discrimination	Enforce Equality Act	Labour, SNP
	Additional pay transparency	Lib Dem, SNP
	Anonymise CVs	Lib Dem, Greens
	Abolish tribunal system	Labour
The 'Mommy' gap	Back to work support	UKIP, Lib Dem
	Strengthen law on women's/maternity discrimination	Labour, SNP, Greens
Gender segregated employment market	Better value women's work,	Labour, PC
	Gender and apprenticeships,	Lib Dem, SNP
	Gender and entrepreneurs,	Lib Dem, Greens
	Education, careers, segregation	Lab, Lib Dem, SNP, PC, UKIP
	Public sector acceleration programme	Lib Dem
Women's low pay	Raise minimum wage,	Labour, SNP
	Enforce living wage	PC
Women's part-time work/flexibility	End zero hours,	PC
	Importance of flexible working	Con, Lib Dem

tion of large company gender pay gap data. This pledge addresses women's part-time work – 'removing barriers that stop women' being included. One might add under 'gender discrimination', parties' pledges on paternity leave and pay: the Conservatives are quiet on this.[52]

Four policy areas address women in their biological capacity as *mothers*. The Conservative Party spoke to the need for greater attention to maternal mental health and mothers' well-being (alongside the Lib Dems, Greens and UKIP). Table 11.7 lists the policy pledges relating to maternity, paternity, and parental leave and pay in more detailed. Note the emphasis given to 'shared' parenting, and the focus by Labour on increasing paternity leave and pay and the Liberal Democrat's 'use it or lose it month'. These are both policies that aim to enhance the likelihood that men will take paternity leave, in practice. The Conservative offering was minimal here – relating to exempting working-age benefits caps from maternity and paternity leave; neither Plaid Cymru nor UKIP address this issue.

Turning to childcare, the Conservatives' commitment to increase free childcare for 3- and 4-year-olds to 30 hours, announced prior to the start of the short campaign, was a key moment when the party placed a gender challenge *in front* of Labour, who offered 25 hours for same age groups; SNP offered 30 hours for 3- and 4-year-olds, and eligible 2-year-olds; the Liberal Democrats, 20 hours

Table 11.7 Maternity, paternity and parental leave pledges

	Maternity leave	Maternity pay	Paternity leave	Paternity pay	Parental leave
Labour	Strengthen law against maternity discrimination		Double, from 2 weeks to 4 weeks	Increase by more than £100 to £260 per week (national minimum wage)	Consult on grandparents' leave
Conservative		We will freeze working age benefits … with exemptions for disability and pensioner benefits – as at present – as well as maternity allowance, statutory maternity pay …		We will freeze working age benefits … with exemptions for … statutory paternity pay	
Liberal Democrat			'Use it or lose it month'; ambition to see paternity leave a 'day one' right		Ambition to see shared parental leave a 'day one' right
SNP	Tighten law on maternity discrimination		Increased		
Greens	Properly enforce discrimination law	Continue to receive statutory maternity pay		Continue to receive statutory paternity pay	

for 2- to 4-year olds and 20 hours for all working parents with children aged 9 months–2 years; Greens, free but voluntary from birth to age 7; Plaid Cymru, 3- and 4-year olds; and UKIP who would maintain 15 hours for 3- and 4-year-olds.

As in 2010, the Conservative Party manifesto addressed the institution of marriage (gay and straight). In so doing, they formally signal their agnosticism about whether individuals choose to stay home, and arguably,[53] also reveal a preference for 'mother care' and the 1.5 worker model, given that it is mostly likely middle-class women who would take up this option. MTA would rise in line with the personal allowance. UKIP agreed with the Tories that MTA should be increased; Labour and the SNP would end MTA.

In documenting, once again, the pledges 'for women' included in the 2015 Conservative Party manifesto, it is possible to position them both against the position of other parties, in respect of their 2010 manifesto, and against the backdrop of the 2010–15 Coalition. If one assumes that the Conservative manifesto is a truer reflection of the party's intent that its record in government, we might conclude that on what we have previously considered to be 'safe' issues – not least VAWAG and gender and international development – the party is continuing in its liberally feminist direction. At the same time it also remains committed to MTA, what can be regarded as a socially conservative position. Some feminist critics will moreover likely continue in explicating what they see as the ideological underpinnings of the parties' childcare policy pledges – assumptions about single mothers and paid work, poor women's inadequate parenting, and role of the state not to provide for childcare, but to remove 'regulations' to maximise childcare provision.

Hanging over all this was the expected £12 billion cuts to welfare. This commitment had been seen as a 'negotiating' commitment; something to be whittled away in a second set of Coalition negotiations with the Liberal Democrats. With a majority in the House, David Cameron did not seek to walk away from this; rather by bringing back into government Iain Duncan Smith MP, Cameron's resolution that the cuts would be pursued was made clear. It was widely expected that the welfare cuts would fall disproportionately once again on (young) mothers.

Conservative women at the polls

We can use the British Election Study (BES) 2015 to evaluate whether the Conservative Party was able to secure women's votes in the election.[54] Unlike the overwhelming majority of opinion polls published in the run up to the 2015 general election, the research council funded large-scale random sample social surveys. The BES and the British Social Attitudes (BSA) survey produced party of vote reports that were within a one per cent margin of the actual difference between the two main parties. As such the BES provides a reliable source to compare men's and women's vote choice in 2015. Figure 11.1 demonstrates that, overall, more women than men reported voting for the Labour, Conservative and

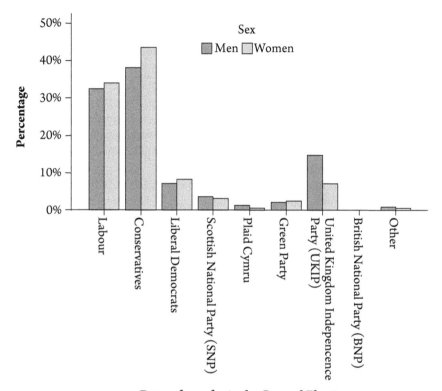

Party of vote for in the General Election
Cases weighted by Combined main study weight (capped selection
plus capped demographic weights)

Notes: N=1238 Validated voters only
The British Election Study includes a voter validation exercise where the electoral register
is checked to establish whether respondents did in fact vote in the General Election.

Figure 11.1 Party of vote by sex, BES face-to-face survey 2015

Liberal Democrat parties, while there was a greater proportion of men among
UKIP voters; in total 15 per cent of men and 7 per cent of women reported voting
for UKIP.

However, Figure 11.2 shows that the aggregate level sex differences in
Conservative vote varies within age groups. The pattern is somewhat mixed among
the under 45s and low sample size issues in the 18 to 25-year-old group would
suggest treating the large gender gap with caution. However, among the over
45s the traditional gender gap holds with a greater proportion of women voting
Conservative. Figure 11.3, however, illustrates where perhaps the most profound
differences between men and women were evident; UKIP drew a disproportionate share of its vote from men aged over 45. The evidence suggests that in 2015 the

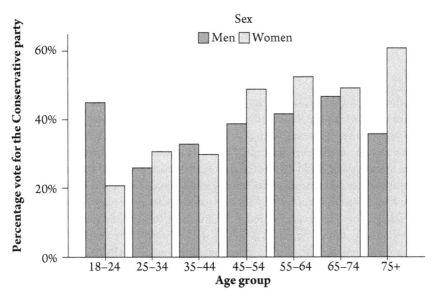

Note: N=1238 Validated voters only

Figure 11.2 Percentage Conservative vote by sex and age group, BES face-to-face survey 2015

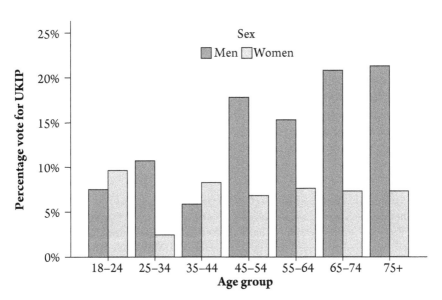

Note: N=1238 Validated voters only

Figure 11.3 Percentage UKIP vote by sex and age group, BES face-to-face survey 2015

Conservatives did not suffer a 'woman problem' and in fact it continued to do well among women, particularly among the older generations.

Conclusion

The election of David Cameron as the leader of the Conservative Party marked a critical moment for the feminisation of the party. Women activists *already* mobilised within the party were able to secure gains in terms of both the descriptive and substantive representation of women. Their claim that women's votes were essential to the party and could be secured through feminisation – and that feminisation and environmentalism were useful ideologies to signal the decontamination of the party brand – were embraced by the then new leader in the run-up to the 2010 general election. However, the vocal commitment to gender equality has waned somewhat over time. The extent to which the party might be described as feminised is contested as relatively more women Conservative MPs have been elected (although the party is still far behind Labour and the SNP in terms of the proportion of women on its benches) and a range of liberal feminist policy positions have been adopted. However, many of these gains have not been formally institutionalised and depend on ongoing negotiation within the party. Furthermore, the impact of public sector spending cuts on women has been an area of feminist criticism of the Coalition and now the 2015 Conservative government. The extent to which women voters responded to the feminisation of the Conservative Party is difficult to disentangle from the effects of UKIP securing a disproportionate number of men's votes but it is evident that the public spending cuts did not lead to a mass exodus to Labour from the Conservatives among women voters in 2015. Feminist academics and practitioners alike will be closely watching the 2017–2022 Conservative government, led for now by a woman leader who has worn the Fawcett Society's 'This is what a feminist looks like' T-shirt[55] to assess whether the party's feminisation continues, stalls, or goes into reverse.

Notes

1 J. Lovenduski, *Feminizing Politics* (Cambridge: Polity Press, 2015).
2 The section on women's substantive representation draws on R. Campbell and S. Childs, 'What the Coalition Did for Women: A New Gender Consensus, Coalition Division and Gendered Austerity', in Anthony Seldon and Mike Finn (eds), *The Coalition Effect, 2010–2015* (Cambridge: Cambridge University Press, 2015), pp. 397–499 and R. Campbell and S. Childs, 'Conservatism, feminisation and the representation of women in UK politics', *British Politics*, 10: 2 (2015), 148–68.
3 See for example, the Women's Budget Group, www.wbg.org (accessed 20 March 2017).
4 K. Celis and S. Childs, 'The Substantive Representation of Women: What to do with Conservative Claims?', *Political Studies*, 60: 1 (2012), 213–25.

5 This section derives largely from S. Childs and P. Webb, *Sex, Gender and the Conservative Party* (London: Palgrave Macmillan, 2012). Note, there is no study of the Conservative Party of the 1990s against which one can compare the party of the 2000s.

6 Although there has been considerable academic study of Thatcher and Thatcherism there has been much less feminist academic analysis. Crudely, while deploying traditional gender roles when it suited her, at other times Thatcher would deny the relevance of gender and reject feminism. See for a summary S. Childs, 'Thatcher's Gender Trouble: Ambivalence and the Thatcher Legacy', Political Studies Association blog, 17 April 2013, www.psa.ac.uk/political-insight/blog/thatcher%E2%80%99s-gender-trouble-ambivalence-and-thatcher-legacy (accessed 20 March 2017).

7 R. Campbell and S. Childs, '"Wags", "Wives" and "Mothers" … But what about Women Politicians?' in Andrew Geddes and Jonathon Tonge (eds), *The UK Votes: The 2010 General Election* (Oxford: Oxford University Press, 2015).

8 Childs and Webb, *Sex, Gender*.

9 *Ibid.* A full analysis of the party's women's organisation lies beyond this chapter; it would require the kind of in-depth qualitative research upon which the previous study was conducted, and which was funded by the ESRC.

10 Campbell and Childs, '"Wags", "Wives" and "Mothers"'.

11 This concern remains.

12 Summarising Rosie Campbell, 'What do we Really Know About Women Voters? Gender, Elections and Public Opinion', *The Political Quarterly*, 83: 4 (2012), 703–10.

13 Campbell and Childs, '"Wags", "Wives" and "Mothers"'.

14 M. Parris, 'Women need more Swagger to Become MPs', *The Times*, 5 July 2014, www.the-times.co.uk/tto/opinion/columnists/article4139436.ece (accessed 20 March 2017); S. Childs, 'Swaggering in a Gendered Attribute: It won't Help Women get Selected as Parliamentary Candidates', British Politics Group blog (14 July 2014), http://brit-ishpoliticsgroup.blogspot.co.uk/2014/07/swaggering-is-gendered-attribute-it.html (accessed 20 March 2017).

15 Nigel Morris, 'Tories Quietly drop David Cameron's "A-list" for Minority Candidates', *Independent*, 5 October 2012, www.independent.co.uk/news/uk/politics/tories-quietly-drop-david-camerons-alistfor-minority-candidates-8199985.html (accessed 17 March 2017).

16 Anne Jenkins, 'Anne Jenkin & Brooks Newmark MP: The Party Needs more Women Candidates – and Here's how to get Them', *Conservative Home*, 28 April 2014, www.conservativehome.com/platform/2014/04/from-anne-jenkin-tweetbrooks-the-party-needs-more-women-candidates-and-heres-how-to-get-them.html (accessed 17 March 2017); 'Caroline Spelman Joins Calls for All-Women Tory Shortlists', *BBC News*, www.bbc.co.uk/news/uk-politics-26177763 (accessed 17 March 2017).

17 Rowena Mason, 'Too Little Progress on Female MPs, says Senior Tory', *Guardian*, 5 February 2015, www.theguardian.com/politics/2015/feb/05/tories-female-mps-bernard-jenkin (accessed 17 March 2017).

18 When a shortlist just happens to be a shortlist of women this does not count as an AWS in the formal sense of a systematic quota policy.

19 See Childs and Webb, *Sex, Gender*.

20 Lovenduski, *Feminizing Politics*, p. 60.

21 Rowena Mason, 'Conservatives Slap Down Women's Minister over All-Female Shortlists', *Guardian*, 27 June 2014, www.theguardian.com/politics/2014/jun/27/ tories-downplay-nick-morgan-all-female-shortlists (accessed 17 March 2017).

22 'Women and Equalities Oral Evidence: Women in the House of Commons after the 2020 Election', HC 630, 12 October 2016, data.parliament.uk/writtenevidence/com mitteeevidence.svc/evidencedocument/women-and-equalities-committee/women-in-the-house-of-commons-after-the-2020–election/oral/41062.html (accessed 17 March 2017).

23 S. Childs, 'The Good Parliament', report, July 2016, www.bristol.ac.uk/media-library/ sites/news/2016/july/20%20Jul%20Prof%20Sarah%20Childs%20The%20Good%20 Parliament%20report.pdf (accessed 17 March 2017).

24 'Good Parliament Report', *Hansard* 616, 2 November 2016, https://hansard.parlia-ment.uk/commons/2016–11–02/debates/114A85D7–72D2–43A7–A52E-F4262 BA2C5B0/GoodParliamentReport (accessed 20 March 2017).

25 The role of the Women and Equalities Committee is described at: www.parliament. uk/business/committees/committees-a-z/commons-select/women-and-equalities-committee/role (accessed 20 March 2017).

26 wow.southbankcentre.co.uk (accessed 20 March 2017).

27 The Women and Equalities Committee: www.parliament.uk/business/committees/ committees-a-z/commons-select/women-and-equalities-committee/ (accessed 20 March 2017)

28 The transcript of the House of Common's debate on the Good Parliament Report, November 2016, can be found at: https://hansard.parliament.uk/commons/2016–11– 02/debates/114A85D7–72D2–43A7–A52E-F4262BA2C5B0/GoodParliament Report (accessed 20 March 2017)

29 Childs and Webb, *Sex, Gender*; D. Dodson, *The Impact of Women in Congress* (Oxford: Oxford University Press, 2006); B. Reingold, *Legislative Women: Getting Elected, Getting Ahead* (Boulder, CO: Lynne Rienner, 2008).

30 T. Heppell, 'Cameron and Liberal Conservatism: Attitudes within the Parliamentary Conservative Party and Conservative Ministers', *The British Journal of Politics & International Relations*, 15: 3 (2013), 340–61.

31 Childs and Webb, *Sex, Gender*; R. Campbell and S. Childs, 'All Aboard the Pink Battle Bus? Women Voters, Candidates and Party Leaders, and Women's Issues at the 2015 General Election', *Parliamentary Affairs*, 68: 1 (2015), 206–23.

32 B. Campbell, *End of Equality, Manifestos for the 21st Century* (London: Seagull Books, 2014). See E. Evans, *The Politics of Third Wave Feminisms: Neoliberalism, Intersectionality and the State in Britain and the US* (Basingstoke: Palgrave, 2015).

33 Campbell and Childs, '"Wags", "Wives" and "Mothers"'.

34 Childs and Webb, *Sex, Gender*.

35 Campbell and Childs, *All Aboard the Pink Battle Bus*; Campbell and Childs, *What the Coalition Did for Women*.

36 For a summary of developments since the 2002 Employment Act, see House of Commons Library (2014) Paper SN01086. 'Flexible working applies to all employ-ees with 26 weeks continuous employment … removes the procedural requirements for employers responses to the request' in favour of dealing 'with the application in a

reasonable manner' and notify employees of the decision within three month period, or 'such longer as is agreed by the parties' (SN01086, 2014, 5). Note here, both an expansion of a right coupled with a lessening of associated regulation.

37 For example, in 2011 the then Secretary of State for International Development Austin Mitchell set out the UK's framework for improving reproductive, maternal and newborn health in the developing world, which was an overtly women and child centred policy. 'Maternal Health – An International Cause Worth Fighting for', www.theguardian.com/ global-development/poverty-matters/2011/jan/18/maternal-health-uk-government-framework.

38 See T. Heppell and S. Lightfoot, '"We Will Not Balance the Books on the Backs of the Poorest People in the World": Understanding Conservative Party Strategy on International Aid', *Political Quarterly*, 83: 1 (2012), 130–8.

39 It has not been possible to subject all women's policy areas to such analysis. These two were selected on the grounds that they are widely considered to be 'women's issues' and because they are part of the inter-party consensus.

40 V. Bryson, 'As Austerity Measures Begin to Take Full Effect, The Gap Between the Conservative Party's "Woman-Friendly" Rhetoric and Reality will Become more Apparent', LSE blog, 23 April 2012, blogs.lse.ac.uk/politicsandpolicy/category/ valerie-bryson/ www2.ohchr.org/english/bodies/cedaw/docs/CEDAW.C.GBR.7.pdf (accessed 20 March 2017); 'United Nations Convention on the Elimination of All Forms of Discrimination against Women', seventh periodic report of States parties United Kingdom of Great Britain and Northern Ireland, CEDAW/C/GBR/7, 15 June 2011, www2.ohchr.org/english/bodies/cedaw/docs/CEDAW.C.GBR.7.pdf (accessed 20 March 2017).

41 House of Commons 2014 SN/HA/4324. See also 'United Nations Convention on the Elimination of All Forms of Discrimination against Women'.

42 'United Nations Convention on the Elimination of All Forms of Discrimination against Women'.

43 Campbell and Childs, *All Aboard the Pink Battle Bus*.

44 See J. MacLeavy, 'A "New Politics" of Austerity, Workfare and Gender? The UK Coalition Government's Welfare Reform Proposals', *Cambridge Journal of Regions, Economy and Society*, 4: 3 (2011), 289–302; and Campbell and Childs, *All Aboard the Pink Battle Bus*.

45 Such criticism speaks, of course, to the already noted feminist debates regarding neo-liberalism.

46 See Campbell and Childs, *Conservatism, Feminism*.

47 E. Miliband, 'David Cameron Wants a Return to the Days of Tory Arrogance', *Guardian*, 24 October 2010, www.theguardian.com/commentisfree/2010/oct/24/ed-miliband-coalition-spending-cuts (accessed 20 March 2017).

48 V. Bryson and T. Heppell, 'Conservatism and Feminism: The Case of the British Conservative Party', *Journal of Political Ideologies*, 15: 1 (2010), 31–50; B. Campbell, *Iron Ladies* (London: Virago, 1987).

49 Admittedly these are subjective groupings although they are informed by previous research. Campbell and Childs, 'What the Coalition Did for Women; S. Childs, P. Webb and S. Marthaler, 'Constituting and Substantively Representing Women:

Applying New Approaches to a UK Case Study', *Politics & Gender*, 6: 2 (2010), 199–223.

50 NB: these are pledges explicitly linked to women. Hence political parties may address some of these issues elsewhere in their manifestos but we are interested in when they are specifically framed 'for women'.

51 This summarises a longer discussion in Campbell and Childs, *What the Coalition Did for Women*.

52 UKIP is the outlier. See Campbell and Childs, *What the Coalition Did for Women*.

53 Campbell and Childs, '"Wags", "Wives" and "Mothers"'.

54 E. Fieldhouse, J. Green, G. Evans, H. Schmitt, C. van der Eijk, J. Mellon, C. Prosser, (2016) 'British Election Study, 2015: Face-to-Face Post-Election Survey' [data collection]. UK Data Service. SN: 7972, www.britishelectionstudy.com/bes-resources/f2f-v1-0-release-note/#.W.

55 R. Sanghani, 'Is Theresa May Britain's most Feminist Prime Minister ever?', *Telegraph*, 13 July 2016, www.telegraph.co.uk/women/politics/is-theresa-may-the-most-feminist-prime-minister-ever (accessed 17 March 2017).

12

Conserving Conservative women:
a view from the archives

Jeremy McIlwaine

This volume emerges from a joint effort between academics and the Conservative Party Archive at the Bodleian Library, Oxford, and the shared initiative to better define, analytically and empirically, the history of women and gender issues in the party from the period of the its modernisation in the later nineteenth century to the present.[1] The purpose of this chapter is to set out some of the challenges – and successes – facing the preservation of the archival legacy relating to Conservative women, from my perspective as the archivist who has been responsible for the Conservative Party Archive (CPA)[2] since 2006.

As with any area of history, the growing scholarship on Conservative women is dependent on the availability of primary source material. Archives, in whatever medium, are the raw material of history, and in that respect historians are dependent on archivists fulfilling three key roles: *first*, identifying material worthy of permanent preservation, and ensuring that it is preserved in an appropriate special collections library or archival repository; *second*, appraising and cataloguing that material in an accessible and intelligible form, including background information on its historical context, so that it can be made available for research; and, *third*, publicising its existence and significance in order to bring it to the attention of the wider academic community so that it may be exploited for research.

Each of these three roles presents its own challenges and archivists have had varying degrees of success in achieving them, and these issues are addressed here. Some of the challenges, certainly, suggest a gloomy future ahead for the survival, acquisition and preservation of the records generated by women and women's organisations in the Conservative Party – which can equally well apply to virtually any other area of Conservative Party activity – yet there are some grounds for optimism.

Identification and preservation of primary source material

What material survives?

The survival of archival material documenting Conservative women is patchy, but despite some significant gaps, much of the archival record relating to the progress of Conservative women since the late nineteenth century has survived in one form or another.

Antecedents of women's suffrage and the Women's Unionist Organisation
The Primrose League, formed in 1883, was the first mass-membership organisation to admit and utilise women as members. While not formally a part of the Conservative Party organisation, its records up to the 1980s are held by the Bodleian Library.

Between 1883 and 1918, a plethora of single-issue groups emerged with which Conservative women were often involved, owing to the Primrose League's reluctance to take a position on controversial issues. Unfortunately, the records of such groups, where they survive at all, are scattered. Even the records of those groups specifically for Conservative women, such as the Women's Unionist and Tariff Reform Association (founded in 1906) and Conservative and Unionist Women's Franchise Association (1908), suffered from being outside the formal party organisation, although it has been possible to piece together their activities through the private papers of key members involved[3] and through the pages of *The Times* and the CUWFA's newsletter, *The Conservative & Unionist Women's Franchise Review*, some copies of which have survived.

Despite women not formally being admitted as members of the Conservative Party until 1918, in certain areas their involvement with the party was officially sanctioned, or at least tolerated.

Within the National Union of Conservative & Constitutional Association's Midland Union, for instance, which represented ten counties, Lady Adelaide Sawyer, wife of the chairman of the Midland Union, Sir James Sawyer, was able to establish the Ladies Auxiliary Council, which held its inaugural meeting in Shrewsbury on 4 August, 1887. While the men of the Midland Union met on the morning of 4 August, and passed a resolution in support of women's suffrage, the afternoon saw the women under Lady Adelaide, form the Ladies Auxiliary Council, the primary purpose of which was to provide a 'flying column' of women canvassers during election campaigns due to the Primrose League's Grand Council instructing its habitations to hibernate during elections. The records of the Ladies Auxiliary Council, which lasted until 1890, are preserved as part of the CPA.

The Women's Unionist Organisation

The incorporation of the Women's Amalgamated Unionist and Tariff Reform Association (WAUTRA) and its branches into the Conservative Party in 1918, where it metamorphosed into the Women's Unionist Association (WUA) – provided the party with an established existing organisation upon which to build. Unfortunately, no records of the WUA at the national level survive from this period, other than the newsletter which it published from September 1920, *Home and Politics*.[4]

Similarly, the records of the executive body of the WUA (from 1951 known as the Women's National Advisory Committee, and from 1982 as the Conservative Women's National Committee), do not survive in the Conservative Party Archive until 1935,[5] other than reports of its meetings which were published in *Home and Politics*. However, some of the WUA's records at the regional level – known as Area Women's Advisory Committees[6] – survive back to 1920, while the records of a surprisingly large number of local WUA branches survive in local authority record offices around the country, many of them dating back to 1920 or even earlier.[7]

Conservative Central Office

Within Conservative Central Office, Miss Marjorie Maxse was appointed administrator for the WUA in 1924 – effectively providing a secretariat to the Central Women's Advisory Committee and the basis of what would later be referred to rather grandly as the Women's Department. While the majority of pre-war working papers of Conservative Central Office were destroyed, evidence of Maxse's struggles to establish equality for women within the party can be gleaned from the pages of *The Conservative Agents' Journal*. Writing in June 1924, for instance, she said, 'It is to be regretted that it is only within the ranks of the Conservative Party that this attitude of distrust and veiled hostility to women still exists. It is dying fast, but there is still a sufficient number of old-fashioned Associations to justify these remarks.'

The successful advance of women into senior positions in the Conservative Party is probably no better demonstrated than the appointment of Lady Iveagh as the party's first woman vice-chairman in 1930 – though she and her successors in post as the party's senior executive woman were tasked specifically with overseeing the party's women's organisation and its youth wing, rather than gaining control over other spheres of party activity.[8] Unfortunately, the papers of Iveagh and her successors do not survive in any quantity until Barbara Brooke was appointed to the post in 1951.[9]

Generally speaking, the archival record for the whole of the Conservative Party in the period from the late 1940s to the early 1980s is particularly rich, having been a virtual golden age for record-keeping within the Conservative Party: its centralised filing registry ensured that every single memorandum, no matter how trivial, was systematically kept, and often in duplicate, giving us tantalising insight into the functioning of the party machine and the associational culture at Central Office. In conjunction with the papers of the Chairman's Office at Conservative Central Office the Woman Vice-chairmen's papers can provide an insight into the attitude towards women within the party at this time. For instance, while Rab Butler was able to ignore the complaint of a deputation of women MPs unhappy at the lack of women members appointed to his Post-War Problems Central Committee in 1942. However, a beleaguered Macmillan could not afford to do likewise when Evelyn Emmet, Vice-chair of the Conservative Backbench Foreign Affairs Committee and one of the few women in a senior position within the party at the time, took issue in May 1963 with the lack of women at a recent meeting at Chequers. The papers show Macmillan to have been stung into action, as he instructed the Joint Party Chairmen and Chief Whip to address the problem.

Another Conservative Central Office department for which relevant records survive on Conservative women, is the Candidates' Department. Detailed files survive on the majority of those applying to become prospective parliamentary candidates between the 1940s and 1990s. Although subject to access restrictions under the Data Protection Act, they are an invaluable source of information on the perception of women candidates by local selection committees, and indeed by Conservative Central Office. For instance, while Margaret Thatcher's file shows that senior party officials – both male and female – clearly recognised her talent and were unanimous in supporting her to find a safe seat to represent, it also contains letters from her complaining about the misogyny she faced within Finchley Conservative Association, even after she was elected to Parliament in 1959. Thirty years' later, Theresa May's file shows that selection processes had not evolved very much, and women candidates were still being judged firstly on presentation and secondly on substance, while for male candidates it was the other way around.

Much can also be gleaned from the election addresses issued during elections by each prospective candidate. Thanks to the assiduous efforts of Conservative Central Office staff, election addresses of all candidates, from all parties, and all constituencies, have been preserved in the Conservative Party Archive covering all general and by-elections since 1922.

Private papers
An institutional archive such as the Conservative Party Archive can only tell part of the story of Conservative women, so to fill the gap one must look to the personal or private papers of individuals.

The Bodleian Library is just one of a large range of institutions which collect and preserve the papers of prominent politicians, and no comprehensive survey has yet been undertaken to track down the whereabouts of records of all such collections known to be held by institutions within the UK.[10] However, in any institution there is likely to be – as with the Bodleian's collections – an acute imbalance between the numbers of those held for men as opposed to women, and the papers of only a handful of prominent Conservative women have made it into the Bodleian. These include those for Baroness Emmet (Conservative MP, 1955–65 and Conservative peer 1965–80); Baroness Young (Conservative peer 1971–2002, and Cabinet Minister); Baroness Nicholson (Conservative MP (1987–95, and former Liberal Democrat/now Conservative peer); Baroness Hornsby-Smith (Conservative MP, 1950–66 and 1970–74, and Conservative peer, 1974–85); and, recently acquired, the papers of Lady Hodgson (Conservative peer since 2013, and formerly chair of the Conservative Women's Organisation, 2005–8).

The limitations of the archival record: The loss of records through destruction
The wealth of material which has survived to form the CPA is very much due to the longevity of the party's occupation of its Smith Square premises and the considerable space enjoyed there. However, between 2004 and 2014, CCHQ (formerly Conservative Central Office) moved no less than four times, often with next to no warning being given to the Bodleian Library and, no doubt, with associated destruction of records.

In addition, the fortunes of the party's archives, prior to the establishment of the CPA at the Bodleian Library in 1978, were always subject to the depredations of its staff. Few members of staff had as much interest in, and appreciation of, the party's history as the Conservative Research Department's Geoffrey Block, who wrote extensively about it in the 1960s and 1970s,[11] and material relating to prominent individuals – Churchill for instance – found its way into private hands before the creation of the CPA.

But this is not to suggest that there was widespread pilfering, or weeding, rather a lack of appreciation of its long-term significance.[12] Often the removal of historical material was officially sanctioned. One such case came to light in 2012 when a retiring academic 'donated' a substantial quantity of material relating to the party's trade unionist organisation dating back to the 1920s and 1930s, which he had been allowed to remove while an intern at Conservative Central Office in the 1970s as he was writing his PhD on this subject.[13]

The wilful destruction of records has been a more serious problem, and not simply the well-intentioned pulping of the papers of Central Office which took place during the Second World War. When the late John Ramsden described his early ventures into Conservative Central Office as part of his Nuffield College-funded project to record contemporary British political archives in the 1970s, he discovered widespread destruction of old papers by panicked staff attempting to avoid the obligations implied by its recording. That discovery led directly to the establishment of the CPA.[14]

Even the existence of the CPA has not prevented the loss of further records inevitably of interest to historians. An interesting series of files in the CPA documents the relationship between Conservative Central Office and each individual local Conservative association dating back to 1945, including many invaluable (and at the time, confidential) reports on the state of the local organisation and the effectiveness of its MP or parliamentary candidate. This series has yielded some exceptional material on the early career of several future party leaders and prime ministers, including the struggle of a 23-year-old Margaret Roberts to be selected as a parliamentary candidate, and the misogyny she experienced in the process. Unfortunately, this series ceases in 1982 because the files from the years since then were destroyed in the mistaken belief that they were of no importance.

This illustrates one of the key difficulties which archivists face, in that we generally deal with records long since out of current use, rather than at the creation stage. The Conservative Party is a constantly evolving electoral machine, as is the nature of the daily political battle, as it tries to take account of new technologies, changing cultures and the whims of an increasingly apathetic electorate. Consequently, the material it produces is constantly changing as it adapts to the latest challenge. In order to preserve the documentary output of the party, then, archivists need to stay ahead of the game and anticipate what will be relevant to scholars in the future in order to ensure that material of historical value is retained. Instead, we are often forced to play catch-up, with the inevitable loss of material that that involves.

The limitation of the archival record: Ambiguity of ownership of records created by senior party officials
Another difficulty in the context of what is missing from the CPA is the uncertainty over ownership of records created in an official party capacity by individuals who go on to have a successful parliamentary career outside the party machine.

Although the office of Party Chairman was created in 1911, the papers of that office only exist in any quantity within the CPA from the time of Lord Woolton (Party Chairman 1946–55), and even then they are not complete. The papers of successive chairmen were retained by them as their own personal papers upon leaving office, often removing key material on the history of the party. Only a fraction of these have since found their way into the public domain through acquisition by special collections libraries, while the rest are presumed lost.

The private papers of J. C. C. Davidson, Party Chairman from 1926 to 1930, are a typical example. In what were crucial years in the integration of women into the Conservative Party, there is much important material on the party organisation in this period among his private papers – fortunately held by the Parliamentary Archives – which, in view of the wartime destruction of the records of Conservative Central Office, means that Davidson's papers contain the key primary source material on the party organisation in this period. The fortunes of other party chairmen's papers have not been so good, many having disappeared without trace.

The same applies to other holders of party offices, such as the Deputy Chairmen and Vice-Chairmen, who went on to become parliamentarians or other holders of public office. Since 1930 there has been a woman Vice-Chairman of the party, a role held by Marjorie Maxse (1944–50), Sylvia Maxwell Fyfe (1951–54), Barbara Brooke (1954–64), Susan Walker (1964–68), Katharine Macmillan (1968–71), Sara Morrison (1971–75), Janet Young (1975–83) and Emma Nicholson (1983–87). Marjorie Maxse left her mark throughout the papers in the CPA, though there is not a vast amount of material and certainly not one distinct series of them. But of the others, only a small quantity of papers and correspondence testifying to their time in office survives in the CPA.

Even papers created by successive Conservative whips have not been prevented by any jurisdictional claim on them from the party from disappearing into the private papers of at least some of the holders of that office, despite the potentially sensitive nature of the material. So for instance, Sir Edward Heath's private papers, held by the Bodleian Library, includes Whip's Office material dating back to 1941, even though he was Chief Whip only from 1955 to 1959, and there are numerous other examples.

Clearly, there is no demarcation between what constitutes personal papers and what, strictly speaking, should be viewed as the institutional papers of the Conservative Party. To some, perhaps, the question of ownership is irrelevant as long as the records themselves survive, and the provenance is beyond doubt. But unless institutional papers are afforded some kind of protection in the same way that records of government are classed as 'public records', obligating their transfer to the National Archives, then the risk of loss through omission, negligence or even wilful destruction will continue. At the same time, until the party constitution is amended to make provision for the records created on its behalf, such records will continue to be at risk and the diaspora of records created by senior party officials will continue, making it even more difficult to track down relevant material. There have already been calls to give greater statutory protection to the papers of former prime ministers,[15] but there are many more categories of archives generally for which there is minimal or no protection from destruction or export.

The limitations of the archival record: web archives
With the impact on the availability of source material on contemporary politics brought about by compliance legislation and the transition to electronic record creation (for more details, see below), there seems to be a growing trend on the part of some scholars to rely solely on material that is available online, rather than digging out relevant archival material not so readily available. While archiving relevant web-pages as a source of information may be just as valid as archiving the working papers of Conservative Central Office,[16] reliance on websites alone means relying on the political propaganda disseminated by government departments and political parties. For some years journalists have adopted the lazy practice of quoting politicians' opinions as expressed by their public relations teams' output on Facebook or Twitter, rather than engaging directly with their subjects. But even with the availability of web archives to protect against the transitional nature of many websites,

there is an increasing proliferation of non-static URLs being cited in academic texts, which cannot stand up to peer review.

The limitations of the archival record: identifying complementary sources
Lord Lexden, the Conservative Party's official historian and a long-standing advocate of the CPA, has done some preliminary work in tracking down and recording in interview the reminiscences of retired party officials, some of them women, who have devoted their lives to the party cause but did not progress on to a parliamentary career, and often did not consider themselves so significant that they documented their own careers. Such oral history recordings are often the only record of the careers of middle-ranking women within the party organisation and the contributions they made,[17] and more work of this type needs to be undertaken.

This is, perhaps, just one obvious way in which the apparent gaps in the written record can be filled, but archivists must look for new and increasingly innovative ways in which to do this. Here, academic suggestions as to *what* might be acquired to fill the gap in the written record would be welcome. Indeed, this enterprise can only be successful by establishing triangular relationships between the CPA, Central Office and historians, and working towards the shared goal of preserving the record, especially of those traditionally under-represented within it, namely Conservative women. It was just this conversation that began at the 'Rethinking Right-Wing Women' conference in June 2015, where historians, political scientists and sociologists, came together with the CPA, Stephen Parkinson (editor of the *Conservative History Journal*), and Baroness Jenkin of Women2Win to devise strategies to conserve Conservative women.

The problems facing preservation: Changing methods of political communication
Arguably the Conservative Party has been one of the most successful at taking advantage of, and adapting to, new methods of communication. Whether it be the 'daylight cinema vans' and major speeches distributed in the form of gramophone recording in the 1920s, the use of television for party political broadcasts from the 1950s, or the use of YouTube, Twitter and the internet generally in the twenty-first century, we have to be prepared to capture and preserve this output. The CPA is not solely a paper archive, and multiple media types are represented within it, each presenting its own preservation challenges.

The problems facing preservation: The impact of the 'paperless office'
The Bodleian Library has been at the forefront in developing the capability of archivists to capture and preserve electronic records, which is timely, as the majority of material that is transferred to the CPA these days is 'born-digital'. Yet having the infrastructure to process electronic records does not mean that we have satisfactorily adapted to the changing culture of record-keeping which the paperless office has also ushered in. As Central Office's Filing Registry and large teams of typists

gave way to individuals' capacity to create their own documents, along with barely regulated networked servers, the justification for keeping everything no longer exists.

When I speak to undergraduates about to venture into the use of archival sources for the first time, I give them a demonstration of the impact that the digital revolution and its consequences has had on the availability of source material. I show them the plethora of information available on the formulation of the Conservative Party's 1970 election manifesto in the CPA: as well as the proceedings of four separate committees involved in bringing together policy proposals and at least six early drafts of the manifesto available besides the final published version, there is also correspondence of senior party figures who were each asked to review it. By contrast, the 2010 election manifesto evolved digitally: it was disseminated and reviewed by email, and superseded early drafts were simply deleted. By chance, one copy of an early draft of the manifesto was printed out, before being consigned to a wastepaper bin. This copy, annotated with comments by David Cameron and George Osborne, was fortunately rescued and sent to the Archive and therefore provides us with a single snapshot of just *how* that manifesto came into being. But frustratingly, this state-of-affairs now appears to be the norm as regards the party's record-keeping, and the tendency to delete superseded versions of electronic documents is ingrained, the ease with which it can be done ensures that it *is* done, all too regularly. Recalling the disaster which befell the archival record in 2010, in 2015 I contacted the party barely a week after the launch of the 2015 manifesto, requesting early drafts for the Archive. They had already been destroyed, regarded as of no historic importance.

Clearly, the headquarters' staff of any political party is likely to see a constant turnover, especially at election times, and one crucial task of the archivist is to educate staff about what is worthy of permanent preservation. My experience is that, while party officials are only too pleased to support the work of the CPA, what is generally offered to it is the public-facing propaganda material produced by the party: its leaflets, posters and published policy proposals. While these clearly do need to be kept, the idea that working papers and early drafts of policy documents are equally if not more significant is not always immediately apparent.

The problems facing preservation: compliance legislation
Another, more worrying way in which changing record-keeping culture has impacted adversely on the historical record is the impact of compliance legislation such as the Data Protection Act and the Freedom of Information Act.

As a private citizen one can appreciate the value of both pieces of legislation for their contribution to the accountability and democratisation of government, but the consequence for the historical record has been nothing less than catastrophic. Had Freedom of Information (FoI) been in existence 50 years ago, we would not have the vast amount of detailed and hard-hitting reports today which makes up the bulk of the CPA. No politician or local activist would have risked putting down in writing – *confidentially* – what would have been exposed to public scrutiny just a few years' later, and few will do so today. The history of record-keeping since the advent of FoI is simply the story of finding increasingly clever ways to avoid making records public. Government departments routinely delete emails after three months, while some departmental officials initially tried to bypass FoI by sending confidential information via SMS message or private web-based email accounts instead of departmental channels, until this was overruled by the Information Commissioner in 2011.[18] As a last resort, civil servants and others simply avoid writing things down altogether,[19] so the quality of *written* records transferred to the Archive in the twenty-first century in terms of their historical worth is usually very poor, which can only have a detrimental effect on the academic research of the future.

As the Conservative Party is effectively a private not a public body, its Archive is not subject to FoI, but the cross-over of party and government relationships means that the impact is the same. Similarly, Data Protection has taken its toll on the readiness of political parties to transfer email correspondence into the custody of archival repositories. Despite libraries' and record offices' long track record of dealing with Data Protection rules since its first inception in pre-digital 1984 via the use of time-limited access restrictions to protect personal, sensitive information, the ever-present threat of sanction from the Information Commissioner means that political parties are much more careful about how they handle such data. As well they should be: but it simply means that the long series of correspondence dating from the 1940s which exists in the CPA is now absent for the period since the 1990s. Rather than being eventually opened up to historical research, it is much more likely that this material will instead be retained for a limited number of years before being destroyed, which inevitably affects the future viability of the Archive, including its value as a resource on Conservative women.

The general trend has been to put fewer and fewer details in writing, although there are some notable exceptions which, thankfully, buck the general trend – such as the detailed minutes of the Board of the Conservative Party, which was established in 1998. Minutes of the various Conservative Party committee meetings which still find their way to the CPA have mostly undergone a transformation since the 1980s from being detailed and informative, to brief and formulaic. The minutes of the 1922 Committee – often sought after by students aware of its importance within the Conservative Party – exemplify this change, often simply recording that '[X] number of MPs attended', and 'A discussion took place.'

The problems facing preservation: The decentralisation of record creation
One last challenge to mention here, is the impact of the decentralisation of much of the Conservative Party organisation since 1998. The fact that so much historical material relating to the party's history survives is due in no small part to its former centralised structure, and to the stability which this gave to record-keeping.[20]

Much of the proselytising work previously undertaken by the party is now carried out by a plethora of autonomous groups affiliated to the party, with a much weaker link to Conservative Central Office. New groups come and go, and many seem to have no longevity at all. Their autonomy from Central Office means that there is even less likelihood that records will be preserved. It is also hard to keep track of them on existing resources. Fortunately the Conservative Women's Organisation is still considered an integral part of the Party organisation and, at the time of writing, the records of Women2Win[21] are being prepared for transfer to the CPA.

The problems facing preservation: resources
As explained, there is much material which was created by the Conservative Party but which for various reasons is missing from the Archive.

The dispersal and loss of archives puts the onus on to archivists to identify other sources to supplement and fill the gaps in the existing record. Like vultures, the big collecting libraries and archival repositories have to keep an eye on the obituary pages and make a timely approach to the family of prominent deceased politicians in the hope of securing their papers. Yet this belies the existence of the resources to do this in the ever-stringent financial times in which we now operate, when even the cost of archiving such papers in acid-free boxes and storing them according to modern international storage standards can be prohibitive. Often only those very prominent politicians are afforded the honour of a proactive approach for the acquisition of their papers before they die. In most cases archivists can only be reactive, and take in records which have been offered, rather than actively seeking out those records which ought to be preserved.

The problem is exacerbated when important archival collections are put up for sale. Without an acquisitions budget libraries are forced to organise huge fund-raising campaigns in order to prevent their export abroad. Edward Heath's archive, for instance, was bought by the Bodleian Library in 2011 at a cost of £825,000, and that was far below the initial asking price.[22] It goes without saying that this kind of fund-raising effort is only possible in extremely rare cases. All of the collections of private papers held by the Bodleian Library of prominent Conservative women have been donated to the Library rather than purchased.

Processing of archival material

Besides identifying and preserving primary source material on Conservative women, the job of the archivist is also to appraise and catalogue that material in an accessible and intelligible form, including background information on its historical context, so that it can be made available for research.

Resources

This again, touches on the question of resources mentioned above. Every archival institution, including the Bodleian Library, has a sizeable quantity of material which it has acquired, but has yet to process and make available. Consequently, much potentially relevant material around the country is still inaccessible, and may not be until such time as external funding bids come to fruition. The same applies to the CPA where approximately 40 per cent of material acquired has not yet been catalogued and made available, and more material is being acquired all the time. Some of this material naturally includes Conservative women, and falling into this category are papers of Emma Nicholson and Janet Young as vice-chairmen of the Conservative Party, and Angela Hooper as the party's senior woman executive at Central Office in the 1970s. Increasingly though, students are volunteering to take on work-experience projects with the CPA, and some preliminary listing work has already been undertaken on these collections, enabling them to be made available for research soon.

The majority of archivists working at the Bodleian, and no doubt in other institutions as well,[23] are funded to work on the cataloguing of a specific collection only. Competing with other institutions for a share of the limited pool of funding available requires ever more innovative and multi-faceted applications. The upshot is that the highly detailed (and time-consuming) descriptive catalogues which archivists used to produce are no longer considered financially viable, and are being replaced by less useful box-lists which do not provide researchers with the information that they need to make an informed decision as to whether a collection will be relevant or not.

There is much to be done on proactively acquiring the records of Conservative women, and other areas of the party's history, but since it was established in 1978 there have been only a handful of years in which there was sufficient funding to employ one archivist to work on the papers, let alone the team that is needed. Fortunately, at the end of 2015 the Conservative Party accepted financial responsibility for the maintenance of the CPA for the first time, which bodes well for the future.

Publicising the availability of archival material

Preservation of archival material is, obviously, a key aspect of an archivist's job, but another is ensuring that this archival material is made available for academic research. This is perhaps the area of archival work in which the most progress has been made since the mid-1990s.

Steady progress in establishing nationally and internationally accepted standards for archival cataloguing, combined with the automation and sharing of catalogues between institutions via the internet now means that archival material held in the vast array of archival-holding institutions around the country[24] is increasingly identifiable through a single web portal.[25] This gives a huge advantage to those trying to locate relevant material on a particular subject or individual, particularly when considering the diaspora of private papers mentioned. Without a doubt, locating relevant source material has never been easier. For instance, anyone searching for records of Caroline Bridgeman's appointment as the first woman chairman of the National Union's Central Council in May 1926 would find that the CPA, holds only the minutes of that body, and no papers relating to J. C. C. Davidson's appointing her to that role. But, besides Davidson's papers, a search of the National Archive's *Discovery* portal would instantly highlight the existence of Bridgeman's own diaries, correspondence and other papers held at the Shropshire Archives in Shrewsbury.

The standardisation and increasing professionalism of archival cataloguing has brought us to the point where relevant material held in the obscurest of private collections can be found with a minimum of effort.

The future

Clearly, there are substantial challenges facing the conservation of Conservative women's papers, but there are also grounds for cautious optimism as steps *are* being taken to improve the situation. The Party's decision to accept financial responsibility for the CPA is the most positive contribution towards preservation of its own archival record since the CPA was established in 1978. With it has come encouragement for party members at all levels to take interest in and pride in the CPA: a 'Friends of the Conservative Party Archive' was launched at the Annual Conservative Party Conference in October 2015, and the Review Panel examining the party's organisation and structure even recommended in March 2016 that 'gold'-level members should be entitled to tours of the CPA.[26] A permanent exhibition of historic party material within Conservative campaign headquarters itself is, as the time of writing, under consideration. And for party activists at all levels, party-funding of the CPA has helped to emphasise our status as the 'official' party archive. A direct result of this has been a marked rise in the number of party groups visiting the Bodleian to learn about the CPA, whether from local Conservative associations, Conservative campaign headquarters, or groups affiliated to the party.

Considering the electoral success of the Conservative Party and the assumption that it would want to actively preserve its history and set the agenda for its legacy, the party's history has been surprisingly neglected in recent years in its publicity and marketing. This is now being redressed by, for instance, giving the CPA a key role to play at the Annual Conservative Party Conference which will help to reconnect party activists with their party's history. Even at a senior level there has been progress: Conference organisers in 2015 arranged for the then Prime Minister David

Cameron to have a private view of key items from the CPA, while Theresa May was a regular visitor to the CPA's exhibition stand at previous party conferences while she was Home Secretary.

This party-wide enthusiasm for the CPA – if it is sustained – can only be of benefit, and should help to ensure that there are no further losses of important material due to ignorance in the future. It is also helping to strengthen the relationship between the Bodleian Library and the Conservative Party, which is necessary to ensure that as much historical material as possible makes its way into the CPA.

But there is much that academic users of the CPA can also do to help, particularly in bringing our attention to obvious gaps in the collections and helping us to generate some acquisition priorities. Those who have developed relationships with key women politicians as part of their research can also help by encouraging them to gift their records to an appropriate repository, and to help us in our funding bids to get those records catalogued. The diverse nature of the Conservative Party in the twenty-first century, the fast pace of change of communications technology and the transformation in record-keeping culture all culminate in making for a much more difficult record-keeping environment than has ever existed before.

The editors of this volume have begun this process of encouraging greater collaboration between the academic and archival. As part of the project which led to this book, a post-doctoral researcher was funded to survey holdings on Conservative women within the CPA and to report back on where the gaps are prior to putting together a strategy paper which can be presented to the party on how to prevent such gaps arising in the future. This work is only in its infancy, and needs to be expanded to the wider Conservative-related private collections held both by the Bodleian Library and in other institutions so that a central register of records relating to Conservative women can be established. Some of this work has already been done. For instance, Stuart Ball's survey of pre-1945 local Conservative association and regional party records includes many references to surviving records of local Conservative women's committees held in local authority record offices. Commercially, there is a great deal of interest in digitising much of the material in the CPA and making it available online on a subscription basis. If the proposed plans come to fruition, this will do much towards opening up the collection more fully to research and making it available to a much wider audience, from as early as 2018.

Finally, archivists' own attitude towards acquisitions should also be reviewed. While no systematic analysis of the Bodleian's holdings of private papers of politicians, journalists, diplomats and broadcasters has been undertaken, those relating to women are obviously under-represented. Of the 183 most important collections noted in 1994, only five had been generated by women.[27] Women often do feature as correspondents in private papers, but this lack of representation makes it all the more important that we consider why this imbalance still persists in the twenty-first century, and what we can do to address this.

Notes

1 The Conference, *Re-Writing Conservative Women*, was held at the Weston Library, Oxford, on 29–30 June 2015.

2 The Conservative Party Archive (CPA) is the official archive of the Conservative Party and was established at the Bodleian Library in 1978, where it complements one of the foremost collections of manuscripts in the UK relating to modern British politics, including the papers of eight former prime ministers. It is held on deposit at the Library, but is owned by the Conservative Party Archive Trust on behalf of the Conservative Party: web.archive.org/web/20170118184637/www.bodleian.ox.ac.uk/cpa.

3 For instance, Mitzi Auchterlonie in her book, *Conservative Suffragists: The Women's Vote and the Tory Party* (London: Tauris Academic Studies, 2007), has identified the journals of Lady Knightley of Fawsley as a key resource.

4 *Home and Politics* was the first of a series of newsletters published exclusively for Conservative women, which were produced at least up to the mid-1980s. See catalogue: https://web.archive.org/web/20160229215615/www.bodley.ox.ac.uk/dept/scwmss/wmss/online/modern/cpa/library/pubm.html#pubm.A.

5 See catalogue: https://web.archive.org/web/20160528160117/www.bodley.ox.ac.uk/dept/scwmss/wmss/online/modern/cpa/cco/cco170.html.

6 Known initially as Women's Parliamentary Liaison Committees, these were typically meetings of the wives of Conservative Members of Parliament before transforming into advisory committees consisting of elected representatives of local women's branches. See catalogue: https://web.archive.org/web/20160303195744/www.bodley.ox.ac.uk/dept/scwmss/wmss/online/modern/cpa/are/are.html.

7 The records of local Conservative associations, including women's branches, are not generally held in the Conservative Party Archive at the Bodleian Library, and are usually to be found preserved in the relevant county record office. Dr Stuart Ball's *Summary List of Conservative Party Regional and Constituency Records, 1867–1945* helpfully records the whereabouts of those known to exist. A copy can be supplied upon request by the CPA.

8 Theresa May was the Conservative Party's first woman Party Chairman, appointed in 2002.

9 For the available records, see: https://web.archive.org/web/20170118174939/www.bodley.ox.ac.uk/dept/scwmss/wmss/online/modern/cpa/cco/cco60.html#cco60.D.

10 The Royal Historical Society's *A Guide to the Papers of British Cabinet Ministers 1900–1964* (Cambridge: Cambridge University Press, 1996) is an extremely useful start to this work but is limited in scope, only three women having held Cabinet positions by 1964, and junior ministers beyond its remit.

11 As well as writing several authoritative books on the history of the party – including *A Source Book of Conservatism* (London: Conservative Political Centre, 1964), *About the Conservative Party* (London: Conservative Political Centre, 1965), *British General Election Campaign Guides, 1885–1950* (Hassocks: Harvester Press, 1976), Block's length of service with the Conservative Research Department (1946–76) and interest in history meant that he dealt with all academic enquiries about the party's archives prior to the establishment of the CPA, gave lectures on the party's history, and was doubtless largely responsible for keeping so much of it intact.

12 Emily Robinson's *History, Heritage and Tradition in Contemporary British Politics* (Manchester: Manchester University Press, 2012) demonstrates how all political parties, not just the Conservatives, have been guilty of undervaluing their own legacy as preserved in their own archives.

13 A copy of Professor Greenwood's 1981 PhD thesis for Reading University, *Central Control and Constituency Autonomy in the Conservative Party. The organisation of 'Labour' and Trade Unionist support, 1918–1970*, is available in the Conservative Party Archive.

14 Professor Ramsden was very keen to set the record straight after reading the much more anodyne version of the Conservative Party Archive's creation, which was published on the CPA's website. A copy of Ramsden's account can be supplied upon request.

15 www.theguardian.com/commentisfree/2015/jun/19/guardian-view-on-margaret-thatcher-papers-too-important-tax-break.

16 The Internet Archive has existed since 1996, and both the British Library and the Bodleian Library have been selectively archiving websites relevant to their special collections (including the Conservative Party) for some years, while UK websites came under the protection of Legal Deposit rules in 2013.

17 For instance, Dorothy Brant (1906–2009), who as a party agent in Durham helped Ramsay MacDonald retain his seat in 1931, and later ran the Conservative Women's Organisation in the 1960s. See Alistair Cooke, *Tory Heroin: Dorothy Brant and the rise of Conservative Women* (Eastbourne: Sumfield & Day, 2008).

18 Martin Rosenbaum, 'Private Email Accounts are Covered by Information Law', *BBC News*, 15 December 2011, www.bbc.co.uk/news/uk-politics-16189461 (accessed 7 March 2017).

19 Gus O'Donnell (Lord O'Donnell of Clapham, former Cabinet Secretary), 'Civil Servants are Mentally Working on Brexit Plans to Avoid FOI', *Telegraph*, 17 January 2016, www.telegraph.co.uk/news/newstopics/eureferendum/12104609/Civil-servants-are-mentally-working-on-Brexit-plans-to-avoid-FOI-says-Gus-ODonnell.html (accessed 7 March 2017).

20 Compare this with the much poorer survival rate of the much more decentralised Liberal Party during the nineteenth and twentieth centuries. The Liberal Party archives are held by the Library of the London School of Economics.

21 Women2Win was co-founded by Baroness Jenkin of Kennington and Theresa May in 2005 as a Conservative pressure group to increase the number of Conservative women in Parliament and in public life.

22 https://web.archive.org/web/20161008024401/www.nhmf.org.uk/LatestNews/Pages/BodleianLibrariesacquireSirEdwardHeathArchive.aspx.

23 The Bodleian Library is but one of a number of national centres for the collection and preservation of modern British political papers, including the British Library, London School of Economics Library, Churchill Archives Centre and the People's History Museum, to name but a few. In addition, there are numerous other specialist libraries and museums which also collect archives, as well as a network of local authority-funded record offices around the country which collect political papers relevant to their local area.

24 For a list of these see: https://web.archive.org/web/20170125085022/discovery.nationalarchives.gov.uk/find-an-archive.

25 https://web.archive.org/web/20170209024948/discovery.nationalarchives.gov.uk/.
26 www.conservatives.com/partyreview.
27 Helen Langley, *Modern Political Papers in the Bodleian Library* (Oxford: Bodleian Library, 1996), p. 8.

13

Women2Win and the feminisation of the UK Conservative Party

Baroness Anne Jenkin

Introduction by Sarah Childs

Summer 2005. BBC Radio 4's *Woman's Hour* is discussing the under-representation of women in British politics. The general election had seen the re-election of a Labour Government under Tony Blair. Using a party quota once again – All Women Shortlists – the Labour parliamentary benches were 28 per cent female, with 98 Labour women MPs. Opposite them, the Conservative benches remained overwhelmingly male: there were only 17 Conservative women MPs, constituting a mere 9 per cent of the Conservative parliamentary party. An asymmetry of women's descriptive representation, one that had been marked since 1997, when the number of women MPs doubled overnight from 60 to 120 with 101 Labour women, remained stark in 2005. There was a lot of ground to make up. With the Conservative Party in the process of electing a new party leader – David Cameron would ultimately be successful in autumn 2005 – there was an opportunity for women in the party, many of whom had been unhappy for some time about their under-representation and marginalisation, to first gender the party leadership election and, thereafter, to feminise their party. Anne Jenkin also a guest on *Woman's Hour* that day made party feminisation her mission; she recognised the window of opportunity; she also recognised that she was perhaps uniquely positioned, and could play a critical role. Anne is happy to admit that 'others were there at the start, and on the journey, and by my side', but she is also correct to point out that she is the 'only one of the team who has been there through thick and thin'. In the 2015 Parliament, ten years from the launch of Women2Win, there are more Conservative women MPs in Parliament than ever. Following the 2015 general election, there are 68 Conservative women MPs, some 20 per cent. An awful lot of effort was expended within the party by those committed to a more female friendly party; this did not happen by chance. There was nothing inevitable about the feminisation of the party at the last general election. And there is still much more to do, even with the second Conservative woman Prime Minister, Theresa May: at the 2015 general election the Labour Party, again using AWS, returned a parliamentary party that was over 40 per cent female. Anne's essay importantly tells 'the story' of Women2Win – gets it 'on the record'. It is, moreover, an opportunity 'to reflect on progress' to date and the progress that still needs to take place.

So, how did it all start? Well it probably starts with where I come from. My maternal great grandfather (himself the son and grandson of MPs), Sir Willoughby Dickinson, was the Liberal MP for St Pancras North and introduced the Women's Enfranchisement Bill in February 1907, because he was so outraged that his sister, a doctor, didn't have the same opportunity as him. He later became a Labour member of the House of Lords, and his daughter, my grandmother became the MP for Hemel Hempstead in 1937 until 1959, and was in fact the only Conservative woman MP elected in 1945. I work with people in the House of Lords who still remember her. Some readers who don't follow Parliament closely may think that it is normal for me to have been whip to my father-in-law (the late Patrick Jenkin, Baron Jenkin of Roding), and that my own husband (Bernard Jenkin, MP for Harwich and North Essex) has been an MP now for 23 years. But despite the fact that I stood once for Parliament, in Glasgow in 1987, I really remain a very reluctant politician. But we will come to that later.

My first job was in Conservative Central Office (as it was then) and over the next ten years or so I worked as PA – we didn't have researchers in those days – for half a dozen or so MPs. So the Westminster village became my world. There was no plan. I just stumbled into it and despite a temporary escape or two for a couple of years here or there, it remains my world. It can be a pretty vicious and unpleasant world, with a higher than average number of sad people with unhappy lives, but I understand and know the place and its inhabitants.

By the time of the general election of 2005 (when the leader of the Conservative Party was Michael Howard), I knew a lot of people in the party and in Parliament. Senior people. Bernard had been an MP and in the Shadow Cabinet for a number of years. I had worked for him for about ten years. Our generation had reached the top. I also knew a lot of journalists. Soon before that election two Conservative women candidates were de-selected. I think they were in Colne Valley and Calder Valley. One de-selection was something to do with her skirt being too short, or perhaps not short enough, and the other had, I think, slept with her chairman. Someone, I think Alice Thomson, a journalist for the *Times* newspaper, asked me for a quote. The journey towards Women2Win started there. Of course, I had noticed how badly we did with women. That election saw no increase at all in the number of Conservative women MPs. We stuck at 17 – just 9 per cent. I wrote an article for the *Sunday Times* on the selection procedure. I asked around. What did people think? I recommended a Gold List/A List, call it what you like, but short of AWS it seemed to me a reasonably fair way to level the playing field.

After the election, because by now I was in the cuttings, *Woman's Hour* asked me on to comment on the lack of progress. I remember sitting in the Green Room at the BBC when the researcher came in to talk to the woman following on after me.

A comedian I think. 'You are on after a piece about women and the Conservative Party', she said. And they both chortled. I felt ashamed of my party. That confirmed to me there was much work to do. I told that story on air with Jenni Murray. Also on the programme was Theresa May, formerly Party Chairman, and of course now our second Conservative woman Prime Minister, and down the line from Bristol was Professor Sarah Childs. Although not, I think, a professor then, she was already well known to those following the debate about women in Parliament. Which I was not! I waffled on about encouragement, support and so on. She was clear that more radical action was needed.

I could have stopped there. But, I let curiosity get the better of me and when I got home I Googled her, sent her an email and asked for a private seminar about what the Conservative Party could and should be doing to attract more women candidates, get them selected and then elected. Sarah may remember that lunch. It was a bit of an eye opener for me. Of course by then I was more focused on what Labour was doing and what little progress we were making. She rightly pointed out that if we were going to do anything, this was the time. With a leadership election under way, it was an opportunity to leverage influence. I remember Liam Fox coming over for a chat and promoting primaries. I barely knew what primaries were!

But then, in May or June 2005, it looked as though David Davis MP was going to romp home as leader, and did I really have the energy and commitment to spend my summer campaigning on something that just wasn't going to happen?

Some dates are clear in my mind: 7/7 was Michael Ancram's (a senior Conservative party politician) 60th birthday, and he celebrated with a breakfast party. Theresa May MP and I had our first proper conversation about what our pressure group might look like and do. Other senior women were there too. Finally, the answer to my regular question, 'When will someone do something about the women?' was answered. It was staring me in the face: me. But here I should acknowledge generations of people in the party who had done their best. Doreen Miller, Trish Morris and even Iain Duncan Smith and Michael Howard were aware of the problem, but they weren't strong enough to know what to do.

We started meeting weekly. I wish I could remember exactly who was there, but certainly the late lamented Shireen Ritchie who died so tragically young in 2012. Laura Sandys who, when she came runner-up to Nick Herbert as the candidate for Arundel, overheard one old trout saying, 'Well, he may be a homosexual, but at least we didn't get a woman' – enough to radicalise any female candidate! And Theresa's chief of Staff, Andrew Griffiths.

We spent the early autumn preparing for the launch in November. We wrote round to all MPs asking if they supported our aims. It got back to me that one senior MP, subsequently a Cabinet minister, was dismissive. I rang his wife. She told me she'd be waiting for him with a rolling pin. He signed up next day. A number then, and many more now, realised that their daughters are in many cases still struggling against prejudice in their chosen professions. Some have daughters who aspire to be MPs. Recently, I was surprised to see Sir Oliver Heald, a long-standing, rather traditional MP photographed a '50:50 Parliament' T-shirt. But of course his very able daughter Sarah is on the candidates list and I can confidently predict that she will be an MP in the not too distant future.

I can't recall the exact date of the launch, but it was the end of November in the Lewis PR auditorium at the bottom of Millbank Tower. I had written an article for the *Sunday Express*, which paid for the event. I remember Steve Hilton, adviser to David Cameron, saying that it was the first Conservative event he had attended which looked populated by real, normal people. Jackie Ashley of the *Guardian* chaired it. Theresa spoke, a losing candidate spoke, Sarah Childs, and Jenny Watson of the EOC took us through the sobering statistics. We had good press coverage and I think it was a wake-up call to David Cameron who was elected leader of the party just two weeks later.

And here I break off the story to pay tribute to a number of the men who have embraced our cause. Andrew Griffiths was up all that night printing leaflets on his home printer. He is the Godfather of Women2Win. Although not actively involved any more, he and I made it happen at the beginning. One of the nicest compliments I have ever received came from him. 'Most people in politics talk about doing things. You do them.' He subsequently went on to coach the woman who beat him for the seat he had been working to get for most of his adult life. He has been the MP for Burton since 2005. My own husband Bernard comes next. When David Cameron became leader he made Bernard Deputy Chairman for Candidates. A difficult job at the best of time, managing the candidate and selection process, but Bernard also had to implement the A list, the Gold list and it was not an easy task.[1] It didn't play to his strengths. I don't remember exactly when it was that he said, 'You won't get anywhere unless you get buy in from the men.' And he was right. We lobbied but were pushing at an open door. David Cameron supported us and came to events. Indeed, in the first speech he made as leader, he talked about how the parliamentary party must become more representative of Britain as a whole.

Other men came forward to help. Many male MPs volunteered as mentors. They know how to get selected. Some became quite competitive. 'I got my woman an interview', and so on. Many of them spent time working on speeches, Q&A practice, working with candidates on their strengths and weaknesses. They weren't all too sure about how to approach the hair and clothes issues, but they were great. As were my three co-chairs, Brooks Newmark, Guy Opperman and Mark Garnier, all of whom have spent much time and energy on this cause. In 2016 Will Quince became co-Chair.

I would also like to thank Lorraine Fulbrook, Amanda Sater (now Deputy Chairman of the Party), Alexandra Robson and most recently Ellen Miller, for their commitment as 'Director' since 2006, most of whom on a voluntary basis. We have always had a small but very willing, enthusiastic and 'can do' team, all treated as equals, which has helped to make the campaign such a pleasure to work on.

But back to 2006. I took a year out, working pretty well full time on getting our kitchen table operation up and going. I wasn't a gender politics expert. I didn't really know what I was doing, but we got things done. We ran a number of 'Introduction to Politics' sessions hosted by women head hunters, including Virginia Bottomley who had been an MP and Cabinet Minister. On the panels we had MPs, candidates, councillors, party activists and others who could explain the journey and how to navigate the maze to the green benches. The party selected early in the key target seats in advance of the 2010 general election, which we hoped to take off Labour, and many of the brightest stars off the 'A' List – Amber Rudd, Margot James, Jane Ellison, Tracey Crouch, Karen Bradley, Louise Mensch, for example, were chosen for these challenging seats. We had no idea at that stage that the parliamentary expenses scandal of 2009 would produce so many extra plum seats nearer the election; by then our pipeline of good candidates had begun to tail off.

And the pipeline (supply of women candidates) remains an issue. Thirty per cent of all those who come forward to do the Parliamentary Assessment Board (all candidates need to be approved by the party) and get on to the candidate list are women, a percentage which has remained more or less static since 2006. It remains a big challenge on which we intend to focus over the next few years, to hunt out more women who are interested in starting that journey. Thirty per cent get on to the candidate list and many of them don't do enough to promote themselves or become more active once they are on that list. Again, we intend to work on that.

Between 2005 and 2010 Women2Win organised many events, was active at the Conservative Party conference and fund-raised enough to employ an assistant for one day a week. We launched a Business Supporters Club with Lady Thatcher in about 2008 which has successfully kept us ticking over since then. We fund-raised to support candidates. In 2010 we were able to donate £1k to fifty different candidates' campaigns. In 2015 we supported every single woman candidate with a minimum of £300, and those in the target seats or those trying to hang on to difficult seats got more. But we are frugal. We don't waste money and many people have volunteered their time and expertise for free. I held home cooked lunches at my home for women candidates to meet women from the parliamentary lobby and other journalists. I still do.

After the election in 2010 the number of Conservative Women MPs increased from 17 to 49 MPs, from 9 per cent of the parliamentary party to 16 per cent – better, but not good enough. We started early to identify the stars who we thought were likely to make it in 2015. Panels consisting of the 2010 intake of MPs, senior volunteers and others who knew what it takes to be an MP, interviewed candidates to find out where they needed support. Relationships with Conservative Party headquarters (CCHQ) were very good. We kept in close touch with Carlyn Chisholm, the senior party volunteer who chaired the candidates committee, and who was later joined by Sarah Newton MP, who had herself won Truro and Falmouth in 2010 with a majority of 435 (over 14,000 in 2015). We had regular meetings and updates with the party's women's organisation, the CWO, and eventually worked out that they would focus their efforts with their development programme for women at an early stage of the process, and that we at Women2Win would take over once those women had passed their Parliamentary Assessment Board. To be honest to professional trainers and organisers it might have seemed amateurish and unprofessional, but it worked. Almost every Monday evening we would hold a training session. Early on, they all came together and we rehearsed questions and answers. Later, once selections were under way, we worked one to one with those women who had got selection interviews. Many of them set up smaller groups and worked together. We held mock selections, with real audiences in the offices of the Conservative Association in Ebury Street, where candidates were marked as if at a real selection and the results fed back. Interesting how many ambitious men turned up in the audience for those sessions.

Selections for retirement seats were slow for women and we were anxious. I admit to the odd tear of disappointment and more tears of joy. On Saturday nights of finals for retirement seats I would brace myself for the texts and calls from candidates: 'Sorry Anne, I have let you down (again)' – never! And then the words of encouragement for them to pick themselves up and dust themselves down and set off for the next one.

Here I add a word about the process. It became clear that primaries weren't working for women.[2] The local bloke could, and did, pack the room. Local candidates are increasingly important, and especially in marginal and target seats. But we have to find a balance. The rock-solid safe seats, and this applies to any party, can afford to choose any star of the future. And they should.

After several finals, the wonderful Vicky Atkins had failed to get the one we thought was in the bag. One man and three women in the final and you can guess who got it. We were all a bit despondent. She was tempted to pack it in and wait until her son was older. Off she went to Lincolnshire where the Father of the House (this term refers to the longest-sitting MP), Sir Peter Tapsell, was retiring in his 80s. She knew it was a long shot, relaxed and went for it. I ate my proverbial hat. And shed a tear.

I am so full of admiration for those who go into public life. For most candidates, male and female, the road can be rocky and bumpy and bearing in mind the candidates list usually has over 600 people on it, for the majority it also ends in failure.

Things did not go all smoothly by any means. At times it felt like two steps forward, one step back. A year before the 2015 election I became truly anxious that we might end up with fewer seats after the election. And said so. Publicly. Actually all I said was that if we went backwards, all options should be on the table. You might have thought I was advocating slaughter of first-born males from the reaction from some. I personally would have no problems with All Women Shortlists (AWS) and would be fighting for them now if we had not moved forward so significantly in May 2015. But there are other easier battles to fight. And we are split on the subject in my team.

Whilst we have never taken a Women2Win view on AWS I think there were by choice ten all women voluntary finals, including towards the end, some of the best seats in 2015. I asked someone I knew who had been present at the Faversham final whether people there had minded having just four women to choose from. She said not. It made it easier. No pressure on them. And I think that's part of the problem. I heard from someone else at another final that they saw three women first. Great response. All fabulous. And then in came the bloke. 'But there's our MP.' But that will change. Sarah Newton reported that when she went to visit Conservative Associations to discuss their selection, many of them said: 'We want one like Esther McVey' – sadly one of the three women MP casualties in May 2015.

There was another low moment when three of the women MPs elected in 2010 announced quite early on that they weren't going to stand again. They announced early because they were being responsible. The press picked this up and it became a story. In the end, thrity-five Conservative MPs retired. Three of them were women. So, not exactly a story. But some mud stuck.

Louise Mensch has many qualities. Self-promotion is one. Unfortunately, when she left Parliament after only a couple of years, causing a by-election in Corby ,which we then lost to Labour, anecdotally this proved to be a real deterrent to some constituencies. 'A' list women were perceived to be 'unreliable' 'selfish' and it took a lot of work to get over this perception. We helped CCHQ produce a film about the work of an MP, which showed the life of four very different types of MP, including one BME and two women, which was shown to the audience in advance of selections.

Labour women, especially those in the Lords, like Patricia Hollis who had been actively involved with their campaign for AWS, were interested in how we were getting on, and encouraging. Although they teased me that we would never make progress without it, when I reported during the international women's day debate that well over one third of the retirement seats had selected women they were surprised (see Campbell and Childs 2015 for full analysis of candidate selection by party and seat type).[3] They were even more surprised to find that we had done so well with our BME representation, seven new BME MPs in rock-solid Conservative seats, better I think than the Labour Party, and in places like Richmond (Yorkshire), and Hampshire where there are almost no BME voters.

So as we went into 2015 the general election campaign, I was pretty confident that we would end up with more women MPs than before. But only just. Like everyone else, I was amazed by the actual result.

We were at my husband's count in Colchester as the results came in. Rumours flew. Women dominated the evening. Vince Cable had been beaten – by Dr Tania Mathias, who had worked in the Gaza Strip for the UN as a relief worker, and most recently practised in the NHS as an eye specialist. Mark Reckless, UKIP, had lost to Kelly Tolhurst, and finally, for many Conservatives at least, their favourite moment of the night when Ed Balls lost to the visibly shocked Andrea Jenkyns. We ended the night up from 48 women MPs to 68. There were seats we had not expected to hold, Cannock Chase for example and Erewash. Three of the six we gained from Labour and the mass of Lib Dem seats which fell, many to women candidates, few of whom had been expected to win.

So, what's the plan for Women2Win now and for the next five years? Well we have ambitious plans. Our brilliant new director, Gillian Keegan, was herself elected to the Commons in 2017 whilst our previous talented right-hand woman, Resham Kotecha, 25, fought in Coventry North West. I met Gillian at the theatre, introduced by mutual friends. She is in her 40s. With a successful business career behind her, she is ready for a second career. Since that meeting, she has stood in three elections, twice in Chichester where she was a Cabinet member, and once in St Helens at the general election in 2015. With the experience she has gained she will be more than ready for her new role as MP. The two of them, supported by other mature and young candidates, including Beth, aged 22, who fought Yvette Cooper, put together an outreach and engagement programme to speak and appeal to women's business groups and networks, as well as schools and universities in an effort to improve the 30 per cent pipeline I talked about earlier. We will continue look after the existing women MPs and especially the new ones. They know that I am just a phone call away, but I am pleased the induction process and pastoral support from Parliament and the whips' office is better and more comprehensive than ever before.

We have started fund-raising with a view to a more professional development programme. We would like to support those for whom the economics of standing as a candidate is a deterrent. And I understand CCHQ is working on a bursary system too. This has been a long-held criticism and one which is difficult to resolve. Conservative women MPs elected in May 2015 include a cancer nurse, a teacher, an eye doctor, a carer, a director of a scaffolding business, as well as Tania Mathias. But of course, the stereotypical lawyer is well represented in the current tranche and we must work to appeal to a broader section to come forward and to help them to navigate the journey.

We undertook a survey again with the losing candidates. How was it for them? How could the experience be improved? Are they prepared to go on with the journey? I hope they feel that they can tell us things they may not be prepared to tell the centre.

We will as always be active at Conference, not only with our regular Sunday evening party which is always the most popular of the whole conference – and particularly so as last year's saw people almost coming to blows to get in. In 2016 we held a seminar on 'What to do for the Next Five Years' with a panel of senior Conservative women from MEPs, Councillors, MPs, and so on advertising alternative opportunities and what the journey should include.

And a further celebration: David Cameron and Theresa May were our guests of honour at a big event in November 2015 to celebrate our ten years of achievement.

September 2016 saw the launch of our new campaign 'Daughters2Win' at the Carlton Club, once a Conservative institution that was most definitely not women-friendly. This campaign deploys Conservative male MPs, speaking as fathers and grandfather MPs, to talk about the future they want to see for their daughters and granddaughters – one where these young women face the same opportunities as their brothers. The video was shown at the 2016 party conference. Its message is clear: the Conservative Party must make sure that its selection processes are a level playing field for women prospective candidates.

We will keep our feet firmly on the accelerator. We will build our pipeline, by going out into the regions, and seeking out candidates for the national, local and mayoral and PCC elections. We will find mentors for new parliamentary candidates, and for women who fought in the 2015 and 2017 general elections we will continue our practice of matching them up with male MP mentors. Training will be ongoing, and will include Q&A and public speaking skills. And, of course, we will continue to raise the issue of women's under-representation with the party leadership. Despite our significant progress the Conservative Party at many levels does not look like a modern, diverse organisation and will fail to attract modern and diverse candidates until it does. No woman should be left behind as a consequence of the boundary review that will reduce the House of Commons to 600 Members. In 2016 Women2Win held a number of functions, with its founding Chairman of Women2Win – Theresa May – the UK's and the Conservative Party's second woman Prime Minister.

In 2026 I intend to sit in the gallery of the Commons as we double our percentage again to 40 per cent, the Miss Jean Brodie of the Conservative Party, watching a new generation of women take their seats and make their maiden speeches.

As I prepared for this chapter (originally a talk), I have reflected on this past ten years or so, and the extraordinary journey it has been for the Conservative Party, for women in the Conservative Party and of course for me personally. I have mentioned that I am no gender expert. I am of course a feminist, but above all I believe in fairness. When I got angry about the lack of action to support women who wanted to be MPs, I had no expectation or plan that my own journey would take me to Parliament. I genuinely didn't look for or expect any recognition. I just wanted to make a difference, to get things done. To change things for the better.

I hope it isn't unfair to those men who want to be Members of the House of Lords to say that they plan that journey by doing this, this and this.

Well, I did this, this and this, and was totally shocked and very unsure, when after the 2010 election, the Prime Minister asked me to go to the Lords which I did in January 2011. I am still, in a typically female way, out of my comfort zone much of the time. But I am of course pleased and proud that through me the work of Women2Win and the support it has provided for so many candidates, and the cages it has rattled, has been recognised.

Some people still say to me, why does it matter whether we have 10 per cent, 20 per cent or even no women MPs? They should be there on merit and all that guff.

In the end it is simple. Women's life experiences are different to men's. Not inferior, not superior, just different. And it is that difference which continues to need to be better reflected at Westminster.

Notes

1 This list was created to identify the party's top 50 women and top 50 men aspirant candidates. The party's held and vacant seats were expected, but importantly not required, to select from amongst these.
2 See S. Childs and P. Webb, *Sex, Gender and the Conservative Party* (London: Palgrave Macmillan, 2012).
3 See Rosie Campbell and Sarah Childs, 'Conservatism, Feminisation and the Representation of Women in UK Politics', *British Politics*, 10: 2 (2015), 148–68, for full analysis of candidate selection by party and seat type.

Index